Biblical Hebrew Grammar Visualized

Linguistic Studies in Ancient West Semitic

edited by

M. O'Connor†, Cynthia L. Miller-Naudé, and Jacobus A. Naudé

The series Linguistic Studies in Ancient West Semitic is devoted to the ancient West Semitic languages, including Hebrew, Aramaic, Ugaritic, and their near congeners. It includes monographs, collections of essays, and text editions informed by the approaches of linguistic science. The material studied will span from the earliest texts to the rise of Islam.

Biblical Hebrew Grammar Visualized

FRANCIS I. ANDERSEN
and
A. DEAN FORBES

Winona Lake, Indiana
EISENBRAUNS
2012

Library of Congress Cataloging-in-Publication Data

Andersen, Francis I., 1925–
  Biblical Hebrew grammar visualized / Francis I. Andersen and A. Dean Forbes.
    p.   cm. — (Linguistic studies in Ancient West Semitic ; 6)
  Includes bibliographical references and index.
  ISBN 978-1-57506-229-7 (hardback : alk. paper)
  1. Hebrew language—Grammar.   I. Forbes, A. Dean.   II. Title.
  PJ4567.3.A525   2012
  492.4′82421—dc23

                                                                    2012003744

Contents

For Lois† and Ellen

Preface

The enormous amount of work that has been done on the language of the Jewish Bible is still limited in its range. The phonology of Biblical Hebrew (consonants, vowels, accents) and the morphology (the phonetic/phonemic patterns and grammatical structures of words) have been thoroughly described. But as one moves into grammar proper, the work becomes more and more selective and incomplete. Even at the level of small phrases, there are many phenomena that have not been accounted for or even noticed. The familiar constituents of clauses, such as verbs, subjects and objects, have been discussed, of course, but many other clause constituents have not received much attention from Hebraists, compared with the work that linguists have done with other languages. There is not yet a comprehensive, systematic, principled investigation of whole clauses as the basic units of syntax. The rigorous exploration of the grammar of discourse structures larger than clauses is only in its beginning stages.

In addition to incomplete coverage of phenomena, another limitation in previous work is its concentration on the narrative prose texts of the Hebrew Bible, with less attention to prophetic, poetic, and wisdom writings. The challenge is to study the entire text of the Hebrew Bible at every level of grammatical organization, from phoneme to discourse, as completely as possible. This task has become more feasible with the availability of electronic texts for computer-enabled research, assisted by the development of linguistic theories that supply appropriate concepts and terminology. This is the burgeoning field of corpus linguistics.

Compared with other corpora, the evidence for the language used by the people of Israel in biblical times is meager. The Hebrew Bible, supplemented by contemporary inscriptions found by archaeologists and by extra-canonical compositions, such as the Dead Sea Scrolls, proffers about a half million words—the number of words in the Hebrew Bible is a little more than 300,000. Yet a comprehensive investigation of the grammar of these few texts has not yet been achieved.

Corpus linguistics aims at the analysis and description of all the grammatical phenomena in a given body of text in some "canon," such as the complete works of one author. This book takes the first steps toward investigation of the grammar of the Hebrew found in just one version of the Hebrew Bible.

Biblical Hebrew Grammar Visualized (BHGV) is an initial foray, trying out the corpus linguistics way of doing research on the grammar of Biblical Hebrew. While there is much in the book that beginning students of Biblical Hebrew will grasp, it is primarily intended for intermediate and advanced students of Biblical Hebrew, as well as researchers in the area. Its data consist of phrase markers for each and every distinct clause in the Hebrew Bible. Each phrase marker gives a pictorial representation of the constituents of each clause in the form of a structure (a tree or graph) that shows the grammatical functions and semantic roles of clause constituents, along with the grammatical relations that bind the constituents into linguistic structures.

There is virtually no limit to the questions that may be addressed to the data in this form, no limit to the amount of detail that the phrase markers can reveal. Understandably, this book cannot report more than a few small and representative samples of the fruits of the linguistic research that is enabled by our new tools. Many of the results are presented here in the form of tallies of the incidence of selected phenomena, often as bar charts. Close-up details are accessible by interrogating the full database of phrase markers and texts available from Logos Bible Software.

This book sets forth the linguistic theory on which the grammatical analysis is based. It explains the terms used. It presents a few *sample* studies that will illustrate the potential of this approach for research. It suggests topics for further investigation.

Some of the material in this book will be new to students of Biblical Hebrew who do not have a background in contemporary linguistics. This book will supply some of that background. It does not attempt a full-scale discussion of all of the theoretical issues that lurk in its foundations, but it points to the main literature that we draw upon. Nor does it seek "the one true grammar for Biblical Hebrew." We believe that superior insights emerge when scholars approach the text via many paths.

In spite of the seeming complexity of many clauses (some are quite long and convoluted), most clauses are short, and the basic grammatical structures in all of them are actually quite simple. A construction consists of constituents in relationships, many of them binary (with two members joined together in some way). Because so many structures are small and simple, they are accessible to students whose understanding of Hebrew grammar may still be in its early stages. There are numerous simple searches that they can carry out immediately to find small phrases and short clauses. They can narrow the searches by specifying the vocabulary item(s) they wish to be present, enriching familiar "word" searches beyond mere co-occurrence patterns into the grammatical constructions in which some word is used. This is just a beginning. More advanced students and scholars engaged in cutting-edge research may find the investigation of more complex structures more challenging, but all the more rewarding for that.

It is important to make it clear that this book is *not* a user manual for the Andersen-Forbes data as realized by the Logos software. Our simple web site (Andersen-Forbes.org) contains white papers intended to assist would-be searchers of our data plus other useful materials. Nor does the book seek to be a reference grammar.

Because this is an initial foray, there is much in the book that is unfinished and provisional. We try to be upfront about this. Addressing real problems has enhanced our repertoire of grammatical functions and semantic roles; it has also shown the need for further work. The data will be enriched and made more transparent when we have completed the full representation of the grammatical functions and semantic roles of all the clause immediate constituents.

Because discourse grammar and clause syntax are parts of the same fabric of Hebrew grammar, we expect the work on clause syntax presented here to move seamlessly into the discourse grammar that we hope to present in a future volume. The final chapter of this book offers a foretaste of our approach to discourse analysis.

A word about our glosses: The glosses that we supply throughout this book are included to assist readers. They are *type* glosses, not *token* glosses. That is, one gloss is applied to each form (the "type") and is used whenever that form appears in the text (as a "token"). Consequently, the glosses are jarring at times. They in no way attempt to supply an interlinear translation. (For more on our glosses, see Appendix 7, §A7.1.)

Acknowledgments

Frank and Dean are grateful for David Noel Freedman's friendship, provocation, stimulation, and encouragement over many decades.

Frank enjoyed 50 years of inspiration from Kenneth L. Pike. He thanks colleagues at the University of California, Berkeley (especially Anne Kilmer), Macquarie University (especially Edwin Judge), the University of Queensland (especially Gregory Fox and Edward Newing), and the University of Melbourne (especially Antonio Sagona and Terry Falla). He thanks the Australian Research Grants Scheme for financial help with research assistance while at Macquarie University and the University of Queensland.

Dean thanks a succession of managers and colleagues at Hewlett-Packard Laboratories (especially Paul Stoft and Joan Humphreys).

We are deeply grateful to Christo van der Merwe for making the time to read our manuscript. Many substantial improvements to the book resulted from his thoughtful comments and criticisms. We alone are responsible for all errors and wrongheadedness that remain.

We thank Bob Pritchett, President of Logos Bible Software, for his willingness to take on the task of making our data available to others, and we also thank Eli Evans and his colleagues at Logos Bible Software for their responsiveness to our requests for adjustments to the realization of our formalism over the past few years.

We thank Jim Eisenbraun, Beverly McCoy, and the entire Eisenbrauns crew for their professional attention to our book. Its many tables and figures have made its realization a genuine challenge.

Through it all, Lois and Ellen were our constant inspiration. Without their active encouragement, this work would not exist.

FRANCIS I. ANDERSEN
The University of Melbourne
Melbourne

A. DEAN FORBES
Palo Alto

The Structure of This Book

Chapters 1–4 provide readers with important introductory information on our approach: the text adopted, our general linguistic perspective, the syntactic representation used, division of the text into clauses and into individual segments, and our part-of-speech system.

Chapters 5 and 6 provide an extended survey of the basic and complex phrases found in Biblical Hebrew.

Chapters 7 and 8 characterize the clauses and clause-like structures of Biblical Hebrew. We examine both main and embedded structures.

Chapters 9–17 study clause immediate constituents (CICs)—the major constituents that combine to form clauses—from multiple perspectives. We introduce the five disparate types of CICs (Chapter 9) and then focus especially on the semantic roles fulfilled by various CICs (Chapter 10). We introduce methods for assessing the composition, incidence, and ordering of CIC types (Chapter 11). We then use these methods to investigate the characteristics of the clauses based on four very frequently attested verb roots (Chapters 12–15). We next examine the make up of the various CICs (Chapter 16) and then explain the uses of, and computation of, a way of comparing sets of clauses in terms of the incidence patterns of their CICs (Chapter 17).

Chapters 18–21 tie up some loose ends. We examine the characteristics of quasiverbals (Chapter 18) and verbless clauses (Chapter 19). We scrutinize phenomena that significantly complicate syntactic representation (Chapter 20). Finally, we present supra-clausal structures and introduce the rudiments of our approach to discourse analysis (Chapter 21).

The seven appendixes are designed for specialists. Motivated general readers will be able to grasp much of the material but should, with little hesitation, skip over material that seems too technical for them. The appendixes deal with details of text preparation (Appendix 1), our approach to linguistics (Appendix 2), various ways of approaching positional syntax (Appendix 3), alternation of the indirect object form in the אמר corpus (Appendix 4), statistically rigorous compositional analysis (Appendix 5), pairing verbless clauses (Appendix 6), and enhancements of our database, realized and planned (Appendix 7).

The book concludes with a glossary, bibliography, and three kinds of indexes (authors, scripture, and topics).

Global Abbreviations

Abbreviations used throughout the book are included here; locally-used abbreviations are not. Brief definitions of items set in the Eurostile font in the right-hand column may be found in the Glossary.

A   Aleppo Codex
ASV   American Standard Version
BDB   Brown, F.; Driver, S. R.; Briggs, C. A. *A Hebrew and English Lexicon of the Old Testament.* Oxford: Clarendon, 1907.
BHL   Dotan, A., editor. *Biblia Hebraica Leningradensia.* Peabody, MA: Hendrickson, 2001.
BHS   Elliger, K., and Rudolph, W., editors. *Biblia Hebraica Stuttgartensia.* Stuttgart: Deutsche Bibelgesellschaft, 1984.
CCC   cophenetic correlation coefficient
CIC   clause immediate constituent (a central concept)
DA   discourse analysis
DU   discourse unit
EDU   elementary discourse unit
GF   grammatical function (a central concept)
GF/SR   grammatical function/semantic role
GKC   Kautzsch, E., editor. *Gesenius' Hebrew Grammar.* Translated by A. E. Cowley. 2nd ed. Oxford: Oxford University Press, 1910.
KJV   King James Version
L   Leningrad Codex
LXX   Greek Septuagint
MT   Masoretic Text
NIV   New International Version
NJPS   New Jewish Publication Society
NP   noun phrase
NRSV   New Revised Standard Version
POS   part(s) of speech (a central concept)
PP   prepositional phrase
QV   quasiverbal
RRG   role and reference grammar
SR   semantic role (a central concept)
VLC   verbless clause
VP   verb phrase

Note: Terms that are defined in the glossary are flagged in the text by setting them in the Eurostile font when we believe an assist might be helpful.

Labels and Grammatical Abbreviations

1st	first in clause		
2nd obj	second object	F/fem.	feminine
		furn	furniture semantics
abs	absolute		
abst	abstract	gam	Heb. word *gam* 'also'
accmp	accompanier	geog	geographic semantics
acmpl	adjectival complement	GF	grammatical function
adj	adjunct	gram	grammatical knowledge / grammar
anch	anchored		determined
anml	animal semantics		
app	apposition	humn	human semantics
benf	beneficiary	I/ind obj	indirect object
bldg	building semantics	IC	immediate constituents
bnd	bonded	incl	includer
body prt	body part semantics	inf abs	infinitive absolute
		inf abs amp	infinitive absolute amplifier
C	consonant	inf abs int	infinitive absolute intensifier
C	common	inf cst	infinitive construct
c	collective	inf uttr	infinitive of utterance
cau	cause	instr	instrumental
CCC	cophenetic correlation coefficient	inv	inverse modification
CIC	clause immediate constituent	int	intensifier
cl	clause	intrg	interrogative
cmpl	complement		
cmpr	comparison	Janus sc/sb	Janus subject-complement/subject
cogv cmpl	cognitive complement	juxt	juxtaposed
conc	concurrency feature		
cond	condition	laps	lapsii calami
coord cj	coordinating conjunction	lbl	label
crd	cardinal number	loc	locational semantics
cstr	construct	loc distributive	distributive location
D	dual	m/masc.	masculine
d	distributive	mdl	modal
DA	discourse analysis	mix list	mixed list (some items in a list flank
def	definiteness		conjunctions, and others do not)
deprv	deprivation	MN/mnr	manner
dir obj	direct object	mntl	mental semantics
discrs	discourse	mod	modification
disj	disjunction	mvt aim	movement aim
dl and / dl seq *w*	discourse level sequential *waw*	mvt dir	movement direction
DRS	discourse representation structure	mvt orig	movement origins
dstr app	distributed apposition		
dstr obj	distributive object	N/n	noun (phrase)
DU	discourse unit	neb	nebulous
		neg	negative
EDU	elementary discourse units	nested	nested phrase (neither subsetting nor
EN	enriching constituent		supersetting)
excl	exclamative	nmlzr	nominalizer
excl voctv labl	exclamative vocative clause label??	nom	nominalized construction
ext	extent	nom inf	nominalized infinitive constituent

nota acc.	nota accusitivi (definite-object-marker word *'et* in Hebrew)	rstr	restricter
		S/sent	sentence
NP	noun phrase	S/sing	singular
O/obj	object	sbj	subject
obj addr	object of address	sbj addr	subject of address
obj cmpl	object complement	sbj cmpl	subject complement
obj mk	object marking	sbj distr	distributive subject
oblq	obliqueness	sbst	substantive
open intrg	open question	SCCs	supra-clausal constituents
P/pl.	plural	Sem	semantics
part	participle	sent/discrs	sentence licensed in discourse
pdox	paradoxical licensing relation	SP	spatial
pers.	person	sptl	spatial semantics
pers pr	personal pronoun	SR	semantic role
PN	proper noun	subord	subordinate
POS	part of speech	subset	subsetting phrases (from most general to least general)
poss	possessive		
PP	prepositional phrase	suff	suffixation
PR	participant	superset	supersetting phrases (from least general to most general)
prd	predicator		
prep	preposition	susp	suspension
pron	pronoun		
PS	phrase structure	TM	temporal
ptc	participle	tm int	time interval
q closed	closed question	tm pt	time point
qtr	quoter		
qty	semantics of quantity	unanch	unanchored
qual	semantics of quality	undes	undesirable outcome
QV/qv	quasiverbal	utnsl	utensil semantics
refrnt	referential	V/vb	finite verb (predicator)
rem	remainder	val	valuable
resum	resumption	veg	vegetation semantics
rhet	rhetorical question operator	VLC	verbless clause
RRG	role and reference grammar	vocbl	vocable semantics
rslt	result	voctv	vocative
rsn	reason	VP	verb phrase
rsrc	resource	war	war semantics

Chapter 1

Introduction:
What We Mean by "Biblical Hebrew,"
"Grammar," and "Visualized"

1.1 *Biblical Hebrew*

In this book, *Biblical Hebrew* is the language contained in all of the Hebrew portions of the Jewish Bible as attested in the Leningrad Codex (**L**).

1.1.1 Choosing the Text(s)

Biblical Hebrew in our book title reflects the fact that we have limited the corpus here considered to the Jewish תנ״ך minus its Aramaic portions (see §1.1.3.5). Given that early decision, we next had to choose which text(s) of the Jewish Bible to rely upon. We could pick one complete "best" manuscript, or we could select "best portions" drawn from several manuscripts. That is, we could opt for the Leningrad Codex, **L** (dated 1008 C.E.), essentially complete and judged to be of high quality—the text transcribed in the *Biblia Hebraica Stuttgartensia* (BHS). Or we could piece together excellent manuscripts to synthesize a complete text:

- Cairo Codex of the Prophets, **C**, dated 895 C.E.
- Petersburg Codex of the Latter Prophets, **P**, dated 916 C.E.
- Aleppo Codex, **A**, dated ~930 C.E., lacking most of the Torah as well as many Writings
- British Museum Or 4445, **B**, dated ~950 C.E., consisting of Gen 39:20–Deut 1:33
- Various texts from Qumran

Both options were open since each specifically mentioned manuscript (**L, C, P, A, B**) was available, in that its text existed in photographic, transcribed, or facsimile form.

Because it was (essentially) complete and enjoyed wide scholarly acceptance, in 1970 we chose to base our computer-readable text on the Leningrad Codex. To date, we have seen no compelling reason to alter that decision.[1]

1.1.2 Correcting "Obvious Errors" in L

We depart from readings provided by **L** when we judge those readings to be simple scribal errors. Such erroneous readings are typically signaled in the apparatus of BHS by a "sic L" note.

Authors' note: A grasp of this chapter, *especially §1.3*, is vital for understanding this book. We suggest readers first go through the chapter without consulting appendixes. Where more information is desired, consult relevant appendixes during a second pass. Terms in underlined Eurostile font (such as normal) may be found in our glossary.

1. Readers desiring a more detailed discussion of text choice should read appendix §A1.1.

1

Across the whole of BHS, we count 368 "sic L" notes. We change what we consider an erroneous reading 216 times, 59% of the instances.[2]

In addition to correcting about three-fifths of the "sic L" anomalies flagged in BHS, we have made three changes that are not signaled in BHS by a "sic L" note.[3]

We have also restored Josh 21:36–37, as per BHS and Dotan's BHL. This patch is now taken for granted, but one may have misgivings as to the quality of the inserted text. The apparatus of BHS says "exstat in mlt Mss Edd" but does not disclose the source of the text selected. Works of reference, such as those by E. Tov and by Robert G. Boling and G. Ernest Wright, are perfunctory.[4] Benjamin Kennicott reported the turbulent variety in the readings in the sources.[5] He was particularly struck by manuscripts that had four additional Hebrew words in the "missing" text ("to be a city of refuge for the slayer"[6]) and one manuscript with a fifth extra word ("in the wilderness," agreeing with the LXX[7]). These tiny differences in themselves may not seem to matter. But they raise a serious issue. The mystique of the ben Asher tradition, greatly exaggerated by Kahle, and the consequent prestige of the successive editions of *Biblia Hebraica* do not warrant acceptance of **L** as "all we need to know about Biblical Hebrew." In due time, the variants already available in the *Qere/Kethiv* apparatus should be augmented from sources with a claim to be considered "Biblical Hebrew," particularly the biblical texts among the Dead Sea Scrolls.

Early on, we decided that we would not attempt to make emendations. Of course, there are important places where a particular emendation makes excellent sense and rescues the analysis from paralysis. But, in the interest of consistency, we have omitted even these well-justified emendations. The costs paid for our determined avoidance of emendations are rather far-fetched analyses of some damaged passages.

1.1.3 Reducing the Text

Because we knew that production of a syntactic representation of Biblical Hebrew would be a massive undertaking, we decided to limit our initial analysis to a single unequivocal text derived from our chosen manuscript by applying to our minimally corrected text of **L** the following five sorts of reductions:

- Omission of cantillations
- Choice of *Kethiv* readings, setting aside the *Qere* variants
- Resolution of lexical ambiguity
- Resolution of structural ambiguity
- Omission of Aramaic text blocks

---

2. For additional discussion, see appendix §A1.2.1 and §A1.2.2.

3. For the specifics, see appendix §A1.2.3.

4. Emanuel Tov, *Textual Criticism of the Hebrew Bible* (2nd ed.; Minneapolis: Fortress, 2001) 238. Robert G. Boling and G. Ernest Wright, *Joshua* (AB 6: Garden City, NY: Doubleday, 1995) 483.

5. Benjamin Kennicott, *The State of the Printed Hebrew Text of the Old Testament Considered* (Dissertation I, Oxford, 1753: 440, 552; Dissertation II, Oxford, 1759: 285, 330–32, 390, 485, 487, 571).

6. Ibid., I.440, II.332.

7. Ibid., II.332.

1.1.3.1 Omission of Cantillations

We used cantillations in resolving certain homographic normal and construct forms and in resolving the ambiguity of words that differed only in stress position. But, given the turbulence evident in the marking of cantillations and given the limited technical resources available to us early on, we elected not to include cantillations in our text markup.[8]

1.1.3.2 *Kethiv* Text Analyzed

Our computer text includes both the *Qere* and *Kethiv* readings found in **L**, the *Kethiv*s having been vocalized in accordance with Gordis.[9]

The presence of the *Qere / Kethiv* alternate readings presents the corpus grammarian with three options. The very fact that the sages included *Qere / Kethiv* pairs in the text makes them part of the text and also betokens an attitude of neutrality over their respective merits. It cannot be inferred that placing the *Kethiv* in the body of the text gives it a superior claim, especially when we notice that *Qere* and *Kethiv* sometimes swap places.

1. *First option.*   Accept all the data on a level field and make two representations of each clause that contains a *Qere / Kethiv* pair of words that differ in syntax. This procedure is the same in principle as multiple representations of structurally ambiguous clauses (§1.1.3.4).
2. *Second option.*   Choose the better of the two, case by case. This would permit palpably recalcitrant variants to be discarded. However, adopting this policy would involve tricky choices, tantamount to deciding on a single text. This could not be done responsibly without spelling out the reasons for each choice, an onerous task that is best left to specialized *Qere / Kethiv* researchers.[10]
3. *Third option.*   As an interim measure, choose either all of the *Qere* or all of the *Kethiv* variants.

To achieve maximal simplicity in representing syntactic structures, we decided to use all of the *Kethiv* variants, without prejudice relative to the merits of the *Qere* alternatives. A price is paid for this choice. We are left with impossible *Kethiv*s that must be parsed as nebulous (§9.3.1.2).

The first option might be followed later. We emphasize that, because of the shortcomings of L's *Qere / Kethiv* repertoire, our electronic text cannot contribute much to the study of the *Qere / Kethiv* phenomenon.[11]

1.1.3.3 Lexical Ambiguity Resolved

In line with our decision to seek maximal representational simplicity initially, we have resolved lexical ambiguity. A given word may exhibit lexical ambiguity. That is, it may be one of several possible lexemes that share the same spelling. Words of this sort are homographs, "lexemes . . . which have the same spelling but differ in meaning."[12] Of 44,026 entries in our dictionary, at present 6,546 involve homography. Failure to resolve homography where a grapheme appears as *multiple parts of speech* represents an error on our part. Resolution of *within-part-of-speech homography* is an ongoing process carried out when we notice that a particular gloss is misleading at times.[13]

---

8. For more discussion, see appendix §A1.3.1.

9. Robert Gordis, *The Biblical Text in the Making: A Study of the Kethib-Qere* (Jersey City, NJ: Ktav, 1971).

10. Maimon Cohen, *The Kethib and Qeri System in the Biblical Text* (Jerusalem: Magnes, 2007).

11. Readers desiring more detail should consult appendix §A1.3.2.

12. David Crystal, *A Dictionary of Linguistics and Phonetics* (5th ed.; Oxford: Blackwell, 2003) 220.

13. For specific examples and further discussion, see appendix §A1.3.3.

In specifying our text, our policy has been to resolve many instances of lexical ambiguity. At times, this has forced us to resolve fundamental, even intentional ambiguity by over-reader fiat. This policy should not be allowed to negate the claims of other readings.

1.1.3.4 Structural Ambiguity Not Represented Initially

Consider this structurally ambiguous clause from Exod 2:1:

וַיֵּלֶךְ אִישׁ מִבֵּית לֵוִי

and + he-walked + man + from + house-of + Levi

The prepositional phrase (from house-of Levi) can:

1. modify man (a man from the house of Levi walked) [house = tribe],
   or
2. specify the movement origin (a man walked from the house of Levi) [house = building].

Since we have elected for the present to represent only one parse of a structurally ambiguous text, we must decide which of the interpretations is the more salient. In the present instance, we draw on world knowledge to the effect that "house-of Levi" refers to a kinship group and decide that the first option is the preferred one.

The structural ambiguity in the example is easily resolved, but resolution is not always so easy. As is explained in §20.3, we have made provision for the representation of ambiguity in the future.

1.1.3.5 Exclusion of Aramaic Blocks

Our database includes the text and syntactic analysis for all of the תנ״ך. Hence, users of our database have three language options—Hebrew only, Aramaic only, or the entire תנ״ך.

This book is based, however, on only the Hebrew chapters and verses. Our counts and examples are drawn from the Hebrew portions. We omit the following blocks of Aramaic text: Jer 10:11; Dan 2:4b–49 and chaps. 3, 4, 5, 6, and 7; Ezra 4:8–24, chap. 5, 6:1–18, and 7:12–26. The text for these passages contains 4,827 words. Hence, they account for around 1.6% of the census of words in the complete תנ״ך, which consists of 305,520 words.

1.2 *Grammar*

Readers may be assisted by knowing from the outset our stance regarding linguistic theory. In setting out the way our work relates to the Hebrew grammar that is enshrined in the grammars and other works of reference that most students of Biblical Hebrew use, we do not debate the merits of our different ways of doing things, nor do we go into much detail. In this introductory section, we emphasize three critical grammar-related points:

1. We accept and affirm and continue to use as much as we can of previous work on Hebrew grammar.
2. We are eclectics, drawing insights from multiple linguistic formalisms.
3. Too often, statements alleged to be about the syntax of Biblical Hebrew are, in fact, statements about the syntax of translation(s). We try to be very sensitive to this trap, actively seeking to avoid it.

1.2.1 Traditional Approaches to the Syntax of Biblical Hebrew

For the most part, what traditional Hebrew grammar calls *syntax* is restricted to the short-range functions of the various word classes. Our syntax begins where traditional treatments leave off. The two approaches are complementary, and most of what traditional Hebrew grammar has done can stand, especially the extensive treatments of morphology.[14] Taking the "word" as its working unit, traditional Hebrew grammar is rather fragmented. By contrast, our treatment aims to be holistic. Our major working units are whole clauses.

Behind the old mind set was a belief that language was logical, that grammar was consistent, and that Biblical Hebrew grammar was uniform and homogeneous. This was the underlying view, whether one's approach rested on academic scientific rationalism or on the pious belief that sacred Scripture had the unique benefit of divine authorship and therefore was immaculate, its inerrancy preserved by divine providence.

In contradiction to all that, and without any detriment to the qualities of a holy book, we are committed simply to describing what is there, recognizing variety and diversity, and seeking, some-day perhaps, to correlate variety with the numerous variables that likely were at work—date, text type, dialect, register, and so on—with corruption appearing as the last option, reluctantly invoked, when all other explanations fail to convince.[15]

1.2.2 Eclecticism and Modern Linguistics

We have relied on many of the insights and methods developed by modern linguists. Rather than pausing along the way to explain these influences or expecting readers to infer them, we will briefly sketch the major influences here. Our basic stance with regard to modern linguistics is as follows:

1. Our emphases are those of the corpus linguists rather than those of the transformationalists.
2. We are, nonetheless, generativists with a preference for phrase-structure grammars.

1.2.2.1 Emphases Drawn from Modern Linguistics

For us, many of the emphases in renascent corpus linguistics—the linguistic analyses of texts—are superior to those insisted upon by the Chomskyans in the latter decades of the last century. Specifically, for our work, we affirm the priority of:[16]

- Empiricism over rationalism
- Performance over competence
- Language description over language universals
- Quantitative models over qualitative models
- Surface structure over deep structure
- Functional approaches over formal approaches

---

14. Joshua Blau, *Phonology and Morphology of Biblical Hebrew: An Introduction* (Linguistic Studies in Ancient West Semitic 2; Winona Lake, IN: Eisenbrauns, 2010).

15. More detail on traditional approaches to the grammar of Biblical Hebrew can be found in appendix §A2.1.

16. The first four contrasts are adapted from Geoffrey Leech, "Corpora and Theories of Linguistic Performance," in *Directions in Corpus Linguistics* (ed. Jan Svartvik; Berlin: De Gruyter, 1992) 107.

The fiats of the Chomskyans are intelligible once one understands that their goal was the demolition of American structuralism. Since Chomsky and his disciples saw structuralism as misguided in its reliance on empirical methods, they strongly preferred rationalist approaches based on native-speaker intuitions. Description of particular languages was to be supplanted by explanation in terms of language universals. Since they saw language performance as fatally compromised by random phenomena, they focused on language competence and the codification of native-speaker knowledge of language. Since they saw the structuralists' zeal in describing and quantifying the surface details of language performance as a dead-end activity, they opted to reconstruct so-called deep structure. For the Chomskyans, structuralism's reliance on a loose functionalism rendered it unscientific, while rigorous formalism led to genuine scientific progress.

The Chomskyan critique of structuralism did properly skewer many of its excesses, but the Chomskyans went too far, reaching a point where almost nothing in the structuralist program was worth salvaging. Trask is accurate when he asserts that "the early generative linguists came to use 'structuralist' as a term of abuse."[17] The onslaught was withering. "Chomsky had, effectively, put to flight the corpus linguistics of an earlier generation. His view on the inadequacy of corpora, and the adequacy of intuition, became the orthodoxy of a succeeding generation of theoretical linguists."[18]

It took a few decades, but corpus linguistics (or textlinguistics) has been rehabilitated by the computational linguists. The primacy of performance data over native-speaker intuitions has been reasserted. Description has again become defensible, even informative. Powerful statistical methods are flourishing.[19] In short, many of the excesses of early scorched-earth generativism have been or are being redressed.

1.2.2.2 Phrase-Structure Grammars

As data-driven approaches to linguistic study have made a comeback, the previously dismissed methods of phrase-structure grammar have been impressively generalized and shown to be capable of covering a vast array of linguistic phenomena without ever resorting to transformations or positing deep structure. Over time, we have been increasingly drawn to this branch of syntactic theory. According to Matthews, a phrase-structure grammar is:[20]

> Any form of generative grammar consisting only of phrase structure rules. Hence any grammar which assigns to sentences a type of structure that can be represented by a single phrase structure tree.

Our grammars are phrase-structure grammars, since our computational parsing algorithms involve phrase-structure rules[21] and since the resulting phrase markers are usually trees.[22] ("Phrase markers" and "trees" are introduced in §1.3.)

---

17. R. L. Trask, *A Dictionary of Grammatical Terms* (London: Routledge, 1993) 263.

18. Geoffrey Leech, "The State of the Art in Corpus Linguistics," in *English Corpus Linguistics: Studies in Honour of Jan Svartvik* (ed. K. Aijmer and B. Alterberg; London: Longman, 1991) 8.

19. Christopher D. Manning and Heinrich Schütze, *Foundations of Statistical Natural Language Processing* (Cambridge, MA: MIT Press, 1999).

20. P. H. Matthews, *Oxford Concise Dictionary* (Oxford: Oxford University Press, 1997) 280.

21. See appendix §A2.2 for information on our approach to the computer parsing of our text.

22. More precisely, as will be explained in chap. 20, our phrase markers are trees except when we encounter phenomena that force us to generalize from trees to graphs.

1.2.3   The Autonomy of Syntax—Not

In this subsection, we consider the notion of the *autonomy of syntax*: "the doctrine that syntax can and should be studied in isolation from other branches of linguistics and most particularly from semantics."[23] Our rejection of this doctrine is central to our representation of the grammatical functions of Biblical Hebrew. As needed, we bring morphology, semantics, discourse analysis, and world knowledge into our analyses of Biblical Hebrew. Thus, our procedures involve bottom-up syntactic analysis as far as it will take us, but we also engage in top-down analysis when only that enables what seems to us to be a proper overall analysis.[24]

1.2.3.1   The Role of Morphology

Morphological analysis underlies our assignment of parts-of-speech labels to segments and of grammatical characteristics to these segments. We will not discuss morphological analysis in this book, since it is adequately covered in intermediate books on the grammar of Biblical Hebrew.

1.2.3.2   The Role of Semantics

In advancing a strict hierarchy of discovery procedures for inferring grammars, the structuralists argued that the various domains of linguistic inquiry were separate. In their view, syntax was autonomous from morphology and semantics, so "no syntactic analysis could be undertaken until the morphological analysis was complete."[25] Appeals to semantic information were also out of bounds as one did syntactic analysis. This view was maintained, at least by implication, by the generativists. Over time, this strict view of separation has eroded. Of late, "linguists have often been willing to accept that syntactic analysis must, at least sometimes, take note of semantic facts."[26] We go further, including explicit semantic information in our grammatical representations.

1.2.3.3   The Role of Discourse Analysis

The common view among linguists is that the sentence is "the largest unit of grammar,"[27] a view that we do not share. We see grammar as extending above and below[28] the sentence into discourse. We take discourse analysis to be a serious discipline, one that we have begun to address.[29]

Discourse analysts divide into two camps: linguists who see discourse analysis as an endeavor separate from the analysis of syntax ("the disjoint camp") and linguists who see discourse analysis as a continuation of clause-level analysis into the higher reaches of texts ("the unified camp"). We identify with the latter camp, seeing grammatical relations as transitioning smoothly into discourse.

We will encounter situations in which detailed discourse analysis is a prerequisite for doing adequate syntactic analysis.

---

23. Trask, *A Dictionary*, 24.
24. For a few added details on this topic, see appendix §A2.2.
25. R. L. Trask, *A Dictionary*, 263.
26. Ibid., 24.
27. Matthews, *Oxford Concise Dictionary*, 337. This is also the view of, among many others, Trask, *A Dictionary*, 250; Crystal, *A Dictionary*, 414; also, M. G. Dareau, "Glossary," in *Concise Encyclopedia of Grammatical Categories* (ed. Keith Brown and Jim Miller; Oxford: Elsevier, 1999) 436.
28. We note that discourse units are quite commonly embedded in clauses.
29. The next of our planned volumes will deal with the discourse analysis of Biblical Hebrew. For a provisional introduction to our approach, see chap. 21 below.

1.2.4 Filling a Gap in Traditional Treatments

In this book, we attempt to fill a gap in the traditional treatments of Hebrew clause grammar. It is a commonplace in linguistics that the clause is the basic unit of grammar, discrete and integral. However, traditional Hebrew grammars have limited treatments of the internal syntax of whole clauses. The literature provides very few principled, systematic, exhaustive accounts of the grammatical functions and relations operating among all of the constituents in the complete clauses of Biblical Hebrew in all their variety.[30]

When it comes to the clause, traditional Hebrew grammars are partial and disjointed. They list the typical grammatical functions of the various parts of speech, supplying a few illustrations. Most of the text of the Hebrew Bible is never dealt with. So it is misleading to present a work as a grammar of Biblical Hebrew, when all it deals with are selected grammatical functions and constructions as found in only a fraction of the text. Corpus linguistics demands complete coverage.

To make this point, we only need to examine two leading works. What is under scrutiny is the *way* of doing Hebrew grammar inherited from our fathers in the discipline.

Waltke and O'Connor (IBHS).   The first half of *IBHS* reviews the syntactic functions (not always distinguished from "meanings") of nouns, adjectives, numerals, and pronouns. There are four pages on "Aspects of the Syntax of Prepositions." The second half takes up verb stems, whose functions are listed and illustrated. The treatment remains at the level of microsyntax—that is, it deals with small constructions. It does not advance to the study of the full array of constituents that each verb evokes in the clauses in which it is the predicator.

At the end of the treatment of verb syntax, *IBHS* has two short chapters on the subordination and coordination of clauses. These chapters view clauses as units in higher structures (sentences), and their functions are classified along traditional lines as conditional, causal, temporal, and so on. Here we see the beginnings of rudimentary bottom-up discourse grammar. Holistic top-down analysis of clause-internal grammar is nowhere to be found.

Joüon / Muraoka.   Joüon / Muraoka is a general reference grammar in three parts: orthography and phonetics, morphology, and syntax. Because the orthographic "word" is taken as the unit of grammar, some syntax is found in the treatment of morphology, as in the recognition of a pronoun suffix on a verb as its object. Anticipating the traditional treatment of the grammar of nouns under "cases," a little additional syntax is found in the discussion of noun inflection, such as when a construct noun or suffixed stem is said to be "in the genitive" (p. 260).

Part 3 of Joüon / Muraoka ("Syntax") deals with the short-range syntactic functions (microsyntax) of several parts of speech, beginning with the verb. Chapter 1 ("Tenses and Moods") is concerned with the "various semantic values" (p. 350) of the verb forms. *The grammatical significance of the semantics of verb roots is not taken into account.* Otherwise, what is called "verb syntax" is engaged with the problem of tense and aspect in the Hebrew verbal system. These are important parts of Hebrew grammar, but they do not take us very far into syntax and do not even begin to deal with internal clause syntax as such. There is no interest in matters of transitivity or valence in the perspective of the relations of a verb to all the other clause immediate constituents in its clause. Chapter 7 ("Clauses") distinguishes nominal and verbal clauses and then discusses

---

30. Useful treatments, however, are to be found in the work of Wolfgang Richter and his students. See, for example, W. Richter, *Grundlagen einer althebräischer Grammatik*, vol. 3: *Der Satz* (Arbeiten zu Text und Sprache im Alten Testament 13; St. Ottilien: EOS, 1980).

a miscellaneous list of "particular clauses": substantival (with noun-like functions), relative, circumstantial, negative, interrogative, exclamatory, optative, asseverative, curse and oath, temporal, conditional, final, consecutive, causal and explicative, concessive, adversative, exceptive, comparative, disjunctive. There does not seem to be any awareness that these categories occupy several taxonomic dimensions—logical, pragmatic, and text type. This, again, is the traditional approach, as can be seen by comparison with Davidson's syntax of a century earlier. The enduring value of this tradition is appreciated. It takes each clause as a whole, as a discrete unit in discourse, but with little consideration of what is inside it.

The bottom-up treatment of small constructions that never takes a whole clause into its purview and the rudimentary bottom-up discussion of the discourse functions of clauses as units—both of these approaches are limited by endemic binarism. A top-down holistic analysis of the internal syntax of complete clauses is required to fill the gap between these two approaches.

1.3 *Visualizing Structure*

1.3.1 Labeled Bracketing

How the constituents of a phrase combine can be shown via a representation that is much used in linguistics, a *labeled bracketing*. We introduce "labeled bracketing" here because our preferred representation, the phrase marker, evolves nicely from it.

Construction of the labeled bracketing is straightforward. Each sequence of constituents making up a phrase is flanked by paired brackets, and then a label specifying the kind of phrase is placed immediately within the leading bracket. To promote readability and minimize clutter, our illustrations of bracketing will be in English, with the segments in italics.

Let us construct the labeled bracketing for the three-segment word מִפִּרְיוֹ, *from* + *fruit* + *its*. Consider first the common noun *fruit*. The labeled bracketing for *fruit* is [N *fruit*], where N indicates that this segment is a noun. Relying on our recollections of grade-school grammar, we assert that *fruit* and *its* may next be combined to form the larger noun phrase whose structure is [NP [N *fruit*] [pron *its*]], where "pron" indicates that *its* is a pronoun. The syntactic structure of the full prepositional phrase—abbreviated PP—is then represented as in (1.1).

(1.1)   [PP [prep *from*] [NP [N *fruit*] [pron *its*]]]

This bracketing captures the syntactic structure of the prepositional phrase, but correctly pairing the left brackets with their corresponding right brackets can be tedious, especially when the constituents become lengthy. We will overcome this limitation in the next section.

The decoding of labeled brackets only becomes more arduous as more complex constituents are analyzed. For example, consider this six-word clause from 2 Kgs 18:8:

הוּא־הִכָּה אֶת־פְּלִשְׁתִּים עַד־עַזָּה

We translate the six words literally as:

He + *he-hit* + [*nota acc.*] + *Philistines* + *until* + *Gazah.*

The labels needed for representing the structure of this clause are:

Label	Constituent Name
S	sentence
VP	verb phrase
PP	prepositional phrase
PN	proper noun
V	verb
prep	preposition
pron	pronoun[31]

In terms of these labels, the labeled bracketing for this simple clause is as in (1.2).

(1.2) [S [pron *he*][VP [V *he-hit*][PP [prep [*nota acc.*]][PN *Philistines*]][PP [prep *until*][PN *Gazah*]]]]

This is not easy to decipher. Its structure can be made clearer by introducing judicious indenting as is shown in (1.3), that is, by making an *indented list*.

(1.3)   [S

                             [pron *he*]
                             [VP

                                          [V *he-hit*]
                                          [PP

                                                        [prep [*nota acc.*]]
                                                        [PN *Philistines*]

                                          ]
                                          [PP

                                                        [prep *until*]
                                                        [PN *Gazah*]

                                          ]

                             ]

                    ]

In this representation, we keep the words and their part-of-speech labels together with their enclosing brackets on the same vertical line. The constituents in the column immediately to the right of a given constituent down to its closing bracket are called its immediate constituents (ICs). Thus, for example, the immediate constituents of S (the sentence) are a pron (pronoun) and a VP (verb phrase). The VP has three ICs: V (the sentence's verb) plus two PPs (prepositional phrases). The first PP has two ICs: the *nota accusativi* (object marker) and a proper noun. Even this representation is awkward to read. Enter the phrase marker. . . .

1.3.2 The Phrase Marker

Suppose that we link each constituent with each of its immediate constituents via an arrow from the former to the latter and that we do away with the now superfluous brackets. Then the representation in (1.4), mathematically equivalent to a labeled bracketing, is obtained. This is a phrase marker.

---

31. For now, so as to parallel standard works on syntax, we have chosen to name the most inclusive constituent the sentence. However, as our exposition develops below, our major unit of syntactic structure will be termed the clause.

(1.4)

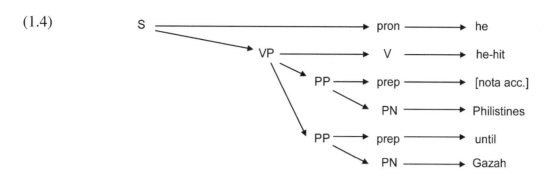

Unlike a labeled bracketing, a phrase marker is easily understood. For example, in phrase marker (1.4), we readily see that the proper noun 'Gazah' combines with a preposition ('until') to form a prepositional phrase (PP = 'until Gazah'), which is one of three immediate constituents of the sentence's verb phrase (VP = 'he-hit [*nota acc.*] Philistines until Gazah').

Mathematically speaking, a phrase marker is a <u>tree</u>. If the phrase marker is counter-rotated by ninety degrees so that the S is at the bottom (the <u>tree root</u>) and the words are at the top (the tree <u>leaves</u>), then the reason for calling the structure a tree will be obvious. In linguistics textbooks, phrase markers are invariably displayed with the root at the top and the leaves at the bottom (i.e., the tree is upside down). We opt for placing the tree on its side with its root to the left so that long clauses can be displayed down the page or screen rather than across.

1.3.3   The Enhanced Phrase Marker

1.3.3.1   Enhancements Made

Being fashioned in the traditional way, phrase markers of the sort presented above show how larger and larger constituents are built up until they finally combine to show the structure of entire clauses.

As we developed our syntactic representation, we asked what additional information might be incorporated in a phrase marker to enhance its usefulness for research. One interesting and well-developed syntactic theory, *lexical functional grammar*, argues that a complete presentation of syntax must supply both a picture of the hierarchical makeup of clauses and a quite separate catalog of essential information regarding grammatical functions. "[Functional]-structure is composed of attributes (features and functions) and their values."[32] Included in functional-structure is information specifying the <u>subject</u>, <u>direct object</u>, <u>tense</u>, and so on, associated with a clause.

Much functional-structure information can be straightforwardly grafted onto traditional phrase markers, as can information regarding the semantic characteristics of the constituents. To accomplish this enrichment (and make our phrase markers more readable), we make these changes and enhancements to traditional phrase markers:

1. Add the Hebrew text to the left of the English glosses.
2. Replace S (sentence) by cl (clause) in the root node at the far left of the phrase markers.
3. Delete the VP (verb phrase) constituent, joining its constituents directly to the root node.
4. Then, to the immediate right of the root node, insert a set of *function-specifying* labels, short yet informative (e.g., dir obj) rather than acronymic (e.g., do), that provide the names

---

32. Y. N. Falk, *Lexical-Functional Grammar: An Introduction to Parallel Constraint-Based Syntax* (Stanford, CA: CSLI, 2001) 16.

of the clause immediate constituents (CICs).[33]

5. Enrich the label information by introducing a two-line format. The upper line describes the *form* or *function* of the constituent. When form is being described, explicit semantic information is included. The lower line gives the licensing relation justifying the assembling of the constituent.

The resulting structures might properly be termed *enhanced phrase markers*, but for brevity we will simply continue to call them phrase markers.

Transforming the traditional phrase marker (1.4) yields the (enhanced) phrase marker (1.5).[34]

(1.5)

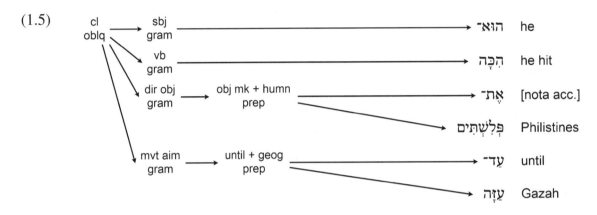

The innovations given in the previous list are realized in this phrase marker as follows:

Item #1:   Hebrew text.   Self evident.

Item #2:   "Clause" as Root Constituent.   In a simple substitution, cl replaces S. Along with the newly minted cl in the upper line of the root node label, a new shortened form has appeared in the lower line: oblq. This is short for obliqueness, a topic taken up in §1.3.3.3.

Item #3:   Deletion of the Verb Phrase.   In most modern textbooks on syntax, one of the fixed points is that the root label (be it symbolized by S or cl) in the phrase marker for a declarative sentence always has two and only two immediate constituents, NP and VP. The former functions as the clause's subject, while the latter functions as the clause's predicate. This is the orthodox view. Practitioners of lexical functional grammar and others, however, suggest that holding this binary view of sentence structure is counterproductive when certain non-English-like languages, so-called nonconfigurational or fluid languages, are being investigated. We address this topic in §7.2 and §7.3.3. We trust that until then readers will, however uneasily, accept our jettisoning of the use of VPs for Biblical Hebrew.

Items #4 and #5:   CIC Insertion and Label Format.   The inclusion of function-specifying labels is a major innovation. This clause has the four clause immediate constituents (CICs) named in the upper lines of the CIC labels. Their expanded names are as follows:

---

33. Clause immediate constituents (CICs) are the major constituents in clauses. They are treated at great length in chaps. 9–16. Clause immediate constituents have also been referred to as *clause-rank constituents* in John H. Connolly, *Constituent Order in Functional Grammar: Synchronic and Diachronic Perspectives* (Berlin: Foris, 1991) 28. The easily pronounced acronym *CIC* ("kick") is our innovation.

34. This and all of the subsequent phrase markers in this book have been exported from the *Andersen-Forbes Phrase Marker Analysis of the Hebrew Bible*, as displayed by the Libronix Digital Library System, Logos Research Systems.

CIC Label	Expanded Name
sbj	subject
vb	finite verb, one kind of predicator
dir obj	direct object
mvt aim	movement aim

The subject is often said to be "what in the clause is already known" (its theme). Traditionally, it is the doer of the action in a clause. The predicator is not the traditional predicate.[35] Rather, it is a verbal or quasiverbal constituent that specifies an equivalence, a state, an activity, or a process. In the present example, the predicator is a finite verb. The direct object is that which is affected by the action specified by the predicator. It is the "undergoer" of the action of the predicator. In Biblical Hebrew, the direct object is often marked by the *nota accusativi*, as it is here. The movement aim is the destination of the activity specified in the clause. The lower lines of the CIC labels each read gram. This indicates that a CIC classification has been assigned on the basis of grammatical knowledge. The significance of this label is discussed in §1.3.3.3.

1.3.3.2   Construction-Identifier Label Formats

The construction-specifying upper lines in the labels on non-CIC nodes come in two flavors: one for prepositional phrases and one for noun phrases.

Prepositional Phrase Construction Format. Our example clause has two other labels to the right of the four CIC labels just explained. These non-CIC labels are in the *prepositional phrase format.* The upper line in the label on the first prepositional phrase constituent '[*nota acc.*] + Philistines' reads obj mk+humn, meaning that the prepositional phrase consists of the object-marking preposition plus (+) a noun having human semantics. The upper line in the label on the prepositional phrase "until + Gazah" reads until+geog, meaning that the prepositional phrase consists of the preposition "until" plus a noun having location/geographic semantics. In both labels, the lower line of the label reads prep, indicating that we are dealing with a prepositional phrase gathered together ("licensed") because of the presence of a preposition.

Noun Phrase Construction Format. The *noun phrase format* is different. Consider phrase-marker fragment (1.6) from 2 Chr 29:32.

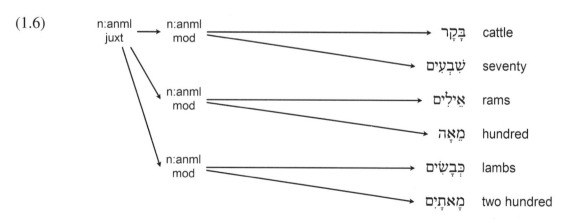

(1.6)

---

35. The term *predicator* has a long history. For example, in 1961, Halliday used it as we do: M. A. K. Halliday, *Categories in the Theory of Grammar* (Indianapolis, IN: Bobs-Merrill, 1961) 257.

The constituent is a noun phrase with animal semantics (n:anml) produced by juxtaposing (juxt) its three subconstituents. Each of the three subconstituents is itself a noun phrase with animal semantics (n:anml) produced by modifying (mod) the first segment in each phrase with the next segment.

The upper line reads n:anml, indicating that the constituent formed is a noun (phrase) further specified (:) as involving animal semantics.

1.3.3.3 The Licensing Relations of Grammar and Obliqueness

When we say that the assembling of a prepositional phrase is licensed by the presence of an initial preposition or that the assembling of a construct phrase is licensed by the presence of an initial substantive in the construct state, the underlying grammatical mechanisms being described are clear. But when we say that the assigning of some label to a clause immediate constituent (CIC) is licensed by *grammar* [gram] or that the assembling of a clause is licensed by *obliqueness* [oblq], the underlying grammatical mechanisms are unspecified.

Given our adoption of a two-line format for the node labels in our phrase markers, we had to assign *some* licensing relations to justify the classification of CICs and the assembling of clauses; but which ones and, more importantly, with what meanings? We might have simply installed the label dummy, explicitly signaling our initial ignorance of the what, how, and why of CIC classification and clause assemblage. Instead, we opted for *grammar* and *obliqueness*, allowing us to search for each licensing relation independently. The relations *grammar* and *obliqueness* stand for the very disparate and still obscure mechanisms that provide the grounds for classifying CICs and assembling them into clauses. Here is the critical point for our work:

> *Gathering the data needed to begin working out the grammatical mechanisms underlying* "grammar" *and* "obliqueness" *is the focus of the latter two-thirds of this book.*

1.4 *Brief Summary*

Text Source. We use the *Kethiv* text of the Leningrad Codex, "obvious errors" having been corrected, cantillations having been omitted, lexical and structural ambiguity having been resolved in favor of "salient readings," and blocks of Aramaic text having been set aside.

Our Grammatical Stance. Where possible, we build on traditional grammars of Biblical Hebrew. With regard to modern linguistics, we are eclectic. We ally ourselves with the corpus linguists but also find much of value in the work of the generativists, especially generalized phrase structure grammar. We reject the notion of the autonomy of syntax and bring in semantics and discourse analysis as needed. We iteratively rely on both bottom-up and top-down analyses.

Visualizing Structure. Phrase markers, suitably extended, allow us to present our analyses graphically. Our phrase markers consist of labeled nodes and their connecting edges. The node labels disclose the functions and forms of constituents, as well as the grammatical principles licensing their creation. Also included is information regarding the semantic classifications of the constituents.

Of critical importance to our investigations are the clause immediate constituents (CICs), the immediate offspring of the clausal nodes ("roots") in the phrase markers. Central foci of our book are the characteristics of two pivotal licensing relations: (1) gram, which guides the specification of the functions of the CICs, and (2) oblq, which constrains the assembling and ordering of the CICs in clauses.

Chapter 2

Text Division

In chap. 1 we used, without comment, some examples wherein the basic units for syntactic analysis were parts of words, a word being conventionally defined as a continuous sequence of Hebrew consonants and vowels bounded by spacers: (white) space, line end, verse-end marker (*sof pasuq*), or dash (*maqqep*). In general, our basic unit of syntactic analysis is the segment. A segment can be a word ("a free morpheme"), a part of a word ("a bound morpheme"), or a sequence of words. (For the place of morphology in our work, see appendix §A2.3.1.)

We dissect prepositions and pronoun suffixes from nouns. For example, above (§1.3.1) we analyzed מִפִּרְיוֹ into three segments וֹ + פִּרְ׳ + מְ׳ 'from' + 'fruit' + 'its'. We also detach definite articles and conjunctions. For example, בַּיּוֹם is made up of three segments:

$$\text{יוֹם} + \_ + \text{ב} \quad \text{'in'} + \text{'the'} + \text{'day'}$$

while וַיִּתְפְּשׂוּם consists of these three segments:

$$\text{ם} + \text{יִתְפְּשׂוּ} + \text{וַ} \quad \text{'and'} + \text{'they-seized'} + \text{'them'}$$

This example shows that we separate one-consonant segments (the conjunction וַ) and object pronoun suffixes from verbs but not the subject pronoun affixes of verbs. Segments are also formed by the ligaturing of words, almost invariably forming proper nouns. For example, in our analysis, we ligature the two-word sequence בֵּית־אֵל to form a single segment glossed 'Bethel'.

It should be clear that we do not accept the lexicalist hypothesis: "the view that rules of syntax may not refer to elements smaller than a single word."[1] As is often the case in Anglo-American linguistics, this hypothesis is "English-o-centric." Rejection of the lexicalist hypothesis is warranted for Biblical Hebrew because its words commonly consist of sequences of morphemes, each having a distinctive role in syntax. For example, were we to treat וּלְאִמָּהּ in Gen 24:53 as a single constituent, important syntactical structure would be hidden. We therefore divide this word into four segments:

$$\text{הָ} + \text{אִמ׳} + \text{לְ׳} + \text{וּ} \quad \text{'and'} + \text{'to'} + \text{'mother'} + \text{'her'}$$

We divide 1,258 four-segment words, 20,759 three-segment words, and 120,007 two-segment words into their segments.

---

1. Robert L. Trask, *A Dictionary of Grammatical Terms in Linguistics* (London: Routledge, 1993) 157.

15

2.1 *Words, Segments, and Ligatures*

Having made the global decision to segment the words making up the biblical text, we were left with a large number of local decisions. We needed to choose which words should be segmented or joined and how. Making these choices required repeatedly answering three questions:

1. *Segmentation.*   Should a given word be segmented or left whole?
2. *Selection of cut-point.*   Where should a multisegment word be sliced?
3. *Ligaturing.*   When should a sequence of words be ligatured?

2.1.1 Segmentation

An example from English may help readers understand what the "segment / no segment" decision involves. Consider the word "tomorrow." This noun evolved from a prepositional phrase.[2] It is instructive to examine this word in Exod 17:9 as printed in three English versions. The KJV uses the term "to morrow," the ASV has "to-morrow," and the RSV has "tomorrow." Were we to perform a syntactic analysis of the verse in English, how would we represent "tomorrow"—as two segments or as one? The answer depends on the word's lexical status when the version was published.

Our decisions regarding word segmentation are mostly intuitive, with a few exceptions.[3] Our segmentation of one sort of word deserves comment. We always segment לִפְנֵי into פְּנֵי + לְ *'to'* + *'face-of'*. We do so because we, and most writers of Biblical Hebrew grammars, view לִפְנֵי as a preposition "prefixed to the substantive פָּנִים in the construct state."[4] The English translation 'before' has lexicalized the compound.[5] Compare "in spite of," "instead of," and "in place of." The preposition לִפְנֵי is not the only word of this kind in Biblical Hebrew.

2.1.2 Selection of Cut-Point

Early in our work, we segmented the texts *ad libitum*, that is, "by the seats-of-our-pants." This approach was indescribably tedious, and the results were unacceptably inconsistent. We therefore enunciated a set of sequentially applied rules that were at first manually implemented. This manual approach increased the tedium and, surprisingly, led to results that were not particularly consistent. Our next gambit was to have the computer enforce consistency. The computer was programmed to move an arrow along through the text, pausing at positions where a word cut might be made, and waiting until the human analyst accepted or rejected the proposed segmentation. If the segmentation was accepted, then an arrow was left in position showing the cut, and the text file was adjusted

---

2. E. C. Traugott, "Grammaticalization and Lexicalization," in *Concise Encyclopedia of Grammatical Categories* (ed. K. Brown and J. Miller; Oxford: Elsevier, 1999) 182.

3. For specifics, see F. I. Andersen and A. D. Forbes, *A Linguistic Concordance of Ruth and Jonah* (Wooster, OH: Biblical Research Associates, 1976) 23–26.

4. Bill T. Arnold and John H. Choi, *A Guide to Biblical Hebrew Syntax* (Cambridge: Cambridge University Press, 2003) 115. Other works referring to the complex nature of לִפְנֵי include GKC, 377; R. J. Williams, *Williams' Hebrew Syntax* (3rd ed.; Toronto: University of Toronto Press, 2007) 135–36; Bruce K. Waltke and M. O'Connor, *An Introduction to Biblical Hebrew Syntax* (hereafter *IBHS*; Winona Lake, IN: Eisenbrauns, 1990) 221. Some treat לִפְנֵי as unitary, as in C. H. J. van der Merwe, Jackie A. Naudé, and Jan H. Kroeze, *A Biblical Hebrew Reference Grammar* (Biblical Languages: Hebrew 3; Sheffield: Sheffield Academic Press, 1999) 287.

5. *Lexicalization* is "the process or result of assigning to a word or phrase the status of a LEXEME," according to R. R. K. Hartmann and Gregory James, *Dictionary of Lexicography* (London: Routledge, 1998) 84.

accordingly. Figure 2.1, a black-and-white photo of our computer monitor screen, was made in early 1971.[6] It shows the opening words of the book of Ruth with the segmenting arrows in place.

Figure 2.1.

The pair of arrows at the beginning of the third line flanks the definite article represented by " ֽ ."

Our final and most accurate approach to segmentation involved "bootstrapping." The computer used the segmentation manifested in a stretch of correctly segmented text to segment new, previously unseen text. There were arrow-insertion criteria and arrow-exclusion criteria. The new results were then manually corrected, and the newly checked results were used to segment the next block of text. And so on. This approach yielded quite high-quality results that were then perfected in the process of building a computerized, lemmatized dictionary for the Hebrew Bible.

2.1.3   Ligaturing

We deal with ligatured words every day. Consider "New York." This proper noun has been lexicalized for a long time and so, in our system, would be declared to be a single segment. In the case of Biblical Hebrew, we have declared hundreds of proper nouns, plus four common nouns and one subordinating conjunction, to be lexicalized. We have joined adjacent words to produce 382 distinct segments. Two-thirds of these appear only once in the MT. The most frequently occurring ligatured item is the subordinating conjunction כִּי אִם 'except' (120×). The second most-frequent is forms of בֵּית־אֵל 'Bethel' (72×), and the third is בֵּית לֶחֶם 'Bethlehem' (41×). By our analysis, Biblical Hebrew contains almost one thousand ligatured segments.

2.2   *Chunking the Text into Clauses*

2.2.1   Rule-Based Clause Onset Detection

For computational parsing, the largest appropriate units are clauses. In our approach, a clause typically consists of a predicator and the constituents that accompany it, a predicator being a verbal or quasiverbal constituent that specifies equivalence, activity, state, or process. A single finite verb can be a whole clause.[7] We have explained elsewhere just how we determined clause boundaries.[8] Here we briefly provide the flavor of that work.

---

6. The pin-cushion distortion in the photo is due to the monitor screen's non-planarity. Four decades later, it is amusing to recall how inordinately pleased we were with our pathetic little unkerned Hebrew stick characters!

7. Even a single constituent can form a "verbless" (or "nominal") clause lacking a predicator. See chap. 19.

8. F. I. Andersen and A. D. Forbes, "On Marking Clause Boundaries," in *Bible et Informatique: Interprétation, Herméneutique, Compétence Informatique* (Paris: Honoré Champion, 1992) 181–202. On the general question, see Marjo C. A. Korpel and Josef Oesch, eds., *Unit Delimitation in Biblical Hebrew and Northwest Semitic Literature* (Pericope 4; Assen: Van Gorcum, 2003).

We relied on a dozen ordered rules for detecting clause onset—clause-offset detection being a more difficult problem. But, of course, a true main clause onset must coincide with a true offset, setting aside the first clause in the Bible. Our rules are highly heuristic. To provide a sense of our approach, we quote four of the rules from our referenced essay, tell how often they were used ("how often they fired"), and tell their individual accuracies across Biblical Hebrew.

1. *Rule A.*   "The quoting formula לֵאמֹר is usually followed immediately by a quoted speech." This rule fired 939 times, 929 of them correctly—a 99% true positive rate. There were 10 places where a speech did not immediately follow the quoting formula.
2. *Rule B.*   "A *waw*-sequential construction usually begins a new clause." In 20,691 of its 20,907 firings a new clause begins—a 99% true positive rate.
3. *Rule F.*   "When the first word in a verse is a predicator, it is likely that it begins a . . . clause." This rule fired 2,520 times, 17 incorrectly—a 97% true positive rate.
4. *Rule L.*   "Each new chapter probably begins a new clause." This rule fired 929 times, once "incorrectly"—a 99.9% true positive rate. The verse prior to Jer 3:1 ends with a complete and well-formed clause. Then Jer 3:1 begins with a stranded לֵאמֹר.

Our suite of rules correctly found almost two-thirds of the clause onsets with very few false onset detections but with a fair number of fragmentary "clauses." Completion of the task of clause isolation required careful human over-reading.

2.2.2 Clause-Boundary Ambiguity

Clause-onset position can be ambiguous. Consider three clauses from Exod 17:9:

וְצֵא הִלָּחֵם בַּעֲמָלֵק מָחָר אָנֹכִי נִצָּב עַל־רֹאשׁ הַגִּבְעָה

The NJPS reads:

". . . go out and do battle with Amalek. Tomorrow I will station myself on the top of the hill . . ."

But it might also be rendered:[9]

". . . go out and do battle with Amalek tomorrow. I will station myself on the top of the hill . . ."

Whether a clause boundary should occur before or after "tomorrow" is formally ambiguous. In circumstances of this sort, we have the choice of either somehow representing both clause divisions or selecting and representing the more compelling division. We decided to provide mechanisms for handling the former option but, in this first pass at analysis, represented only the latter. This choice, however, leaves us to decide which of the several options is preferred. For the present example, we follow the cantillations, as do all seven English Bibles consulted, and divide the clauses before "tomorrow." We let unanimity rule, mindful that neither cantillations nor scholarly consensus is always correct.

---

9. Bear in mind that we have opted not to be constrained by the cantillations. The *athnaḥ* in Exod 17:9 encodes a pause before "tomorrow," indicating that the Masoretes divided the verbs into two clauses at this point. See further Emanuel Tov, *Textual Criticism of the Hebrew Bible* (2nd ed.; Minneapolis: Fortress, 2001) 68–69.

2.3 *Brief Summary*

Segments.   Our basic units of analysis, segments, are whole words ("free morphemes"), parts of words ("bound morphemes"), or ligatured words ("lexicalized phrases"). Delimitation of segments relied on computational "bootstrapping" and consistency enforcement followed by correction by an expert.

Clause Delimitation.   Delimitation of clause boundaries involved computational application of a set of heuristic clause-onset rules followed by correction by an expert.

Chapter 3

Parts of Speech

3.1 *Approaches to Parts-of-Speech Specification*

The grammatical category of a segment is its part of speech. The parts of speech (POSs) in a language form a system. Many are definable only when considered in relation to one another. A systems approach is essential, especially when multiple-part-of-speech homography is considered.

The taxonomic problem requires that the analyst execute three tasks: (1) propose a part-of-speech system, (2) decide when segments need to be formed by word dissection or ligaturing, and (3) assign each resulting segment to its POS category.

Two crucial points need to be appreciated:

- The taxonomic tasks are addressed *iteratively*. One does not deal with task 1 fully, execute task 2 perfectly, and then carry out task 3. Rather, in dealing with tasks 2 and 3, one may discover aspects of the POS system that need adjustment. These adjustments, in turn, may require changes to segmentations and classifications that were made previously.
- Carrying out the work involves sophistication ranging from matching up simple patterns to exegesis and reliance on world knowledge. The pretense of bottom-up analysis is just that—a pretense. In what follows, we will provide many examples illustrating this point.

Parts of speech can be specified in five ways: ostensive (by presenting constrained lists), semantic (based on "meaning"), derivational (transforming a segment affix), paradigmatic (based on form patterns), and distributional (based on segmental environments).[1]

3.1.1 Ostensive Specification

Ostensive (or, ostensible) specification (simple listing) is appropriate for some parts of speech. For example, we may specify the major[2] free pronouns (non-suffixing) by this list and its attendant constraints:

Any of these strings is a free pronoun

הֵנָּה הֵמָּה הִיא הוּא אַתֵּנָה אַתֶּם אַתְּ אַתָּה אֲנַחְנוּ אֲנִי

if it is preceded by [a spacer **or** a form of *and* **or** a ה-form of *the*]
and it is followed by a spacer.

---

1. Robert L. Trask, "Parts of Speech," in *Concise Encyclopedia of Grammatical Categories* (ed. K. Brown and J. Miller; Oxford: Elsevier, 1999) 280–82. We have added "ostensive" to Trask's list.

2. Only one allomorph of each is shown here. In order to specify the free pronouns exhaustively, we would need to add 16 additional character strings that are here omitted from the table for the sake of simplicity.

The foregoing illustrates the holistic nature of taxonomic assignment. The just-stated rule finds the free pronouns, but it does so only if one can reliably find *and* as well as the ה-form of *the*.

Identification of the <u>coordinating conjunction</u> *and* is straightforward:

Any of these forms is an *and* if it follows a spacer in Biblical Hebrew:

וֹ   וְ   וַ   וֶ   וֵ   וִ   וּ

This rule correctly identifies coordinating conjunctions 99.94% of the time. It is incorrect 30 times and correct more than 50,000 times. If we seek perfection, then we should exclude from consideration all 30 occurrences of the following simple segments:

וַשְׁתִּי   וַשֵׁנִי   וָפְסִי   וַנְיָה   וָלָד   וַיְזָתָא   וְוֵי   וָוִים   וָהֵב   וְדָן

The modified rule perfectly isolates all 50,000-plus *and*s in Biblical Hebrew. But the rule is not as simple as it might seem, for we have not discussed on what basis we chose the 10 segments to exclude. Three words in the string just above are common nouns ('child', 'hooks', and 'hooks of'), and the other 7 are proper nouns. But we have not yet provided diagnostics for common and proper nouns. Nor have we discussed how we came to know the possible forms for *and*. Since traditional grammars are most reliable when they deal with functional categories, we accept their identifications of the forms of *and* that are identical with the forms specified above.

The specification of ה-forms of *the* is, unfortunately, quite complex. We accept the traditional view that the ה-forms of the definite article are הָ-, הַ-, and הֶ-. Had we assumed that any word-initial occurrence of these characters should be identified as a definite article, then our false-positive error rate would have been 11%, which is unacceptably high. Having carried out the classification, we know that הָ-, הַ-, and הֶ- are also word-initial in instances of 16 other parts of speech. We need to constrain the rule for the definite article to avoid misfiring in these cases. This assumes that we have worked out criteria for recognizing the alternate categories. Once again, we see the interactions encountered when one attempts to specify the parts of speech and identify their members.

3.1.2 Semantic Specification

Basing part-of-speech classification on meaning is unreliable. According to Trask: "Though popular in the past, this criterion is rejected today, since it is hopelessly misleading: lexical categories are syntactic categories, not semantic ones, and the meaning of a word is at best no more than a rough guide to its likely word class."[3] For the most part, we steer clear of meaning as an approach to classification.

3.1.3 Derivational Specification

Derivational specification is quite rare in Biblical Hebrew. We recognize only two kinds of segment obtained by adding derivational suffixes to other segments.

3.1.3.1 *He* Locale

Adding a ה- onto a noun transforms it. When a common noun is involved, the result is a directional adverb. Example: אַרְצָה 'land-ward'. When a proper noun is involved, the result is a movement

---

3. Trask, "Parts of Speech," 280.

aim or target. Example: מִצְרָיְמָה 'Egypt-ward'. In Biblical Hebrew, we count the former 427 times and the latter 406 times. Of course, ה– is a very common word ending (occurring almost 20,000 times), so we cannot provide a simple rule to identify this phenomenon.

3.1.3.2 Suffixed ָם–

The suffix ָם– is added to a common noun to derive an adverb 114 times. This suffix contributes only these 6 segments to our dictionary:

אָמְנָם truly   אֻמְנָם truly   דּוּמָם silently   חִנָּם freely   יוֹמָם by day   רֵיקָם in vain

Because ָם– is a common word ending, we attempt no rule(s) to identify this phenomenon.

3.1.4   Paradigmatic Specification

Paradigmatic specification relies on form patterns exhibited by various parts of speech. It is the most popular way of specifying parts of speech among the writers of grammars.[4]

Some patterns are precisely diagnostic, while others reduce the possibilities to a manageable few. For example, suppose that we specify the Qal suffixed 1st-pers. sing. verb as follows:

> A segment consisting of a consonant with a *qames*
> > a consonant with a *patah*
> > a consonant with a *šewa*
> > followed by תִּי–
> > *then followed by a spacer*
> is a Qal suffixed 1st-pers. sing. verb.

This rule correctly specifies verbs having the shape אָמַרְתִּי 'I said' in 456 of the 1,390 instances of Qal suffixed 1st-pers. sing. verbs (33%). To specify the remaining two-thirds, additional rules must be written. For example, if we specify words of the shape רָאִיתִי 'I saw', then we classify an additional 280 such verbs (another 20%). And so on through the many paradigms.

3.1.5   Distributional Specification

Distributional specification relies on segment environments to infer the relations among parts of speech. The traditional approach to distributional analysis relies on *frames* and on the judgments of native speakers. A native speaker is provided a frame and asked what items can fill its gap. Taking an example from Crystal,[5] one might be given the frame *"She saw_____box"* and asked what words can fill its gap. Crystal asserts that the words that can fill this gap are determiners: {*the, a, my, one*, etc}. We observe, however, that if *box* is taken to be a verb, then a quite different set of words can fill the gap: {*Joe, boys, men, kangaroos*, etc}. In general, there are better ways to get at distributional patterns than via frames—ways that do not require native-speaker discriminations. In practice, these methods can only be reliably investigated computationally. Forbes has made two

---

4. See the tables of paradigms scattered throughout GKC; through van der Merwe, Naudé, and Kroeze, *A Biblical Hebrew Reference Grammar* (Sheffield: Sheffield Academic Press, 1999); and at the end of Paul Joüon and T. Muraoka, *A Grammar of Biblical Hebrew* (rev. Eng. ed.; Rome: Pontifical Biblical Institute, 2006) 617–49.

5. David Crystal, *A Dictionary of Linguistics and Phonetics* (5th ed.; Oxford: Blackwell, 2003) 188.

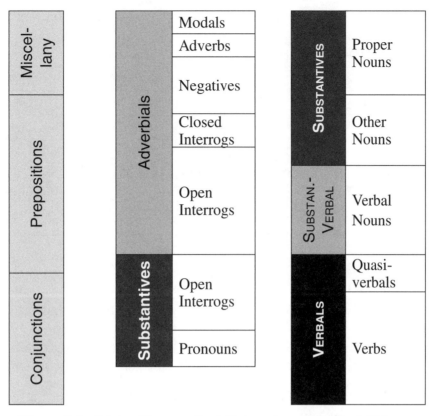

Figure 3.1. Major Grammatical Categories of Biblical Hebrew

forays into this area.[6] If progress in this area continues, it should be possible to combine paradigmatic and distributional specification in ways that will lead to new insights into the interrelationships of the parts of speech of Biblical Hebrew.

3.2 *The Andersen-Forbes Part-of-Speech System*

The darkened boxes in figure 3.1 disclose the top level of our taxonomy of Biblical Hebrew. This seven-category taxonomy (miscellany, prepositions, conjunctions, adverbials, substantives, substantives-verbals, and verbals) is far too coarse-grained for our purposes, so we begin elaborating it by subdividing the adverbials into five subcategories (modals, adverbs, negatives, closed interrogatives, and some open interrogatives), the substantives into four subcategories (some open interrogatives, pronouns, proper nouns, and other nouns), and the verbals into two subcategories (quasiverbals and verbs). There is little in this taxonomy that would surprise the writers of grammars, as examination of GKC, BDB, *IBHS*, Joüon and Muraoka, and van der Merwe et al. has confirmed. Three innovations deserve comment:

---

6. A. Dean Forbes, "Squishes, Clines, and Fuzzy Signs: Mixed and Gradient Categories in the Biblical Hebrew Lexicon," in *Syriac Lexicography I: Foundations for Syriac Lexicography* (ed. A. D. Forbes and D. G. K. Taylor; Piscataway, NJ: Gorgias, 2006) 105–39; idem, "Distributionally Inferred Word and Form Classes in the Hebrew Lexicon," in *Syriac Lexicography II* (ed. Peter Williams; Piscataway, NJ: Gorgias, 2009) 1–34.

Table 3.1. 37 Grammatical Categories for Biblical Hebrew

exclamatives	closed interrogatives	ordinals	quasiverbals	cohortative sequentials
definite articles	open interrogatives	adjectives	pure verb ptcps.	imperative verbs
[nominalizers] אֲשֶׁר	demonstrative pronouns	ethnics	infinitives absolute	insistent imperatives
prepositions	free pronouns	common nouns	suffixed (perfect) verbs	jussive verbs
conjunctions	bound pronouns	pure noun ptcps.	prefixed (imperfect) verbs	cohortative verbs
modals	proper nouns	infinitives construct	prefixed (preterite) verbs	
adverbs	*all* כָּל	noun-verb / noun ptcps.	suffixed sequentials	
negatives	numerals	noun-verb ptcps.	prefixed sequentials	

1. We distinguish closed interrogatives (interrogatives allowing only yes-or-no answers) from open interrogatives (interrogatives allowing answers that are drawn from open sets of possible answers).[7]
2. We recognize a mixed category of verbal nouns: part substantive, part verb.
3. We have also introduced a subclass of verbals that we refer to as quasiverbals.[8]

The expanded set of grammatical categories tabulated above is still too coarse for our work, so we further subdivide categories, obtaining the 37 more fine-grained categories listed in table 3.1. Most of these categories will already be familiar to readers. Four comments may be helpful:

1. We have subdivided the nouns into eight subcategories and the finite verbs into ten subcategories.
2. Because of its odd behavior and to facilitate further study, we have made כָּל 'all' a one-lexeme category.[9]
3. We have subdivided the participles (ptcps.) into four subcategories.
4. Readers wanting a concise definition of a category should consult the glossary.

We go one step further. We further divide various categories into even finer categories, leading to the 76 part-of-speech taxonomy shown in the three-panel display in fig. 3.2. The display consists of three major panels. The right-most entries in each panel disclose the most fine-grained categories, for example, *[lapsii calami]*, modals, demonstratives. With two exceptions,[10] entries that include a Hebrew segment are subcategories of traditional "parental" parts of speech—for example, the many individual prepositions.

Readers may wonder why we have more grammatical categories than is traditional. In the case of the left-most panel in fig. 3.2, why not simply have miscellany, preposition, and conjunction and omit the finer-grained categories? Our splitting of the segments into many categories addresses a

---

7. Some of the open interrogatives are classified as adverbials and others as substantives, as we discuss in §9.3.4.3.

8. Van der Merwe *et al.* (*A Biblical Hebrew Reference Grammar*, 58–59) refer to a subset of what we call quasiverbals as "predicators of (non)existence." Waltke and O'Connor (*IBHS*, 72) refer to these predicators as "quasi-verbal indicators." See chap. 18 for a full treatment of quasiverbals.

9. See Forbes, "Squishes," 121–22.

10. The two exceptions are [nominalizers] אֲשֶׁר and כָּל 'all'.

Miscellany
- [lapsii calami]
- exclamatives
- definite articles
- [nominalizers] אֲשֶׁר
- [object marker] אֵת

Prepositions
- from מִן
- in בְּ '
- like כְּ '
- to לְ '
- with אֵת
- with עִם
- unto אֶל
- upon עַל
- until עַד
- inside תּוֹךְ
- under תַּחַת
- other prepositions

Conjunctions
- coord. conjunction
- and-then וַ '
- also גַּם
- or אוֹ
- because, etc. כִּי
- if אִם
- but indeed אוּלָם
- other conjunctions

Adverbials
- modals
- adverbs

Negatives
- do not אַל
- not בִּלְתִּי
- not לֹא / אִם / אִי

Closed ?
- yes?/no? הֲ
- [question] אִם

Open Interrogatives
- why? מַדּוּעַ
- how? אֵיךְ
- where? אָנָה
- when? מָתַי
- whence? מֵאַיִן
- who? מִי
- what? מָה

Substantives — Pronouns
- demonstratives
- free pronouns
- bound pronouns

Substantives — Proper Nouns
- divine proper nouns
- human proper nouns
- land proper nouns
- mountain proper nouns
- city proper nouns
- river proper nouns
- other geog. proper nouns

Other Nouns
- all כָּל
- cardinal numerals
- ordinal numerals
- adjectives
- ethnics
- common nouns
- pure noun participles

Verbal Nouns
- infinitives construct
- noun-verb / noun participles
- noun-verb participles

Verbals — Quasiverbals
- behold הִנֵּה
- exists יֵשׁ
- still עוֹד
- not-exists אֵין
- where? אַיֵּה [a]

Verbs
- pure verb participles
- infinitives absolute
- suffixed (perfect) verbs
- prefixed (imperfect) verbs
- prefixed (preterite) verbs
- suffixed sequentials
- prefixed sequentials
- cohortative sequentials
- imperative verbs
- insistent imperatives
- jussive verbs
- cohortative verbs

Note: When a grammatical category consists mainly of one lexeme, then the most common allomorph follows an italicized gloss.

Each category is discussed in the text.

[a] This word is both an *open interrogative* and a *quasiverbal.*

Figure 3.2. The Parts of Speech of Biblical Hebrew

question bedeviling taxonomists: should one lump segments into a few shared categories or assign them to many disparate categories? Since it is trivial to merge sets of segments but nontrivial to split them, we have opted to do the splitting work. This way, individuals who want to examine fine details may do so, while those who prefer less fine-grained POSs can merge our categories.

Being "splitters" results in a dilemma. As William Croft put it: "Splitting: where does one stop?"[11] We answered Croft's question on the bases of traditional insights and our practical needs. (1) In recent times, particles were split from verbs and nouns on morphological grounds; they are not inflected. As a default category, particles have diverse grammatical functions. The high ratio of *particle* tokens (segments) in the text to their types (lexemes in the dictionary) indicates that "particles" do a great deal of grammatical work. The most important fact is that particles have diverse grammatical functions and thus belong to a corresponding range of parts of speech. Additionally, each conjunction has characteristic logical functions, so each conjunction is a POS in its own distinctiveness. (2) Verbs share similar grammatical functions by virtue of being predicators. Many nouns have similar grammatical functions on the basis of shared semantics (e.g., animates may be the subjects of clauses). (3) Prepositions have a common grammatical function of "governing" nominals, but each preposition makes a distinctive contribution to the semantic roles of prepositional phrases. Hence each preposition gets its own POS. For practical reasons, we bundled the rarely used prepositions into a default POS called "other prepositions."

3.2.1 Figure 3.2, Left-most Panel: Particles

The category *particles* contributes 108 lexemes to our dictionary, 1.2% of the total. These few entries account for 36% of Biblical Hebrew segments. Many parts of speech making up *particles* involve homography.

3.2.1.1 Miscellany

The miscellany set contains four parts of speech that do not fit well elsewhere.

Lapsii calami.   We have 32 'calamitous lapses'. Lapsus calami is not a genuine part of speech since it is attached to segments, the part of speech of which cannot be determined.

The *lapsii calami* are of two kinds: 23 *Qere welo' Kethiv* plus nine "true" *lapsii calami*.

The *Qere welo' Kethiv* occur in Judg 20:13; 2 Sam 8:3, 16:23, 18:20; 2 Kgs 4:7, 19:31, 19:37; Isa 55:13; Jer 31:38, 50:29; Ezek 9:11; Ps 30:4; Job 2:7; Prov 23:24, 27:24; Ruth 3:5, 3:17; Lam 2:2, 4:16, 5:3, 5:5, 5:7 (2×).

The "true" *lapsii calami* are hapaxes and are distributed as follows:

Gen 30:11	בגד	1 Kgs 12:33	לְבָד	Job 26:12	תובנת
Deut 33:2	אשדת	Ps 10:10	חֶלְכָּאִים	Lam 4:3	כי ענים
1 Sam 4:13	יד	Ps 55:16	יְשִׁימֹות	2 Chr 34:6	בהר בתיהם

Exclamatives.   Our set of exclamatives contains 20 lexemes and accounts for 225 segments in our Biblical Hebrew text. The list shows our dictionary headings along with their glosses.

---

11. William Croft, "Parts of speech as language universals and as language-particular categories," in *Approaches to the Typology of Word Classes* (ed. P. M. Vogel and B. Comrie; Berlin: de Gruyter, 2000) 76.

אֲבוֹי	*alas*	אִי	*oh*	אָנָּא	*O!*	הָהּ	*hah*
אָבִי	*O!*	אֵיךְ	*how!*	בִּי	*O!*	הוֹ	*ho*
אַבְרֵךְ	*abrek*	אַלְלַי	*alas*	הֵא	*hey*	הוֹי	*hoy*
אֲהָהּ	*ahah*	אָמֵן	*amen*	הֶאָח	*hey*	הִנֵּה	*behold!*
אָח	*sigh*	אָמְנָה	*certainly*	הֵד	*oh*	מָה	*how!*

Note that specification of some of the lexemes involves resolution of homography. For example, אָבִי appears as a word—אָבִי 'father-my' [a two-segment word]—and as three different lexemes: אָבִי 'father' [suffixed masc. sing. common noun], אָבִי 'I will bring' [Hiphil active 1st-pers. sing. prefixed verb, variant form], and אָבִי 'O!' [exclamative]. Twice, we have classified אָבִי as an exclamative, in 1 Sam 24:12 and in Job 34:36.

Definite articles. Three ה-form definite articles were specified in §3.1.1 above. The definite article POS also includes three segments that lack the ה: -ַ-, -ָ-, and -ֶ-.

Nominalizers. The principal segment that nominalizes and thereby embeds an immediately following clause, converting the clause into a noun or noun equivalent, is אֲשֶׁר 'which'.[12] Often referred to as a *relative pronoun,* אֲשֶׁר nominalizes 5,451 times. The form also exhibits homography and functions as a subordinating conjunction 51 times. Contrast these clauses:

$$\text{וַיַּצֵּג אֶת־הַמַּקְלוֹת אֲשֶׁר פִּצֵּל} \ldots$$
He set the rods <u>that</u> he had peeled . . . (NRSV, Gen 30:38)

$$\text{נָתַן אֱלֹהִים שְׂכָרִי אֲשֶׁר־נָתַתִּי שִׁפְחָתִי לְאִישִׁי}$$
God has given me my hire <u>because</u> I gave my maid to my husband. (NRSV, Gen 30:18)

In the first clause, אֲשֶׁר nominalizes the following clause, which consists of only a finite verb. In the second (partial) clause, אֲשֶׁר is a subordinating conjunction. The phrase marker (3.1) shows the three clause immediate constituents (CICs) for the clause in Lam 2:17. Note how אֲשֶׁר nominalizes the one-word clause consisting of a finite verb, glossed 'which he planned'.

(3.1)

cl oblq	→	vb gram		עָשָׂה	he made
	↘	sbj gram		יהוה	Yahweh
	↘	dir obj gram	→ nom nom	אֲשֶׁר	which
			↘ cl oblq → vb gram →	זָמַם	he planned

3.2.1.2 Prepositions

Our set of prepositions is smaller than most other grammarians' sets, but none of ours should surprise readers. As usual, there is much homography. For example, various forms of אֵת '[obj]' and אֵת 'with' have been resolved. Regarding segmentation, we left compounds unsegmented *if* their nominal components were never attested with nominal functions and their original literal meaning.

---

12. Our other nominalizers are: זֶה, 8×; זוֹ, 1×; זוּ, 15×; -שֶׁ, 135×. We do not recognize -הַ as a nominalizer.

Hence בִּגְלַל 'on account of' remains intact, since גלל is attested only in this compound (BDB, 164a). But פְּנֵי often means a literal 'face' and so we form לְ + פְּנֵי (these practices alter preposition counts).

For the record, the category called "other prepositions" has these 13 rarely attested members:

אַחַר *after*	בֵּין *between*	בַּעֲבוּר *for sake of*	יַעַן *because*
אֵצֶל *near*	בַּלְעֲדֵי *without*	בְּעַד *through*	לְבַד *except*
בִּגְלַל *on account of*	בִּלְתִּי *except*	זוּלָתִי *except*	לְמַעַן *for*
			קָבְל *before*

3.2.1.3 Conjunctions

Our set of conjunctions involves greater delicacy than is typical. Their behavior is complex. They can operate within phrases, within sentences (joining main clauses), and within discourses. Further, as has been shown elsewhere,[13] forms such as גַּם/גַם exhibit very complex distributional patterns.

Once again, there is ample homography to be described. Three situations are prominent:

1. The various forms of the coordinating conjunction וְ 'and' are assigned in a context-specific way to two subcategories: standard coordination and ו-sequential coordination.[14]
2. The conditional and interrogative functions of אִם: 'if' and '[*question*]' are resolved.
3. The many discourse-level functions of כִּי exemplified by the glosses 'because', 'but', 'that', 'although', 'when', and 'if' are resolved.

The category labeled "other conjunctions" is a mélange of relatively rarely attested conjunctions:

אֲבָל *but*	בַּעֲבוּר *for sake of*	כִּי אִם *except*	מֵאָז *since*
אִלוּ *if*	הֵן *if*	לָהֵן *therefore*	עַד *until*
אַף *also*	זוּלָתִי *except*	לוּלֵי *perhaps*	עַל *because*
אֲשֶׁר *because*	טֶרֶם *before*	לָכֵן *therefore*	עֵקֶב *because*
בְּטֶרֶם *before*	יַעַן *because*	לְמַעַן *for the sake of*	פֶּן *lest*
			שֶׁ *because*

3.2.2 The Middle Panel: Adverbials and Pronouns

The central panel of fig. 3.2 holds 12 ostensively defined categories plus the *modals*, *adverbs*, *demonstratives*, *free pronouns*, and *bound pronouns*.

---

13. C. H. J. van der Merwe, *The Old Hebrew Particle* gam (St. Ottilien: EOS, 1990). Also, Forbes, "Squishes," 135.

14. Some grammars assign multiple quasi-POSs to 'and' (BDB has five), and the NIV gives it many English glosses. See E. W. Goodrick and J. R. Kohlenberger, *Zondervan NIV Exhaustive Concordance* (2nd ed.; Grand Rapids, MI: Zondervan, 1999) 1396–98. By contrast, at present we distinguish only two kinds of 'and'.

3.2.2.1 The Modals

According to our glossary, a modal is a "segment that expresses the speaker's uncertainty or desire with regard to some statement." We recognize seven modal lexemes:[15]

אֲבָל	*surely*	אַחֲלֵי	*would that*	אָכֵן	*surely*	לוּ	*would that*
אוּלַי	*perhaps*	אַךְ	*surely*	כִּי	*surely*		

Note that the segments נָא/אָ '[emphatic]' are not included among our modals. From the perspective of pragmatics, they *do* exhibit modal behavior. But they—unlike the modals listed above—are invariably enclitic. Hence, we have assigned them with reservations to the adverbs category.[16]

3.2.2.2 The Adverbs

We recognize these 35 adverbs:

אָז	*then*	חִישׁ	*quickly*	לְבָד	*apart*	עוֹד	*still*
אָחוֹר	*back*	טֶרֶם	*not yet*	מְאֹד	*very*	עַתָּה	*now*
אַחַר	*afterward*	יַחְדָּו	*together*	מְהֵרָה	*quickly*	פֹּה	*here*
אַחֲרֹנִית	*backwards*	כְּבָר	*already*	מַטָּה	*below*	פִּתְאֹם	*suddenly*
אַךְ	*only*	כֹּה	*thus*[17]	מַעַל	*above*	רַק	*only*
אֵפוֹא	*then*	כָּכָה	*thus*	מַעְלָה	*upwards*	שָׁם	*there*
הָלְאָה	*farther*	כִּי	*very*	נָא	*[emphatic]*	שָׁמָּה	*thither*
הֲלֹם	*here*	כֵּן	*thus*	עֶדֶן	*yet*	תַּחַת	*underneath*
הֵנֵּה	*here*	לֹא	*certainly*	עוֹד	*again*[18]		

3.2.2.3 The Negatives

We recognize 5 negation lexemes:

אִי	*not*	אַל	*do not*	אִם	*not*	בִּלְתִּי	*not*	לֹא	*not*

3.2.2.4 The Interrogatives

There are these 2 closed interrogatives: אִם *[question]* and הֲ' *yes?/no?*

We also distinguish these 11 open interrogatives:

---

15. In addition, we recognize the *idiomatic modal expression* מִי־יִתֵּן, translated 'would that', as a modal. See §15.3.4.4.

16. See GKC, 308 n. 1 and especially n. 2.

17. Van der Merwe (private communication) holds that כֹּה is always "*thus* pointing forward" while כֵּן is "*thus* prototypically pointing backward."

18. We recognize both a durative sense ('still'), concomitant with imperfective aspect, and a repetitive sense ('again'), concomitant with perfective aspect. The word עוֹד has other senses, less prototypical, that we have not yet distinguished.

אַיֵּה *where?* אֵיפֹה *where?* אָנָה *where?* מַדּוּעַ *why?* מֶה *what?* מָתַי *when?*

אֵיךְ *how?* אֶל *where?* מֵאַיִן *whence?* מָה *what?* מִי *who?*

Note that the open interrogatives are not included with the pronouns in fig. 3.2 but, rather, are considered to be adverbials and/or substantives (traditional grammars usually classify "who?" and "what?" as pronouns). Note further that אַיֵּה is classified as both a quasiverbal and an interrogative. Further, several items are classified as interrogatives and as pronouns. Allowing segments to be members of more than one part of speech is a departure from traditional taxonomy. Traditionally, the parts of speech are exhaustive, a constraint that we do enforce. They are also mutually exclusive, a constraint that we jettison to handle segments such as those just listed. One might avoid mixed categories by the expedient of simply renaming the mixed classes. For example, a new set (containing only one part of speech, אַיֵּה) named "quasiverbal-interrogative' might be introduced.

3.2.3 The "Simple" Substantives

At the bottom of the middle panel of fig. 3.2 are three kinds of pronoun. The right-most panel of fig. 3.2 contains 34 categories grouped into 5 supersets: proper nouns, other nouns, verbal nouns, quasiverbals, and verbs. In this subsection, we take up the pronoun, proper noun, and other noun supersets.

3.2.3.1 The Pronouns

Demonstrative Pronoun. We distinguish 5 demonstrative pronoun lexemes in Biblical Hebrew. Their most frequent forms are:

	masc.		*fem.*		*common*	
sing.	זֹו זֶה	*this*	זֹה זֹאת	*this*		
plur.					אֵלֶּה	*these*

Free Pronoun. The most frequent forms of the free pronouns in Biblical Hebrew are shown in the table below.[19] We observe that: (1) הֵמָּה occurs both as 3rd-pers. masc. pl. (275×) and (incorrectly, so BDB, 241) as 3rd-pers. fem. dual (3×: Zech 5:10, Ruth 1:22, Song 6:8); (2) הֵנָּה occurs both as the 3rd-pers. fem. pl. free pronoun (47×) and as the adverb 'here' (51×). (3) The variant form נַחְנוּ is both the 1st-pers. common pl. free pronoun (4×) and a suffixed sequential 1st-pers. common pl. Qal active verb (once, in 2 Sam 17:12, 'we will rest'; see BDB, 628a).

	person	*masc.*		*fem.*		*common*	
sing.	1					אֲנִי	*I*
	2	אַתָּה	*thou*	אַתְּ	*thou*		
	3	הוּא	*he*	הִיא	*she*		
pl.	1					אֲנַחְנוּ	*we*
	2	אַתֶּם	*you*	אַתֵּנָה	*you*		
	3	הֵמָּה	*they*	הֵנָּה	*they*		

---

19. Note that we use *thee* and *thou* for 2nd-person sing. throughout this work and *you* for 2nd-person pl.

Bound Pronoun. Because we dissect pronoun suffixes so as to minimize the proliferation of suffixed forms, we obtain many bound pronoun forms. The table below tallies the number of forms attested for each kind of pronoun suffix. For example, there are five suffixed forms of *us*, and they are: ‐נוֹ (1063×), ‐נֻ (377×), ‐נוּ (4×), ‐נֻ (168×), and ‐נוּ (18×).

	person	masc.		fem.		common	
sing.	1					12	*me*
	2	14	*thee*	9	*thee*		
	3	13	*his / him*	9	*her*		
dual	2			3	*you*		
	3			3	*them*		
pl.	1					5	*us*
	2	5	*you*	6	*you*		
	3	17	*them*	16	*them*		

3.2.3.2 The Proper Nouns

We identify 3,552 distinct proper noun forms that appear a total of 33,963 times in Biblical Hebrew. As is the case with so many other parts of speech, their classification involves the resolution of considerable homography. Example: יָבֵשׁ

'Yabesh' (1×, name of man; 2 Kgs 15:10)
'Yabesh' (5×, name of city; 1 Chr 10:12)
'it dried up' (8×, suffixed Qal active, 3rd-pers. masc. sing.; Josh 9:12)
'it will dry up' (5×, suffixed sequential Qal active, 3rd-pers. masc. sing.; Isa 19:5)
'dry' (6×, adjective of quality, masc. sing.; Josh 9:5).

Some work remains to be done on the proper nouns, in that many eponyms need to be divided into subsets with assignment to appropriate semantic classes. For example, יִשְׂרָאֵל appears 2,506 times, always as the name of a human in our data. It is never classified as a place, and so on.

3.2.3.3 The Other Nouns

We divide the other nouns into seven subgroups: כָּל 'all', cardinal numeral, ordinal numeral, adjective, ethnic, common noun, and pure noun participle. The makeup of all of these parts of speech, except perhaps adjective and pure noun participle, will be well known to readers (if not, they should consult the glossary).

Adjective. Our definition of the category *adjective* is highly restrictive in one sense: with very few exceptions, we require that any adjective modify an immediately preceding substantive. But it is untraditionally inclusive in another sense: demonstrative pronouns and free pronouns, if they are made definite and if they modify an immediately preceding substantive, are also classified as adjectives. For example, in the noun phrase הַ׳יּוֹם הַזֶּה, we classify זֶה as an adjective.

Pure Noun Participle. Participles are nouns. But they also have affinities with verb paradigms, having verbal features such as transitivity and voice. In any context where a participle exhibits only nominal characteristics, we call it a *pure noun participle* and give it noun semantics. We classify

4,475 segment occurrences in our text as pure noun participles. For example, in Jer 4:7, in the clause עָרַיִךְ תִּצֶּינָה מֵאֵין יוֹשֵׁב, the segment יוֹשֵׁב is classified as a pure noun participle and is assigned human semantics, since this participle has only nominal features in this context. We will discuss our taxonomy of participles in greater detail in §3.2.4.2.

3.2.4 Verbal Nouns

The right-most panel of fig. 3.2 contains one mixed superset: verbal nouns. That is, this set of categories concurrently exhibits both nominal and verbal behaviors. Because of their mixed nature, phrase markers with these items have unique characteristics. In this subsection, we take up the verbal noun superset, which consists of: infinitive construct, noun-verb / noun participle, and noun-verb participle.

3.2.4.1 The Infinitive Construct

Our text contains 6,768 infinitives construct. Around nine-tenths have a prefixed preposition, the preposition being some form of prefixed –ל around three-quarters of the time. The critical point is that infinitives construct have functional immediate constituents of their own. That is, they can be central to constructions that exhibit the obliqueness phenomenon mentioned in §1.3.3.1. Phrase marker (3.2) for Gen 37:25a contains an infinitive construct.

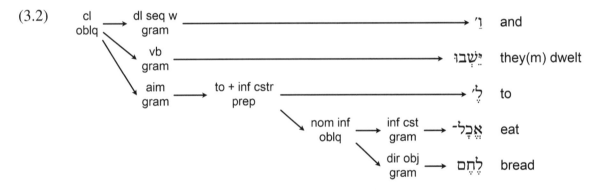

Note that the infinitive construct (inf cst) אֱכָל 'eat' has its own direct object (dir obj) לֶחֶם 'bread'. Together, these form a nominalized infinitive constituent (nom inf), licensed by obliqueness (oblq). The nominalized infinitive constituent combines with the preposition—לְ 'to' to form a prepositional phrase (to+inf cstr). Functionally, this is a CIC (clause immediate constituent) that specifies the aim or purpose for which 'they(m) dwelt' = 'they(m) sat down'.

3.2.4.2 The Four Kinds of Participles

The accepted wisdom is that a participle refers to a person's activity or a state of affairs that is *present*, either coincident (or overlapping) in time with the moment of speech or else occurring at the same time as some past event to which it is circumstantial. The participle is thus supposed by some to be the nearest thing that Classical Hebrew has to a present tense, increasingly having this role as the finite suffixed (perfect) and prefixed (imperfect) verbs settle down to supplying the past tense and future tense, respectively.[20]

---

20. "In Biblical Hebrew the present tense is properly the domain of the predicative participle" (Jan Joosten, "The Predicative Participle in Biblical Hebrew," *Zeitschrift für Althebraistik* 2 [1989] 128–59).

However, scanning the categories in the right-most panel of fig. 3.2 from just above the verbal nouns down through just below the quasiverbals, one notices that we distinguish four functions of participles: *pure noun participles*, *noun-verb participles*, *noun-verb/noun participles*, and *pure verb participles*.[21] We view the traditional participles as functionally inhomogeneous. They profit from subdivision.[22]

We introduced the first kind of participle, the *pure noun participle*, at the end of §3.2.3.3. Recall that participles of this kind exhibit only nominal characteristics.[23]

There are constructions in which a word with the form of a participle has verbal relations with one or more arguments that follow it, making a constituent that is a verbal clause. When a constituent of this sort also functions in nominal relations with a previously occurring segment, we call this second kind of participle a *noun-verb participle*. It is a "noun up-front and a verb out-back." We emphasize that it is the construction as a whole—not just the participle alone—that functions nominally. This fact has been missed in discussions of constructions that involve determination by means of the definite article. In such cases, there is no need to say that the definite article is a relative pronoun, let alone talk about a "relative participle."[24]

The third kind of participle exhibits only verbal characteristics. We call this sort of participle a *pure verb participle*.

There is a fourth category of participle. When a word with the form of a participle has *both* nominal and verbal relations with following segment(s) in a mixed construction, as well as some nominal function with preceding segment(s), then we call it a *noun-[verb/noun] participle*. It is a "noun up-front ('noun-'), and it is a verb *and* noun ('[verb/noun]') out-back!" The example below should make this difficult concept clearer (see יֹשְׁבֵי as a Noun-[Verb/Noun] Participle, p. 35).

The different kinds of participles can be appreciated by comparing phrase markers that contain the segment שֹׁפֵט, which exhibits three of the four participle behaviors. We illustrate the structures involved with the fourth kind of participle by showing a phrase marker with יֹשְׁבֵי 'dwellers of'.

שֹׁפֵט *as a Pure Noun Participle.* In the phrase marker (3.3) from Exod 2:14, the pure noun participle is coordinated with a common noun, שַׂר 'prince', forming a noun phrase with human semantics (n:humn), licensed by the union/disjunction relation (union/disj). Let us look at this in a bit more detail. The coordination phrase (n:humn) is in apposition to אִישׁ 'man', and together they form a larger noun phrase (n:humn) licensed by apposition (app). The resulting noun phrase combines with the preposition לְ 'to' to form a prepositional phrase (to+humn) that functions as the object complement (obj cmp) in the clause. The clause is made up of five CICs: an open interrogative subject (sbj/open intg), a finite verb predicator (vb), a direct object (dir obj), an object complement (obj cmp), and an adjunct, location (loc), 'upon us'.

---

21. Note that the pure noun participles are classified as common nouns and the pure verb participles as verbs.

22. For more discussion, see F. I. Andersen and A. D. Forbes, "The Participle in Biblical Hebrew and the Overlap of Grammar and Lexicon," in *Milk and Honey* (ed. S. Malena and D. Miano; Winona Lake, IN: Eisenbrauns, 2007) 185–212.

23. But note that there are instances where a participle is an old-fashioned predicate adjective that can equally be seen to be either a pure noun or a pure verb. There is much disagreement in the literature as to whether the "predicate adjective" participle is the subject complement in a verbless clause or a predicator in a verbal clause.

24. BDB recognizes a relative definite article only with perfect verbs. With participles, it calls the definite article "resumptive." There is no need for this category either. The definite article with a participle (construction) simply determines it, as it does any other nominal.

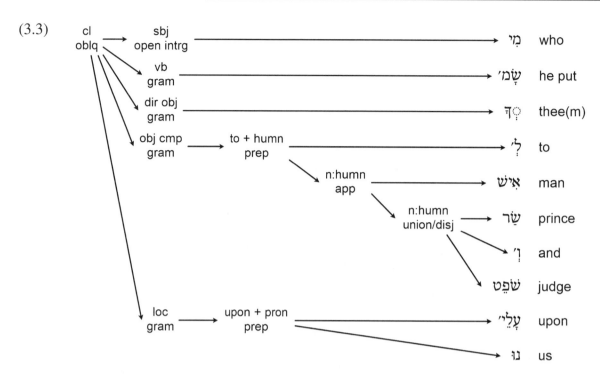

(3.3)

שׁ֫פֵט *as a Noun-Verb Participle.* In the phrase marker (3.4) from 1 Sam 8:1, the noun-verb participle (n-v ptc) has its own beneficiary (benf). The clause has five CICs: a time point (tm pt), a sequential 1 (dl seq w), a finite verb (vb), a direct object (dir obj), and an object complement (obj cmp).

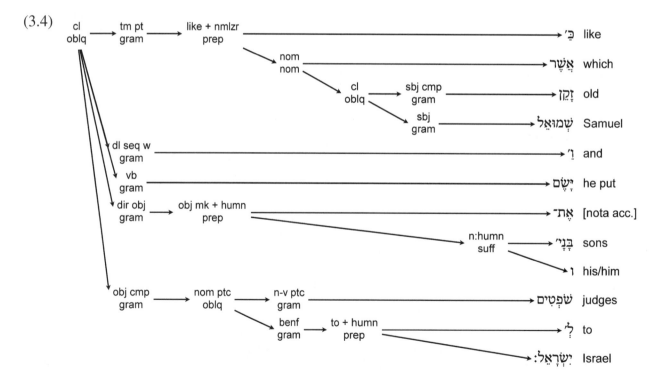

(3.4)

שׁ֫פֵט *as a Pure Verb Participle.* The phrase marker (3.5) from 1 Sam 3:13 shows a clause consisting of five CICs: a pure verb participle (vb ptc), a subject (sbj), a direct object (dir obj), a time aim (tm aim), and a reason (rsn).

(3.5)

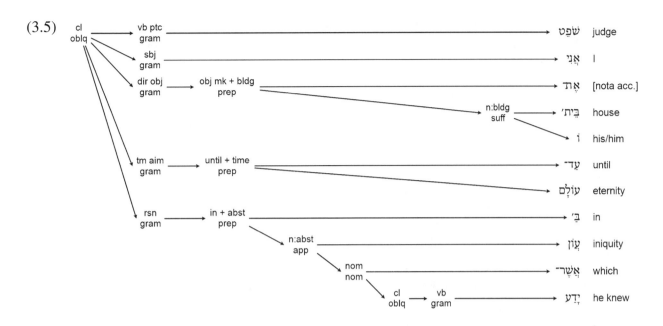

יֹשְׁבֵי *as a Noun-[Verb / Noun] Participle.*   Phrase marker (3.6) for Hos 14:8a exhibits a phenomenon not encountered heretofore. The prepositional phrase label in + thing / prep 'in shadow his' has *two* arrows pointing into it, one from the nom ptc / cstr label and the other from the loc / gram label. As a result, this phrase marker is not a tree. This is an important innovation, but we must defer discussing it until chap. 20, "Non-Tree Phrase Markers." For the present purposes, we note that noun-[verb / noun] participles are rare, there being only 109 in our text, and that our phrase markers represent the syntactic relations that they enter into nicely (for a proper discussion of noun-[verb / noun] participles, see §20.2.1).

(3.6)

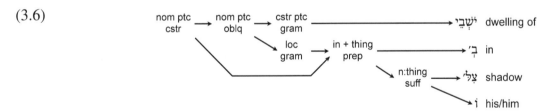

3.2.5 The Quasiverbals

We group these five lexemes in a set that we term the quasiverbals:[25]

אַיֵּה *where?*   אֵין *does not exist*   הִנֵּה *behold*   יֵשׁ *exists*   עוֹד *still*

The literature rarely refers to *quasiverbals*. Waltke and O'Connor do state that "[q]uasi-verbal indicators are particles indicating existence."[26] In chap. 18, we argue for grouping these items.

---

25. F. I. Andersen, "Lo and Behold! Taxonomy and Translation of Biblical Hebrew הִנֵּה," in *Hamlet on a Hill: Semitic and Greek Studies Presented to Professor T. Muraoka on the Occasion of His Sixty-Fifth Birthday* (ed. M. F. J. Baasten and W. T. van Peursen; Leuven: Peeters, 2003) 53.

26. *IBHS*, 72.

Phrase marker (3.7) from Job 9:33 shows an interesting simple clause wherein the existential quasiverbal יֵשׁ 'exists' is the predicator. It is negated, rather than using אַיִן 'does not exist'.

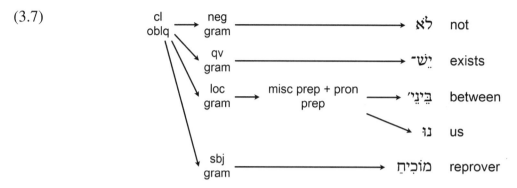

3.2.6 Verbs

At the bottom of the right-most panel of fig. 3.2 are 12 categories of verbs. These categories are for the most part quite traditional. There are only two that are not poly-something (polytense, polyaspect), *wayyiqṭōl* (always sequential preterite and indicative) and imperative (always injunctive). An entry for each verb category may be found in the glossary.

3.2.6.1 The Three Functions of the Infinitive Absolute

Our text contains 860 infinitives absolute. Grammars differ widely in their treatment of the syntax of the infinitive absolute. Joüon/Muraoka provide a detailed analysis, recognizing 9 differing functions for the infinitive absolute.[27] We distinguish 3 functions—predicator, intensifier, and amplifier—and identify each function as a particular CIC.

Infinitive Absolute Predicator. When a clause has no predicator other than an infinitive absolute, we call the infinitive absolute (IA) an *infinitive absolute predicator* (inf abs prd) CIC. Phrase marker (3.8) for Josh 6:3 is an example of this circumstance. This clause has four CICs: the subject

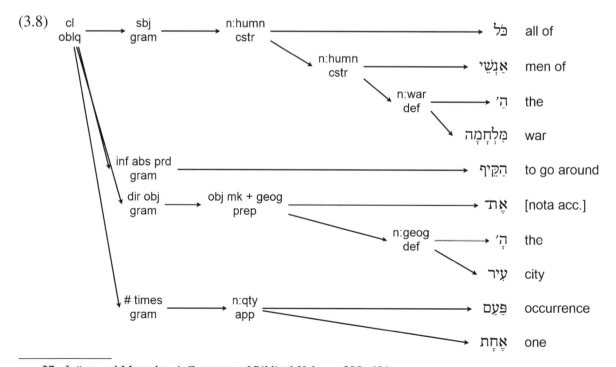

27. Joüon and Muraoka, *A Grammar of Biblical Hebrew*, 390–401.

CIC is a construct chain having human semantics, the predicator CIC is the infinitive absolute, the direct object CIC involves geographic semantics, and there is an adjunct CIC that specifies the number of times.

Infinitive Absolute Intensifier. When a clause has a finite predicator and also has an infinitive absolute having the same "root," then we call the latter an *infinitive absolute intensifier* (inf abs int). Phrase marker (3.9) for 1 Sam 22:16 illustrates this phenomenon.

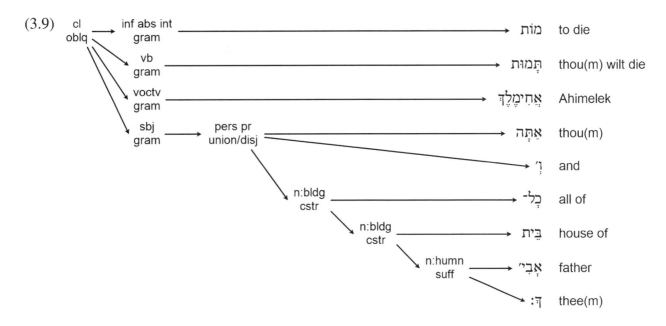

The CICs are the infinitive absolute intensifier, the predicator, a vocative, and the subject.

Infinitive Absolute Amplifier. When a clause has a finite predicator and also an infinitive absolute *but with a different "root,"* then we call the latter an *infinitive absolute amplifier* (inf abs amp). The three-CIC phrase marker (3.10) for Deut 9:12 nicely illustrates this phenomenon.

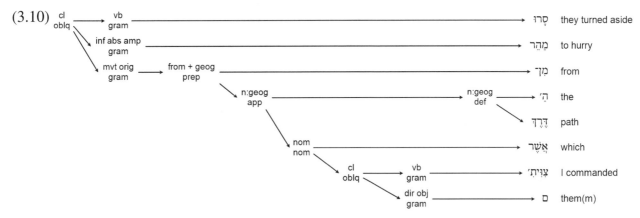

Note that the embedded nominalized clause which is part of the movement origin (mvt orig) CIC is in apposition to 'the path'.

3.2.6.2 The Status of Verb Markup

This inventory of verb groups is a first approximation. There is, to touch on just one illustrative point, a category of "jussive" based in the first place on a morphological distinction (jussives are shorter than normal indicatives). But many prefixed forms are homographs (jussive or indicative),

Table 3.2. The Semantic Codes of Biblical Hebrew

Semantics of PARTICLES			
+	particle	V	vegetation (plant or part, less edibles)
S	spatial and directional	W	work (activity or action)
T	time or season	X	document
		Y	war term (less humans and weapons)
Semantics of SUBSTANTIVES		Z	abstract concept
A	appliance or furniture	#	quantity (numeral / weight / measure / size)
B	building (part / structure)	$	riches (money / transaction / property)
C	creature (bird / insect / fish)	!	vocable (noun)
D	deity	x	undecidable / unknown
E	event		
F	food	**Some Characteristics of VERBS**	
G	geographical name or feature	=	existential (*be* plus most quasiverbals)
H	human (incl. ethnic, community group)	a	verb of attitude (emotional or moral state)
J	jigger (thing)	d	verb of destruction
K	color	j	transitive verb
L	livery (raiment, garment, apparel, jewelry)	k	intransitive verb
M	medical (health term)	l	[temporal locative: 5×]
N	natural substance (incl. light / darkness, weather)	m	verb of movement
O	occipital (mental) state	o	ditransitive Hiphil
P	part (body part, fluid, or excretion)	p	passive verb
Q	noun of quality	r	caused motion
S	spatial and directional	s	stative verb
T	time or season	u	verb of utterance, less אמר
U	utensil (implement / relic / weapon / textile / vehicle)	y	say [אמר]
		z	estimative [קרא]

and so there are many more jussives that need to be identified if the category of jussive as a mood is to be of any use. We have proceeded to resolve the ambiguity.

The assignment of tense and mood—not to mention aspect—is "in process," acceptable as far as it goes in our database, but incomplete. Both tense and aspect are compositional on the clause level, so that tense and aspect are features of clauses as such. That is, the tense and aspect of a clause is determined not only by the characteristics of its verb but also by relations between it and other clauses in the discourse of which it is part. Hence, there is no point in artificially assigning tenses and aspects to the verbs as such, just because people used to think (and traditionalists still think) that verbs, not clauses, have tense and aspect.

3.3 *Part-of-Speech Features*

Grammars assign descriptive features to each segment making up a text. This enables computational parsing, facilitates word-sense assignment, accelerates translation, and aids interpretation.

In the informal grammars presupposed by the traditional reference works, the feature apparatus is extremely simple. Each particle is featureless; it simply is the part of speech that it is. Each substantive is specified by fixing its number, gender, and state. Each verbal is specified by fixing its *binyan*, mood, number, gender, and person. To these traditional features, we add a simplified specification of semantic category where appropriate.

3.3.1 Marking Semantics

The semantics feature was added to our data in the mid-1980s to assist computer parsing. The categories arose willy-nilly, and no effort has yet been made to make them mutually exclusive. We leave our ancient alphabetic mnemonics in table 3.2 to show the "symbol poverty" under which we labored! When we assigned the semantic codes, principled taxonomies were beyond our ken. The introduction of enriched, even multivalued semantic labels is one of our (too-populated) priorities.

3.3.1.1 Semantics of Particles

A few prepositions were assigned spatial semantic values: בֵּין 'between', אַחַר 'after', אֵצֶל 'near', קְבָל 'before', תּוֹךְ 'inside', and תַּחַת 'under(neath)'. In addition, four subordinating conjunctions received temporal semantics: אַחַר 'after', בְּטֶרֶם 'before', טֶרֶם 'before', and מֵאָז 'since'.

3.3.1.2 Semantics of Adverbials

The adverbs listed in §3.2.2.2 are given either no semantic label ("adverbs of manner"[28]):

אַחֲרַנִּית	backward	אֵפוֹא	then (logical)	יַחְדָּו	together	מְאֹד	very
אַךְ	only	דּוּמָם	silently	כֹּה	thus	פִּתְאֹם	suddenly
אָמְנָם	truly	חִישׁ	quickly	כִּי	very	רֵיקָם	in vain
אָמְנָם	truly	חִנָּם	freely	לֹא	certainly	רַק	only

or a temporal label (and are termed "adverbs of time"):

אַחַר	afterwards	טֶרֶם	not yet	כְּבָר	already	עֲדֶן	yet	עוֹד	again
אָז	then	יוֹמָם	by day	מְהֵרָה	quickly	עוֹד	still	עַתָּה	now

or a spatial label (and are termed "adverbs of space"):

אָחוֹר	back	הֲלֹם	here	לְבַד	apart	מֵעַל	above	פֹּה	here	שָׁמָּה	thither
הָלְאָה	farther	הֵנָּה	here	מַטָּה	below	מַעְלָה	upward	שָׁם	there	תַּחַת	underneath

3.3.1.3 Areas for Future Improvement

With regard to semantics, four areas remain for improvement:

1. The characteristics of verbs are crudely defined and crudely implemented.
2. Forcing the semantics feature to have one value is too simple. For example, a *golden branch* should be vegetation (for the branch) and natural substance (for the gold).
3. We have not worked out and applied a theory of figurative / metaphorical language.
4. Reliable work on semantic fields should be used to refine the semantic categories.

---

28. We do not distinguish a "degree modifier" part of speech, consisting in Biblical Hebrew of כִּי 'very' and מְאֹד 'very'. We include these words with the adverbs of manner. See Trask, *A Dictionary*, 74.

3.3.2 The Assigned Features

3.3.2.1 Features of Particles and Adverbials

The parts of speech in supersets *particles* and *adverbials* are featureless, except for those that have a semantic class assigned as described above.

3.3.2.2 Features of Substantives

The features of pronouns are:

Number	S = singular	D = dual	P = plural
Gender	C = common	F = feminine	M = masculine

For free and suffix pronouns, we also give *person* information: 1st, 2nd, 3rd. For demonstratives, we give *state* information of the sort shown below.

The features of proper and common nouns:[29]

Number	S = singular	C = collective	D = dual	P = plural	d = distributive
Gender	C = common	F = feminine	M = masculine		

There are 12 possible state combinations:

	Normal	Pausal	Construct	Suffixed
indefinite	71,007	3,345	30,374	24,676
definite with 'הַ	21,177	1,685	22	6
definite with '_'	5,781	554	4	Isa 24:2

3.3.2.3 Features of Verbal Nouns

For the verbal nouns, we always present the *binyan* and verbal characteristics. This is all that we provide for the infinitives absolute.

The infinitives construct. We also give *state* information, mostly construct or suffixed.

The noun-verb/noun participles. All of the instances ("tokens") are in the construct state.

All but two are masculine. There are 67 plurals and 38 singulars.

The noun-verb participles. We specify the following information:

Number	S = singular	P = plural
Gender	F = feminine	M = masculine
State	as in the extensive specification above	

---

29. There are neither collective nor distributive *proper* nouns.

3.3.2.4   Features of Verbs

For the verbs, we supply their *binyanim* and their verbal semantic / valency information. We also specify the following information:

Number	S = singular	D = dual (3×)	P = plural	
Gender	C = common	F = feminine	M = masculine	
Extended person	1st	2nd	3rd	*definite verb*

The phenomenon of the definite verb (also called the nominalized verb) occurs 52 times. An example is הַֽ׳בָּאָה 'the-she-came' in Job 2:11 in this context:

וַֽ׳יִּשְׁמְע֞וּ שְׁלֹ֣שֶׁת ׀ רֵעֵ֣י אִיּ֗וֹב אֵ֣ת כָּל־הָֽ׳רָעָ֣ה הַ׳זֹּאת֮ הַ׳בָּ֣אָה עָלָי֒׳ו

The noun phrase part of the direct object of this clause is shown in phrase marker (3.11).

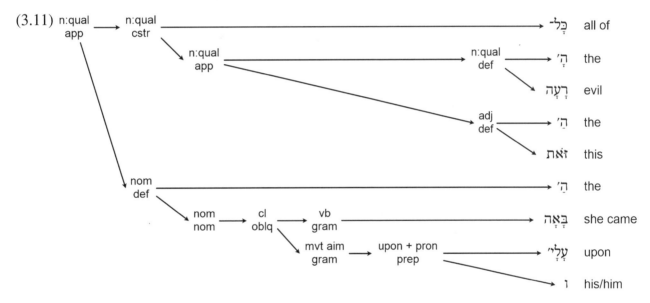

(3.11)

The NJPS translates the direct object as "all these calamities that had befallen him."

3.3.3   Roots versus Identifiers

Each segment type has an associated identifier akin to but sometimes different from the traditional root. In our database, the segments that make up a dictionary entry are identified by a conventional root for verbs or by the consonantal framework for nonverbs. The identifier is thus the lattice of consonants from which the various forms making up an entry can be derived. In specifying the identifier, we ignore *matres lectionis* that are only occasionally used as vowel letters in a lexeme. Thus, for example, the *plene* form כול 'all of' is attested once (as *Kethiv* in Jer 33:8), while the *defective* כל form occurs hundreds of times. Our identifier for this lexeme is therefore כל, not כול. Our approach to lemmatization is strongly descriptive. In this, we are much closer to *HALOT* than to BDB.[30] For example, we are less traditional and more descriptive in that we recognize

---

30. See the introduction to F. I. Andersen and A. D. Forbes, *The Vocabulary of the Old Testament* (Rome: Pontifical Biblical Institute, 1992).

biconsonantal roots. Thus, we use קם rather than קום as the identifier of verbs meaning 'arise', since no word in Biblical Hebrew derived from this root contains the consonant ו as such.[31]

3.4 *Brief Summary*

Top Levels of the Part-of-Speech Hierarchy.   Concordant with modern linguistics, our parts of speech are organized hierarchically (fig. 3.1). Our 7 major categories are largely congruent with those invoked by traditional grammars of Biblical Hebrew. Subdividing these 7 major grammatical categories, we recognize 15 categories (fig. 3.1). We diverge from tradition mainly in: (1) forming the category of *quasiverbals* from lexemes classified by others as adverbials and locating them among the verbals; and (2) distinguishing *closed interrogatives* from the very different *open interrogatives*.

Lower Levels of the Part-of-Speech Hierarchy.   We then subdivide several additional categories, to obtain a list of 37 subcategories (table 3.1). Eight of these are subdivisions of nouns (such as *proper nouns*, *ethnics*, etc.), and 10 are subdivisions of finite verbs (such as *insistent imperatives*, *suffixed sequentials*, etc.). An innovation is our splitting of participles into 4 subtypes: *pure noun*, *noun-verb*, *noun-verb/noun*, and *pure verb*. When we subdivide even more categories, we finally obtain 76 parts of speech (POSs) (fig. 3.2). These parts of speech consist of POSs that are:

- individual lexemes (individual prepositions and conjunctions),
- subsets of traditional POSs (such as nouns [by semantics], verbs [by morphology], and pronouns [free, bound, demonstrative]),
- categories not usually recognized as POSs (such as modals, exclamatives, quasiverbals, closed and open interrogatives, nominalizers [distinguished on syntactic grounds]),
- familiar categories (adverbs, adjectives [albeit with an untraditional definition]).

Part-of-Speech Features.   Tokens of the parts of speech are marked with features standard to the description of Biblical Hebrew: *number*, *gender*, *person*, *state*, and so forth. In addition, we mark substantives with naïve semantic category labels such as *appliance*, *building*, *creature*, *deity*, *event*.

---

31. *Technical detail*: When a verb has more than one (consonantal) alloroot, due to "irregularities" of various kinds in the paradigms, we choose the complete one or the most common one, except for verbs that are historically third *yod*, where the conventional "root" in dictionaries has a nonconsonantal *he'* in third position.

Chapter 4

Phrase Marker Concepts and Terminology

At this point, we need to introduce a few standard ways of describing phrase markers and to specify how information propagates among and within them. Although the basic concepts are simple, the nomenclature will be new to many readers. To assist readers in mastering the terminology, we shall offer multiple occasions to exercise the concepts and terminology in upcoming sections of this book. Readers are reminded that definitions of words and phrases underlined in the text (e.g., root node) may be found in the glossary at the back of the book.

4.1 *Phrase Markers Defined*

A phrase marker is a two-dimensional diagram that displays both the internal hierarchical structure and sequential structure of a clause and its constituents. A phrase marker consists of a set of labeled nodes and the unlabeled directed edges ("arrows") connecting these nodes. The edges show the dominance relations between constituents, pointing from dominating node to dominated node. The precedence relations are implicit, since the (vertical) sequence of the terminal segments is in the same order as the text in the Bible. The concepts underlying phrase markers can best be understood through a simple example.

Phrase marker (4.1) for the first clause in Ruth 2:12 consists of eight edges and nine nodes. Recall that the glosses at the far right of the diagram are supplied as an assistance to readers. They are not part of the phrase marker and thus are not nodes.

(4.1)

The labels on nodes, other than the nodes that contain the text segments, are bipartite. Each node label consists of a construction / constituent identifier and a relation identifier. In displayed phrase markers such as (4.1), the former identifier is spatially above the latter. To save space in running text, we put the construction / constituent identifier and the relation identifier on the same line and separate them by a slash. Hence, the left-most node in the phrase marker above would be presented in text as cl / oblq.

43

A node at the left end of an edge is said to be the mother or parent of a node at the right end, the right node being termed the daughter or child. In phrase marker (4.1), the node cl/oblq is the parent (mother) of three children (daughters): vb/gram, sbj/gram, and dir obj/gram.

With regard to the hierarchical relationship between parent and child, the parent is said to dominate the child *immediately*. The relation between the nodes is said to be one of dominance. In our example, cl/oblq immediately dominates vb/gram, sbj/gram, and dir obj/gram. But it also dominates all of the other nodes in the phrase marker. A node that dominates all of the nodes is said to be the root node or root of the phrase marker. Nodes that have no children—that is, that dominate no other nodes—are called the leaves of the phrase marker. The leaves are the text segments making up the clause that the phrase marker describes.

With regard to the sequential structure of the phrase marker, nodes having the same parent are said to be siblings or sisters. A node that comes earlier in a clause than its sister is said to precede its sister. The relation between the nodes is one of precedence. In the phrase marker above, vb/gram precedes sbj/gram which precedes dir obj/gram.

The upper (or first) part of a node label identifies the structure immediately dominated by this node. There are two kinds of construction/constituent identifiers in our phrase markers. One identifies *major grammatical functions*, and the other specifies the structure of the constituents.

The lower (or second) part of the node label specifies the grammatical relation that licenses (or, justifies) the formation of the structure that its node dominates.

4.2 *Phrase Markers Characterized*

The number of edges that enter a node is called the node's in-degree. The in-degree of a root node is always zero. The in-degree of all of the other nodes is one.[1] The number of edges that leave a node is its out-degree. In example (4.1), the out-degree of the root is three, the out-degree of the text segments is zero, and so on.

There are two very simple ways to characterize the *complexity* of a phrase marker. The phrase marker's *length* is the number of Hebrew segments that it contains. The length of phrase marker (4.1) is four. The phrase marker's *depth* is the maximal number of generations encountered in passing from the root node ("generation 1") to the leaves ("generation N"). In example (4.1), the depth is four.

Until we are forced to generalize them later in this book, our phrase markers will be *labeled*, *directed trees*. Being a tree, any phrase marker obeys these four conditions:[2]

1. *Single-Root Condition.*   There is only one root node.
2. *Single-Mother Condition.*   Any non-root node has only one mother.
3. *Non-tangling Condition.*   Edges may not cross.
4. *Exclusivity Condition.*   For any two nodes in a tree, *either:*

   a. one dominates the other

   or

   b. one precedes the other.

---

1. In chap. 20, we study phenomena for which this is no longer true.
2. Adapted from Robert Trask, *A Dictionary of Grammatical Terms in Linguistics* (London: Routledge, 1993) 285.

Trees have interesting properties.[3] For example, the number of edges is always one less than the number of nodes. Also, between any two nodes, there is always only one path.

4.3 Information Propagation among and within Phrase Markers

The set of phrase markers shown in this book (and made available by Logos Research Systems) has all instances of lexical and structural ambiguity resolved. We do this to produce what we consider the single most-salient parsing of each clause. Usually this policy leads to uncontroversial results. But occasionally it eliminates important, often seemingly intentional ambiguity. We plan to restore and represent ambiguity in later releases of our data.

In this subsection, we will:

- discuss our conventions for resolving ambiguity by propagating information among and within our phrase markers and by relying on world knowledge.
- specify our rules for promoting semantic information within our phrase markers.

4.3.1 Information Sharing among Phrase Markers

What should the gloss on אֵילִים in phrase marker (4.2) from Job 42:8 be? Is 'rams' correct?

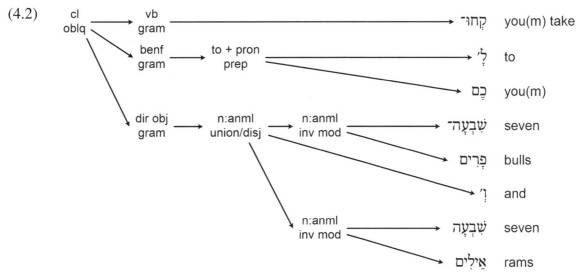

When we encounter the final segment, we consult a lexicon to discover its available semantics. In BDB, we find five entries (pp. 17–18 and 42), each with its own distinctive semantics:

1. 'ram' (semantics: anml) . . . e.g., Isa 1:11
2. 'projecting pillar' or 'pilaster' (semantics: bldg) . . . e.g., Ezek 40:14
3. 'leader, chief' (semantics: humn) . . . e.g., Job 41:17
4. 'terebinth' (semantics: veg) . . . e.g., Isa 1:29
5. 'gods' (semantics: deity) . . . e.g., Exod 15:11

When an analyst selects the semantic category for אֵילִים here, it is very easy to be oblivious to the thought processes and knowledge that constrain the selection. Here, one might proceed as follows:

---

3. Nora Hartsfield and Gerhard Ringel, *Pearls in Graph Theory: A Comprehensive Introduction* (San Diego: Academic, 1994) 17–20.

1. Since the first conjunct in the union phrase making up the direct object has animal semantics, we might decide that the second conjunct should have the same semantics.[4]
2. We might read ahead two clauses and learn that a burnt offering is to be made. Given this fact, we might infer that the אֵילִים are to be part of the offering. Knowing what we know about burnt offerings, we might thereby rule out all semantic categories but the first.[5] In this case, information from a nearby phrase marker plus knowledge of Israelite sacrifices might allow us to make a convincing assignment.

Were we determined initially to work clause-by-clause and then advance higher into discourse, then we might either leave the semantics completely unspecified, or we might under-specify the semantics in a list: Sem = {anml, bldg, humn, veg, deity}. Instead, *we have chosen to consider all available information so as to allow us to select a single value for each semantic feature.*

4.3.2 Semantic Feature Value Propagation within Phrase Markers

Selecting a single value for each semantic feature enables us to enhance our phrase markers by representing the semantics of the syntactic constituents. But to do so, we must specify rules for propagating semantic information in phrase markers. We rely on this modified recursive rule:

Basic Recursive Rule. The semantic feature value for a substantive constituent is the value of its first immediate constituent with the following exceptions:

1. *Definite Phrase Exception.* In a definite phrase, the semantics of the phrase is that of the determined substantive (the second immediate constituent).
2. *Inverted Modification Exception.* In an inverted modification phrase, the phrase semantics are those of the modified constituent (the second immediate constituent).
3. *Construct-Chain Exception.* In a construct chain having one or more *nomina regens* with quantity semantics, the semantics of the final *nomen rectum* are promoted to the level of the earliest quantity *nomen regens*.
4. *Construct-Chain Patch.* In a construct chain, when a *nomen regens* specifying lineage (e.g., "son of," firstborn of," etc.) and having human semantics precedes a *nomen rectum* with animal semantics, the construct phrase gets animal semantics.

An example of each of the parts of this rule may be helpful.

Basic Recursive Rule. Illustrative of the basic recursive rule is the constituent from phrase marker (4.3) for Gen 26:15.

(4.3)
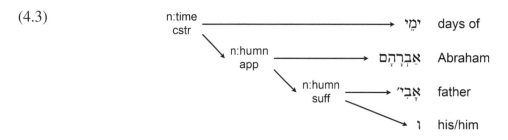

---

4. This inferential leap is on shaky ground. Heterogeneous semantics is common in union phrases. In three-segment union phrases ("X and Y"), the semantics of the conjuncts differ almost a third of the time. Consider these few instances of semantic heterogeneity in union phrases that involve animals: Gen 26:14 (animals and slaves), Exod 14:9 (animals and humans), Zeph 1:3 (people and animals), and 1 Chr 5:21 (animals and animals and animals and humans).

5. This excludes an unfolding tale wherein sacrificial bulls and participating chiefs / leaders are to be taken to Job.

We assign human semantics both to אָבִיו and to אַבְרָהָם אָבִיו. The semantics of the complete noun phrase, יְמֵי אַבְרָהָם אָבִיו, is time.

Definite Phrase Exception.   Consider fragment (4.4) from the phrase marker for Neh 8:7.

(4.4)

n:humn ⟶ הָ׳ the
def ↘ עָם people

The definite noun phrase has human semantics (humn), promoted from below.

Inverted-Modification Exception.   Phrase marker (4.5) from Job 42:8 shows inverted modification.

(4.5)

n:anml ⟶ שִׁבְעָה־ seven
inv mod ↘ פָּרִים bulls

The constituent has the semantics of its second immediate constituent (פָּרִים), namely anml.

Construct-Chain Exception.   The construct chain in (4.6) from Ezek 27:12 illustrates the exception. Both רֹב and כָּל have quantity semantics, so the semantics of the complete chain (val = valuable) is that of the final *nomen rectum* (הוֹן).

(4.6)

n:val ⟶ רֹב multitude of
cstr
    ↘ n:val ⟶ כָּל־ all of
        cstr
            ↘ הוֹן wealth

Construct-Chain Patch.   This patch is necessitated by the limited granularity of our semantics categories. We have no category that covers living beings, be they human or animal. Hence, in a constituent such as פֶּטֶר חֲמוֹר in (4.7) from Exod 34:20, we promote the *nomen rectum* semantics so the noun phrase has animal semantics, thereby avoiding the problem of a noun phrase wherein the firstborn of a donkey would have human semantics (that being the semantics assigned to the lexeme glossed 'firstborn of').

(4.7)

n:anml ⟶ פֶּטֶר firstborn of
cstr ↘ חֲמוֹר donkey

4.4 *The Phrase Marker Creation Process*

Our phrase markers were generated in three steps, with the second and third steps ongoing:

1. Generate phrase markers by designing, implementing, and using a battery of computational parsers (*computer parsing*).[6]

---

6. Our parsing strategy is covered in considerable detail in F. I. Andersen and A. D. Forbes, "Opportune Parsing: Clause Analysis of Deuteronomy 8," in *Bible and Computer: Desk and Discipline* (Paris: Honoré Champion, 1995) 49–75.

2. Extend the phrase markers beyond simple trees and detect/correct parsing errors by repeatedly reading through the phrase markers and by checking instances where the parsing rules were known to be under- or over-productive (*human over-reader correcting*).

3. Make the phrase markers consistent via various strategies (*consistency checking*).

Phrase marker (4.8) from the fable in Judg 9:10 will help us illustrate the process. All of the phrase marker outside the three boxes was correctly generated by the computer parser. The over-reader then assembled the speech into a sentence and made it the daughter of the obj addr node, as shown in the large dotted box. Since trees do not talk, the parser did not identify "the trees" as the subject of "they said." The over-reader recognized that the until-then-unassigned node label in the upper dotted box is *subject* and made the assignment. The parser erroneously assigned the label in the solid-boxed node a value of mvt aim/gram ("movement aim"). The computer was acting on its faulty "knowledge" that "the trees" could not listen but could be a goal of movement. The consistency checker subsequently detected and corrected this error.

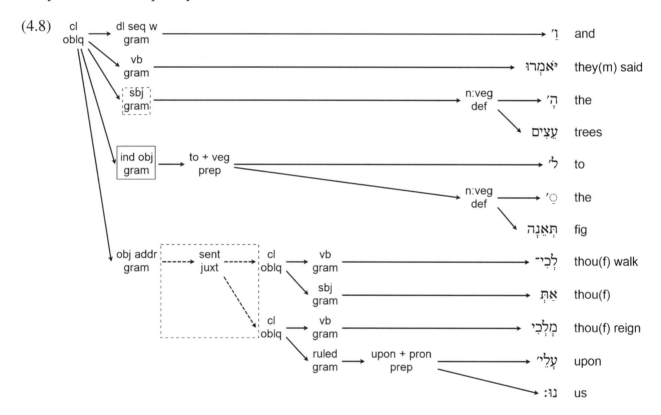

4.5 *Exercise: A Test Case Phrase Marker*

Let us take the phrase-marker concepts out for a bit of exercise. For phrase marker (4.9) from Prov 3:9, what are the answers to these questions? (Answers are supplied below the phrase marker.)

1. How many nodes are there?
2. Without further counting, how many edges are there?
3. Which is the root node?
4. What are the root node's in-degree and its out-degree?
5. What is the depth of the tree?

6. What is the length of the phrase marker?
7. How many children does the from+val/union/disj node have?
8. What node immediately precedes כָּל?
9. What node(s) dominate the segment כָּל?

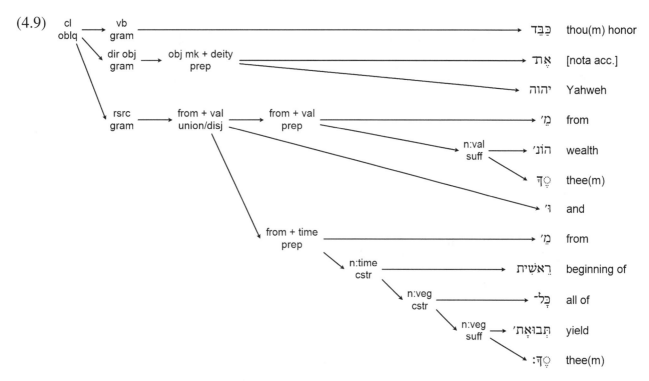

Answer #1: 24 nodes. Answer #2: One less than the number of nodes, namely 23 edges. Answer #3: The node labeled cl/oblq. Answer #4: In-degree = 0; out-degree = 3. Answer #5: depth = 8. Answer #6: length = 12. Answer #7: 3 children. Answer #8: רֵאשִׁית. Answer #9: There are 6 dominating nodes: n:veg/cstr, n:time/cstr, from+time/prep, from+val/union/disj, rsrc/gram, and cl/oblq.

4.6   *Brief Summary*

Vocabulary of Trees.   We introduce the vocabulary for describing phrase marker trees: *node, edge, root, leaf, mother, daughter, sister, in-degree, out-degree, dominance,* and *precedence.*

Trees versus Graphs.   Technically, the vast majority of our phrase markers are *labeled, directed trees.* We explain the conditions that these sorts of structure obey: *single-root, single-mother, non-tangling,* and *exclusivity.*

Information Propagation and Sharing.   A set of conventions governs the propagation of information, especially semantic information, within our phrase markers. The conventions include a basic recursive rule and overrides for handling definite phrases, inverted modification constructions, and construct chains.

The Phrase Marker Creation Process.   The phrase markers were initially created by a battery of incremental computational parsers. Corrections, extensions, and consistency enforcement are the ongoing work of human over-readers.

Chapter 5

The Basic Phrase Types of Biblical Hebrew

5.1 *The Constituent Hierarchy of Biblical Hebrew*

Before studying phrases, we will examine where phrases fit in the constituent hierarchy of Biblical Hebrew. Each level of the hierarchy typically is built up from constituents in the next lower level. We say "typically" because higher-level structures (such as clauses, sentences, and other kinds of discourse units) can be contained ("embedded") within lower-level structures.[1]

Our basic constituent hierarchy has five levels. These are most easily understood by considering an example. In grid-overlain phrase marker (5.1) for Gen 3:21, the columns of the superimposed grid identify the five levels making up the phrase marker. From right to left, these are: segment, phrase, CIC (clause immediate constituent), clausal, and supra-clausal.

The "lowest" (right-most) level of the phrase marker hierarchy consists of the text segments. By now, readers have a good grasp of what a segment is, but a bit of repetition should not be amiss: a segment is a word, part of a word, or a sequence of words that is an ultimate constituent in our syntactic analysis. Segments are the "atoms" of our analyses. Single segments can themselves be phrases or can combine to form more complicated phrases.

5.2 *Basic and Complex Phrases*

This chapter introduces the basic phrase types of Biblical Hebrew. A phrase is *basic* if it contains neither phrase type(s) nor higher-level constituents.[2] Equivalently, a basic phrase contains only one licensing relation. A phrase is *complex* if it contains phrase type(s) or higher-level constituent(s), in which case it must involve more than one licensing relation.

Consider an example: אֵם יַעֲקֹב "mother of Jacob" is a basic phrase, a construct phrase. יַעֲקֹב וְעֵשָׂו "Jacob and Esau" is another type of basic phrase, a union phrase in our parlance. But אֵם יַעֲקֹב וְעֵשָׂו "mother of Jacob and Esau" is a *complex phrase*, since it consists of a union phrase contained in a construct phrase as its *nomen rectum*. Phrase marker (5.2) shows this complex phrase from Gen 28:5.

---

1. Embedding is the focus of chap. 8.

2. Supra-clausal constituents will be dealt with in chap. 21. The higher-level constituents consist of CICs (clause immediate constituents) as well as clausal and supra-clausal constructions.

(5.1)

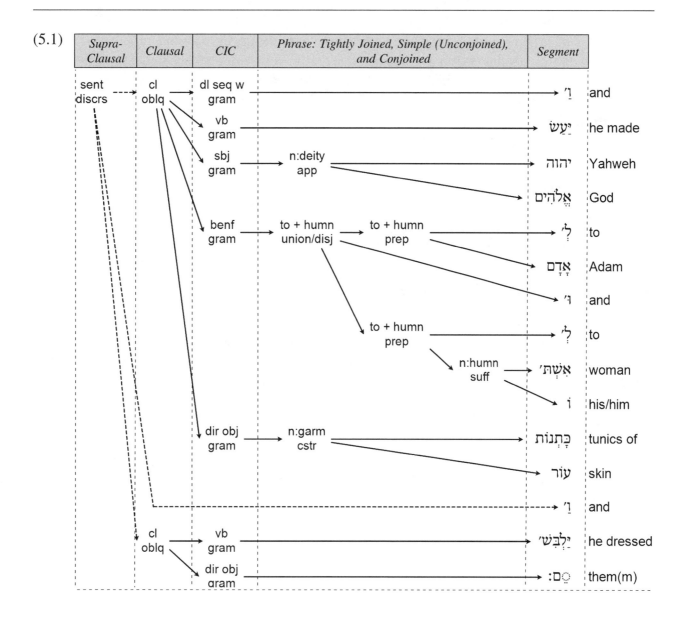

(5.2)

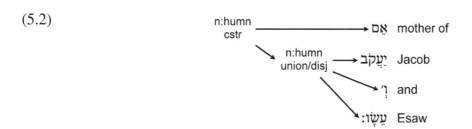

Note that the n:humn / cstr node dominates the n:humn / union/disj node and therefore has included within itself the union construction.

Phrase marker (5.1) has four basic phrases: n:deity/app, the upper to+humn/prep, n:humn/suff, and n:garm/cstr. It contains two complex phrases: to+humn/union/disj and the lower to+humn/prep. The phrase marker is tidy. The "higher" constituents contain the "lower."

We have not yet described the various phrase types and their composition. The basic phrases are straightforward. In this chapter, we describe them. In chap. 6, we take up complex phrases.

We work with three kinds of basic phrases:

1. tightly joined,
2. simple (unconjoined),
3. conjoined.

These phrase types are uniquely defined by the sets of relations *that license their formation.*

5.3 *Basic Tightly Joined Phrases*

A phrase that is declared to be "tightly joined" is licensed either by the relation of suffixation (suff) or by definiteness (def). Both relations are highly local and hence are referred to as "tight." Phrase marker (5.3) for Gen 42:20 contains both types of tight phrase.[3] Nodes licensed by the suff and def relations are usually right-shifted so as to be close to their children segments.

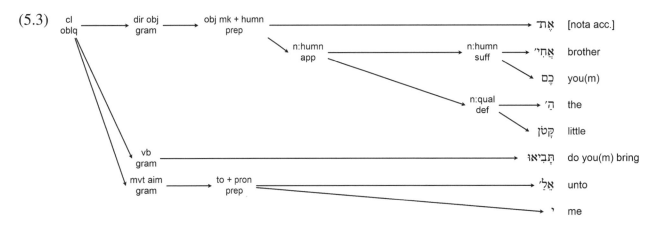

The significance of the structures and labels making up the phrase marker are explained below.

5.3.1 Tight Pronominal Suffixes

Our *Kethiv* text of Biblical Hebrew contains 45,025 pronoun suffixes. More than half of these (55%, or 24,894) are in tight phrases.[4] The table shows the distribution of these pronominal suffixes in terms of the various parts of speech to which they attach.

---

3. Note that what is in apposition in (5.3) is not the "adjective" 'little' but a definite nominal; 'the little' could have been called a definite adjective.

4. We use "tight" rather than "bound" because the meaning of "bound" is often extended in linguistic theory.

Tightly Suffixed Part of Speech	Percentage
Common Noun	95.6%
Pure Noun Participle	3.0%
All -כָּל	0.9%
Cardinal / Ordinal Number	0.5%

One exception aside,[5] each of the pronominal suffixes that is a constituent in a tight phrase combines only with its preceding segment, making this pronominal suffix relationship highly local.

The pronominal suffix *in a tight phrase* functions as a "possessive" pronoun or akin to one.[6] For example, in the phrase marker above, the n:humn/suff node dominates the noun אֲחִי and the suffix כֶם–, yielding a constituent that may be translated 'your [masc. pl.] brother'.

5.3.2 Determined Segments

Our *Kethiv* text of Biblical Hebrew contains 30,298 definite articles. A prefixed article segment *usually* combines immediately and only with a single following segment. This is the situation in the vast majority of cases, 29,166 times (96.3%). In these cases, the relationships are local—that is, *tight*. The remaining 3.7% of the definite articles (1,132 in all) are constituents in phrases that, strictly speaking, are not tight. These constructions are complex. Their exposition is given in chap. 6.

5.4 *Basic Unconjoined Phrases*

Included among the basic unconjoined phrases are all manner of prepositional and nominal phrases that involve neither tight suffixation nor definiteness nor explicit conjoining via conjunctions nor implicit conjoining via juxtaposition. We identify four basic unconjoined phrase types:[7]

1. prepositional phrases,
2. construct phrases,
3. simple modification,
4. inverted modification.

The first two phrase types are consistent with traditional analyses and will be dealt with only briefly. The final two may be less well known and thus will be treated in greater detail.

5.4.1 Prepositional Phrases

A basic prepositional phrase is licensed by the relation of preposition (prep), and itself contains no basic phrase types or higher-level constituents. Of the 74,058 prepositions in Biblical Hebrew,[8] 24,973 (34%) are part of basic prepositional phrases.[9] The prepositions in basic prepositional phrases combine with sibling segments of the sorts indicated in the table.

---

5. The exception is in Ps 89:3. This fascinating verse is discussed at the end of §20.2.3.4, phrase marker (20.17).

6. We write "akin to one," because in a tight phrase such as מַלְכִּי 'my king', the speaker is not claiming to own the king.

7. We recognize two other unconjoined phrase types: nominalized clauses (§8.1) and distributed apposition (§20.2.2).

8. This total includes the direct object markers.

9. Almost 2,900 are segments in compound prepositions, the creation of which is licensed by the juxt relation. See §5.5.3.

Sibling of Preposition	Representative Gloss	Percentage
Pronoun Suffix	"to him"	51.2%
Noun	"to Adam"	43.8%
Adverbial	"from there"	3.3%
Demonstrative Pronoun	"like these"	1.1%
Pure Noun Participle	"to captured-ones"	0.5%
Other	"until them," "to become-many"	0.1%

The constituent from Job 34:31 in (5.4) illustrates the appearance of a basic prepositional phrase. The constituent consists of the preposition אֶל 'unto' (to) followed by (+) the proper noun אֵל 'God' (deity). The construction is licensed by the relation preposition (prep).

(5.4)

to + deity		
prep	→ אֶל-	unto
	→ אֵל	God

5.4.2 Construct Phrases

A basic construct phrase is licensed by the relation of construct (cstr) and itself contains no basic phrase types or higher-level constituents. A construct relation licenses the assembly of a construct construction (or "chain"). A noun in the construct state always forms a construct phrase by pairing with a following noun, noun phrase, or nominalized constituent.

Of the 34,384 construct state segments in Biblical Hebrew, 16,925 (49%) are the lead-items (*nomina regens*)[10] in basic construct phrases. The table shows the parts of speech of the *nomina regens* in the basic construct phrases.

Part of Speech of Nomina Regens	Representative Gloss	Percentage
Common Noun	"sons of [Noah]"	93.2%
"all"	"all of [unclean thing]"	4.9%
Proper Noun	"Ur of [Chaldeans]"	1.9%

Phrase marker (5.5) from Neh 9:7 has אוּר כַּשְׂדִּים "Ur of Chaldeans" (two proper nouns!). Licensed by the relation of construct (cstr), a basic construct noun phrase having geographic semantics (n:geog) is shown.

(5.5)

n:geog		
cstr	→ אוּר	Ur of
	→ כַּשְׂדִּים	Chaldeans

---

10. *Nomina regens* = 'reigning nouns'.

5.4.3 Simple Modification

A basic modification phrase is licensed by the relation of modification (mod), and itself contains no basic phrase types or higher-level constituents. The modification relation licenses a construction where the first constituent is characterized more precisely by the second. The second constituent adds information. Example: "the water under the earth."

Of the 4,086 modification constructions in Biblical Hebrew, the vast majority involve prepositional phrases, and these will be taken up in chap. 6. Only 442 (11%) are in basic modification phrases. In a basic modification phrase, the second constituent may be an adverbial (as in "big very"), a numeral (as in "cows six"), or a common noun (as in "filled [with] incense").

Phrase marker (5.6) from 1 Sam 1:24 showing פָּרִים שְׁלֹשָׁה 'bulls three' involves a basic modification noun phrase with animal semantics (n:anml), its assembly being licensed by the modification relation (mod).

(5.6)

| n:anml mod | ⟶ | פָּרִים | bulls |
| | ⟶ | שְׁלֹשָׁה | three |

5.4.4 Inverted Modification

A basic inverted modification phrase is licensed by the relation of inverted modification (inv mod) and contains no basic phrase types or higher-level constituents. The inverted modification relation licenses a construction in which the second constituent is characterized more precisely by the first. The first constituent adds information about the second. Example: "six cows."

Of the 3,537 inverted modification constructions in Biblical Hebrew, 2,138 (60%) are in basic inverted modification phrases. The table provides the census of the main inverted modifiers.

Inverted Modifier Part of Speech	*Representative Gloss*	*Percentage*
Cardinal Number	"thirty [years]"	42.3%
Quasiverbal	"behold [I gave]"	34.6%
"also" גַם	"also [I]"	10.8%
Negative	"not [good]"	7.2%
Other	—	5.1%

This table involves very disparate kinds of constituents, lumped together by being licensed by the inverted modification relation. (Quasiverbals are thoroughly dealt with in chap. 18. Discontinuous inverted modification involving quasiverbals is taken up toward the end of §20.1.2.)

Phrase marker (5.7) from Gen 11:18 has a basic inverted modifier phrase involving the cardinal number 'thirty'.

(5.7)

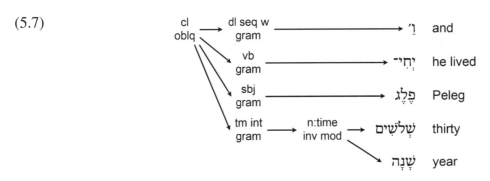

Or, consider phrase marker (5.8) from Gen 27:31. It contains a basic inverted modification phrase, a *clause-internal* instance of inverted modification by גַּם.

(5.8)

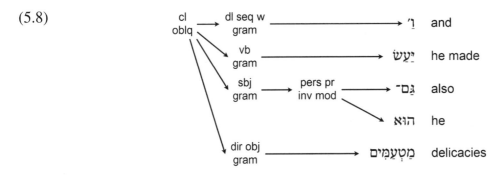

5.5 *Basic Structurally Defined Conjoined Phrases*

Conjoined phrases are created by joining constituents via a particular set of licensing relations. We distinguish two subtypes of conjoined phrases: phrases the assembling of which is based on structural criteria, and phrases the assembling of which is based on semantic criteria. As we will see in §5.6, the semantically defined phrases involve refined specification of the structurally defined phrases.

We distinguish three types of structural conjoining:

1. union ("and") or disjoint ("or") phrases (union/disj),
2. gathered (mixed list) phrases (mix list),
3. joined phrases (juxt).

5.5.1 Union or Disjoint Phrases

Often called a *coordinate phrase*, a union (or disjoint) phrase consists of a series of constituents, connected by coordinating conjunctions: "X and Y and Z" (or disjunctive conjunctions: "X or Y or Z"). Across Biblical Hebrew, the union relation is used 14,633 times, most of them resulting in complex coordinate phrases. In addition to its principal use in licensing the assembling of coordinate phrases (9,511 times), the union relation also licenses the combining of clauses into sentences (5,049 times).[11] We count 2,293 basic (single licensing relation) coordinate phrases in Biblical Hebrew. Most (2,052 or 89%) contain only two conjuncts.[12] Phrase marker (5.9) for a basic coordinate

---

11. Very rarely, there is compounding of clause adjuncts (ca. 30 times). On *adjuncts*, see §7.3.1.

12. The longest basic conjoined phrase contains 14 city names (for 13 cities) in a list in Josh 19:2–6.

(5.9)

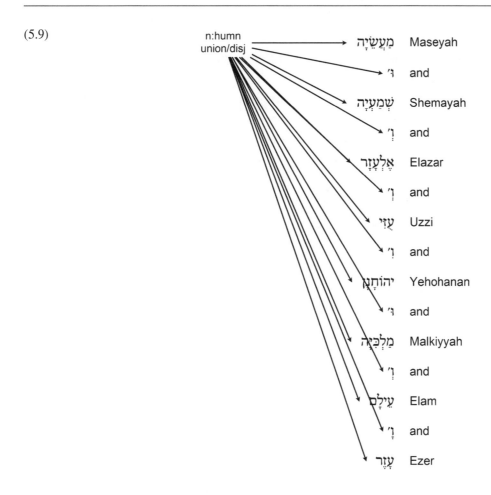

מַעֲשֵׂיָה	Maseyah
וְ'	and
שְׁמַעְיָה	Shemayah
וְ'	and
אֶלְעָזָר	Elazar
וְ'	and
עֻזִּי	Uzzi
וְ'	and
יְהוֹחָנָן	Yehohanan
וְ'	and
מַלְכִּיָּה	Malkiyyah
וְ'	and
עֵילָם	Elam
וְ'	and
עָזֶר	Ezer

phrase (licensed by union/disj) consists of a list of names of humans and is taken from Neh 12:42. The resulting noun phrase has human semantics.

5.5.2   Gathered (Mixed List) Phrases

(5.10)

שֵׁם	Shem
חָם	Ham
וָ'	and
יָפֶת	Yapeth

If one deletes some (but not all) of the conjunctions in a coordinate phrase, then the resulting construction is a gathered phrase or a mixed list. This specification entails that a basic mixed list must contain at least three conjuncts plus at least one coordinating conjunction. The licensing relation for a mixed list is mix list. Phrase marker (5.10) shows a basic mixed list of names of humans from Gen 10:1. These names appear elsewhere as basic coordination phrases (union/disj) in Gen 7:13 and 9:18.

We invoke this licensing relation 930 times across Biblical Hebrew. In 30% of its appearances, the relation gathers clauses together to form sentences. In 20%, the mixed lists consist of human names. The relation occurs in basic mixed lists 157 times and in non-tree phrase markers 27 times.

5.5.3 Joined Phrases

If one deletes all of the conjunctions in a coordinate phrase, then the resulting construction is a joined phrase or, more loosely, a juxtaposed phrase (juxt). This specification entails that a joined phrase contain at least two "conjuncts" and no coordinating conjunctions. Phrase marker (5.11) from Ezra 8:24 shows a basic two-segment juxtaposed phrase. The syntax of the clause of which the two segments are a part is quite complicated, but it is clear that they are part of a single basic joined phrase.

(5.11)

Joined phrases also occur when prepositions or parts of numerals are immediately adjacent. Phrase marker (5.12) from Ezek 10:2 contains a pair of triple-preposition constructions.

(5.12)

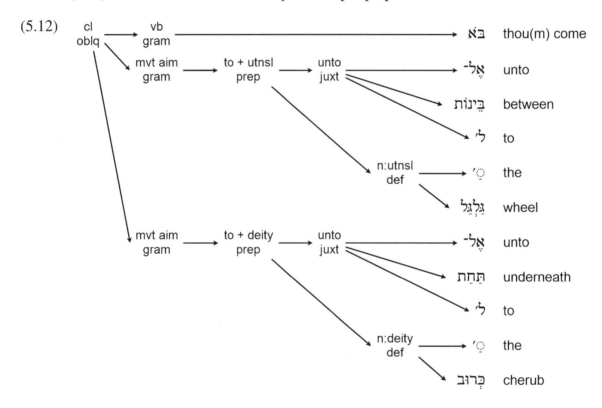

All told, there are 5,015 juxt relations in Biblical Hebrew. Of these, 1,833 appear as licensing relations in the formation of sentences, leaving about 3,200 in phrasal constructions. 138 of these occur in non-tree phrase markers. The 3,200 constructions are divvied up between basic and complex joined phrases. Over two-fifths (1,440) appear in joined prepositions, of which the most common first preposition (around 63%) is -מֵ or other forms of 'from'. There are 1,367 basic joined phrases that consist of two juxtaposed prepositions, 45 basic joined phrases that consist of three juxtaposed prepositions, and two that consist of four juxtaposed prepositions (1 Sam 7:11 'until from under to' and 1 Kgs 7:32 'to from under to'). The combining of cardinal numbers is often licensed by juxt. There is one basic joined phrase having four adjacent numerals (Neh 7:11), 42 having three adjacent numerals, and 577 having two. The remaining joined phrases are a variety of other noun phrases.

5.6   *Basic Semantically Defined Conjoined Phrases*

The pair of *basic* conjoined noun phrases in (5.13) and (5.14) is drawn from Gen 2:21 and Exod 3:4.

(5.13)
     n:deity
     app
         יהוה   Yahweh
         אֱלֹהִים   God

(5.14)
     n:humn
     echo
         מֹשֶׁה   Moses
         מֹשֶׁה   Moses

Examination of the texts from which these constructions are extracted discloses that a proper parsing of each requires that the pairs of segments combine to form basic two-segment phrases. The structural relation of juxtaposition (juxt) would be a valid licensing relation for each phrase. The segments are, after all, juxtaposed in the text. However, we have elected to enhance our representation by introducing five specialized licensing relations. Two of these can appear in basic phrases: echo (echo) and apposition (app).[13] While *juxtaposition* seemingly requires only adjacency,[14] *apposition* requires identical reference and *echo* requires identical form, function, and reference.[15] In the next two subsections, we will examine these two types of basic semantically defined conjoined phrases.

5.6.1   Echo Phrases

"Echo" refers to the *exact* repetition of some constituent within a clause in such a way that all of the repeated constituents combine to form an echo construction. The morphologically identical constituents are usually adjacent, but adjacency is not sufficient since adjacent morphologically identical segments may be in different clauses and/or may exercise different functions in their clause(s). For example, consider (5.15) showing two consecutive clauses from Qoh 7:3–4.

---

13. The other three types of semantically defined conjoined phrases are always complex: strictly subsetting, strictly supersetting, and nested. These types are taken up in chap. 6.

14. The licensing relation of juxtaposition is rarely invoked when the joined constituents are not adjacent. Nonadjacency occurs in less than two percent of the cases licensed by juxt.

15. Strictly speaking, two successive segments might be homographs having the same form but differing functions. In such a case, the items would not combine to form a single conjoined constituent. We know of no actual case of this phenomenon in the Hebrew Bible, and so an example from English must suffice: "I saw the duck duck."

(5.15)

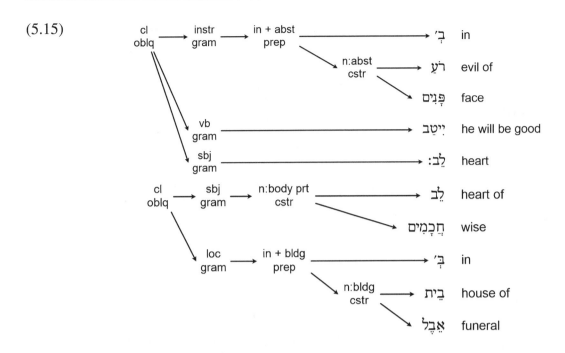

The sequence לֵב׃לֵב spans the boundary between the clauses. The first לֵב is in the normal state, while the second is in the construct state. They cannot form an echo phrase for two reasons: They span a clause boundary, and they have differing functions. Thus we see, perhaps surprisingly, that even the recognition of echo phrases can require a considerable amount of analysis.

We find 229 echo phrases in Biblical Hebrew. There are 161 basic echo phrases and 68 complex echo phrases. There are 18 that require non-trees for their representation.

Most echo phrases contain two sisters (218 instances, 95.2%). Among the basic two-sister echo phrases, we find:

• סָבִיב 'around' echoed 27 times—phrase marker (5.16) from Ezek 37:2, for example:

(5.16)

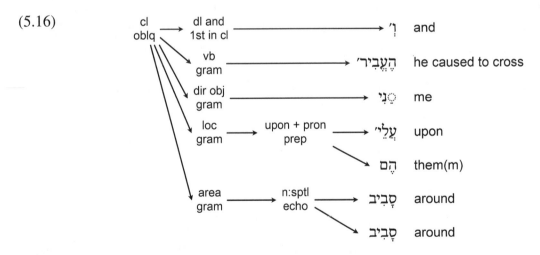

• אִישׁ 'man' echoed 16 times—phrase marker (5.17) from Num 1:4, for example:

(5.17)

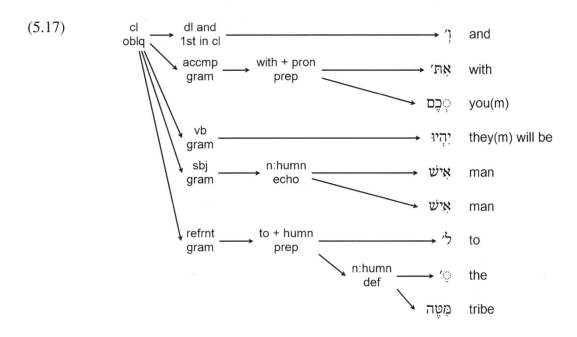

• Numerals echoed 14 times—phrase marker (5.18) from Ezek 10:21, for example:

(5.18)

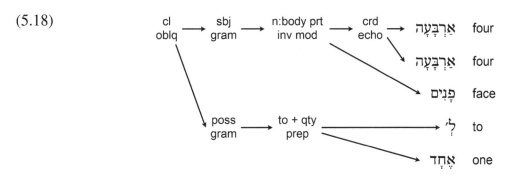

• מְאֹד 'very' echoed 12 times—see phrase marker (5.19) from Gen 7:19:

(5.19)

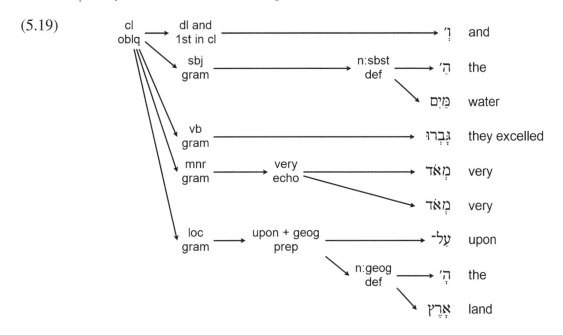

There are four echo phrases having three sisters: Isa 6:3 ('holy, holy, holy'), Jer 7:4 ('Temple of Yahweh, Temple of Yahweh, Temple of Yahweh', a complex echo phrase), Jer 22:29 ('land, land, land'), and Ezek 21:32 ('ruin, ruin, ruin'). Phrase marker (5.20) shows Ezek 21:32a:

(5.20)

```
cl ──→ obj cmp ──→ n:bldg ──→ עַוָּה   ruin
oblq     gram       echo
                           ↘  עַוָּה   ruin
                           
                           ↘  עַוָּה   ruin
          ↓ vb
            gram  ────────────→  אֲשִׂימֶ׳  I shall put
          ↓ dir obj
            gram  ────────────→  נָּה     her
```

The object complement (obj cmp/gram)[16] in this clause is a basic triple-echo phrase, a noun phrase with building semantics (n:bldg/echo).[17]

5.6.2 Apposition Phrases

An apposition phrase is a construction wherein two or more constituents have an identical reference. An apposition phrase is basic if its constituents are all segments. There are 17,961 apposition phrases in Biblical Hebrew. Of these, 676 require non-tree representation. There are 2,207 basic two-segment apposition phrases and 19 basic three-segment apposition phrases. Thus, we see that the vast majority of apposition phrases are complex.

Phrase marker fragment (5.21) from Jer 5:8 is a basic three-segment apposition phrase:

(5.21)

```
n:anml ──→ סוּסִים    horses
app
       ↘  מְיֻזָּנִים  lustful ones
       
       ↘  מַשְׁכִּים  lusty ones
```

5.7 *Brief Summary*

The Constituent Hierarchy. Our constituent hierarchy has these five levels (each taken up in the chapters indicated):

supra-clausal	→	clause	→	clause immediate constituent	→	phrase	→	segment
chap. 21		chaps. 7–8		chaps. 9–16		chaps. 5–6		chap. 3

We define two types of phrases. A *basic phrase* involves only one licensing relation, while a *complex phrase* involves more than one licensing relation. This chapter provides a census, with example phrase markers, of the various kinds of basic phrases attested in Biblical Hebrew.

Basic Tight Phrases. Basic tight phrases consist of a pronoun suffix or a definite article plus a single-segment substantive. Overwhelmingly, the substantive is a common noun.

---

16. The identification of most <u>clause immediate constituents</u> is licensed by the nonspecific relation gram "<u>grammar determined</u>."

17. That is, the noun has the semantics of a "building."

Basic Unconjoined Phrases. Basic unconjoined phrases involve neither suffixation nor definiteness nor explicit joining via conjunctions nor implicit joining via juxtaposition. Basic unconjoined phrases are of four sorts: prepositional phrases ("to David"), construct phrases ("sons-of Noah"), simple modification phrases ("bulls three"), and inverted modification phrases ("three bulls").

Basic Structurally Defined Conjoined Phrases. Basic structurally defined conjoined phrases are of three sorts: union phrases ("Shem and Ham and Yapeth"), mixed lists ("Shem, Ham, and Yapeth"), and juxtaposed lists ("Shem, Ham, Yapeth").

Basic Semantically Defined Conjoined Phrases. Basic semantically defined conjoined phrases are of two sorts: echo phrases ("ruin, ruin, ruin") and apposition phrases ("man Canaanite").

Chapter 6

Complex Phrases in Biblical Hebrew

6.1 *Embedding*

Language allows, indeed relies upon, abundant embedding, whereby "higher" constituents are contained in "lower" constituents.[1] Consider phrase marker (6.1), which shows the syntactic structure of part of the direct object of the main clause in Deut 29:25. Reading diagonally down the left-hand edge of the phrase marker, we see that we are dealing with a noun phrase, a "lower" constituent, having divine semantics (n:deity). We also see that the first segment (אֱלֹהִים) joins with the nominalized construction (nom / nom) because the latter is in apposition (app) to the former.[2] The construction that is explicitly nominalized by אֲשֶׁר is a sentence (sent), a "higher" constituent, formed by conjoining two clauses (both cl / oblq) by "and," licensed by the union (or disjunction) relation (union / disj).[3] The details need not detain us. The point is that this sort of construction, wherein clausal and supra-clausal (that is, "higher" than the clause) constituents are contained within otherwise straightforward noun phrases or other constituents, is rather common (see (6.1)).

If readers who have an appetite for bizarre examples and who have access to a rendition of our database bring up the Andersen-Forbes phrase marker analysis and have a look at Jer 11:1–5a, they will encounter a main clause that we believe is the champion for *iterated* embedding of sentences, clauses, and infinitives construct.[4] A suitable path begins in Jer 11:1, where the reader encounters 14 embedded predicator structures:

11:1 {clause {clause {inf. constr.
      11:2 {sent {sent
           11:3 {clause {clause {clause {clause
                11:4 {clause {inf. constr. {sent {clause {clause
                        }}}}}}}}}}}}}}

---

1. Our five-level hierarchy of constituents is shown and discussed at the beginning of §5.1. In phrase marker (5.1), higher-level constituents are to the left of lower-level constituents.

2. We discuss the nominalized clause construction (nom / nom) in §8.1.

3. In this phrase marker, we encounter *dotted edges*. They signal that the supra-clausal construction of which they are part is an interim makeshift that we hope to replace by a proper discourse-analytic construction one day.

4. We thank Eli Evans of Logos Research Systems for searching out this monumental syntactic structure for us.

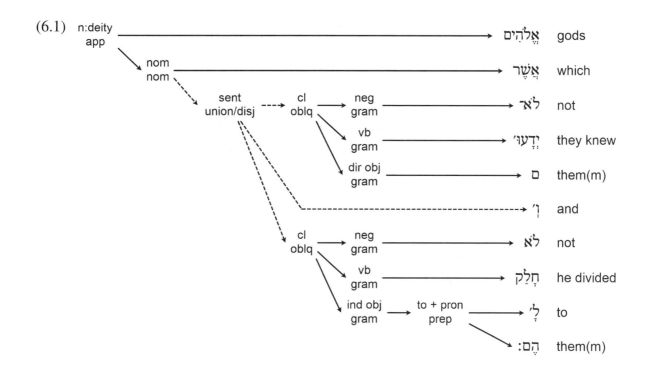

(6.1)

6.2   Complex Phrases

In our parsing of Biblical Hebrew, there are almost 2,000 distinct node labels corresponding to almost 2,000 different constituents. To describe every distinct constituent would be quite beyond the scope of the present volume. The constituents may, however, all be searched for and studied using our database. Our goal in this chapter is rather modest: simply to describe and provide examples for each major complex phrase type.

We simplify terminology and classify the constituents making up a construction as *segments* and / or *phrases*.[5] Given this simplified definition, complex phrases divide into four configurations:

1. *Segment-segment.*   A segment and following segment(s) combine to form a *basic* phrase (covered in chap. 5).
2. *Segment-phrase.*   A segment and following phrase combine to form a complex phrase.
3. *Phrase-phrase.*   A phrase and following phrase combine to form a complex phrase.
4. *Phrase-segment.*   A phrase and a following segment combine to form a complex phrase.

6.3   Complex Tight Phrases

6.3.1   Complex Suffixed Phrases

There are 11 instances of complex suffixed phrases (for basic suffixed phrases, see §5.3). Two cases have a pronominal suffix as the first constituent of a union phrase (Jer 51:35 and Ezek 23:43). Phrase marker (6.2) for Jer 51:35 has the segment-phrase configuration. The complex suffix phrase

---

5. A segment is, in fact, a single-constituent phrase. Rather than refer to one-constituent phrases and multiple-constituent phrases, we elect to refer to the former as segments and the latter as phrases.

(n:work / suff) is formed by joining a segment (חָמָס 'violence') with a following union phrase (pers pr / union / disj).[6]

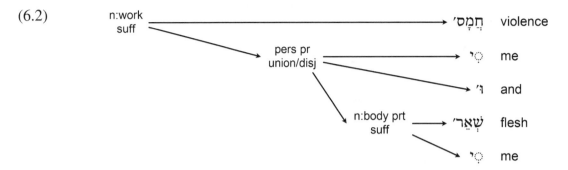

The other nine instances each involve making the suffix the first constituent in an apposition phrase. Phrase marker (6.3) for Prov 23:15 is typical (note that alternate parses are also defensible).

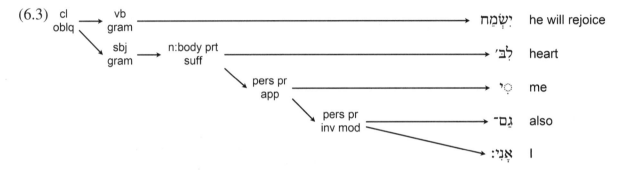

The suffix is the first constituent of a segment-phrase configuration. The second constituent of the complex apposition phrase is a basic inverted modification phrase (the other instances are found in Deut 4:47; Jer 3:11; Ps 9:7, 49:14, 71:16, 103:2; 1 Chr 6:11, 25:7).

6.3.2 Complex Definite Phrases

Here, we list the number of definite complex phrases. Below, we shall provide an example of each phrase type.

Phrase Type	Count
"Possessive"	7
Prepositional Phrase	1
Nominalized Clause	51
Noun-Verb Participle	998
Infinitive Construct	3
Other Complex Noun Phrases	72

---

6. The semantics of the basic suffix phrase consisting of שְׁאֵרִי 'my flesh' is literal and thus is *body part* (body prt) rather than *human*. We have made no effort to provide special handling for figurative usages.

6.3.2.1   The Bizarre Phrase Types: "Possessive" and Prepositional Phrase

This subtype of complex definite phrase consists of eight rather bizarre cases. We present two examples. Phrase marker (6.4) shows a noun phrase from Josh 7:21, which translates literally as 'the-tent-me'. This noun phrase is of the segment-phrase configuration.

(6.4)

n:bldg def ⟶	הָ'	the
↘ n:bldg suff ⟶	אֹהֳלִ'	tent
↘	יֹ	me

The other six "definite possessives" appear in Lev 27:23 (twice), Josh 8:33, 2 Kgs 15:16, Isa 24:2, and Mic 2:12.

The second subtype is, so far as we know, unique to 1 Sam 9:24: a *definite prepositional phrase* 'the-upon-her'. Phrase marker (6.5) is of the segment-phrase configuration.

(6.5)

upon + pron def ⟶	הֶ'	the
↘ upon + pron prep ⟶	עָלֶי'	upon
↘	הָ	her

6.3.2.2   The Nominalized Phrase Types

There are 998 complex definite phrases that involve nominalized predicative constructions. Nominalized predicative structures are not discussed until §8.4. As their name implies, they are noun phrases that contain predications. There are four types: nominalized clauses, noun-verb participles, infinitives construct, and *other*. We shall illustrate our points using an example of each type. All have the segment-phrase configuration.

Nominalized Clauses.   There are 51 clauses nominalized by a definite article. The nominal phrase in (6.6) from Gen 18:21 is an example. The clause (cl / oblq) consists of a finite verb (vb / gram) and a movement aim (mvt aim / gram). The NJPS translates the phrase 'that has reached Me'.

(6.6)
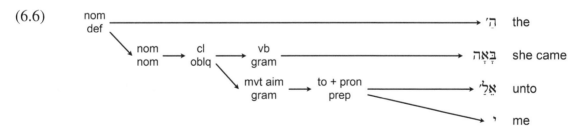

The critical point here is that *the entire clause is nominalized* (nom / nom). The definite article operates upon the entire nominalized clause, making it definite.

Noun-Verb Participles.   There are 998 instances of this phenomenon. The nominal phrase from Isa 62:6 in (6.7) shows a typical construction. As was explained in §3.2.4.2, noun-verb participles are so called because they behave as nouns with regard to pre-context but as verbs with regard to post-context. In the present example, the entire participle phrase is definite (as a noun might be), but the participle has an explicitly marked direct object (such as a verb might have).

(6.7)

nom ptc def	──────────────────────────→	הַ'	the
	↘ nom ptc oblq → n-v ptc gram ─────────────→	מַזְכִּרִים	mentioning
	↘ dir obj gram → obj mk + deity prep ──→	אֶת־	[nota acc.]
	↘	יהוה	Yahweh

Infinitives Construct. In our markup of the text, there are only three instances of the phenomenon in Biblical Hebrew in which an infinitive construct is nominalized and made definite. Phrase marker (6.8) shows the infinitive construct in Jer 22:16.

(6.8)

nom inf def	──────────────────────────→	הַ'	the
	↘ nom inf oblq → inf cst gram ─────────────→	דַּעַת	know
	↘ dir obj gram → obj mk + pron prep ──→	אֹת'	[nota acc.]
	↘	יֹ	me

Were there no explicitly marked direct object, דַּעַת might well be classified as a noun.

Other Complex Noun Phrases. There are 72 other complex noun phrases. Most are quite straightforward, similar to the simple example from 1 Chr 24:6 in (6.9).

(6.9)

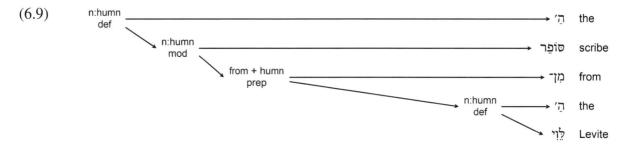

Here we have a basic definite phrase ("the Levite") contained in a prepositional phrase contained in a modification phrase contained in a definite phrase.

6.4 *Complex Unconjoined Phrases*

Included among the complex unconjoined phrases are all manner of prepositional and nominal phrases that do not involve tight suffixation, definiteness, explicit conjoining via conjunctions, or implicit conjoining via juxtaposition. We consider five complex unconjoined phrase types:[7]

---

7. We recognize two other unconjoined phrase types: nominalized clauses and distributed apposition. The former involves a clause and is discussed in chap. 8. The latter involves non–tree behavior and is discussed in chap. 20.

1. prepositional phrases,
2. construct phrases,
3. modification,
4. inverted modification,
5. bonded substantives.

The first two phrase types are consistent with traditional analyses and so will be dealt with only briefly. The final three are less well known and so will be treated in greater detail.

6.4.1 Complex Prepositional Phrases

A prepositional phrase can be complex because its preposition is compound (1,420 times), because its noun phrase is not a simple segment, because the preposition combines with a nominalized constituent, or any combination of the foregoing. We illustrate each situation.

6.4.1.1 Compound Prepositions

Phrase marker (6.10) from Exod 5:20 illustrates how a compound preposition inevitably yields a complex prepositional phrase. The prepositional phrase contains a joined phrase consisting of two prepositions. The phrase marker has a phrase-segment configuration:

(6.10)

```
from + humn ──→ from ──────→ מֵ׳     from
   prep          juxt
                      ↘        אֶת     with

                               ↘     פַּרְעֹה׃   Pharaoh
```

6.4.1.2 Non-Segment Noun Phrase

The most common instance of this phenomenon occurs when a preposition combines with a definite phrase in a segment-phrase configuration, as in phrase marker (6.11) from Gen 1:1:

(6.11)

```
obj mk + geog ──────────────────────→ אֵת    [nota acc.]
   prep
         ↘              n:geog ──────→ הַ׳    the
                         def
                              ↘    שָׁמַיִם   heaven
```

6.4.1.3 Nominalized Constituent

The predominant instances of this phenomenon are infinitive construct nominal phrases, as phrase marker (6.12) for Gen 2:5 illustrates. The infinitive construct (inf cst/gram) and its direct object (dir obj/gram) form a nominal predicative construction (nom inf/oblq), which combines with the preposition to form a prepositional phrase (to+inf cstr/prep).

(6.12)

```
to + inf cstr ──────────────────────────────────→ לְ׳      to
   prep
      ↘    nom inf ──→ inf cst ──────────────────→ עֲבֹד    serve
            oblq        gram
               ↘    dir obj ──→ obj mk + geog ────→ אֶת־    [nota acc.]
                     gram          prep
                                       ↘   n:geog ──→ הָ׳   the
                                            def
                                               ↘  אֲדָמָה׃  land
```

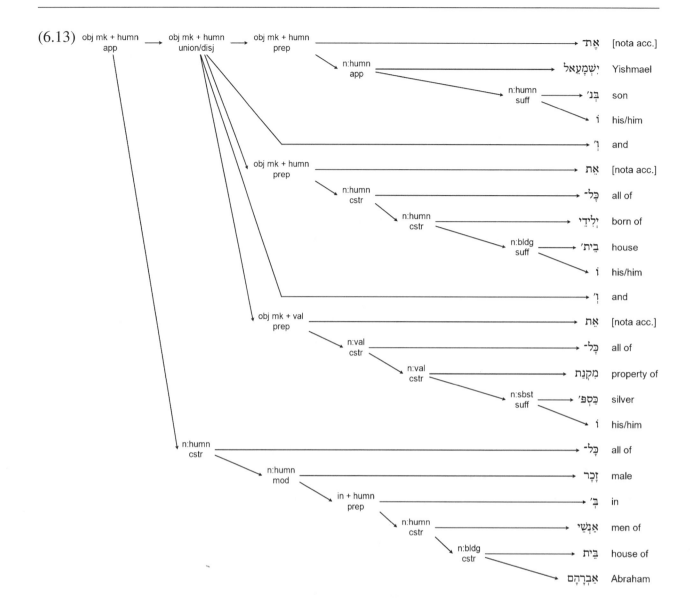

6.4.1.4 Elaborations

As has been noted previously, constructions can become very (disconcertingly?) elaborate. Consider the prepositional-phrase portion of the direct object from Gen 17:23 shown in (6.13). This phrase contains 40 nodes, is 22 segments long, and is 7 levels deep.

More elaborate prepositional phrases exist. Readers with access to our database can examine some truly extensive prepositional phrases. For example, they can inspect the long prepositional phrase in the phrase marker for 1 Chr 28:11–15, a phrase 132 segments long and 14 levels deep.

6.4.2 Complex Construct Phrases

6.4.2.1 Two-Relation Complex Construct Phrases

If we limit a search to construct phrases that consist of a single-segment *nomen regens* plus any other two-segment phrase (constructions consisting of a segment and a phrase), then we find 12,334 instances in Biblical Hebrew. The three top contributors with this structure consist of a construct of a definite phrase (6,145 times or 49.8%; see [6.14]), a construct of a suffixed phrase (3,866 or

31.3%; see [6.15]), and a construct of a construct phrase (1,979 times or 16.1%; see [6.16]). This leaves 344 instances (2.8%) not accounted for. We illustrate the three major phenomena via phrase markers from Genesis 34.

Construct of Definite Phrase.　　Phrase marker (6.14) is a fragment from Gen 34:3:

(6.14)

obj mk + humn prep	⟶	אֶת־	[nota acc.]
	↘ n:humn def	⟶ הַ׳	the
		↘ נַעֲרָ	girl {V}

Construct of Suffixed Phrase.　　Phrase marker (6.15) is a fragment from Gen 34:20:

(6.15)

n:bldg cstr	⟶	שַׁעַר	gate of
	↘ n:geog suff	⟶ עִיר׳	city
		↘ ם֑	them(m)

Construct of Construct Phrase.　　Consider the fragment from Gen 34:25 in (6.16):

(6.16)

n:humn cstr	⟶	שְׁנֵי־	two of
	↘ n:humn cstr	⟶ בְּנֵי־	sons of
		↘ יַעֲקֹב	Jacob

If we require each "contained node" to have more than two daughters, then we find 629 instances of such coordinated phrases. Phrase marker (6.17) from Job 20:17 shows a simple conjoined phrase contained within a construct phrase.

(6.17)

n:geog cstr	⟶	נַחֲלֵי	wadis of
	↘ n:food union/disj	⟶ דְּבַשׁ	honey
		↘ וְ׳	and
		↘ חֶמְאָה:	butter

6.4.2.2　More Elaborate Construct Phrases

Construct phrases with an intricate structure are also common. For example, in phrase marker (6.18) for Exod 3:8, the *nomen rectum* is a coordinate phrase with six conjuncts, each a definite phrase.[8]

---

8. Contrary to initial impressions, (6.18) is a tree. The four edges that cross other edges do so only because of layout engine flaws. Were the break-points moved to the right by appropriate amounts, there would be no crossing edges.

(6.18)

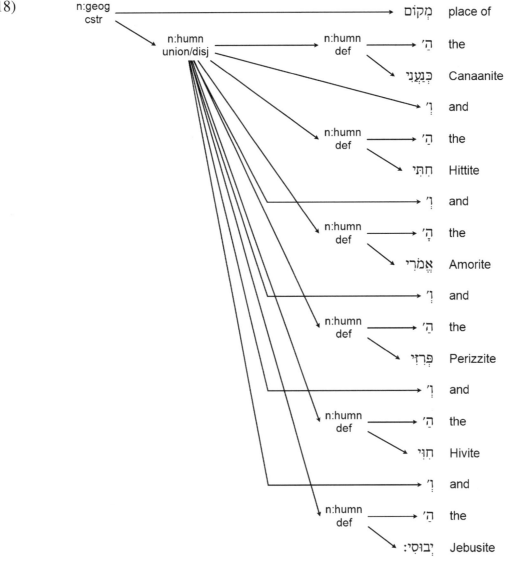

Many complex construct phrases involve recursive structures. Example: the genealogy in 1 Chr 6:18–23 contains a very long structure, in which apposition phrases contain construct phrases over and over ("A son of B son of C . . ."). This page is too narrow to show the phrase marker.

6.4.3 Complex Modification Phrases

442 (11%) of the modification phrases are simple; 3,644 (89%) are complex. Of the complex phrases, 97% involve a modification node with an out-degree of two. The remaining 3% have an out-degree greater than two. We show a phrase marker for each of the three main types of complex modification phrases of out-degree two (in §5.4.3, we discuss basic modification phrases).

6.4.3.1 Segment-Phrase

Segment-phrase types occur 1,617 times. The involved phrase is typically a prepositional phrase (87%). To allow readers to exercise concepts and to make a point about unambiguous parsing, phrase marker (6.19) for the final complete clause in 2 Kgs 14:2 is shown below.[9] Note that the complex modification phrase consists of the mother's name יְהוֹעַדִּין 'Yehoaddin', modified by מִן־ יְרוּשָׁלָם 'from Jerusalem' (the structure dominated by the sbj cmp / gram node). The modification of the proper noun by the following prepositional phrase is indicated with confidence in this context. There is nowhere else for the prepositional phrase to alight. In chap. 20, we discuss contexts with syntactic ambiguity.

(6.19)

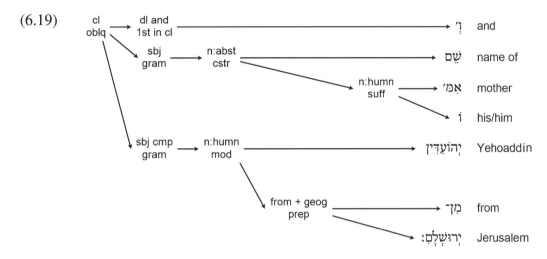

6.4.3.2   Phrase-Phrase

This construction type occurs 1,588 times. Many types of phrase occupy the lead position. Phrase marker (6.20) from 1 Sam 14:3 is typical. The construct phrase is modified by a prepositional phrase.

(6.20)

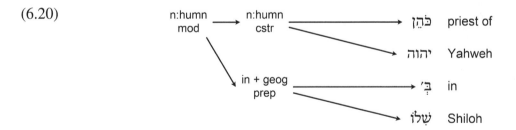

6.4.3.3   Phrase-Segment

This type of construction occurs only 266 times. The instance from Gen 24:16 in (6.21) should suffice.

(6.21)

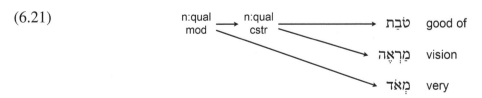

---

9. The *Kethiv* text is shown. The gap at the third position from the end of the clause exists because the *Qere* is not shown.

Here a noun phrase having semantics of quality (n:qual) is built up by modifying (mod) a noun phrase of quality, the latter having been licensed by the relation of construct (cstr).

6.4.4 Complex Inverted Modification Phrases[10]

6.4.4.1 Segment-Phrase

This construction type occurs 623 times. Phrase marker (6.22) from 2 Kgs 23:33 is typical:

(6.22)

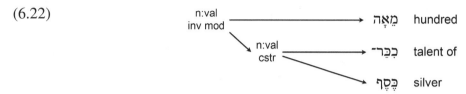

6.4.4.2 Phrase-Phrase

The phrase-phrase construction type occurs 218 times. Phrase marker (6.23) from Judg 20:17 is typical.

(6.23)

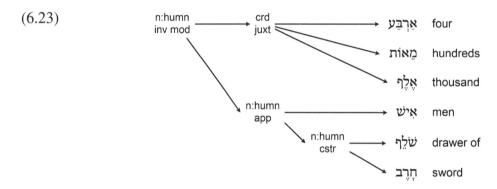

6.4.4.3 Phrase-Segment

The phrase-segment construction type occurs 541 times. Phrase marker (6.24) is typical, drawn from Amos 4:8.

(6.24)

6.4.5 Complex Bonded Substantives

One of the least frequently occurring and most specialized of the licensing relations is a type that we refer to as *bonding* or *bonded correlation*. This relation licenses constructions that approximate the form "not X, but Y" or "X and not Y." Across Biblical Hebrew, there are 62 constituents the formation of which is licensed in our parsing as involving bonding.

Often one part of the bonded construction is negated in an inverted modification structure, as in the bonded "X and not Y" phrase from Jer 18:17 shown in (6.25).

---

10. See §5.4.4 for an explanation of "inverted."

(6.25)

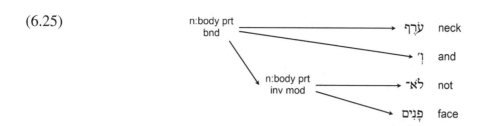

For another example, consider the bonded phrase "in X except in Y" in the prepositional phrase from 2 Kgs 5:15 that appears in (6.26).

(6.26)

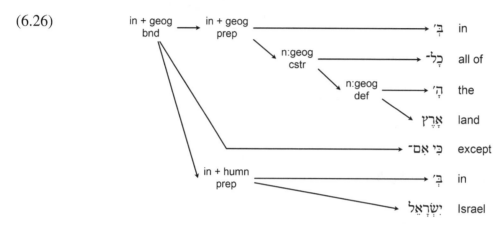

6.5   *Complex Structurally Defined Conjoined Phrases*

In taking up complex structurally defined conjoined phrases, we potentially enter a combinatoric thicket, since the number of combinations of constituents and their "glue" can be enormous. How this occurs is easy to see. Symbolize a segment by S, a phrase by P, a conjunction (usually ֝ו "and") by +, and an absent conjunction by 0. Then we can concisely represent each of the possible conjoined constructions. For example, a segment followed by a phrase joined by a conjunction is symbolized by S+P. Three phrases joined by juxtaposition (with no conjunctions as glue) are symbolized by P0P0P. And so on.

Consider the construction types possible for a two-constituent phrase. The table specifies the subtypes and gives their incidences. There are 8 possible two-constituent subtypes.

	Phrase Complexity			
	Complex			Basic
Union	P+P	P+S	S+P	S+S
	4,402	247	739	2,052
Joined	P0P	P0S	S0P	S0S
	499	51	28	2,169

With a three-constituent coordinated phrase, these 32 patterns are possible:

Phrase Complexity							
Complex							Basic
P+P+P	P+P+S	P+S+P	P+S+S	S+P+P	S+P+S	S+S+P	S+S+S
623	12	20	21	83	7	47	134

Union corresponds to the first data row above.

	P+P0P	P+P0S	P+S0P	P+S0S	S+P0P	S+P0S	S+S0P	S+S0S
Mixed List	23	0	0	0	1	0	1	5
	P0P+P	P0P+S	P0S+P	P0S+S	S0P+P	S0P+S	S0S+P	S0S+S
	141	3	2	17	30	4	8	77

| | P0P0P | P0P0S | P0S0P | P0S0S | S0P0P | S0P0S | S0S0P | S0S0S |
| *Joined* | 102 | 1 | 4 | 0 | 8 | 2 | 4 | 98 |

6.5.1   Compound Conjunctions by Juxtaposition

Juxtaposed conjunctions acting as glue in coordination phrases are quite rare. We find only 13 juxtaposed conjunctions within phrases in Biblical Hebrew. Seven occur in tree phrase markers,[11] and 6 occur in non-tree phrase markers.[12] There are 11 instances of וְגַם 'and also'. Phrase marker (6.27) from Qoh 11:2 shows one of the 'and also' constructions.

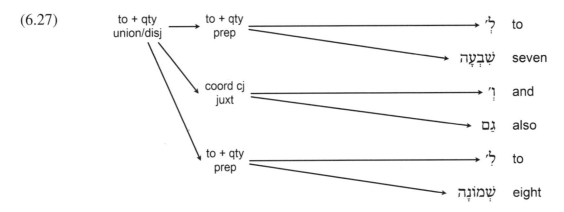

(6.27)

It is important to bear in mind that complex clauses allow for multiple acceptable parses. Consider phrase marker (6.28) from 2 Chr 21:17. The complex coordination phrase was parsed to yield a three-constituent structure P+P+P. One might argue with perhaps superior force that its final five segments form a natural substructure and should be gathered to form a distinct coordination phrase: בָּנָיו וְנָשָׁיו 'his sons and his wives'. Had we adopted this parse, the larger phrase would have had the two-constituent structure P+P. *The critical points are these*: In the building up of complex phrases, multiple equally valid parses are often possible. The consistency with which we have made parsing decisions, especially in forming elaborate constructions, is uncertain. Only with the use and adjustment of our database will consistent parsing of elaborate constructions finally be achieved.[13]

---

11. They are in Gen 6:4 and 14:7, Ezek 21:14, Qoh 11:2, Neh 2:18, 1 Chr 10:13, and 2 Chr 21:17.

12. These occur in 2 Kgs 24:3–4; Zech 9:1–2; Dan 11:22; Neh 6:14, 13:15; and 2 Chr 21:4.

13. The parsing of simple constructions should be fairly consistent, because these structures were created via computational methods and rarely have required adjusting by human over-readers. For a discussion of our approaches to

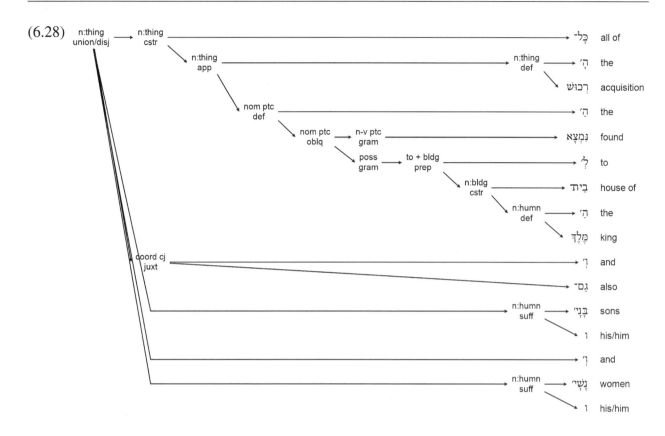

Note the presence of the not-uncommon phenomenon of *semantic heterogeneity*: the first constituent has "thing" semantics while the second and third have human semantics.

6.5.2 Complex Union or Disjoint Phrases

The number of constituents in a complex coordination phrase runs from 2 through 18. We will make no effort to catalog the union/disjoint phrases exhaustively. Rather, we will simply provide illustrative examples of the major subtypes.

As our example of an extended coordinated phrase, consider (6.29) (p. 78), a 5-constituent coordinated phrase from Gen 15:9 with the structure P+P+P+S+S.

The grand total of coordinated phrase subtypes possible for 2–18 constituents exceeds half a million.[14] Very few of these possibilities are realized. The table shows the subtypes attested for 10 constituents and higher in tree-structured union/disjoint phrase markers. Of the myriad possible coordinated phrase subtype patterns, only 17 are attested. Being rare, the large coordinated phrases only feebly sample the range of possibilities.

---

computational parsing, see F. I. Andersen and A. D. Forbes, "Opportune Parsing: Clause Analysis of Deuteronomy 8," in *Bible and Computer: Desk and Discipline* (Paris: Honoré Champion Éditeur, 1995) 49–75.

14. For the "numerically curious": the possible grand total is $2^{19} - 2^2 = 524,284$.

(6.29)

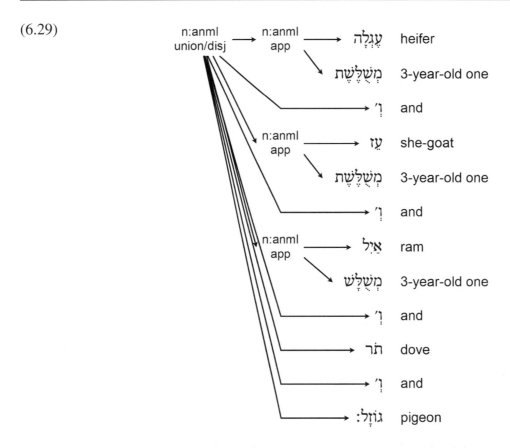

Number of Constituents	Possible Subtypes	Attested Subtypes	Number of Instances	Instance References
10	1,024	3	5	Gen 15:19–21; Num 3:36–37; 1 Chr 9:36–37; 2 Chr 4:19–22, 31:13
11	2,048	3	9	Gen 10:15–18; Exod 30:26–28; Josh 7:24, 15:48–51; 2 Sam 5:14–16; 1 Chr 1:13–16, 4:28–31, 8:22–25, 28:11–15
12	4,096	2	3	Josh 18:21–24; 1 Kgs 7:48–50; Jer 48:21–24
13	8,192	3	4	Gen 10:26–29; Josh 19:18–21; 1 Chr 1:20–23, 4:34–37
14	16,384	3	3	Josh 19:2–6; 1 Sam 30:27–31; 2 Sam 17:28–29
15	32,768	1	1	Exod 35:5–9 [pattern: $S(+S)^4+P(+S)^2(+P)^7$]
16	65,536	0	0	—
17	131,072	1	1	Josh 19:41–46 [pattern: $S(+S)^{15}+P$]
18	262,144	1	1	Exod 31:7–11 [pattern: $P(+P)^{17}$]

6.5.3 Complex Mixed Lists

There are far more ways to realize a mixed list involving constituents than there are ways to realize the corresponding union/disjunct construction or joined construction. The 6-constituent phrase marker (6.30) from Neh 9:8 is typical. Its pattern is P0P0P+P+P+P. Since only 647 instances of mixed phrases are attested in Biblical Hebrew, it is not surprising that few of the lengthy subtypes are attested and that of the subtypes attested, very few are seen more than once. The table at the bottom of the page shows the number of times that mixed lists of a given length are encountered. Basic and complex phrases are included.

(6.30)

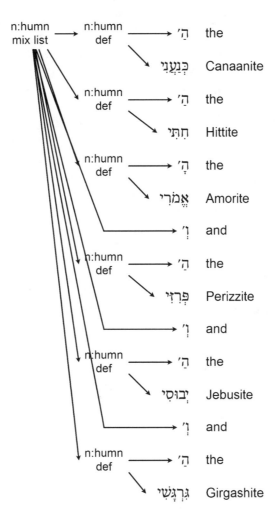

The four longest mixed lists are in 1 Chr 11:26–47 (45 constituents), Neh 10:15–28 (44 constituents), Exod 35:11–19 (41 constituents), and Exod 39:33–41 (41 constituents).

Child Count	Incidence	Child Count	Incidence
4	333	13	1
5	55	14	4
6	87	15	3
7	30	16	8
8	46	17	2
9	17	18	5
10	16	19	0
11	7	20	2
12	9	>20	22

6.5.4 Complex Joined Phrases

The final complex structurally defined conjoined phrase is the *joined phrase*. Recall that this is the type of complex phrase with constituents (at least one of them is itself a phrase and none of them is a conjunction) that gather to form a conjoined construction licensed by juxt. There are 806 of these phrases.

There is evidence that lengthy joined phrases achieve integrity through identity of contained constituent type (segment or phrase) and through identity of constituent structure labeling. For the 55 joined phrases having 5–35 constituents, we find:

1. With two exceptions, they are "monotypic." That is, they are either all segments or all phrases.[15]
2. For 40 of the 49 phrases (82%), the structure labeling is invariant. 70% of these invariant labels involve human semantics.

The 9 phrases exhibiting structure-label variation are an interesting group. For example, among the 25 seven-constituent or longer phrases, only Ps 148:7–12 exhibits variation. Here a joined vocative mostly consists of 'and'-joined pairs praising Yahweh: sea creatures and ocean depths, fire and hail, snow and cloud, mountains and hills, fruit trees and cedars, animals and cattle, creepers and birds, kings and peoples, princes and judges, young men and young women, elders *with* youths.

The incidences of complex joined phrases are as shown below.

Child Count	Incidence	Child Count	Incidence	Child Count	Incidence	Child Count	Incidence
2	594	6	8	10	2	14	1
3	122	7	5	11	4	31	2
4	47	8	0	12	2	32	1
5	17	9	0	13	0	35	1

The four longest complex joined phrases are in Ezra 2:43–54 (35 constituents), Neh 7:46–56 (32), Josh 12:9–24 (31), and 2 Sam 23:24–39 (31).

The 5-constituent phrase marker (6.31) (p. 81) from Josh 10:5 is typical of the complex joined phrases.

6.6 *Complex Semantically Defined Conjoined Phrases*

The distinctions between structurally defined and semantically defined conjoined phrases were presented in §5.6. There is no need to expand on the materials presented there.

6.6.1 Complex Echo Phrases

Basic echo phrases were discussed in some detail in §5.6.1. All we need to do here is provide a brief survey of complex echo phrases and show a parade example. We find 61 complex echo

---

15. In Neh 7:66, the 5-conjunct number "42,300" has the pattern SOSOSOSOP. In 2 Sam 23:32, the 18th conjunct is a segment, unlike the other 30 phrasal conjuncts. The parallel in 1 Chr 11:34 suggests that בֶּן 'son of' has been lost from the text of Samuel. Its restoration in 2 Sam 23:32 would recover the expected all-P pattern from the present very unusual POPOPOPOPOPOPOPOPOPOPOPOPOPOPOPOPOSOPOPOPOPOPOPOPOPOPOPOPOP pattern.

(6.31)

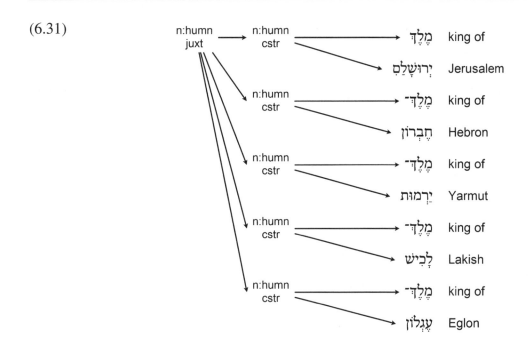

phrases in Biblical Hebrew. Fifty-two are represented by tree phrase markers and 9 by non-tree. There is only one complex triple echo, in Jer 7:4, as shown in phrase marker (6.32).

(6.32)

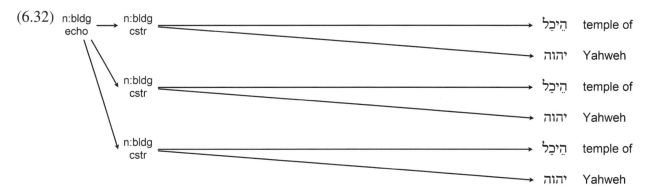

6.6.2   Complex Apposition Phrases

Apposition was introduced in §5.6.2. Below we provide the tallies for the apposition phrases classified by child count. Both tree and non–tree phrase markers are included.

Child Count	Complex	Basic
2	16,850	2,207
3	783	19

Child Count	Complex	Basic
4	77	0
5	14	0

Child Count	Complex	Basic
6	3	0

Many of the complex apposition phrases include nominalized constituents, be they nominalized clauses (nom/nom), nominalized infinitives (nom inf/oblq), or noun-verb participles (nom ptc/oblq). Nominalized constructions are not discussed in this book until chap. 8. We expect that readers will grasp the following material nevertheless. If not, they should consult the glossary or sample chap. 8 and then return to this point. Phrase marker (6.33) from Prov 21:24 shows a phrase-terminal nominalized clause.

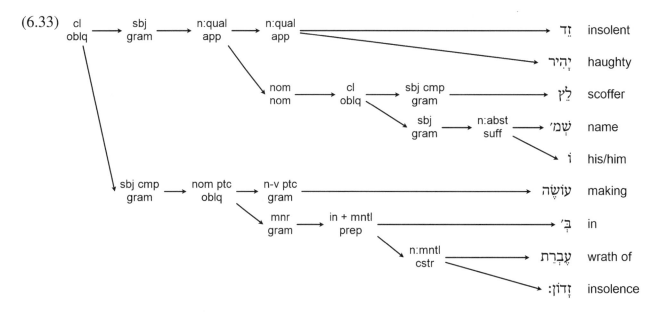

As the following figures reveal, nominalized constituents have a strong tendency to come at the end of complex apposition phrases.

Child Count	Number Initial	Number Terminal
2	56	4,097
3	3	288
4	0	26
5	0	4
6	0	1
2–6	59	4,416

In Biblical Hebrew, nominalized constituents in complex apposition phrases are almost 75 times more likely to be phrase-terminal than to be phrase-initial.

When addressed at all, the traditional treatment of constructions such as we are examining here is to make a general statement (to the effect that nominalized constituents in apposition phrases [almost always] come at the end of the phrase), provide a few examples, and leave the matter. Having all of the data analyzed allows us to investigate atypical instances and question why they are the way they are: are the exceptions clustered in the text; does their incidence seem to be controlled by identifiable factors; is their occurrence associated with genre; is it random?

Phrase marker (6.34) from 1 Kgs 7:48 shows a nominalized clause (nom/nom) followed by a single segment in apposition to the definite phrase (n:furn/def) leading off the apposition trio. Why is this phrase structured this way? We note that 1 Kings has the largest number of these atypical instances of any book—seven in all.

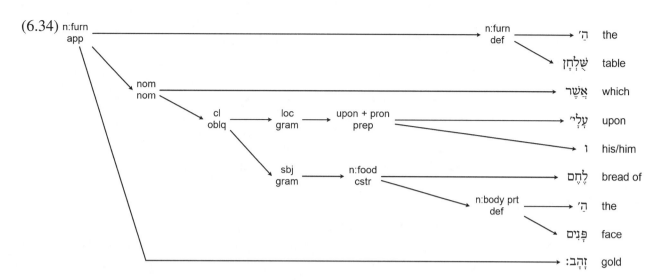

6.6.3 Strictly Subsetting Phrases

The final trio of related complex phrases consists of:

1. strictly subsetting phrases (210×),
2. strictly supersetting phrases (185×),
3. nested phrases (16×).

These phrase types are investigational and are to date incompletely identified in our phrase markers.[16] Whether they prove worth completing or whether they should revert to structurally defined phrase types remains to be seen. They are semantic replacements for the union/disjoint, mixed list, and joined phrase types, relying on the hypernym/hyponym (superclass/subclass) distinction. A strictly subsetting phrase is made up of constituents the order of which runs from most general to least. In this type of phrase, hyponym follows hypernym. For example, the first constituent of phrase marker (6.35) from Gen 24:10 specifies the *land*, and the second specifies the *city*, a subset of the former. Num 9:11 has a three-child subsetting consisting of *month*, *day*, and *time of day* ("evening").

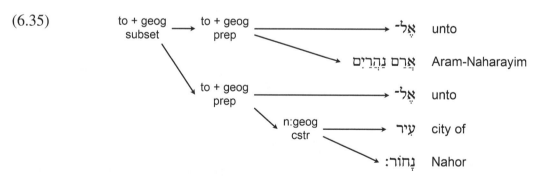

6.6.4 Strictly Supersetting Phrases

In strictly supersetting phrases, hypernym follows hyponym. The order runs from least general to most. Phrase marker (6.36) from Judg 10:1 conveys the structure. Here, *city* precedes *region*.

---

16. Hence the counts provided above are tentative at best.

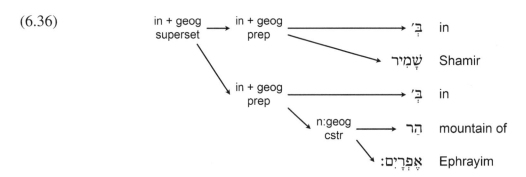

6.6.5 Nested Phrases

When there are three or more immediate phrasal constituents, the constituents might form a hypernym/hyponym set, but the ordering may be neither subsetting nor supersetting. We refer to these phrases as *nested*. Phrase marker (6.37) from Deut 34:6 shows this sort of structure. Here we have *valley, land, city*—a non-monotonic sequence.

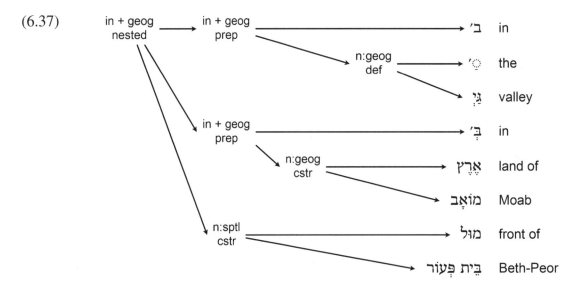

6.7 *Brief Summary*

Complex Phrases.   A complex phrase involves more than one licensing relation. This chapter provides a census, with example phrase markers, of the various kinds of complex phrases attested in Biblical Hebrew.

Complex Tight Phrases.   Unlike the very rare complex suffixed phrases (10×) and the few bizarre complex definite phrases (8×), there are many "well-formed" complex definite phrases (1,107×), the great majority involving noun-verb participles (89%).

Complex Unconjoined Phrases.   Complex unconjoined phrases are of *five* sorts: prepositional phrases ("from the Levite"), construct phrases ("two-of sons-of Jacob"), modification phrases ("priest-of Yahweh in Shiloh"), inverted modification phrases ("hundred talent-of silver"), and bonded substantives ("neck and not face").

Complex Structurally Defined Conjoined Phrases.   Taking up complex structurally defined conjoined phrases lands us in a combinatoric nightmare since there are a great many possible combinations of segments, phrases, and connectives. In practice, however, few are realized. As with basic structurally defined conjoined phrases, there are three sorts: union phrases ("heifer three-year-old one and she-goat three-year-old one"), mixed lists ("the Canaanite, the Hittite, the Amorite, and the Perizzite"), and juxtaposed lists ("king of Jerusalem, king of Hebron, king of Yarmut, king of Lakish, king of Eglon").

Complex Semantically Defined Conjoined Phrases.   Complex semantically defined conjoined phrases are of five sorts: echo phrases ("Temple of Yahweh, Temple of Yahweh, Temple of Yahweh"), apposition phrases ("David the king"), strictly subsetting phrases ("in the year the second, in the month the second, in twenty in the month"), strictly supersetting phrases ("in day of twenty and four to the month, in the sixth, in year of two to Darius the king"), and nested phrases ("in the month the first, in the year the second, in one to the month").

Chapter 7

Main Clauses

We expound on clauses by characterizing and providing examples of main clauses (chap. 7) and embedded clauses (chap. 8).

7.1 *The Clause*

7.1.1 Our Previous References to the Clause

Assuming that readers came to our book with a serviceable concept of the clause, we have already used the word clause about 180 times. We have now reached the point where we can and should explain what we mean by a clause. Our glossary entry for clause reads:

> *clause*—Typically, a syntactic unit that includes a predicator and the clause immediate constituents that accompany it. In Biblical Hebrew, a subject plus some other constituent[s] can constitute a clause that has no predicator (traditionally called "nominal"; in recent literature, "verbless" or "nonverbal").[1]

There is characteristically a need to define the foundational terms of an area using other foundational terms from the same area. This is due to the fact that the terms together form an interrelated system. For example, readers who looked up our glossary entry for clause, provided above, may have felt the need to consult a fair number of additional glossary entries: predicator, verbal, quasiverbal, clause immediate constituent, constituent, subject, segment, and so on.

7.1.2 Definitions of "Clause" in the Literature

We see the interrelated-system phenomenon also in the definitions of the clause offered in traditional books on the syntax of Biblical Hebrew:

> A clause normally consists of a subject and a predicate. Depending on whether the predicate is a noun or a verb, a clause is said to be *nominal* or *verbal.*[2]

> In this grammar a clause is regarded as a meaningful series of words that has a subject and a predicate.[3]

---

1. As shown in chap. 19, some "clauses" lack both predicators and subjects! The terms in underlined Eurostile in our definition have all been introduced by now, so our definition should be intelligible to readers.

2. Paul Joüon and T. Muraoka, *A Grammar of Biblical Hebrew* (rev. Eng. ed.; Rome: Pontifical Biblical Institute, 2006) 525.

3. Christo H. J. van der Merwe, Jackie A. Naudé, and Jan H. Kroeze, *A Biblical Hebrew Reference Grammar* (Sheffield: Sheffield Academic Press, 1999) 355.

A clause is a set of words with a subject, a predicate, and any words that modify them. The subject or predicate can be implied rather than stated, and the modifiers can be absent.[4]

We also observe the interrelated-system phenomenon in reference works on general linguistics:

clause A clause is a phrase that includes a predicate and all of its arguments and modifiers.[5]

clause (n.) A term used in some models of grammar to refer to a unit of grammatical organization smaller than the sentence, but larger than phrases, words, or morphemes.[6]

clause . . . Any constituent dominated by the initial symbol S, particularly one which forms part of a larger structure. Clauses are conventionally divided into main clauses and subordinate clauses.[7]

None of these definitions inclines us to alter our glossary definition, given above.

7.1.3 Concepts Relevant to Clause Characterization

What is needed, however, is the explanation, integration, and extension of a concept that was mentioned previously with its discussion deferred until now: *configurational* versus *nonconfigurational languages* (mentioned in §1.3.3, Item #3, p. 12). We now take up this concept, discussing its relation to the classification and characterization of the clauses and clause immediate constituents of Biblical Hebrew.

7.2 *Configurational versus Nonconfigurational Languages*

According to Crystal, configurational languages have "a fairly fixed word-order and hierarchical constituent structure"[8] while nonconfigurational languages exhibit "fairly free word-order and seemingly 'flat' constituent structure."[9] The distinction was introduced into linguistics by Kenneth Hale.[10] As David Golumbia convincingly argues,[11] the existence of nonconfigurational languages represented a serious impediment to the transformationalists' quest for Universal Grammar. As a result, the nature and frequency of nonconfigurational languages were and remain contentious areas of research. In the following subsections, we will answer two questions:

1. Is Biblical Hebrew a nonconfigurational language?
2. If it is nonconfigurational, what difference does this make to syntactic description?

---

4. Ronald J. Williams and John C. Beckman, *Williams' Hebrew Syntax* (3rd ed.; Toronto: University of Toronto Press, 2007) 172.

5. Ivan A. Sag, Thomas Wasow, and Emily M. Bender, *Syntactic Theory: A Formal Introduction* (2nd ed.; Stanford, CA: CSLI, 2003) 557.

6. David Crystal, *A Dictionary of Linguistics and Phonetics* (5th ed.; Oxford: Blackwell, 2003) 74.

7. Robert L. Trask, *A Dictionary of Grammatical Terms* (London: Routledge, 1993) 44. This definition strikes us as minimally helpful.

8. Crystal, *A Dictionary*, 95.

9. Ibid., 315. Elsewhere (p. 182), Crystal explains that "sentences have a flat structure if they lack the [noun phrase–verb phrase] configuration."

10. Kenneth Hale, "Warlpiri and the grammar of non-configurational languages," *Natural Language and Linguistic Theory* 1 (1983) 5–47.

11. David Golumbia, "The interpretation of nonconfigurationality," *Language and Community* 24 (2004) 1–22.

Hale characterized nonconfigurational languages as involving: "(i) free word order, (ii) the use of syntactically discontinuous expressions, (iii) extensive use of null anaphora."[12]

The data discussed below indicate to us that Biblical Hebrew exhibits Hale's three defining characteristics. Saying this, however, does not mean that we accept any "non-configurationality program." Givón has registered important cautions regarding "so-called non-configurationality."[13]

7.2.1 Free Word Order?

Crystal makes the difference between fixed and free word-order languages quite clear: "Fairly fixed word-order" languages "rely on word-order as a means of expressing grammatical relationships within constructions."[14] Crystal's distinction can be refined by accepting Steinberger's observation that "[m]ost languages known as *free word order languages* are in fact languages with *partially free word order* . . . , or rather *free phrase order*. . . ."[15]

Does Biblical Hebrew exhibit partially free phrase order, or in our parlance, *partially free CIC order*? Let us first consider a concrete example and then examine the ordering of the three major clause constituents across all of Biblical Hebrew.

7.2.1.1 The Ordering of S, V, O, and B ("Beneficiary") CICs in עשׂה Clauses

When we search Biblical Hebrew for all clauses containing a subject (S), a direct object (O), a "beneficiary" CIC (B), and an עשׂה-based finite verb (V), we find 21 clauses.[16] In the table below, we provide an example of each of the eight different orderings of S, V, O, and B attested.

Pattern							Citation[a]
V		S		O		B		Num 6:11
V		S		B		O		Gen 3:11
V		B		S		O		Josh 5:3
O		V		S	ind obj	B	src	2 Chr 4:16
O		V		B		S		2 Sam 7:11
V		B		O		S	loc	Neh 8:16
S	neg	V	tm int	O		B		Exod 36:6
S	voc	V		B		O		Ezek 12:3

a. Each verb-initial clause shown involves a sequential finite verb. The interpolated constituents represented in lowercase are: neg = negative, voc = vocative, tm int = time interval, ind obj = indirect object, src = source of supply, and loc = location (see the glossary for definitions).

---

12. Hale, "Warlpiri and the grammar of non-configurational languages," 5. More-recent references characterize *configurational* languages along complementary lines. For example, Trask (*A Dictionary*, 55–56) asserts that configurational languages "are usually characterized by fairly rigid word order and by the infrequency of discontinuous constituents."

13. Talmy Givón, *Syntax: An Introduction* (rev. ed.; Amsterdam: Benjamins, 2001) 279–83.

14. Crystal, *A Dictionary*, 503.

15. Ralf Steinberger, "Treating 'Free Word Order' in Machine Translation," *Proceedings of the 15th Conference on Computational Linguistics* (Stroudsburg, PA: Association for Computational Linguistics, 1994) 69.

16. We dismiss from consideration a clause in 1 Sam 20:2 purporting to have the pattern "loc B V S O" because the beneficiary CIC is forced due to our use of the *Kethiv* text.

Out of a possible 24 permutations of 4 constituent types, only 8 are attested. Three of the 4 constituents are attested at each clause position. This example exhibits partial free CIC ordering.

7.2.1.2 The Ordering of S, V, O in the Clauses of Biblical Hebrew

Next, consider the ordering of S, V, and O across all of the clauses of Biblical Hebrew.[17]

SVO	VSO	OSV
2,420 (33.5%)	3,085 (42.7%)	166 (2.3%)
SOV	VOS	OVS
145 (2.0%)	1,043 (14.4%)	364 (5.0%)

For these data, the oft-repeated assertion that Biblical Hebrew is a VSO language is an insufficient description. The VSO sequence occurs in only 43% of the clauses containing an S, a V, and an O.

In passing, consider ordering in the subset of these sorts of clauses having *unanchored predicators* (see §11.2). For these, our tallies yield:

SVO	VSO	OSV
2,387 (44.8%)	1,611 (30.2%)	166 (3.1%)
SOV	VOS	OVS
143 (2.7%)	662 (12.4%)	364 (6.8%)

These clauses are predicator initial ("V-initial") 43% of the time.[18]

Biblical Hebrew *does* exhibit substantial free CIC ordering.[19] Hale's characteristic (i), "free word order," is true of Biblical Hebrew.

7.2.2 Syntactically Discontinuous Expressions?

In §4.2, the third of the four conditions that a tree-structured phrase marker must obey was:

3. *Non-tangling Condition.*   Edges may not cross.

When edges are tangled (i.e., when they *inescapably* cross one another), then the underlying constituents are said to exhibit discontinuity.[20] Every phrase marker shown until now, with one exception, has been a tree and has not exhibited tangling.[21] This is because we have selected phrase markers to make it so. But, consider phrase marker (7.1) from Ruth 1:1b.

At issue here is the extent of the subject of the clause. There is concord between the finite verb segment יֵלֶךְ and the following segment אִישׁ, which clearly is at least part of the subject. The problem is what to do with the trailing coordinate phrase: הוּא וְאִשְׁתּוֹ וּשְׁנֵי בָנָיו. The segment הוּא in

---

17. In obtaining these tallies, we set aside indirect objects, complements, objects and subjects of address, and peripheral elements. See §11.3.2.5.

18. When we examine clauses with an unanchored predicator plus either a subject or an object, initial-predicator incidence increases substantially. The VO sequence occurs in 80% of cases, and the VS sequence occurs in 62% of cases.

19. We say more about all this in §11.3, where we take up *positional syntax.*

20. For example, in the clause "Wake him up," one analysis takes the finite verb "wake up" to be rendered discontinuous by the interposed direct object "him."

21. Because of imperfections in graphic layout, some phrase markers contain edges that cross one another but that would not do so were the layout better. The single tangled phrase marker is at the end of §3.2.4, phrase marker (3.6).

this coordinate phrase is co-referential with אִישׁ, and so they might each be given an index to indicate identity of reference, yielding אִישׁ$_i$ and הוּא$_i$. This is a standard technique for identifying items without having to introduce crossing edges. But the coordinate phrase ("he and his wife and his two sons") is *not* co-referential with אִישׁ, so this simple artifice is not immediately available. Since we are not constrained to use only trees for our phrase markers, we rely on tangling in situations such as this. We dominate both אִישׁ and הוּא וְאִשְׁתּוֹ וּשְׁנֵי בָנָיו with a node showing that they combine to form a noun phrase having human semantics, the semantic licensing relation between the two dominated constituents being that of superset (n:humn / superset). That is to say, הוּא וְאִשְׁתּוֹ וּשְׁנֵי בָנָיו refers to a superset of the referent of אִישׁ. Note that we have relied on semantic relations in the formation of our phrase markers.

(7.1)

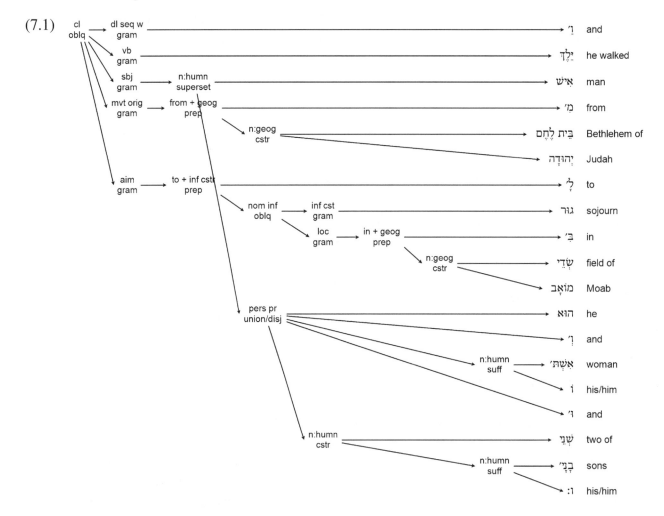

In addition to the introduction of indexation, other strategies for avoiding overt representation of discontinuity have been devised over the years. Chomsky introduced "a second level of description defined by transformations to account for facts which his predecessors had employed discontinuity to handle."[22] Another avoidance strategy "assumes that noncontiguous syntactic elements cannot form a syntactic constituent, although they may be mapped onto a semantic representation

22. Geoffrey J. Huck and A. E. Ojeda, *Syntax and Semantics: Discontinuous Constituency* (Orlando, FL: Academic, 1987) 3.

in which their translations form a unit."[23] Our approach strives to supply a What-You-See-Is-What-You-Get representation, avoiding these sorts of multiple levels of representation.

Discontinuity is also associated with a second phenomenon: distributed apposition, wherein a later constituent is in apposition to two or more earlier constituents considered *together*. Consider the direct object clause immediate constituent (CIC) in (7.2) from 1 Sam 31:2.

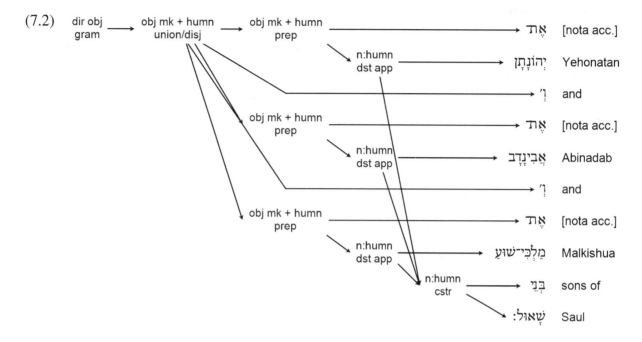

The referent of 'Yehonatan', 'Abinadab', and 'Malkishua' *taken together* is 'sons of Saul'. The resulting constituents transgress the tangling condition.[24] Syntactic representation of Biblical Hebrew involves discontinuous constituents. For a table showing the relative incidence of discontinuity as a function of licensing relation, see §20.1.2. There we see that discontinuity occurs in 9.8% of the instances of "interruptable constituents."[25] Hale's characteristic (ii), "the use of syntactically discontinuous expressions," is true of Biblical Hebrew.

7.2.3 Null Anaphora?

According to Hale, the third characteristic of nonconfigurational languages is "extensive use of null anaphora," by which he refers "to constructions in which an argument (i.e., subject or object of a verb) is not represented by an overt nominal expression in [Phrase Structure]."[26]

---

23. Ibid., 5.

24. Since the n:humn / cstr node has three mother nodes, this phrase marker also disobeys the *Single-Mother Condition* for trees: *any non-root node has only one mother.* In Biblical Hebrew, distributed apposition is uncommon but real. It occurs 155 times.

25. The following licensing relations intrinsically do not permit discontinuity: *definite, preposition, suffixation,* and (with 9 exceptions) *construct.*

26. As reported by Golumbia, "The interpretation," 6.

7.2.3.1 Null Subjects

With regard to the subject, there is no question that Biblical Hebrew exhibits extensive null anaphora since it "is a prototypical example of a *pro-drop language.*"[27] As Cote puts it: "[I]n languages with 'strong' inflection, the subject case may be absorbed by the inflective morphology, eliminating the need for an overt subject."[28] This phenomenon is very common in Biblical Hebrew. For example, we find 2,272 clauses in Biblical Hebrew that consist of only a finite verb. In this book, phrase markers for clauses lacking overt subjects are, among others, (3.2), (4.2), (4.9), and (5.3). Recall that our definition of clause does not stipulate that it must include an overt subject.

7.2.3.2 Null Objects

Non-overt direct objects in Biblical Hebrew do exist. Consider the case of עֲשׂוּ. This imperative verb form occurs 30 times in Biblical Hebrew, 21 times with a direct object. Thus, it is typically transitive. Four times the clause in which the imperative occurs involves a <u>comparison</u> (Gen 19:8; Jer 26:14, 50:15, 50:29), and three times the imperative is part of a set expression (Hag 2:4; 2 Chr 19:7, 19:11), וַחֲזַק . . . וַעֲשׂוּ "be strong and do!" (twice) and שִׁמְרוּ וַעֲשׂוּ "keep and do!" (once). The remaining two instances (2 Sam 3:18 and 1 Kgs 18:25) involve non-overt direct objects. Consider phrase marker (7.3) from 1 Kgs 18:25.

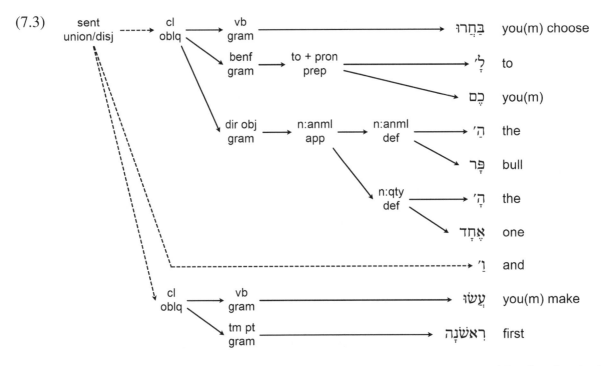

In the second clause, it is "the one bull" that Elijah commands the prophets of Baal to "make," even though this is not evident from the phrase marker as presently configured.[29]

---

27. Robert D. Holmstedt, *The Relative Clause in Biblical Hebrew: A Linguistic Analysis* (Ph.D. diss., Univ. of Wisconsin, 2002) 185–86. According to Trask, *A Dictionary*, 219: "pro-drop . . . The phenomenon in which an argument position of a verb, particularly subject position, can be left empty."

28. Sharon A. Cote, *Grammatical and Discourse Properties of Null-Arguments in English* (Ph.D. diss., University of Pennsylvania, 1996) 10.

29. In chap. 20, we will see that drawing an edge from the lower cl / oblq up to dir obj / gram encodes this situation but violates the *Single-Mother Condition* (since dir obj / gram will have two mothers), making the phrase marker a graph.

Perhaps a second example will prove helpful. Consider phrase marker (7.4) for Ps 78:21a.

(7.4)

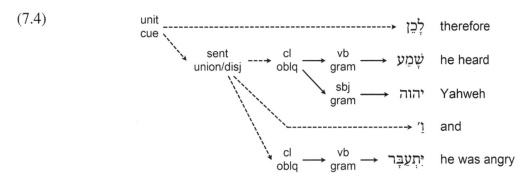

The suffixed Qal active verb שָׁמַע is transitive in a little over one-third of its occurrences (transitive 28 times out of 74 occurrences). When transitive, it is usually translated 'he heard'; when it is intransitive, it is often translated 'he listened'. In Ps 78:21a above, it is (properly) translated as transitive, even though there is no overt direct object. The antecedent of the non-overt direct object is the accusation that the people spoke against יהוה in vv. 19 and 20:

הֲיוּכַל אֵל לַעֲרֹךְ שֻׁלְחָן בַּמִּדְבָּר׃ הֵן הִכָּה־צוּר וַיָּזוּבוּ מַיִם

וּנְחָלִים יִשְׁטֹפוּ הֲגַם־לֶחֶם יוּכַל תֵּת אִם־יָכִין שְׁאֵר לְעַמּוֹ׃

Since there is extensive use of null anaphora in Biblical Hebrew, Hale's characteristic (iii), "extensive use of null anaphora," is met.

There is considerable evidence that "languages exhibit different mixtures of morphological and / or structural marking of functional information, yielding a continuous scale along the dimension of (non-)configurationality."[30] Since all three of Hale's characteristics are found, we conclude that Biblical Hebrew is, to some yet-to-be-determined extent, a nonconfigurational language. Where Biblical Hebrew lies on the nonconfigurationality gradient is a topic for research.

That Biblical Hebrew exhibits each of the characteristics of nonconfigurational languages has implications for the way that we represent and describe the constituents making up clauses.

7.2.4   Implications of Free Phrase Order

Given that Biblical Hebrew exhibits some free CIC order, the topic of constituent order is much broader than is the case for configurational languages. We take up *constituent order* in chap. 11.

7.2.5   Implications of Representing Discontinuity

Discontinuity throws up technical challenges when it comes to storing and searching the resulting phrase markers. These issues are beyond the scope of this book and have, in any case, already been dealt with by the database implementers. Because the tree conditions listed in §4.2 are violated, we are required to decide which phenomena we will represent via non–tree phrase markers. See chap. 20.

---

30. Anette Frank, "Projecting LFG F-Structure from Chunks—or (Non-)Configurationality from a Different Point of View," *Proc LFG03 Conference* (2003) 217–37; on the web at http://cslipublications.stanford.edu/LFG/8/lfg03.pdf. See also Carl Pollard and Ivan A. Sag, *Information-Based Syntax and Semantics*, vol. 1: *Fundamentals* (Stanford, CA: CSLI, 1987) 188.

7.2.6 Implications of Null Anaphora

The existence of null anaphora affects both the theory and terminology that we adopt for describing clause immediate constituents (CICs), as will be seen in chaps. 9 and 10.

7.3 *Complements and Adjuncts*

We conclude this chapter by turning to the distinction between clausal complements and adjuncts.

7.3.1 The Standard Definitions

We begin by introducing the distinction between complements and adjuncts. A common partitioning of CICs is embodied in these definitions from van der Merwe, Naudé, and Kroeze: [31]

> Complement . . . this term refers to an obligatory element in a construction. On the syntactic level complements refer to obligatory, non-omissible, non-verbal parts of the predicate or verb phrase (VP).
>
> Adjunct . . . The term . . . refers to an optional or secondary element in a construction. On the syntactic level adjuncts refer to optional, omissible, non-verbal elements in the predicate or verb phrase (VP).

The definitions provided by Waltke and O'Connor assert a similar contrast: [32]

> [Complement:] an element in a grammatical construction that completes the predicate, notable types being objects and some adverbials.
>
> [Adjunct:] an optional or less important element in a grammatical construction, notable groups of adjuncts being adverbs and some prepositional phrases.

How these four definitions, plus additional definitions supplied by four linguistics authorities, [33] characterize the complement-adjunct distinction is summarized in the following table.

Authority	*Complements Obligatory?*	*Reference to Predicate?*	*Distinction Made Specific?*
van der Merwe et al.	Yes	Yes	No
Waltke and O'Connor	Yes	Yes	No
Crystal	Yes	Yes	No
Matthews	Yes	Yes	No
Trask	Not All	Yes	No
Pollard and Sag	Not All	Yes	Attempted

The consensus is that:

1. Complements are obligatory.
2. The domain of complements and adjuncts is the predicate.

---

31. Van der Merwe, Naudé, and Kroeze, *Biblical Hebrew Reference Grammar*, 355.

32. Waltke and O'Connor, *IBHS*, 690 and 689. Elsewhere (p. 163), they observe that "a strict delimitation [between complement and adjunct] is not possible."

33. Crystal, *A Dictionary*, 88 and 11. P. H. Matthews, *Oxford Concise Dictionary of Linguistics* (Oxford: Oxford University Press, 2005) 63 and 8. Trask, *A Dictionary*, 51 and 8. Pollard and Sag, *Information-Based Syntax*, 134–39.

3. The distinction between complements and adjuncts is, in practice, vague.

We now discuss our reservations about each of these assertions.

7.3.2   Optional Complements

The existence of null objects in Biblical Hebrew (§7.2.3.2) renders the *obligatoriness* assertion inexact. Optionality has been commented on in more-general contexts. For example, in a book section entitled "Optional Complements," Pollard and Sag observe that "[c]ertain complements are associated with semantic roles that are *ontologically necessary*, so that even when the complement in question is not overtly expressed, the situation described must be one where some object plays the role in question."[34] The usual clause used to exemplify ontological necessity is "He ate." Something must have been eaten, even if its nature is not explicit in the clause. *In Biblical Hebrew, complements may be optional.*

7.3.3   The Domain of Complements and Adjuncts

In §1.3.3, Item #5 (p. 12), we retired the concept of "verb phrase" but not the concept of predicate. It is the invariant practice of writers explaining complements and adjuncts to locate their domain in the predicate portion of the clause. The critical observation for our purposes, however, is this: in nonconfigurational languages such as Biblical Hebrew, a predicate construction is not useful in the way that it is for configurational languages. This is because "in [Biblical Hebrew] we have an example of a language in which sbj and obj are rather similar to the same concept in more familiar languages, but cannot be distinguished in terms of being part of a VP complement."[35] As remarked in §7.2, nonconfigurational languages have phrase markers, the top levels of which are flat structures. In them, it is not helpful to analyze a clause into an NP subject and a VP predicate. As a result, we assert: *for Biblical Hebrew, the domain of complements and adjuncts is the clause.*[36]

7.3.4   Making the Complement-Adjunct Distinction Specific

Most texts vaguely describe adjuncts as being "secondary to" or "less important than" complements. They do not provide operational diagnostics for distinguishing complements from adjuncts. One exception to this nonspecificity is provided by Pollard and Sag.[37] They give "a number of rough-and-ready syntactic and semantic diagnostics which usually serve to make the distinction" between complements and adjuncts. Here, *in their own words*, are their diagnostics:

1. *Order-dependence of content*: The contribution of adjuncts to semantic content can depend upon their relative order in a way that does not apply to optional complements.[38]
2. *Constancy of semantic contribution*: In general, a given adjunct can occur with a relatively broad range of [verbs] while seeming to make a more-or-less uniform contribution to

---

34. Ibid., 132–34. See also Kordula De Kuthy and W. Ditmar Meurers, "Dealing with Optional Complements in HPSG-Based Grammar Implementations," *Proc. HPSG2003 Conf.*, 88–96.

35. Y. N. Falk, *Lexical-Functional Grammar: An Introduction to Parallel Constraint-Based Syntax* (Stanford, CA: CSLI, 2001) 21. *We have replaced "Wambaya" in the quotation with "Biblical Hebrew."*

36. With regard to complements and adjuncts, however, the clause can be usefully—up to a point—subdivided into a nucleus, a core, and a periphery. See §11.3.2 and §19.2.

37. Carl Pollard and Ivan A. Sag, *Information-Based Syntax*, 135–39.

38. Idem, adjunct examples: "Kim jogs reluctantly twice a day" versus "Kim jogs twice a day reluctantly." Optional complement examples: "Kim complained about the neighbors to the landlord" versus "Kim complained to the landlord about the neighbors."

semantic content across that range. A given optional complement, by contrast, is typically limited in its distribution to co-occurrence with a small (and often semantically restricted) class of [verbs] (possibly even a single item).[39]

3. *Iterability*: In general, two or more instances of the same adjunct type can occur with the same [verb], but this is impossible for complements.[40]
4. *Relative order*: In English, some adjuncts tend to be ordered after complements.[41]
5. *Possibility of internal gaps*:[42] At least some adjuncts appear to generally disallow unbounded internal traces. . . . Complements, by contrast, generally allow internal gaps.[43]

Note that practical application of these diagnostics presupposes that one has reliable methods for judging "contribution to semantic content" and sufficient data to assess patterns of occurrence "in general." While it might be possible to devise methods for judging "contribution to semantic content," the amount of data available for Biblical Hebrew is limited. Hence, statistically significant inferences about complements versus adjuncts are limited. For example, of the 1,573 verb lexemes in our dictionary for Biblical Hebrew, 1,007 occur 10 times or fewer times. Given so few instances, reliable inferences will not be possible for two-thirds of the verb lexemes. We will be able to make robust inferences for the verb lexemes that appear frequently, and this may be sufficient. One hundred fourteen of the verb lexemes (7.2%) occur more than 100 times. For these, it should be possible to investigate the complement-adjunct distinction reliably.

7.4   *An Alert regarding "Marginal Analyses"*

The second table of §7.2.1.2 is reproduced below. It was presented above to make the point that—for unanchored verbs across the totality of Biblical Hebrew—the grammatical function sequence VSO is *not* preferred over the SVO sequence but, rather, the reverse is true:

SVO	VSO	OSV
2,387 (44.8%)	1,611 (30.2%)	166 (3.1%)
SOV	VOS	OVS
143 (2.7%)	662 (12.4%)	364 (6.8%)

The examination of the GF sequence might have gone further. We might have searched out the factors that affect the sequences observed. To dig deeper into the GF-ordering puzzle, we might next have inquired whether *text type* had any effect on GF ordering. We might have tallied, as a function

---

39. Adjunct example: "Kim camps / jogs / meditates on the hill." Optional complement example: "Kim depends / relies on Sandy."

40. Adjunct example: "Kim and Sandy met in Baltimore in the lobby of the Hyatt in July." Optional complement negative example: "*Yes we have no bananas, pineapples."

41. Adjunct example: "Butch apologized to his computational ichthyology seminar because coelocanths were undecidable." Optional complement negative example: "*Butch apologized because coelocanths were undecidable to his computational ichthyology seminar."

42. Trask, *A Dictionary*, 114: "*gap* . . . A location in a sentence in which no element is overtly present even though some element appears to be in some sense grammatically required."

43. Adjunct negative example: "*Which endangered species did Sandy meet someone [fond of __]?" Complement example: "Which endangered species did Kim impress you as being most [fond of __]?"

of gross text type, the incidence of clauses found to be subject-initial, predicator-initial, or object-initial. This would have led to a table of the sort shown below.

Gross Text Type	Subject-Initial	Predicator-Initial	Object-Initial	Row Total
Narrative	367	386	104	857
Human-to-human speech	812	583	165	1,560
Human-to-God speech	312	200	49	561
Divine speech	768	512	123	1,403
Column Total	2,259	1,681	441	4,381

We would observe, for narrative, that initial-subject clauses are slightly outnumbered by initial-predicator clauses but that, for the other three text types, the initial-subject clauses outnumber the initial-predicator clauses by significant amounts.[44] Further exploration would be called for to determine why this should be.

Usually in this book, we reduce the complexity of the situations being described in order to simplify exposition. This is standard practice when one is doing "exploratory data analysis," as we are in general. To probe our data fully would have unduly expanded and delayed the publication of this volume. Readers are urged to keep this author-imposed limitation in mind and encouraged to view it as an invitation to further research.

7.5 *Brief Summary*

Our Definition of "Clause."   Our definition of clause stands up well when compared with those found in grammars of Biblical Hebrew and in reference works on general linguistics.

On Nonconfigurationality.   Biblical Hebrew meets all three of Hale's characteristics of nonconfigurational languages: free phrase order, use of discontinuous constituents, and frequent use of null anaphora. Free phrase order is seen across the corpus, especially when unanchored predicators are involved. Discontinuity occurs about 10% of the time in constituents where it is admissible. And, Biblical Hebrew, being a pro-drop language, exhibits frequent null anaphora.

Complements and Adjuncts.   The distinction between complements and adjuncts is vague but useful if one allows complements to be optional, as we do—contrary to the usual definition. Ways of making the distinction semirigorous have been proposed but have not yet been successful.

Marginal Analyses.   We are all-too-well aware that some readers will be frustrated by our not examining the influences of potentially relevant explanatory variables on the phenomena described in this volume.

---

44. Technical note: This impression is validated by contingency table analysis. For narrative, the standardized residuals for initial-subject clauses are significantly positive, while individuals for the initial-predicator clauses are significantly negative (chi-squared test with 6 degrees of freedom and at the 99% confidence level).

Chapter 8

Embedded Clauses

In chap. 7, we focused on *main clauses*. Here, we take up four kinds of embedded clause:

1. nominalized clauses (with and without אֲשֶׁר),
2. clausal complements,
3. subordinated clauses,
4. clause-like structures.

8.1 *Nominalized Clauses*

A few of the phrase markers shown thus far contain embedded nominalized clause constituents, identified by their telltale dominating nom / nom nodes. See phrase markers (3.1), (3.4), (3.5), (3.10), (6.1), (6.6), (6.33), and (6.34).

8.1.1 The Representation of Nominalized Clauses

In Biblical Hebrew, we find 6,873 nominalized clauses.[1] They divide into two groups:

Group #1: clauses preceded by an overt nominalizer, usually אֲשֶׁר,[2]
Group #2: clauses not preceded by an overt nominalizer.[3]

The constituent in (8.1) from Gen 3:1 shows a Group #1 nominalized clause (hence, marked by a preceding אֲשֶׁר). Note that our practice is to place the אֲשֶׁר outside the embedded clause. We view אֲשֶׁר as an operator[4] that nominalizes a following clause or sentence.[5]

---

1. We studied simple nominalizer incidence in Francis I. Andersen and A. Dean Forbes, " 'Prose Particle' Counts in the Hebrew Bible," in *The Word of the Lord Shall Go Forth: Essays in Honor of David Noel Freedman in Celebration of His Sixtieth Birthday* (ed. Carol L. Meyers and M. O'Connor; Winona Lake, IN: Eisenbrauns, 1983) 165–83.

2. R. D. Holmstedt, *The Relative Clause in Biblical Hebrew* (Ph.D. diss., University of Wisconsin, 2002) addresses clauses introduced by segments other than אֲשֶׁר (e.g., -זוּ, זוֹ, זֶה, הַ, and -שֶׁ), a topic that we do not take up except for -הַ as a nominalizer (§6.3.2.2). These alternate nominalizers are marked and hence searchable but are not discussed by us (see §3.2.1.1).

3. This would be referred to as the "null relative word case" by Holmstedt, *The Relative Clause*, v.

4. R. L. Trask, *A Dictionary of Grammatical Terms* (London: Routledge, 1993) 195: "Any grammatical element which bears a scope relation to some part of a sentence."

5. A nominalizer may scope more than a clause. In phrase marker (6.1), the nominalizer scopes a sentence.

(8.1)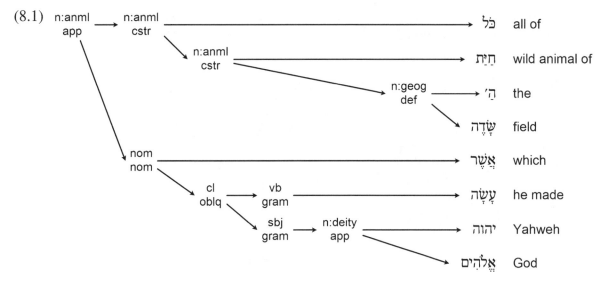

The constituent in (8.2) from Ps 118:24 contains a nominalized clause from Group #2. It lacks an אֲשֶׁר.

(8.2)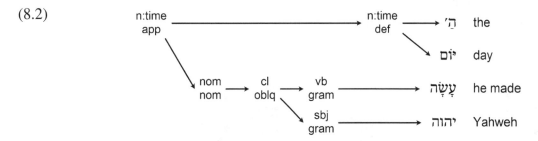

8.1.2 The Distribution of Nominalized Clauses

The distribution of Group #1 ("Overt Nominalizer") and Group #2 ("Null Nominalizer") clauses across Biblical Hebrew can be presented graphically. To do so, we first gather the data shown in the following table. ("Section Size" is the total number of clauses of any type found in the section.)

	Overt Nominalizer	*Null Nominalizer*	*Incidence Counts*	*Section Size*
Torah	2,084	117	2,201	19,593
Former Prophets	1,728	95	1,823	17,847
Latter Prophets	1,164	250	1,414	19,658
Poetry	217	185	402	11,462
Other Writings	929	104	1,033	10,215
Total	6,122	751	6,873	78,775

We then compensate for the effects of section size by dividing the overall incidence of nominalized clauses in a portion by a measure of the section's size ("Relative Incidence").[6] We let the number of

---

6. That is, the relative incidence measures the frequency of nominalized clauses as a proportion of the total number of clauses in the section.

clauses in each section of the MT measure its size. The effects of section size may also be removed by forming the ratio of overt nominalizer to null nominalizer counts ("Overt-to-Null Ratio"). The following pair of indicators results.

	Relative Incidence	*Overt-to-Null Ratio*
Torah	0.11	17.81
Former Prophets	0.10	18.19
Latter Prophets	0.07	4.66
Poetry	0.03	1.17
Other Writings	0.10	8.93
Overall	0.09	8.15

To grasp the significance of these measures, consider the situation observed for the Torah. There we find that one in 10 clauses is a nominalized clause. We also find that 18 times as many nominalized clauses have an overt nominalizer segment as clauses that do not. Figures 8.1 and 8.2 make the comparative situation across Biblical Hebrew more immediately obvious.

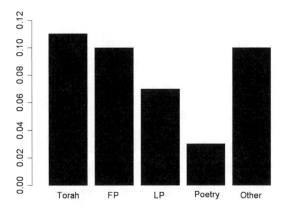 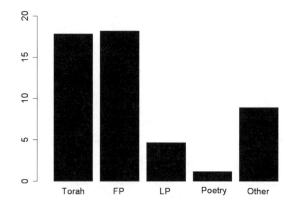

Fig. 8.1. Relative Incidence of Nominalized Clauses.

Fig. 8.2. Overt-to-Null Nominalizer Ratio.

In the Poetry section (Psalms, Job, and Proverbs):

1. Embedded nominalized clauses occur far less frequently in the poetry section than they do elsewhere (left plot). For example, they occur almost four times less frequently in the poetry section than in the Torah section.
2. Overt-nominalizer clauses occur far less frequently than null-nominalizer clauses as compared with other sections of Biblical Hebrew (right plot). For example, they occur more than 15 times less frequently in the poetry section than in the Torah section.

8.1.3   Other Characteristics of Nominalized Clauses

Taking our lead from Holmstedt, we consider these four topics related to nominalized clauses:[7]

1. overtly and covertly headed nominalized clauses ("dependent" versus "independent"),
2. restrictive and nonrestrictive nominalized clauses ("essential" versus "non-essential"),
3. the resumption phenomenon wherein a pronoun in a nominalized clause refers back to the substantive that the nominalized clause apposes,
4. nominalized clause extraposition wherein the nominalized clause does not immediately follow the substantive that it apposes.

Dealing with these phenomena in detail is beyond the scope of this volume, but we will provide phrase markers illustrating each. Readers desiring comprehensive information should consult a standard grammar or, better, Holmstedt's thesis.

8.1.3.1   Overtly and Covertly Headed Nominalized Clauses[8]

In phrase marker (8.2) from Ps 118:24 (above), the nominalized clause is in apposition with an immediately preceding *overt head*—namely הַיּוֹם 'the day'. The nominalized clause is dependent. By contrast, phrase marker fragment (8.3) from Gen 18:19 provides an example of an *independent* nominalized clause. It is in relation to no preceding substantive.

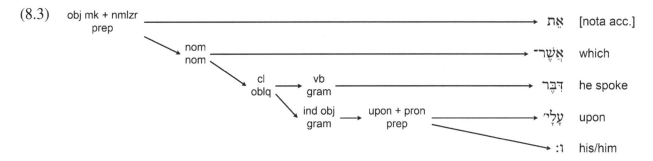

8.1.3.2   Restrictive and Nonrestrictive Nominalized Clauses[9]

Holmstedt contrasts restrictive and nonrestrictive clauses as follows:

[A] restrictive [nominalized clause] provides information about its head which is necessary for identifying the exact referent of the head; a non-restrictive [nominalized clause] presents additional information about its head that is non-crucial for identifying the referent of the head.[10]

As instances of the phenomenon of restrictiveness, we use two examples that are discussed by Holmstedt.[11] As an instance of a *restrictive* nominalized clause, he supplies Gen 1:7. The relevant phrase marker fragment shown in (8.4) has an overt head and an overt nominalizer.

---

7. Holmstedt, *The Relative Clause*, passim. We uniformly replace Holmstedt's "relative clause" with "nominalized clause."

8. Ibid., 66–79.

9. Ibid., 114–25.

10. Ibid., 114.

11. Ibid., 115.

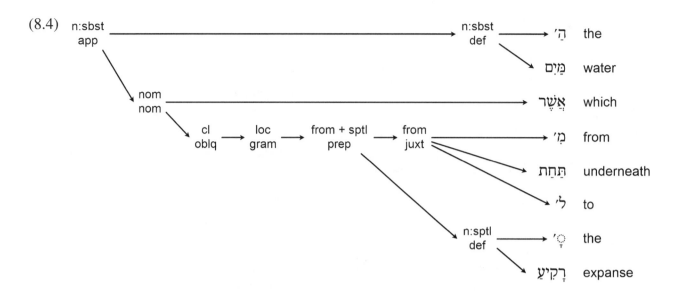

The nominalized clause clearly restricts the reference of הַמַּיִם 'the waters'. As a nonrestrictive example, consider (8.5) from Exod 18:9, which has an overt head and an overt nominalizer. The nominalized clause is non-restrictive, since יִשְׂרָאֵל is a proper noun and, as such, is not eligible for restriction.

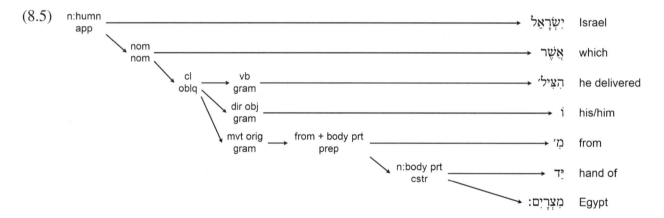

8.1.3.3 Resumption Phenomena

As noted at the outset of §8.1.3, the resumptive phenomenon[12] involves a pronoun in a nominalized clause that refers back to the substantive to which the nominalized clause is in apposition. Consider phrase marker (8.6) from Isa 37:34 (p. 103). Here, the nominalized clause is in apposition to דֶּרֶךְ 'the path'. But הָ- 'her' is the anaphor of 'the path'. Thus, by the definition, this construction is "resumptive" (it also has an overt head, an overt nominalizer, and is restrictive).

---

12. Ibid., 90–107.

(8.6)

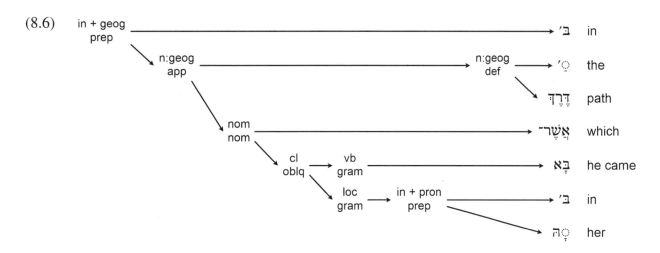

8.1.3.4   Nominalized Clause Extraposition[13]

According to Crystal,[14] extraposition "refers to the process or result of moving (or extraposing) an element from its normal position to a position at or near the end of a sentence." Holmstedt gives the locations of 139 instances of extraposed nominalized clauses.[15] In 63 of his cases, we do not find an extraposed nominalized clause. These divergences result from differing analyses, especially our allowing phrases to be heads for nominalized clauses. Consider phrase marker (8.7) from Gen 1:11. Our analysis makes the phrase פְּרִי לְמִינוֹ the head for the nominalized clause. As a result, the (restrictive) nominalized clause (nom/nom) is not extraposed from its head.

(8.7)

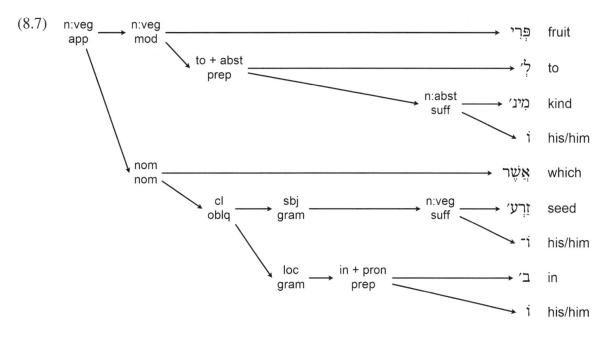

We find 94 instances of extraposed nominalized clauses that are not in Holmstedt's list. Each involves <u>distributed apposition</u> (introduced toward the end of §7.2.2). Phrase marker fragment (8.8)

---

13. Ibid., 290–93, 301–5.

14. David Crystal, *A Dictionary of Linguistics and Phonetics* (5th ed.; Oxford: Blackwell, 2003) 174. Emphases removed.

15. Holmstedt, *The Relative Clause*, 301, footnote.

from 1 Chr 22:13 shows the phenomenon. Both הַחֻקִּים and הַמִּשְׁפָּטִים are in *distributed apposition* to the following restrictive nominalized clause. Because of the presence of וְאֶת־הַמִּשְׁפָּטִים, the nominalized clause is not adjacent to הַחֻקִּים. It is inherently extraposed.

(8.8)

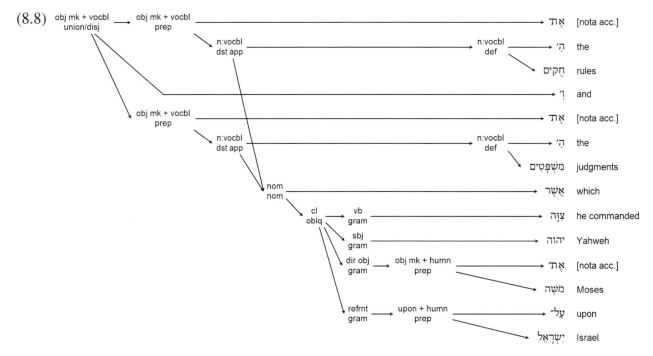

8.2   *Clausal Complements*

A second kind of embedded clause is the clausal complement. When a cognitive / mental verb is involved, its clause is commonly said to encode "indirect speech."[16] We have identified 872 of these embedded clauses in Biblical Hebrew. They are of three sorts. We classify them as:

1. clausal <u>cognitive complements</u> of cognitive / mental verbs (805×),
2. clausal complements in interrogative expressions (54×),
3. paradoxical clausal complements in verbless clauses (13×).

8.2.1   Clausal Cognitive Complements of Cognitive / Mental Verbs

The repertoire of cognitive / mental verbs encountered is fairly small. Most often seen in these constructions are verbs having the roots זכר 'remember', ידע 'know', ראה 'see', and שמע 'hear', but others put in appearances—even היה 'be', once.[17] A complement of a cognitive / mental verb CIC is usually labeled cogv cmpl / cue ("cognitive complement"). Here, the licensing relation is cue, which indicates that the CIC includes a cue phrase—a segment that signals the onset of an embedded discourse unit.[18] The cue phrase used with complements of cognitive / mental verbs is almost always the complementizer כִּי 'that'. Phrase marker (8.9) provides an example, taken from Jer 16:21, of a clausal cognitive complement of the cognitive / mental verb יְדְעוּ 'they will know':

---

16. Trask, *A Dictionary*, 140: "The reporting of what someone else has said without using his / her exact words."

17. Since we work with the *Kethiv* text, we treat Judg 16:25 as involving a clausal complement.

18. Also termed a "discourse marker" or "discourse particle." See Kerstin Fischer, ed., *Approaches to Discourse Particles* (Bingley, UK: JAI, 2008).

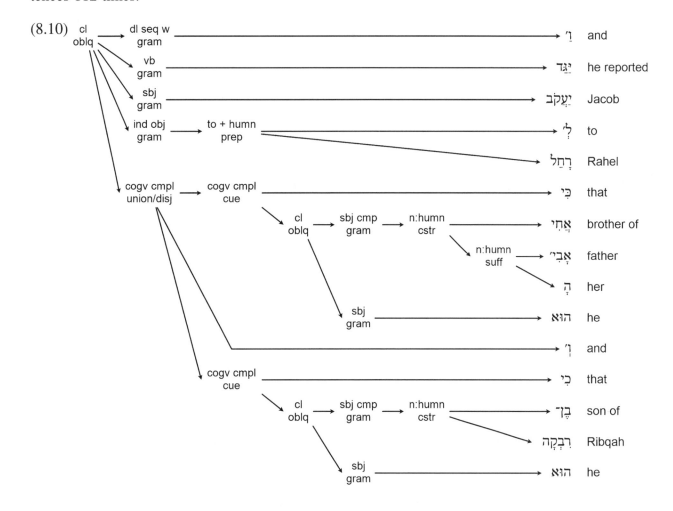

(8.9)

Here, the embedded clause is verbless (verbless clauses are taken up in chap. 19).

There are compound complements 16 times.[19] In these cases, the complementizer (כִּי) is repeated in a coordinated structure dominated by a cogv cmpl / union / disj node. Phrase marker (8.10) is an example from Gen 29:12. The embedded structures are usually simple clauses but are sentences 112 times.

(8.10)

---

19. These may be found in Gen 3:6, 29:12; Exod 3:11, 4:31; Josh 2:9, 8:21, 10:1; 1 Sam 31:7; 2 Sam 5:12, 16:10; 1 Kgs 11:21; Jer 40:7, 40:11; Job 7:17, 31:25; and 1 Chr 10:7.

8.2.2 Clausal Complements in Interrogative Expressions

We have classified 54 interrogative expressions as involving clausal complements. The basic structure is as seen in phrase marker (8.11), a verbless clause from Job 21:15:

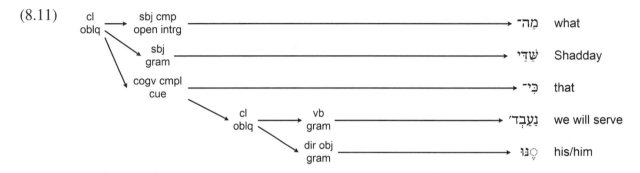

8.2.3 Clausal Complements in Verbless Clauses

We have classified 13 verbless clauses as involving clausal complements.[20] The structure is as seen in phrase marker (8.12) from Ps 119:71:

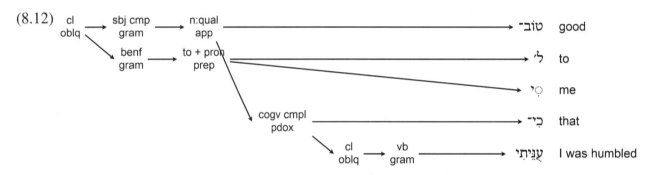

That the CIC dominating this clausal complement is **cogv cmpl / pdox** is an abuse of terminology again occasioned by our desire to avoid undue proliferation of CIC categories. Just how the constituents combine, and to what effect, is unclear to us. Hence our introduction of the paradoxical licensing relation, **pdox**. The parse shown here could also be used for situations similar to (8.11). Note that the phrase marker exhibits tangling and therefore is not a tree (see chap. 20).

8.3 *Adverbial Subordinated Clauses*

In §8.1, we dealt with one sort of subordinated clause, the nominalized (or relative) clause, which usually is in apposition to a noun phrase. Then in §8.2, we dealt with another sort of subordinated clause, the verb-complement clause, which is usually the complement of a cognitive / mental verb. We turn now to the third kind of subordinated clause, the adverbial clause:

> A subordinate clause which bears to its main clause any of a range of semantic relations similar to those borne by adverbs, such as time, manner, place, instrument, circumstance, concession, purpose, result, cause or condition.[21]

---

20. See Exod 3:12, 5:2; Josh 22:34, 24:22; 1 Sam 12:5, 21:16; 2 Kgs 20:9; Jer 44:29; Ps 119:71; Prov 22:8; Ruth 4:9; Qoh 9:3; Lam 3:27.

21. Trask, *A Dictionary*, 10.

Readers who have access to our data may have noticed that the syntax search interface for CICs contains this set of eight "mixed-level constituents" (five of which appear as instances in Trask's definition of the adverbial clause above):

Aim / Purpose	Condition	Reason	Time Point
Concessive	Discourse-Level Sequential-ן[181]	Result	Undesired Outcome

These CICs are called *mixed-level* because they can occur within clauses as phrasal CICs or as supra-clausal elementary discourse units (EDUs). Consider the *reason* CIC (rsn / gram) in phrase marker (8.13) from 2 Chr 29:9. The final CIC is structurally a prepositional phrase. Functionally, it provides the *reason* for the state of affairs. The clause is translated by the NJPS as 'and our sons and daughters and wives are in captivity on account of this'.

(8.13)

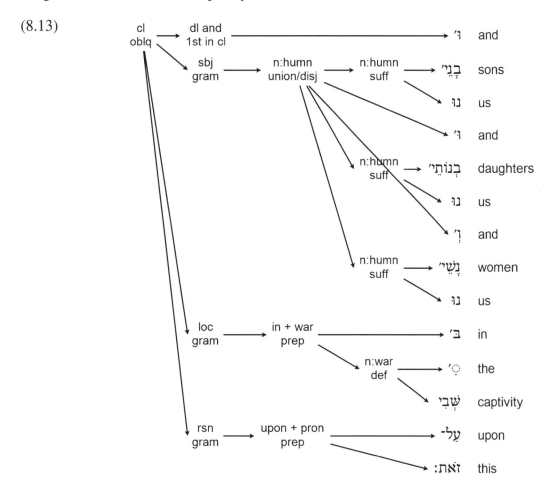

Compare phrase marker (8.14) from Gen 43:30:

---

22. Strictly speaking, this is an interim mispositioned cue phrase rather than a true CIC.

(8.14)

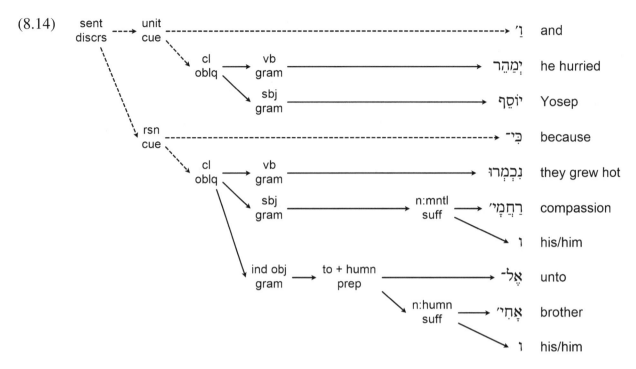

Here, we have represented the *reason* (rsn / cue) as a supra-clausal elementary discourse unit (EDU). We discuss the supra-clausal domain in chap. 21. For now, we simply note that the main clause with its subordinated adverbial clause has been analyzed into two elementary discourse units. The first is simply called a "unit" (unit / cue), our way of indicating that it has the status of an EDU in discourse but that we have not yet decided its precise EDU class. The second unit is truly a *reason* EDU (rsn / cue) and is marked as such by the cue phrase כִּי, glossed 'because'. The two EDUs combine to form a discourse unit represented at this tentative stage of our analysis by the node having the nondescript label sent / discrs (sentence licensed in discourse). In a perhaps jarring departure from convention, we have promoted the subordinated clause and its subordinating conjunction to discourse level in preparation for proper handling by discourse analysis.

8.4 *Embedded Clause-Like Types*

Above, we have discussed traditional embedded clauses. In addition to those, we have already seen two other kinds of construction involving embedding that exhibit clause-like behavior: nominalized participles and nominalized infinitives construct. Take a look at the following phrase markers:

Clause-Like Type	Locations of Phrase Markers			
Noun-Verb Participle	(3.4) 1 Sam 8:1	(6.7) Isa 62:6	(6.33) Prov 21:24	
Noun-[Verb / Noun] Participle	(3.6) Hos 14:8			
Infinitive Construct	(3.2) Gen 37:25	(6.8) Jer 22:16	(6.12) Gen 2:5	(7.1) Ruth 1:1

In each case, the participle or infinitive construct behaves as a noun "up-front" and as a verb "out-back" (put technically, it behaves exocentrically as a noun and endocentrically as a verb). In the next two subsections, we discuss the verbal nouns and show a few interesting phrase markers.

8.4.1 Noun-Verb Participles

Based on our classification, there are 2,413 constructions containing noun-verb and noun-[verb/noun] participles in Biblical Hebrew.[23] Of these, 29 participles are parts of non-tree phrase markers, 27 having two mothers and two having three mothers (in Ps 106:21 and Ps 136:7). Consider phrase marker (8.15) for the three-mother instance in Ps 106:21–22.

We make four generalizations about participial constructions:

1. The participles almost always have a single parent.
2. The participles are almost always the first CIC in their construction.[24]
3. The subject of the participial construction is almost always null ("covert").[25]
4. The most common participial construction has two CICs.[26]

(8.15)

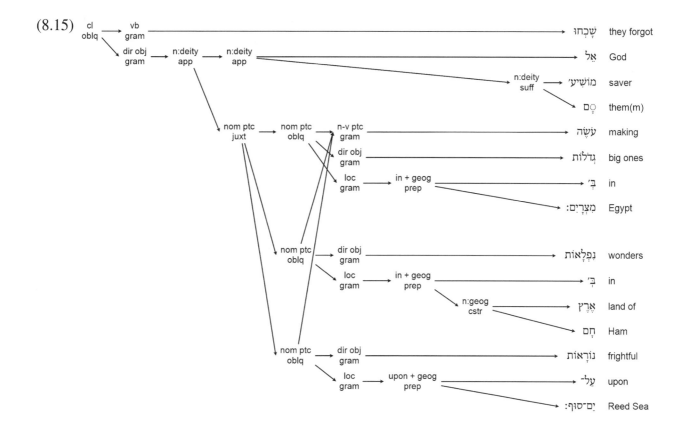

---

23. The census is as follows: 2,383 have 1 parent; 27 have 2 parents distributed as follows: 2 in Deuteronomy, 11 in Isaiah, 3 in Jeremiah, 4 in the Minor Prophets, 6 in Psalms, and 1 in Job. Two have 3 parents as noted in the text above.

24. After all, the nominal front of the verbal noun must plug in to something contiguous. The participle comes first 2,401 times out of 2,413 instances (99.5%). The participle is preceded by another CIC 12 times: location (4×), direct object (3×), negative (2×), subject (1×), subject complement (1×), and instrument (1×). See §11.1.3.3.

25. We find 4 distributive subjects (1 Sam 25:10, Jer 23:30, Ezek 3:13, and 2 Chr 18:9) and 16 subjects. One might argue that, in general, the identity of the subject inheres in the semantics of the nominal aspects of the participles.

26. There are 1,869 two-CIC participial constructions out of 2,454 (76%).

This is how many CICs the noun-verb and noun-[verb/noun] participle constructions have:

CIC Count	Incidence
1	26
2	1,861
3	452
4	65
5	7 [27]
6	1 [28]
7	1 [29]

In almost 80% of the two-CIC instances, the participle is followed by either a *direct object* CIC (×705, 37.8%), a *location* CIC (×568, 30.5%), a movement origin CIC (×106, 5.7%), or an *instrument* CIC (×90, 4.8%). Of the 705 direct object CICs, 69 (10%) are pronoun suffixes on the participle and 28 (4%) appear as pronoun suffixes on object markers, leaving 608 (86%) as other freestanding phrases. Of the 564 location CICs, 509 (90%) are prepositional phrases. The preposition is בְּ 318 times (62%) and אֶל 162 times (32%).

8.4.2 Nominalized Infinitives Construct

Based on our classification, there are 6,682 nominalized infinitive construct constructions in Biblical Hebrew, none having more than one mother. Phrase marker (8.16) from Judg 16:23 is typical.

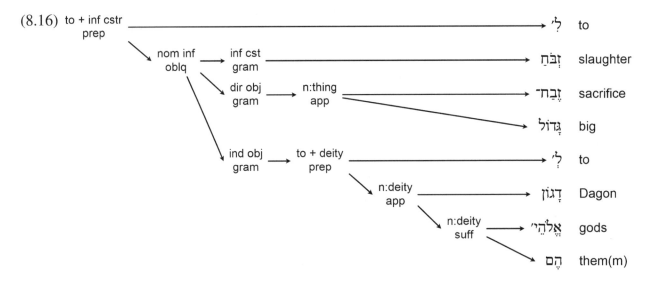

We make four generalizations regarding infinitive construct constructions:

---

27. See Num 3:38, Deut 8:16 (2×), Isa 49:5, Hab 2:9, Prov 27:14, and 1 Chr 11:10.
28. See Jer 2:6, which exhibits the CIC order: n-v ptc, dir obj, loc, loc, loc.
29. See Deut 1:33, which exhibits the CIC order: n-v ptc, loc, loc, aim, loc, tm pt, aim.

1. The infinitive construct always has a single parent.
2. The infinitive construct almost always is the first CIC in its construction.[30]
3. The subject of the construction is typically null (74% of the time).[31]
4. The most common infinitive construct construction has two CICs.[32]

The infinitive construct preceded by a negative CIC in (8.17) from Gen 3:11 may be of interest.[33]

(8.17)

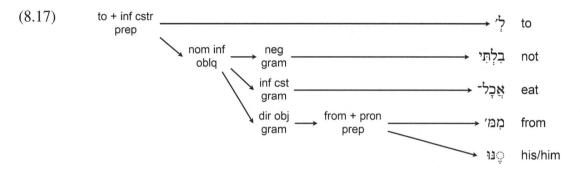

This table shows how many CICs the infinitive construct clause-like constructions have in Biblical Hebrew:

CIC Count	Incidence
1	593
2	3,805
3	1,718
4	480
5	75
6	9 [34]
7	1 [35]
8	1 [36]

With regard to the "pre-contexts" of the infinitives construct, 6,000 are preceded by prepositions (90% of the infinitives construct). The preposition is some form of -לְ 4,520 times (75% of the preposed prepositions).

---

30. The infinitives construct are initial 6,547 times out of 6,682 instances (98%). They are preceded by a negative CIC 97 times.

31. We find 1,736 subjects and four distributive subjects (Num 32:18; Jer 34:9; Esth 9:19, 9:22). Noted in passing: only two subjects come before their infinitives construct, those in Isa 30:7 and in Zech 8:9.

32. There are 3,805 two-CIC infinitive construct constructions out of 6,682 (57%).

33. On negation of the infinitive construct, see: C. H. J. van der Merwe, J. A. Naudé, and J. H. Kroeze, *A Biblical Hebrew Reference Grammar* (Sheffield: Sheffield Academic Press, 1999) 153; P. Joüon and T. Muraoka, *A Grammar of Biblical Hebrew* (rev. ed.; Rome: Pontifical Biblical Institute, 2002) 402.

34. These are at Exod 16:3, 16:8; Lev 7:36; Deut 4:34; 1 Kgs 11:36; Jer 45:1; Dan 11:1; Neh 10:35; and 1 Chr 16:40.

35. See Lev 23:37–38, which exhibits the CIC order: inf cst, obj cmp, ind obj, dir obj, obj cmp, tm pt, accomp.

36. See 1 Chr 23:31, which exhibits the CIC order: inf cst, dir obj, ind obj, tm aim, # times, cmpr, mnr, loc.

8.5 *Brief Summary*

Embedded Clauses.   We distinguish four kinds of embedded clause: *nominalized clauses, clausal complements, subordinated clauses,* and *clause-like structures.*

Nominalized Clauses.   Both the overall incidence of nominalized clauses and their use of an explicit nominalizer are very significantly depressed in the poetry books and, to a lesser extent, in the Latter Prophets. Following Holmstedt, we provide examples of several interesting kinds of nominalized clause: overtly and covertly headed, restrictive and nonrestrictive, resumptive, and extraposed (where our analysis differs significantly from Holmstedt's).

Clausal Complements.   In our analysis, clausal complements appear in three contexts: as cognitive complements of cognitive / mental verbs, in interrogative expressions, and in verbless clauses. Clausal complements are usually marked by the complementizer כִּי 'that'.

Adverbial Subordinated Clauses.   Adverbial subordinated clauses are introduced here for completeness but discussed in §21.3.

Embedded Clause-Like Structures.   These are mostly noun-verb participles and infinitives construct. The noun-verb participle structures are usually two (1,861×) or three CICs (452×) long. They mainly involve: a direct object (38%), a location (30%), or a movement origin (6%). The nominalized infinitive construct structures are usually two (3,805×) or three CICs (1,718×) long.

Chapter 9

Classifying Clause Immediate Constituents

We begin this chapter with a reminder of some concepts introduced at the end of chap. 1. In §1.3.3.3, we discussed our first full-fledged phrase marker (from 2 Kgs 18:8, reproduced here).

(1.5)

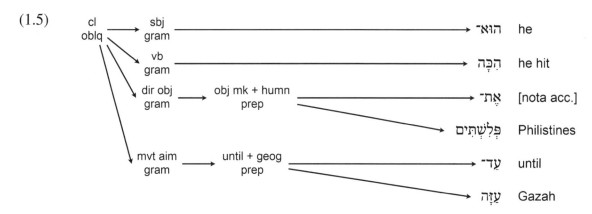

Specifically, we touched on the ubiquitous licensing relations gram and oblq:

> [W]hen we say that the assigning of some label to a clause immediate constituent (CIC) is licensed by *grammar* [gram] or that the assembling of a clause is licensed by *obliqueness* [oblq], the underlying grammatical mechanisms are unspecified. . . . The relations *grammar* and *obliqueness* stand for the very disparate, and still obscure, mechanisms that provide the grounds for classifying CICs and assembling them into clauses. . . . Here is the critical point for us:
>
> > *Gathering the data needed to begin working out the grammatical mechanisms underlying "grammar" and "obliqueness" is the focus of the latter two-thirds of this book.*

The point has arrived to begin making good on this last assertion. To this end:

1. First, we consider the nature of the grammar licensing relation with regard to the taxonomy of CICs, their classification, and their recognition.

   - In this chapter (9), we define five major *subtypes of CICs* and then discuss all but the second part of the fifth subtype (*semantic roles*) at length.
   - In chap. 10, we take up *semantic role*s in detail.

2. Second, we gather data that shed light on the nature of the obliqueness licensing relation with regard to the incidence, ordering, and makeup of the CICs in various kinds of clauses.

   - In chap. 11, we set out the methods and structures that we use to analyze specific verb root corpora.

- In chaps. 12–15, we study the composition, incidence, and ordering of CICs in the corpora defined by four very frequent verb roots in Biblical Hebrew.
- In chap. 16, we examine the *structures* of the various CIC subtypes.

9.1 *The Clause-Immediate-Constituent Subtype Taxonomy*

It is very helpful to view the clause immediate constituents (CICs) in terms of the following simple taxonomy:

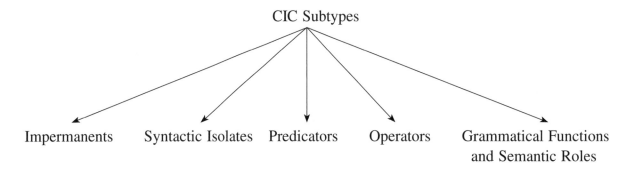

Each CIC falls into one of the five exhaustive and mutually exclusive subtypes.

9.2 *Excursus: The Mixed and Full Approaches to Representation*

9.2.1 The Mixed Representation

It is important to understand how grammatical function and semantic role are displayed in our system. Our simple labeling of phrase marker nodes with semantic category information (§3.3.1 and §4.3.2) broadens our phrase markers beyond those standardly used to depict syntactic relationships (§1.3.2). To enhance further our representation of clauses, we include information concerning the "three rudimentary categories all of which play a particularly crucial role in the understanding of human language: (a) parts of speech, (b) semantic roles, and (c) grammatical relations."[1] We use these informal definitions of each category type, taken from our glossary:

- *Part of speech.* The grammatical class or grammatical category of a segment. The specifics of our part-of-speech categories are given in chap. 3.
- *Semantic role.* The semantic relation exhibited by a participant in a clause. For example, in "Gorgou smote the wee gozingpol," "Gorgou" has the semantic role of doer and "the wee gozingpol" has the semantic role of patient. Also known as the *logical role, thematic role, theta role, thematic relation, case role,* and *deep case relation.*[2] As we will see in detail in chap. 10, many of the CIC labels in our phrase markers specify semantic roles.
- *Grammatical relation.* The syntactic function of a clause constituent in relation to other constituents in its clause. Examples: subject, predicator, direct object. "Any one of several

1. Lindsay J. Whaley, *Introduction to Typology: The Unity and Diversity of Language* (Thousand Oaks, CA: Sage, 1997) 54. The terms *grammatical relation* and *grammatical function* are used preferentially in "certain frameworks" (so R. L. Trask, *A Dictionary of Grammatical Terms* [London: Routledge, 1993] 122). We use *grammatical function* (GF) in our work.

2. Whaley, *Introduction*, 75.

specific grammatical relations which a noun phrase can bear within its [clause]. The most widely recognized grammatical relations are subject, direct object, indirect object and oblique object."[3]

An example may help. In "and Jacob broke camp Sukkot-ward" (Gen 33:17), "Jacob" has the part of speech *proper noun*, semantic role *agent*, and grammatical function *subject*. One might configure one's representation so that the node label information would include all three. This sort of representation might be termed *full*. Instead, on an interim basis, we use a *mixed representation*. The rules governing the mixed representation are:

- The part of speech and semantic category of each segment are indicated.[4]
- Any major grammatical function[5] exhibited by a CIC is preferentially shown.
- If a CIC has no major grammatical function, then its semantic role is displayed.

Phrase marker (9.1) from Lev 17:11 illustrates our *mixed representation*. Labels sbj, dir obj, and ind obj assign grammatical functions (GFs), while labels loc and aim reveal semantic roles (SRs).

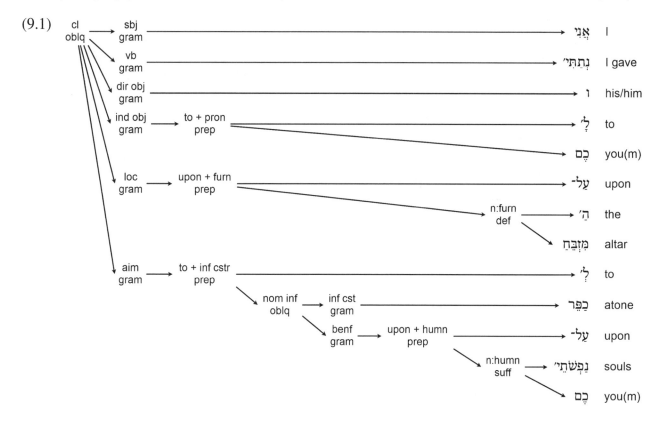

---

3. Trask, *A Dictionary*, 123. Avery D. Andrews, "The Major Functions of the Noun Phrase," in *Language Typology and Syntactic Description*, vol. 1: *Clause Structure* (2nd ed.; ed. Timothy Shopen; Cambridge: Cambridge University Press, 2007) 134: "In the literature, the term 'grammatical relation' is used as a virtual synonym of 'grammatical function.'"

4. In the Logos embodiment of our data, the part of speech and semantic category information pop up when the cursor hovers over a segment. For example, hovering over מִזְבֵּחַ 'altar' in Lev 17:11 discloses that this segment is a common noun having the semantic category "appliance / furniture."

5. John H. Connolly (*Constituent Order in Functional Grammar: Synchronic and Diachronic Perspectives* [Berlin: Foris, 1991] 29) has the major clause elements "subject, predicator, object and complement."

Our rules presuppose ways of discerning whether or not a CIC has a grammatical function in a given clause. This is not necessarily easy, since the identification of grammatical functions—especially in flexible phrase–order languages such as Biblical Hebrew—often involves more than a simple syntactic analysis of the clause immediate constituents. As Connolly observes:

> We must differentiate between the strictly syntactic and semantic aspects of the terms 'subject' and 'object.' Generally in linguistics these two terms are employed in a syntactic sense which, as with syntactic functional terms in general, designates their grammatical relationship to other elements in the same construction. . . . In [functional grammar], however, . . . they are used in an essentially semantic sense, to represent different vantage points or perspectives in the presentation of the state of affairs.[6]

9.2.2 The Full Representation

A price is exacted when semantic role information is squeezed out by grammatical function information. The specifics of the semantic role information may be important. For example, a constituent that functions as an indirect object "can bear a number of semantic roles such as recipient. . . , experiencer. . . , and source."[7] When the loss of information is unacceptable, then a full representation is preferable.

A *full representation* for the clause in Lev 17:11 might be as in phrase marker (9.2). We have replaced the uninformative licensing relation gram ("grammar determined") by a semantic role in the sbj, dir obj, and ind obj CICs. Also, we have declared the grammatical function of the loc and aim CICs to be adjunct, moving the semantic role declarations onto the lower lines in the node labels. Hence, the upper line of each CIC label gives its grammatical function, and the lower line gives its semantic role.

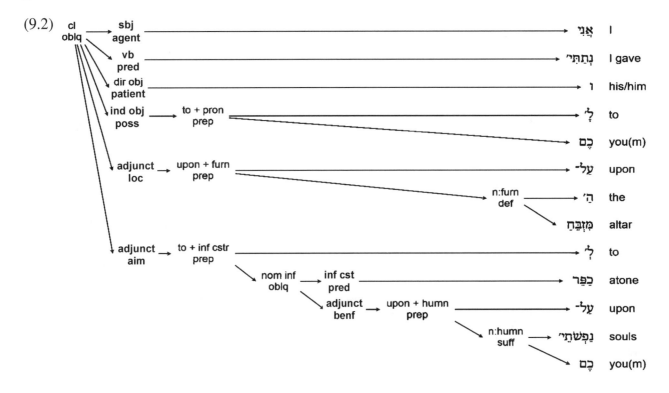

---

6. Ibid., 47.
7. Whaley, *Introduction to Typology*, 70.

9.3 *Five Types of Clause Immediate Constituent*

In the next five subsections, we discuss most of our CIC subtypes. We devote chap. 10 to the second aspect of the fifth subtype, semantic roles.

9.3.1 Impermanent Clause Immediate Constituents

The impermanent CICs are incomplete or recalcitrant items and are either: (1) *underspecified* "and" *cue phrases* (incomplete) or (2) *indeterminate constituents* (recalcitrant). Eventually, the former will move into discourse level, while the latter will remain indeterminate until we emend them.

9.3.1.1 Underspecified "And" Cue Phrases

Many phrase markers in this book begin with a coordinating conjunction CIC labeled dl seq w/gram (*discourse level sequential w*; see phrase marker [8.10]) or dl and/1st in cl (*first in clause discourse level "and"*; see phrase marker [8.13]). In our present database, the former occurs 17,429 times, and the latter occurs 9,138 times. Ostensive rules for identifying all instances of *"and"* are given in §3.1.1. The *underspecified "and" cue phrases* are an easily delimited subset of these.

Although diagrammed as CICs at the beginning of clauses, the underspecified *"ands"* are supra-clausal cue phrases (§21.3.2.1), the polysemy of which we have not yet resolved by discourse analysis. We consider them to be impermanent interlopers at clause beginnings. They are not true CICs.

9.3.1.2 Indeterminate Constituents

There are two small sets of indeterminate CICs: the 24 *lapsus calami* CICs and the 33 *nebulous* CICs. These CICs should eventually be reclassified as a result of suitable emendation, exegetical insight, or fiat. We listed our set of *lapsus calami* in §3.2.1.1. The CICs labeled *nebulous* (neb/gram) are a hodgepodge.[8] Consider, as an example, phrase marker (9.3) from 1 Sam 2:32:

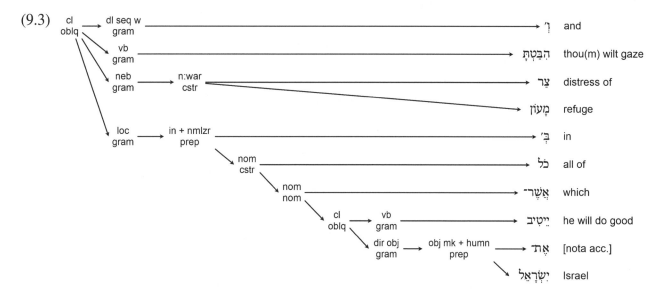

The clause, with its problematic צַר מָעוֹן, has received disparate translations, including:

---

8. They are in 1 Sam 2:32; 2 Sam 7:23 (2×), 14:26, 16:11, 17:3, 19:7; 1 Kgs 8:31, 11:15, 11:25; 2 Kgs 9:25; Isa 8:6, 41:4, 43:14, 47:9; Jer 3:10, 8:15 (2×); Ezek 14:4, 27:19, 45:5; Mic 6:12; Hab 2:5; Ps 39:7, 59:13, 68:14, 104:15, 141:5, 148:13; Prov 14:25; Qoh 5:6; Dan 11:18; and 1 Chr 26:16. Being so rare, they have no significant effect overall.

KJV   And thou shalt see <u>an enemy in my habitation</u>, in all the wealth which God shall
       give Israel.

RSV   Then in <u>distress</u> you will look <u>with envious eye</u> on all the prosperity which shall be
       bestowed upon Israel.

ASV   And thou shalt behold <u>the affliction of my habitation</u>, in all the wealth which God
       shall give Israel.

9.3.2 Syntactically Isolated Clause Immediate Constituents

Zwicky recognizes a curious kind of noun phrase (NP):[9] "Isolated NPs, standing alone (*Hey,
idiot!*) or interrupting sentences (*I'm afraid,* you idiot, *that your hair is on fire*)." He sees "two
kinds of uses for isolated NPs: vocative/exclamative, telegraphic," distinguishing two types of
vocatives (*address* and *call*) and three types of exclamatives (*epithet, dismay,* and *astonishment*).
He displays six telegraphic uses, which he sees as "shading off from fragment NPs": *offer, request,
hot news, identification of type, identification of individual,* and *discourse topic*. McCawley lucidly
lays the situation out under the heading "Extrasentential Discourse Units."

> There are a variety of linguistic units that are not obviously constituents of sentences, though they are
> in many cases loosely linked to particular sentences. . . . The absence, to my knowledge, of any respect
> in which vocatives behave like syntactic constituents of linguistic units that they appear in suggests
> that . . . either they are combined with the host S at the top of the syntactic structure . . . or they simply
> do not make up syntactic units with the host S. . . . Other types of linguistic units that often have host
> Ss but are not obviously constituents of the host Ss include many of the quite diverse items that are
> often indiscriminately lumped under the term "interjection."[10]

We recognize three kinds of *syntactically isolated* CICs or <u>isolates</u>: <u>vocatives</u>, <u>exclamatives</u>, and
<u>labels</u> (this last being akin to Zwicky's identification of telegraphic uses).

9.3.2.1 Vocative CICs

As our glossary states, a <u>vocative</u> is "a constituent in direct speech intended specifically to attract the attention of the one addressed." Here, we display vocatives in three kinds of context.

A vocative can be the only CIC in an utterance, a *stand-alone*, truly isolated NP. For example,
consider phrase marker (9.4) from Exod 3:4:

(9.4)

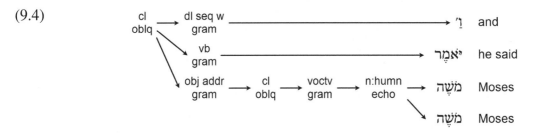

Alternatively, a vocative can interrupt a clause, which is what happens in phrase marker (9.5) from
Deut 33:7:

---

9. Arnold M. Zwicky, "Isolated NPs," http://www-csli.stanford.edu/~zwicky/isolated.hnd.pdf. See also Kerstin
Fischer, ed., *Approaches to Discourse Particles* (Bingley, UK: JAI, 2008) 8–9, where "integratedness" is discussed.

10. James D. McCawley, *The Syntactic Phenomena of English* (2nd ed.; Chicago: University of Chicago Press,
1998) 750–53.

(9.5)

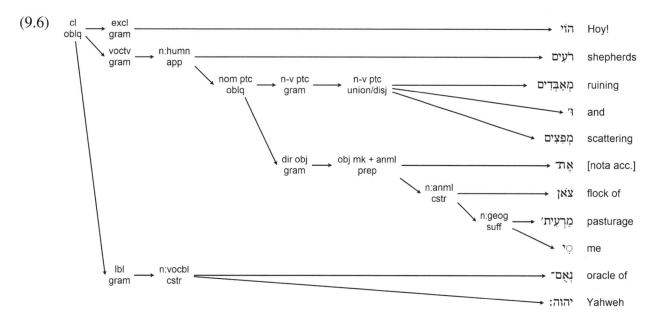

More typically, the vocative is clause initial or final. Once, in Jer 23:1, a vocative combines with two other isolates to produce an **excl voctv labl** clause. Phrase marker (9.6) shows this clause:

(9.6)

9.3.2.2 Exclamative CICs

According to our glossary, an <u>exclamative</u> is "a <u>constituent</u> that expresses a sudden or strong emotion." The constituent may be a single segment drawn from the list in §3.2.1.1 or may involve the echoing of one of these segments. As an example, consider phrase marker (9.7) from Isa 10:5:

(9.7)

The constituent may be a complex noun phrase, as in phrase marker (9.8) from 2 Kgs 4:19:

(9.8)

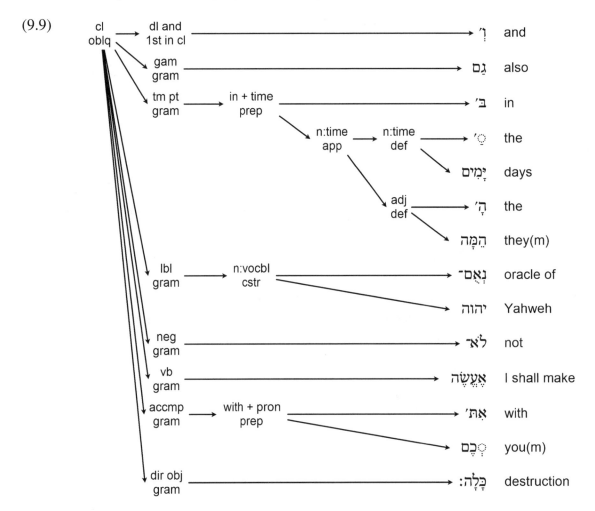

About one-third of the exclamatives occur in single-CIC clauses as stand-alone isolates.

9.3.2.3 Label CICs

There are 199 instances of stand-alone isolated *labels*. This leaves 482 instances where a label CIC does not stand alone. The label is the first CIC in these clauses 13% of the time and is last 73% of the time. In phrase marker (9.9) for Jer 5:18, the label is medial:

(9.9)

9.3.3 Predicator CICs

Our glossary definition of a <u>predicator</u> is "a <u>verbal</u> or <u>quasiverbal</u> <u>constituent</u> that specifies equivalence, activity, state, or process." The predicators are the focus of chaps. 11–15 and 18.

9.3.4 Operator CICs

We next take up what we term operator CICs. An *operator* is a "grammatical element which bears a *scoping* relation to some part of its [text]. Examples include determiners and quantifiers, negation, tense, aspect and mood."[11] The *scope* of an operator refers "to that stretch of language affected by the meaning of a particular form. . . . As a general illustration, in English the scope of negation typically extends from the negative word until the end of the clause."[12] For Biblical Hebrew, certain operators have as their scope a phrase, an entire clause, or even multiple clauses. Each involves a single part of speech. Our six operator CICs, along with their definitions, are:

- <u>negative</u>.   A segment that negates a constituent or constituents.
- <u>closed interrogative</u>.   A <u>segment</u> that asks a yes-no question about a <u>constituent</u>.
- גַּם /גַם 'also'.   When functioning within a <u>clause</u>, this distributionally complex <u>segment</u> expresses inclusion of some number of following <u>constituents</u>. We keep this lexeme separate from the includer group for reasons given in §3.2.1.3.
- <u>includer</u> (אַף 'also').   When functioning within a clause, this segment expresses *inclusion* of some number of following <u>constituents</u>.
- <u>restricter</u> (רַק 'only' and many instances of אַךְ).   When functioning within a <u>clause</u>, these <u>segments</u> express *restriction* of some number of following <u>constituents</u>.
- <u>modal</u>.   A <u>segment</u> or idiom that expresses the speaker's (un)certainty or desire with regard to some statement.

The operator CICs exhibit disparate characteristics. While *negative, (closed) interrogative*, and to a lesser extent גַם 'also', *includer*, and *restricter* CICs exhibit classical variable scoping, the scoping of *modal* CICs is often difficult to establish with confidence (see §9.3.4.4).

9.3.4.1 Negative CICs

The negative part of speech was defined ostensively in §3.2.2.3. For the purposes of this subsection, we present a trio of phrase markers illustrating the progression of scoping of a negative operator from phrase to clause to multiple clauses.

Phrasal Negative Operators.   A negative can operate upon a noun phrase to produce a constituent consisting of a negative operator and a noun phrase licensed by inverted modification (inv mod). The scope of negation is not necessarily to the end of the clause. Phrase marker (9.10) from Jer 5:7 contains the negated noun phrase לֹא אֱלֹהִים 'not gods':

(9.10)
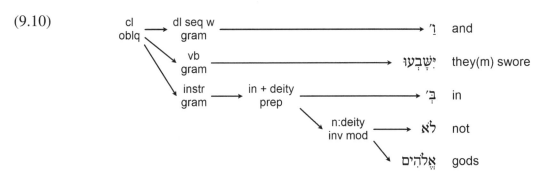

---

11. Trask, *A Dictionary*, 195. To align with Biblical Hebrew practice, we have replaced Trask's "sentence" with "text" in the definition.

12. David Crystal, *A Dictionary of Linguistics and Phonetics* (5th ed.; Oxford: Blackwell, 2003) 407.

Clausal Negative Operators.   There are 5,316 instances in which a negative operator immediately precedes a predicator, such as in (9.11) from 2 Chr 20:33:

(9.11)

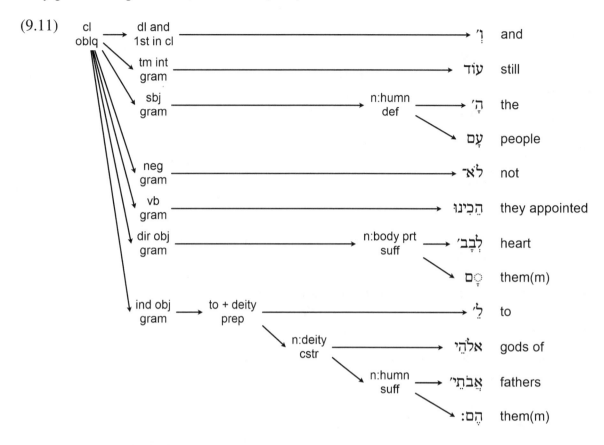

Given this very common adjacency behavior, one might be tempted to treat the negative as operating at phrase level to form a negative verbal constituent licensed by inverted modification. For two reasons, we prefer to treat such negatives as operating upon their entire clauses:

1. There are 279 instances in which the negative operator is not adjacent to the predicator. Any representation of negative operators must handle this sort of separation. Phrase marker (9.12) from Ps 6:2 illustrates the behavior to which we refer:

(9.12)

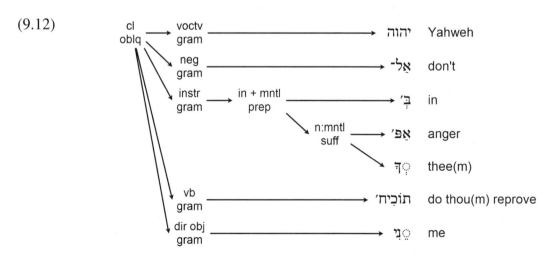

Combining the negative and the verb to form a constituent would involve "tangling," producing a non-tree phrase marker (§4.2). We avoid this complication where possible.

2. *Polarity* is a characteristic of the *clause* in discourse analysis, where one encounters assertions such as: "Clause$_1$ and Clause$_2$ differ in polarity (i.e., one clause is positive and the other negative)."[13] Given our interest in discourse analysis, we assign polarity to the clause.

Multiple-Clause Negative Operators.   The scope of a negative operator can extend over multiple clauses. Consider phrase marker (9.13) for a pair of juxtaposed clauses from Isa 38:18:

(9.13)

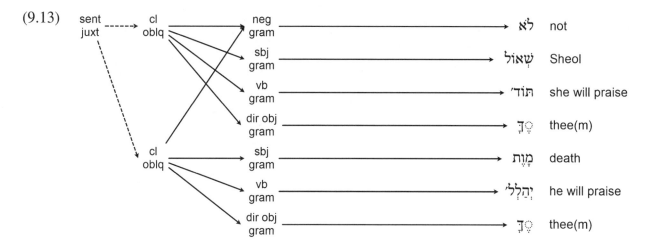

In this and similar instances, we have used the mechanism of multidominance to indicate the extended scope of the negative operator. As a result, the phrase marker is not a tree (this matter is discussed in §20.2).

As an additional example, consider this interesting phrase marker (9.14) from Isa 23:4 (see p. 124).

9.3.4.2   Closed Interrogative CICs

The interrogative part of speech was defined ostensively in §3.2.2.4. Closed interrogatives are operators in that they, like negatives, can exhibit phrasal, clausal, or multi-clausal scoping.[14]

In Biblical Hebrew, the interrogative operators for closed questions are -הֲ 'yes-no?' and אִם '[question]'. Only if we were to introduce a rhetorical question operator, הֲלֹא- 'is not...?' (rhet/gram),[15] would the interrogative operator be a *phrase level* constituent of the rhetorical operator. Phrase markers (9.15a) and (9.15b) from Job 10:20 show the two approaches.

---

13. Simon Corston-Oliver, "Beyond String Matching and Cue Phrases: Improving Efficiency and Coverage in Discourse Analysis," Microsoft Research Tech Report, November 1998, 4. http://www.research.microsoft.com/apps/pubs/default.aspx?id=69677.

14. Andrew Radford, *Syntax: A Minimalist Introduction* (Cambridge: Cambridge University Press, 1997) 130–47.

15. We have not yet decided whether to introduce a rhetorical operator CIC.

(9.14)

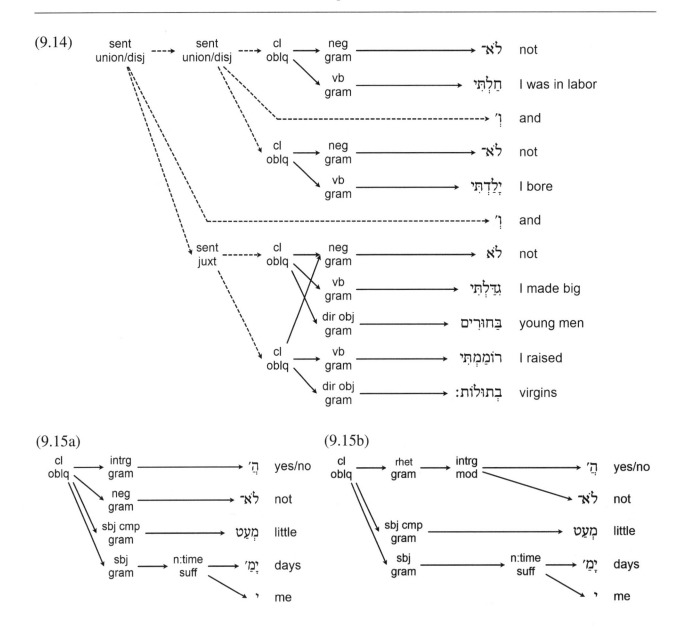

(9.15a)

(9.15b)

Most translations render the clause as a rhetorical question: "Are not the days of my life few?" (NRSV). The NJPS translates it as having indicative modality: "My days are few."

Usually, a closed interrogative scopes a single clause, as in (9.16) from Ruth 1:19:

(9.16)

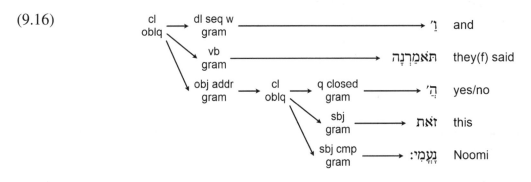

A closed interrogative can also scope multiple clauses. For example, in phrase marker (9.17) from Jer 49:7, the interrogative operator scopes the three juxtaposed clauses making up the sentence.

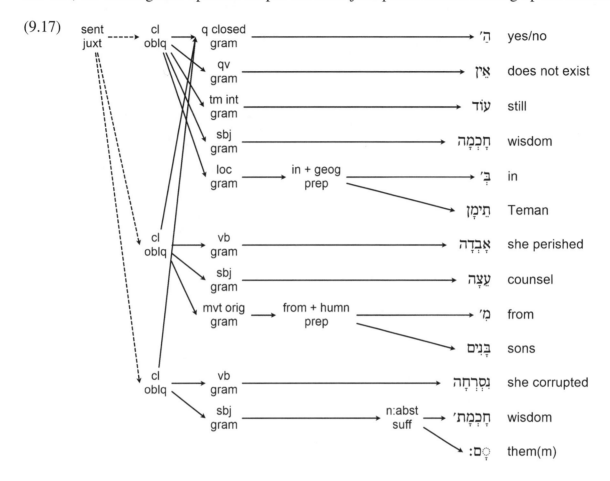

9.3.4.3 Quantifier CICs

A group of operator CICs, known as *quantifiers* or *focus particles*, specifies the domain of inclusion ("includers") or restriction ("restricters") of the constituents upon which they operate. Because "their meaning always indicates that the referent to which they refer *is an addition to or limitation of another referent*,"[16] they are termed *focus particles* by some. We prefer to call them *quantifiers*.

Includer CICs גַּם/גַם '*Also*' *and* אַף '*Also*'.   These were touched on in §3.2.1.3. We find phrasal instances, as in phrase marker (9.18) from Gen 47:3:

16. C. H. J. van der Merwe, J. A. Naudé, and J. H. Kroeze, *A Biblical Hebrew Reference Grammar* (Sheffield: Sheffield Academic Press, 1999) 311.

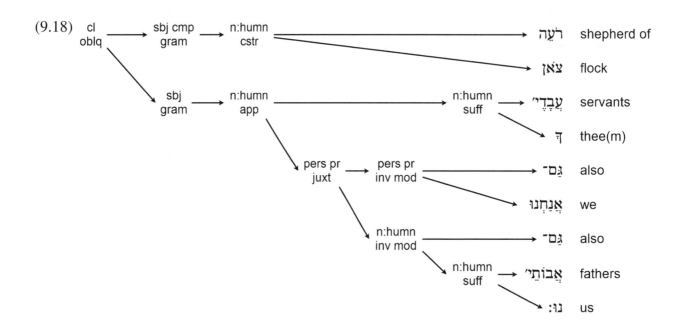

We find גַּם /גַם having single-clause scope, as in phrase marker (9.19) from Exod 2:19:

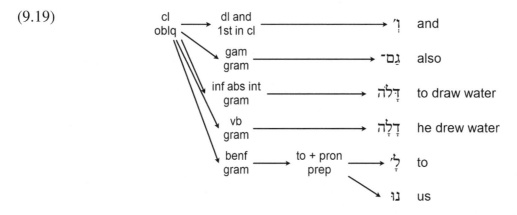

And we find גַּם /גַם with multiple-clause scope, such as in phrase marker (9.20) from 1 Sam 15:29. In this extensive multi-clause phrase marker, גַּם /גַם is a supra-clausal cue phrase (this notion is discussed in chap. 21). As noted in §3.2.1.3, the uses of גַּם /גַם are many and complex. Consequently, in practice, we have left גַּם /גַם as the sole member of its own class (see (9.20), p. 127).

Restricter CICs אַךְ *'Only' and* רַק *'Only'.* We have divided אַךְ into two classes, epistemic modal adverb ('surely', 62×, §3.2.2.1) and restrictive adverb (99×, §3.2.2.2). Each CIC רַק (25×) is classified as a restrictive adverb (§3.2.2.2). With one exception (Deut 28:13), the restrictives are clause initial.[17] Phrase marker (9.21) from Num 12:2 uniquely includes both kinds of restricter.

---

17. However, in Josh 6:18, רַק follows "and."

(9.20)

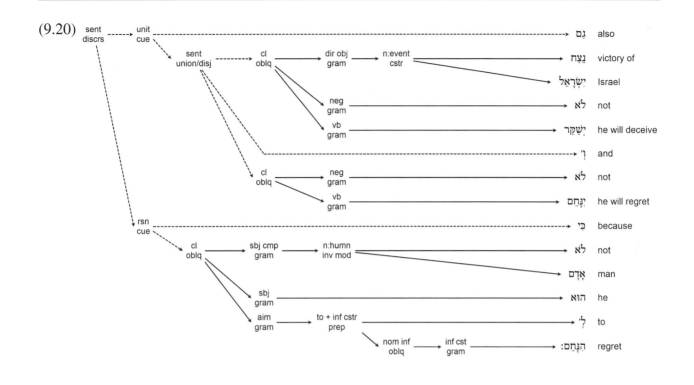

(9.21)

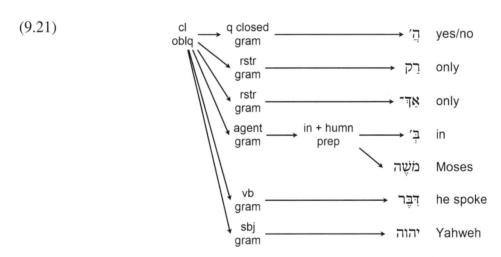

9.3.4.4 Modal CICs

A modal is a segment that expresses the speaker's uncertainty or desire with regard to a particular statement. As defined ostensively in §3.2.2.1, our modals consist of seven lexemes. We know of no modal that operates at phrase level. Single-clause scoping is typical. Multiple-clause scoping is less common. As an example, consider phrase marker (9.22) from 1 Kgs 18:5, which contains an instance of the modal אוּלַי 'perhaps'. With modals, we encounter a kind of multiple-clause scoping that differs from what we have seen with the previous operator CICs. With the other operators, the extent of scoping is fairly clear-cut in any given case. But with the modals, operator scope is less obvious. What is the scope of the modal in (9.22)? Since the clauses form a discourse unit, the scope of the modal is all three clauses. Hence, in a proper discourse representation, the modal will be supra-clausal.

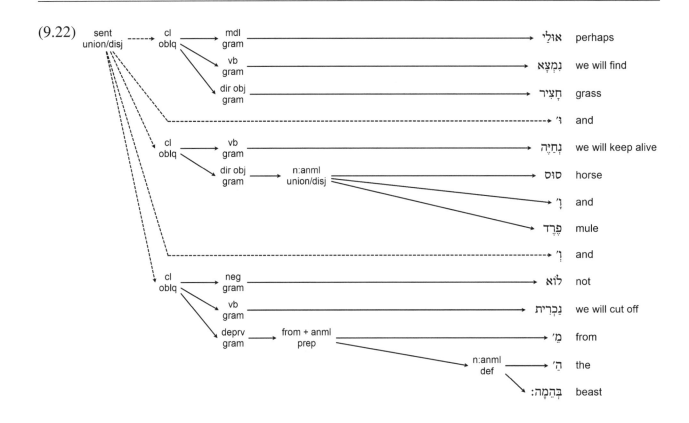

Since the modals appear only in direct speech, we always know the upper bound on the extent of scoping—the end of the speech. But the actual extent of the scope typically needs working out.

Since multiple-clause scoping is really an issue at discourse level, the working out of the best way of representing scoping can wait until we get into formal discourse analysis. For now, it is enough to alert readers to scoping issues so they can be attentive as they work with the texts.

9.3.5 The Grammatical Function and Semantic Role CICs

In this subsection we discuss the grammatical function aspect of clause immediate constituents, deferring the discussion of the semantic roles until chap. 10.

9.3.5.1 Our Repertoire of Grammatical Function CICs

Whaley portrays linguistic opinion regarding the primary grammatical functions as follows:

> Both in traditional grammar and in several contemporary syntactic theories . . . , it is assumed that there are three primary grammatical relations that can be held by noun phrases in a clause: subject, direct object, and indirect object. . . . The[se] entities specified by the verb are called *arguments*.[18]

As long as we use a mixed representation (§9.2.1), we subdivide two of the primary grammatical functions and thereby obtain these seven interim grammatical function CICs:[19]

---

18. Whaley, *Introduction to Typology*, 68–69. We use "grammatical relation" and "grammatical function" interchangeably (see Trask, *A Dictionary*, 122).

19. The *subject complement* and *object complement* are *not* complements of the predicator but rather of the subject and object, respectively, and so are not included in our table. See Crystal, *A Dictionary*, 88.

Master Category	Subsidiary Categories	Master Category	Subsidiary Categories
subject	subject (sbj)	*direct object*	direct object (dir obj)
	subject-of-address (sbj addr)		object-of-address (obj addr)
	Janus sbj-cmp / sbj (Janus sc / sb)		second object (2nd obj)
		indirect object	indirect object (ind obj)

We have already provided examples of several of the CICs in this group:

1. For subject, see phrase marker (9.1) in §9.2.1.
2. The subject-of-address CIC has a speech as the subject of a Niphal passive of an utterance verb. As an example, consider phrase marker (9.23) from Gen 22:14:

(9.23)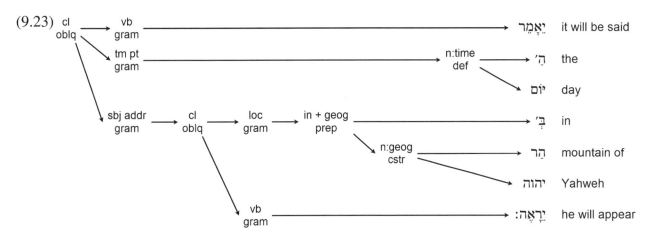

3. Phrase marker (9.24) shows a Janus sc / sb in 1 Chr 6:2. On this CIC type, see Appendix 6.

(9.24)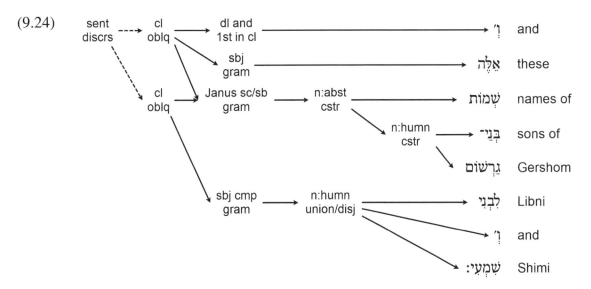

4. For examples of direct objects, see phrase markers (1.5), (4.1), (4.2), (5.1), and so on.
5. For an instance of an object-of-address, see phrase marker (9.4).

6. Second objects go with ditransitive verbs as in phrase marker (9.25) from Gen 41:39:

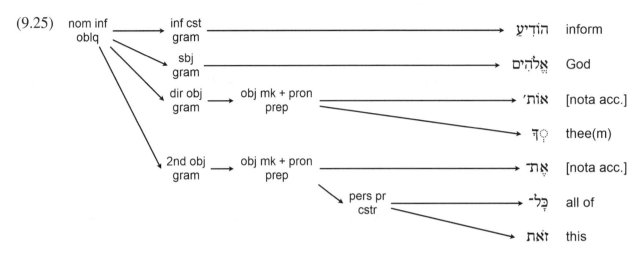

7. For indirect objects, see phrase markers (8.10), (8.14), (8.16), (9.1), among others.

9.3.5.2 Special Characteristics of Some Grammatical Function CICs

In addition to supplying CIC labels and the vague gram licensing relation, we flag four CIC phenomena: suspension (881×), resumption (733×), distribution (698×), and open interrogation (1,460×). Interestingly, with one maddening exception, these phenomena never occur simultaneously.[20]

Suspension and Resumption.   Sometimes a grammatical function is repeated ("resumed"), usually by a pronoun. Phrase marker (9.26) from Gen 3:12 shows a suspended and resumed subject. CICs other than grammatical functions also exhibit suspension and resumption. Phrase marker (9.27) from Jer 50:21 shows a pair of location CICs exhibiting suspension / resumption.

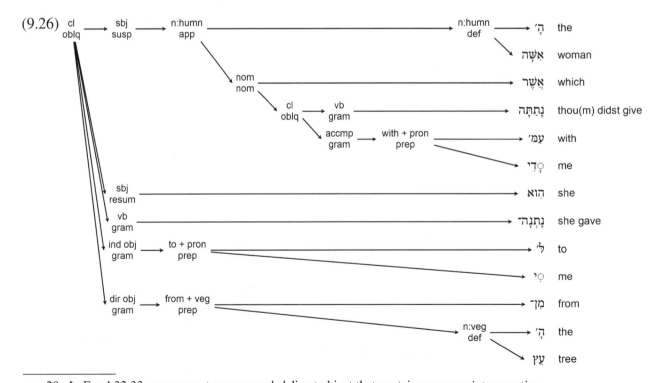

---

20. In Exod 32:33, we encounter a *suspended* direct object that contains an *open interrogative*.

(9.27)

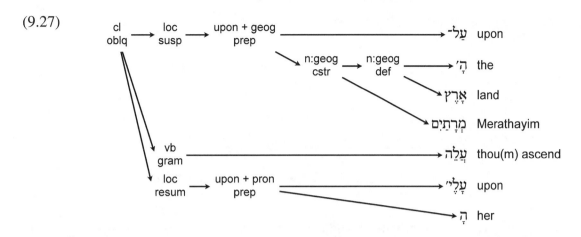

Distribution. As our glossary has it, a distributive subject is "[a] singular nominal subject that refers separately to each and every member of a plural subject. Example: 'They . . . each man.'" And similarly for other kinds of CICs. Phrase marker (9.28) from Exod 33:4 includes a distributive subject, a distributive object, and a distributive location CIC:

(9.28)

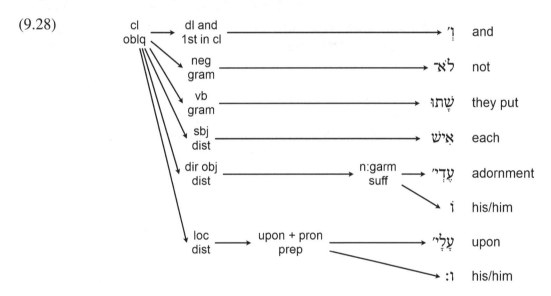

Open Interrogation. Two interrogative parts of speech were defined ostensively in §3.2.2.4. Questions are of two sorts, closed and open.[21] The former "ask questions with a closed set of answers,"[22] while the latter involve "questions where the set of answers is open-ended."[23] Closed interrogatives were taken up in §9.3.4.2. Here, we focus on open interrogatives. Regarding open interrogatives, Huddleston comments:

> The grammatically distinctive property of open interrogatives is the presence of an interrogative word: *who*, *what*, *which*, *why*, etc. . . . The interrogative words . . . combine two roles: one as a marker of open interrogative clause type, one as a pronoun, determiner, temporal adverb, etc., with functions that can also be filled by noninterrogative words.[24]

---

21. R. D. Huddleston, "Sentence Types and Clause Subordination," in *Concise Encyclopedia of Grammatical Categories* (ed. K. Brown and J. Miller; Amsterdam: Elsevier, 1999) 334–37.
22. Ibid., 334.
23. Ibid., 335.
24. Ibid.

What Huddleston is getting at can readily be seen by considering a concrete example. Consider phrase marker (9.29) from Prov 6:9:

(9.29)

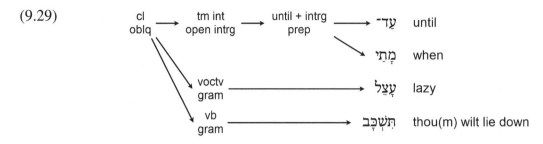

As its first role, the interrogative מָתַי 'when?' indicates that the clause involves an open question. As its second role, the CIC is part of a time interval (tm int) adjunct. Our representation shows that the CIC is a time adjunct, a tm int, and also indicates that the clause is the interrogative (open intrg).

Many open-interrogative segments are not immediately dominated by a CIC-node but, rather, are parts of phrases. These constructions are usually set phrases well on their way to being lexicalized. Example: לָ׳מָה 'to what?' = 'why?' Three hundred eighty-two open interrogatives are parts of basic phrases such as this. In addition, there are 19 atypical phrasal interrogatives.[25] The phrasal interrogative is never deeply embedded,[26] and so we may represent the situation as before. Phrase marker (9.30) from Job 38:29 illustrates our representation in these sorts of cases:

(9.30)

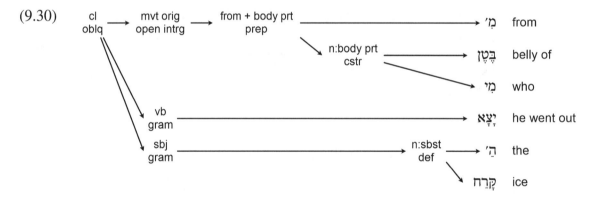

9.4 *On Recognizing CIC-Types*

Having devised and displayed an exhaustive top-level taxonomy of CIC-types and having specified the kinds of CICs that belong to each subtype,[27] producing at least one example of each, we now need only to comment on how each CIC is recognized and assigned to its proper subtype. In other words, what principles and rules does the gram licensing relation subsume?

---

25. An open interrogative is a *nomen rectum* in Gen 24:23; 24:47; 1 Sam 12:3 (3×); 17:55, 56, 58; Jer 8:9; 44:28; Job 26:4, 7; 38:29. Coordinated interrogatives are found in Exod 10:8; 1 Kgs 2:36, 2:42; 2 Kgs 5:25. A discontinuous echo is found in 2 Kgs 9:32. The construction in Job 26:7 (עַל-בְּלִי-מָה) is unique.

26. The open interrogative CIC dominates a basic phrase (§5.2), except in Job 26:7 and 38:29 (each of which involves a prepositional phrase).

27. Recall that any CIC belongs to one of the following five exhaustive and mutually exclusive subtypes: impermanent, syntactic isolate, predicator, operator, {grammatical function and semantic role}.

The CIC category of a few kinds of CICs is readily evident. For example, the exclamatives and modals involve little homography and thus are for the most part easily classified.[28] But the recognition of most CIC categories presupposes that the clause of which they are a part has been fully parsed. In these cases, the gram licensing relation subsumes a full grammar of Biblical Hebrew and then some.

Consider, for example, recognition of grammatical function. While Whaley asserts in effect that the grammatical function subtype is "identifiable by special morphological and syntactic marking,"[29] this is not true for Biblical Hebrew where, for instance, direct objects, especially in poetry, are often unmarked. Another approach examines noun-phrase position relative to the predicator. For example, Gildea and Jurafsky "expect . . . [position] to be highly correlated with grammatical function, since subjects will generally appear before a verb, and objects after."[30] This assumes fixed constituent ordering, and so it is not very useful for Biblical Hebrew. In our computer parsing, we found that comparing predicator semantics and gender with noun-phrase semantics and gender was quite useful in distinguishing subjects from direct objects.[31] In fact, in determining the grammatical functions of CICs, we have often had to draw intuitively on non-local information and on world knowledge.[32] The phrase markers that we analyze incorporate varying amounts of extrasyntactic information. Homographs have been resolved wherever we have become aware of their existence. This means, for example, that the forms of the object marker (אֶת, אֵת, אוֹת׳, and אֵת׳) have been classified differently from the identical forms functioning as 'with'. As a consequence, more than 800 CICs have been predetermined to have an accompanier semantic role rather than having the grammatical function of *direct object*. We take advantage of all such assistance in this investigation of grammatical functions and semantic roles.

9.5 *Brief Summary*

Excursus: Mixed versus Full Representation.   The phrase markers in this book (and, at present, in our database) supply a *mixed representation* of the syntactic / semantic phenomena exhibited by Biblical Hebrew. They privilege display of GF information over display of SR information. In our planned *full representation*, both GF and SR information will always be displayed.

The Top Levels of the CIC-Subtype Taxonomy.   Clause immediate constituents are divided into these five subtypes:

1. *Impermanents.*   CICs that will, in due course, be assigned to other CIC classes.
2. *Syntactic isolates.*   NPs that are syntactically isolated—vocatives, exclamatives, and labels.
3. *Predicators.*   the verbal or quasiverbal nuclei of their clauses.

---

28. Homography can be daunting. Consider the exclamative אֲבִי 'O!' (found in four different lexemes!, §3.2.1.1) or the modal כִּי 'surely' (found in seven different lexemes!, §3.2.2.1).

29. Whaley, *Introduction to Typology*, 67.

30. Daniel Gildea and Daniel Jurafsky, "Automatic Labeling of Semantic Roles," *Comparative Linguistics* 28 (2002) 257.

31. F. I. Andersen and A. D. Forbes, "Opportune Parsing," in *Bible and Computer* (Paris: Honoré Champion, 1995) 61.

32. For example, in determining the CIC label of a pronominal constituent, one must know its possibly-remote anaphor.

4. *Operators.* CICs that exert their influence over phrases, clauses, or multiple clauses—negatives, closed interrogatives, quantifiers (also known as "focus particles"), and modals.
5. *Grammatical functions / semantic roles.* We recognize three basic GFs: subject, direct object, and indirect object. SRs are considered in chap. 10.

Special Features of Some GFs / SRs. A CIC may exhibit the following special features:

1. It may be *suspended* and later *resumed*, usually by a free pronoun.
2. It may exhibit *distribution.*
3. It may perform *open interrogation.*

These phenomena are mutually exclusive, with one curious exception.

Chapter 10

Semantic Role CICs

As we noted in chap. 9, nominal CICs can be described by their semantic roles—"the semantic relationship that a nominal bears to the rest of the clause."[1] Note that the nominal may be embedded in a prepositional phrase constituent. Indeed, some theories view prepositions as particles that simply mark their associated nominals for various roles:[2] "'dependent marking' [signals] the existence of a grammatical relation between two elements of a sentence . . . by a marker placed on the dependent term." In this chapter, we discuss our set of semantic roles, their taxonomy, and their recognition.

Semantic role analysis is part of many grammatical theories. The degree of refinement of an analysis depends on the importance that the roles have in a given theory. According to Van Valin:

> [In Government Binding Theory] nothing depends on which [semantic] role an argument receives, as long as it receives one (and only one), whereas in [Lexical Functional Grammar] the validity of the syntactic analysis depends crucially in many instances on the identity of the [semantic] role assigned.[3]

Not surprisingly, role analysis in Government Binding Theory is much less developed than in Lexical Functional Grammar.[4]

The various analyses differ with regard to role repertoire, role taxonomy, and role recognition criteria. We review typical approaches to these three issues, concluding each review with a sketch of our stance.

10.1 *Semantic Role Repertoire*

10.1.1 Representative Approaches

The number of semantic roles defined in grammars varies vastly, from just a few to many hundreds.[5] This is because the extent of the repertoire depends on how the roles are used:

> [If the roles are] part of the system of lexical representation, wherein they represent aspects of the verb's meaning . . . , then a large number will be needed to express the great variety of

---

1. Lindsay J. Whaley, *Introduction to Typology* (Thousand Oaks, CA: Sage, 1997) 290.

2. Avery D. Andrews, "The Major Functions of the Noun Phrase," in *Language Typology and Syntactic Description*, vol. 1: *Clause Structure* (2nd ed.; ed. T. Shopen; Cambridge: Cambridge University Press, 2007) 143.

3. R. D. Van Valin Jr., "Functional Relations," in *Concise Encyclopedia of Grammatical Categories* (ed. K. Brown and J. Miller; Amsterdam: Elsevier, 1999) 154. We have replaced *θ-role* with *semantic role*.

4. Trask complains that "[t]he proponents of [Government Binding Theory] have been remarkably unforthcoming about precisely which [semantic roles] are posited in the framework" (R. L. Trask, *A Dictionary of Grammatical Terms* [London: Routledge, 1993] 278).

5. Daniel Gildea and Daniel Jurafsky, "Automatic Labeling," *Computational Linguistics* 28 (2002) 247.

verbal semantic contrasts. . . . [If they] play a role in the statement of grammatical rules, principles, or constraints . . . , then only as many will be needed as the syntax requires, and this is a much smaller number than that required for a lexical representation function."[6]

The fullest lexical representation is that of FrameNet II, which tailors over 800 semantic roles specifically verb-by-verb.[7] By contrast, a typical abstract representation has "between eight and twenty unique roles."[8] Connolly (following Dik) provides the following list of 22 semantic functions (to use Connolly's terminology), with an English example of each.[9]

Connolly's Semantic Functions

Semantic Function	English Example
Time	*at midnight*
Duration	*for an hour*
Place	*in Abergynolwyn*
Comitative	*in his friend's company*
Manner	*slowly*
Instrument	*with a hammer*
Attendant circumstance	*without looking*
Agent	*[watched] by a neighbor*
Position	*[retained] by the lender*
Force	*[demolished] by a storm*
Degree	*to a large extent*
Comparison	*than you*
Cause	*because of his personality*
Result	*with predictable consequences*
Purpose	*for his own ends*
Beneficiary	*for our sake*
Condition	*if in doubt*
Concession	*despite this*
Negative / restrictive	*seldom*
Focusing	*only*
Disjunct	*probably*
Conjunct	*therefore*

Gildea and Jurafsky suggest these 18 "abstract semantic roles": *agent, cause, degree, experiencer, force, goal, instrument, location, manner, null, path, patient, percept, proposition, result, source,*

---

6. Van Valin, "Functional Relations," 151, text interleaved.

7. Josef Ruppenhofer et al., *FrameNet II: Extended Theory and Practice*, 25 August 2006. http://framenet.icsi .berkeley.edu. In FrameNet II parlance, *semantic roles* are *frame elements*.

8. Whaley, *Introduction to Typology*, 67.

9. John H. Connolly, *Constituent Order in Functional Grammar* (Berlin: Foris, 1991) 71–72.

state, and *topic;*[10] Van Valin proffers these 11 "thematic relations": *agent, experiencer, instrument, force, patient, theme, recipient, goal, source, locative,* and *path;*[11] and Whaley puts forward these 13 roles: *agent, benefactive, comitative, experiencer, goal, instrumental, locative, patient, purposive, recipient, source, temporal,* and *theme.*[12] We note that:

1. Some items appear in all four lists. For example: *instrument(al)* and *place* (Connolly) ≈ *location* (Gildea and Jurafsky) ≈ *locative* (Van Valin, Whaley).[13]
2. Some items appear in only one list. For example, Gildea and Jurafsky include *percept,* not found in other lists.
3. Some distinctions do not withstand scrutiny. For example, Van Valin defines *force* as "involuntary causal participant which, unlike an instrument, cannot be manipulated. They can include things like *tornados, storms,* and *acts of God,* as in *The flood washed away the village.*"[14] But contrast these clauses:

    a. Due to poor levee maintenance, *the flood* washed away the village. (Instrument?)
    b. As Divine retribution, *the flood* washed away the village.[15] (Force?)

10.1.2 Our Approach to the Role Repertoire

We have followed the usual approach, namely, "to posit as few roles as possible, identifying a new role only when it seems to be required."[16] Over time, we have added roles, reaching our present tally of 44 semantic roles.[17] The table on p. 138 shows our categories compared with others' categories. Of our 44 semantic role (SR) categories, 21 are not used by our four reference works. We have found that they need to be available for real distinctions arising from the combined effects of the semantics of verbs, prepositions, and nominals in Hebrew composition. The SRs peculiar to our work fall into several natural groups:

- Two geometrical SRs:
    area
    length
- Path specifier SRs:
    movement bearing and movement origin
    time aim and time origin
- "Balancing SRs":
    harmed one (opposite of beneficiary)
    undesired outcome (equating result to "desired outcome")[18]

---

10. Gildea and Jurafsky, "Automatic Labeling," 279.

11. Van Valin, "Functional Relations," 152. What Van Valin and others call "theme," we call "exocentric absolute" to avoid confusion with the more usual definition. See §21.1.2.3.

12. Whaley, *Introduction to Typology,* 65.

13. The definitions of *agent* differ.

14. Van Valin, "Functional Relations," 152.

15. By our present conventions (§9.2.1), we will label *the flood* as the subject in both clauses, hiding its semantic role(s).

16. Whaley, *Introduction to Typology,* 66.

17. Three of these SRs will appear later in our full representation: doer, experiencer, and patient (see §9.2.2).

18. This is one area of our system where we may have gone too far. A result may be neither a desirable nor an undesirable outcome. It may be wise to remove undesired outcome from our collection of semantic roles or to add

Andersen-Forbes' Compared with Others' Semantic Roles (SRs)

A-F SR	*Others' SR*	*Used by* [a]	*A-F SR*	*Others' SR*	*Used by*
Accompanier	Comitative	*C, W*	Material/composition		
Agential	Agent	*C, W*	Movement aim	Goal	*G, V, W*
Aim/purpose	Purpose	*C*	Movement bearing		
Alternate/surrogate			Movement interval	Path	*G, V*
Area			Movement origin		
Beneficiary	Beneficiary	*C, W*	Number count		
"But-rather"			Number of times		
Cause	Cause	*C, G*	Patient	Patient	*G, V, W*
Comparison	Comparison	*C*	Possessor	Recipient	*V, W*
Concessive	Concession	*C*	Quantity/quantifier		
Condition	Condition	*C*	Quoter		
Cost			Reason	Purposive	*W*
Deprivation			Reference		
Doer	Agent	*G, V*	Resource/supply	Source	*G, V, W*
Exocentric absolute	Topic/Theme(2×)	*G, V, W*	Result	Result	*C, G*
Experiencer	Experiencer	*G, V, W*	Ruled-over one		
Harmed one			Separation (ablative)		
Instrument	Instrument	*C, G, V, W*	Time aim/goal		
Involved ones			Time interval	Duration	*C*
Length			Time origin		
Location	Place	*C, G, V, W*	Time point	Time/Temporal	*C, W*
Manner	Manner	*C, G*	Undesired outcome		

a. *C* = Connolly, *G* = Gildea and Jurafsky, *V* = Van Valin, *W* = Whaley.

- Miscellaneous SRs:

alternate	number of times
"but-rather"	quantity
cost	quoter
deprivation	reference
involved ones	ruled-over one
material/composition	separation
number count	

For the record, the four references use a dozen SRs that we have not (yet) had occasion to introduce:

desired outcome as a balancing item.

SR Terminology	English Example	Used by
Attendant circumstance	*without looking*	C
Conjunct	*therefore*	C
Degree	*to a large extent*	C, G
Disjunct	*probably*	C
Focusing	*only*	C
Force	*[demolished] by a storm*	C, G, V
Negative / restrictive	*seldom*	C
Null	it *would be foolish*	G
Percept	*It is apparent that . . .*	G
Position	*[retained] by the lender*	C
Proposition	*that does show freedom*	G
State	*he was hollering at them*	G

Several of these seem unattested in Biblical Hebrew. For example, we know of no null constructions ("dummy elements" as in English "*It* is raining") in Biblical Hebrew.

10.2 *Representative Approaches to Semantic Role Taxonomy*

Here we arrive at the central matter of this chapter, the taxonomy of semantic roles. Underlying classification is a dilemma common to classification systems: *category splitting*.[19] When should one subdivide a category? The literature suggests three ways of handling the "split / quit" dilemma:

1. *Map categories onto a line.*   Thereby, avoid discrete categories.
2. *Manual approach.*   Split maximally and then group hierarchically.
3. *Algorithmic approach.*   Use data to cluster the categories and then use a threshold to determine category granularity.

10.2.1 Map Categories onto a Line

The first option finesses the "split or quit" dilemma but suffers from arbitrariness. According to Van Valin, in the "continuum of [semantic roles], agent defines one end and patient the other; all of the other [semantic roles] represent points along the continuum."[20] He then presents (10.1) to illustrate the positioning of his semantic roles:

(10.1)
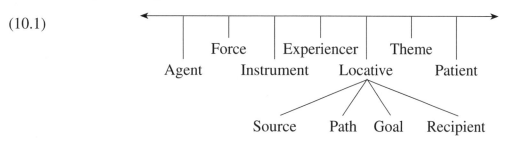

---

19. This issue is discussed for lexical categories by William Croft, "Parts of speech as language universals and as language-particular categories," in *Approaches to the Typology of Word Classes* (ed. P. M. Vogel and B. Comrie; Berlin: Mouton de Gruyter, 2000) 76–79. See also our §3.2 above.

20. Van Valin, "Functional Relations," 151. For consistency with our usage, we have replaced Van Valin's "thematic relations" with our "semantic roles."

This assumes that the roles lie in a one-dimensional space, but they may not. It also spaces them out uniformly, although this sort of spacing may be a distortion of the data. Forbes has shown that there are ways of determining whether textual data imply category positioning along a line and that there are ways of assigning data-derived distances between linearly ordered categories.[21] Techniques of this sort have not yet been applied to semantic roles, to say nothing of the roles appropriate to Biblical Hebrew.

10.2.2 Manual Approach: Split Maximally, Then Group Hierarchically

In the second option, one introduces as many categories as seem meaningful—the more the merrier. One then uses text characteristics to group the categories.

This is the option that is typically adopted and the one that we used. It has the virtue of simplicity but leads to an uneven taxonomy wherein the categories exhibit differing granularity. As the initial attempt at defining semantic roles, it is useful, but ultimately a rule-based computational approach may provide superior results.

The manual/intuitive approach to hierarchical grouping of semantic roles is common in the literature. For example, Van Valin presents the hierarchy of semantic roles shown in (10.2):[22]

(10.2)

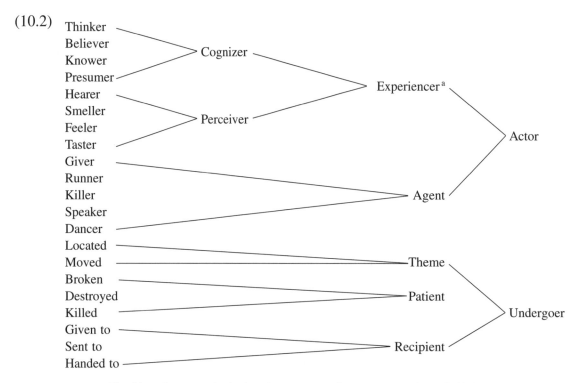

a. The idea, for example, is that the category of *cognizer* consists of *thinker, believer, knower,* and *presumer* and that *cognizer* and *perceiver* together form the category of *experiencer*; and so on.

---

21. A. Dean Forbes, "Squishes, Clines, and Fuzzy Signs: Mixed and Gradient Categories in the Biblical Hebrew Lexicon," in *Syriac Lexicography I: Foundations for Syriac Lexicography* (ed. A. D. Forbes and D. G. K. Taylor; Piscataway, NJ: Gorgias, 2006) 123–28.

22. Van Valin, "Functional Relations," 154. See also Connolly, *Constituent Order*, 71–72, where a two-level hierarchy is given.

When we intuitively group our semantic roles to form a hierarchy, we obtain this provisional taxonomy:

Major Participants	Spatial	Phrasal Discourse Units
Doer	Area	Cause
Experiencer	Length	Comparison
Patient	Location	Deprivation
Other Participants	Separation ("ablative")	Quoter
Accompanier	**Temporal**	**Mixed-Level**
Agential	Time aim/goal	Aim/purpose
Alternate/surrogate	Time interval	"But-rather"
Beneficiary	Time origin	Concessive
Exocentric absolute	Time point	Condition
Harmed one	**Enriching Constituents**	Reason
Involved ones	Cost	Result
Possessor	Instrument	Undesired outcome
Ruled-over ones	Manner	
Movement	Material/composition	
Movement aim (target)	Number count	
Movement bearing (direction)	Number of times	
Movement interval	Reference	
Movement origin	Resource/supply source	
	Quantity/quantifier	

10.2.3   Algorithmic Approach: Cluster and Threshold

An intuitively fashioned hierarchy may seem exhaustively and appropriately descriptive, but it ultimately suffers from not being directly and explicitly based on measured text characteristics (for proposed text characteristics, see §10.3.4). In any event, investigating algorithmic approaches is beyond the scope of this volume.

10.3   *Semantic Role Classification Criteria*

Once we have settled on a set of semantic roles and grouped them hierarchically, we must devise methods of assigning semantic role categories to clause immediate constituents.

10.3.1   Representative Classification Criteria

Bornkessel et al. nicely summarize the challenges that we, as definers of semantic roles, face:

[T]here is still no fully satisfactory model of how the syntax-to-semantics linking is accomplished. One reason for this appears to lie in the problems regarding the definition and scope of semantic roles that have continually reappeared since the very beginnings of research in this domain. . . . For example, researchers have vastly differed with regard to how many semantic roles should be assumed, how these should be characterised both in semantic and in syntactic terms, how the different roles should be dissociated from one another, and which syntactic phenomena should be derivable from them. . . . From the earliest approaches to semantic roles and their interface character between syntax and semantics, a central research focus has lain on defining the relation between these roles (both individual and generalised) and their corresponding syntactic categories. [23]

It is to the last mentioned topic that we now turn. What is the relation between the semantic roles and their corresponding syntactic categories? Or, putting the emphasis on classification, is it possible to classify CICs on the basis of their syntactic properties? Much work has been done in this area. Unfortunately, the work that we are aware of presupposes fixed phrase order at some point, a presupposition we are not prepared to make. Work on semantic-role classification criteria falls into two areas: manual and computational.

Manual classification is carried out by humans following analysis-constraining handbooks, [24] with research invariably done on a verb-by-verb basis. The resulting sets of semantic roles are dauntingly extensive. One benefit of having the manually classified semantic roles is that they can be, and are, used to enable and evaluate computational analyses. [25]

Computational classification uses algorithms embodying standard methods of pattern recognition based on sets of features derived from the texts analyzed. [26] The goal of this analysis is to "infer role labels, given sentence constituents and a word from the sentence that is the *predicator*, which takes semantic arguments." [27]

10.3.2 The Complement-Adjunct Distinction

In §7.3.4, we provided criteria for distinguishing complements and adjuncts taken from Pollard and Sag. We concluded that, given the limited size of our corpus, the criteria were of practical significance only for the frequently occurring verbs. In this subsection, we take up the distinction afresh, this time approaching it from the semantic role perspective.

The FrameNet II formalism distinguishes three "levels of centrality" for semantic roles: core, peripheral, and extra-thematic. [28] These are defined as:

- "A core [semantic role] is one that instantiates a conceptually necessary component of a frame, while making the frame unique and different from other frames.
- "[Semantic roles] that do not introduce additional, independent or distinct events from the main reported event are characterized as peripheral. Peripheral [semantic roles] mark such notions as *time*, *place*, *manner*, *means*, *degree*, and the like.

---

23. Ina Bornkessel et al., eds., *Semantic Role Universals and Argument Linking: Theoretical, Typological, and Psycholinguistic Perspectives* (Berlin: de Gruyter, 2006) 1–3.

24. Two well-developed manual projects are Ruppenhofer et al., *FrameNet II*; and Martha Palmer, Daniel Gildea, and Paul Kingsbury, "The Proposition Bank," *Computational Linguistics* 31 (2005) 71–106.

25. Having labeled instances of the semantic roles allows algorithms to select and weight syntactic features using the standard methods of statistical pattern recognition. (See "supervised learning" in any book on pattern recognition.)

26. See Gildea and Jurafsky, "Automatic Labeling"; Cynthia A. Thompson, Roger Levy, and Christopher D. Manning, "A Generative Model for Semantic Role Labeling," *Proc. ECML-2003*; Kristina Toutanova et al., "Joint Learning Improves Semantic Role Labeling," *Proc. 43rd Meeting of ACL*; Trond Grenager and Christopher D. Manning, "Unsupervised Discovery," in *Proceedings of the 2006 Conference on Empirical Methods in Natural Language Processing*.

27. Thompson, Levy, and Manning, "A Generative Model," 1.

28. Although the FrameNet II terminology implies a particular positioning, the definitions of terms do not. Hence, the distinctions are relevant to both fixed and free phrase order languages.

- "Extra-thematic [semantic roles] situate an event against a backdrop of another state of affairs, either an actual event or state of the same type . . . or by evoking a larger frame within which the reported state of affairs is embedded."[29]

Within this framework, Manning and co-workers propose a useful distinction between arguments and adjuncts: "while core arguments must be associated with a semantic role that is verb specific . . . , [peripheral] adjuncts are generated by a role that is verb independent."[30]

Palmer et al. provide a table of "general, adjunct-like arguments."[31] Deleting three pseudo-roles,[32] we present their table 1, which looks like this:

loc: location	tmp: time
ext: extent	pnc: purpose [*sic*]
adv: general purpose	mnr: manner
cau: cause	dir: direction

10.3.3 Linking Functions to Constructions

By way of reminder, the daughters of the clause root node are the clause immediate constituents (CICs; see §5.1). Each CIC dominates a daughter node, its label specifying a construction. The exercise in this subsection is to "link" the CIC *function* labels to the CIC daughter *construction* labels—that is, to see how the function and form labels correlate. Two examples will make this notion concrete.

Invariable Linking. Let us first examine a situation in which a construction is invariably linked to a particular CIC. Consider the construct phrase נְאֻם־יהוה 'oracle of Yahweh' (236×). Its form is n:vocbl/cstr. Its semantics (vocable) make it eligible to label a specimen of prophetic text, and so the form is, with one exception,[33] immediately dominated by a lbl/gram CIC node, as in phrase marker (10.3):

(10.3)

(10.4)

Multiple Linkings. The prepositional phrase לְדָוִד or לְדָוִיד 'to David' occurs 147 times in Biblical Hebrew, 85 times as a CIC daughter. The *linking question* is: "What grammatical functions (GFs) and semantic roles (SRs) does this construction exercise and under what circumstances?"

---

29. A (semantic) frame is "a script-like conceptual structure that describes a particular type of situation, object, or event along with its participants and props" (Ruppenhofer et al., *FrameNet II*, 5).

30. Grenager and Manning, "Unsupervised Discovery," 3. Also Kristina Toutanova et al., "Joint Learning," 590.

31. Palmer, Gildea, and Kingsbury, "The Proposition Bank," 76–77.

32. The deleted items are: DIS: discourse connective, NEG: negative, MOD: modal.

33. In Isa 31:9, the construct phrase is in apposition to a nominalized clause, the combined structure being a label CIC.

The phrase is linked to either of two grammatical functions (ind obj [42×] and dir obj [1×]) or any of six semantic roles (refrnt [9×], lbl [14×], poss [13×], benf [4×], mvt aim [1×], and mvt dir [1×]). Phrase marker (10.5) shows a typical ind obj instance from 1 Chr 11:5:

(10.5)

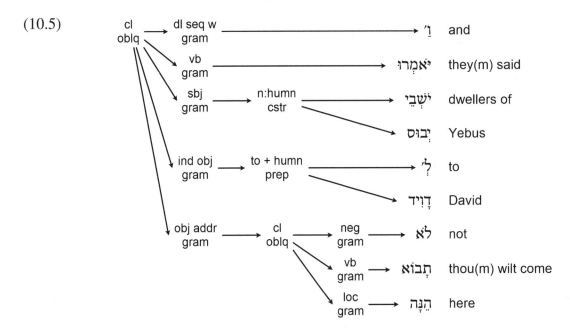

The predicator is יֹאמְרוּ 'they(m) said'. As we will see in §12.4.3.5, if the predicator root is אמר, then a לְ+<human> prepositional phrase is an ind obj 97.3% of the time.

The single dir obj is shown in (10.6) from 1 Chr 18:6, where the verb is a Hiphil of ישע:[34]

(10.6)

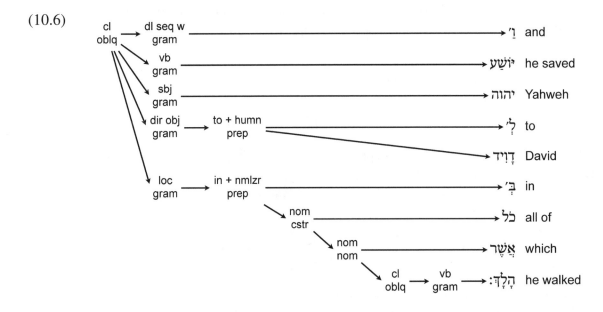

Our phrase is a label (lbl) CIC 14 times, always in a psalm, as in (10.7) from Ps 26:1:

---

34. Overall in ישע clauses, the phrase לְדָוִד occurs twice as dir obj (Ps 86:16 and 1 Chr 18:6). The direct object is marked instead with an object marker in very similar passages in 2 Sam 8:6, 14; and 1 Chr 18:13.

(10.7)

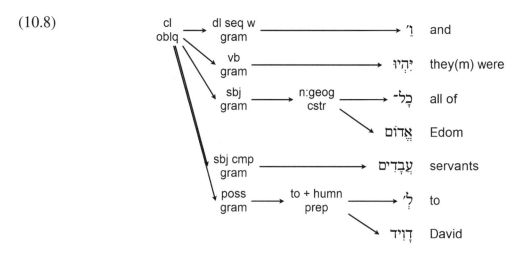

The possessor role occurs 13 times. In phrase marker (10.8) for 1 Chr 18:13, the predicator is יָהְיוּ 'they-were'. About 40% of the לְ+ <human> phrases in היה clauses are possessors (poss).

(10.8)

MISPLACED

We find four places[35] where לְדָוִד has the semantic role beneficiary (benf). In phrase marker (10.9) from 2 Sam 5:11, the clause predicator is יִבְנוּ 'they built' with root בנה.

(10.9)

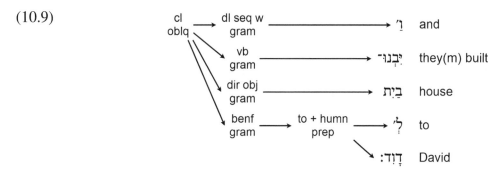

Approximately half (54.5%) of the לְ + <human> phrases in בנה clauses function as beneficiaries (benf).

The semantic role movement aim (mvt aim) is seen once, in 1 Chr 12:17, phrase marker (10.10). The predicator root is בא 'to come'. In clauses having this root, phrases of the shape לְ + <human> have movement aim (mvt aim) as their function almost two-thirds of the time (63.5%).

---

35. These are: 2 Sam 5:11; 1 Kgs 11:38; Jer 22:4, and 33:15.

(10.10)

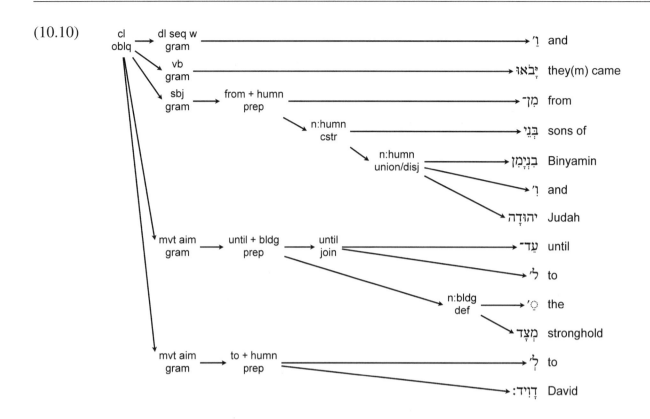

We have seen that grammatical function and semantic role are not necessarily intrinsic to syntactic form as such. Rather GF/SR correlate with the semantics of the verbs with which they are associated.

10.3.4 Proposed Semantic Role Syntactic Correspondences

Important work has been done on describing "the relation between semantic roles and their syntactic realization . . . [the goal being] . . . to learn to recognize semantic relationships from syntactic cues, given examples with both types of information."[36] What is being described here is called "supervised learning." By having a subset of one's data marked up with both the independent and dependent categories of interest,[37] one can exploit standard methods of pattern recognition to infer rules for assigning the dependent categories, given the independent categories. Typically, the inferred rules are probabilistic, and one is engaging in statistical pattern recognition.[38]

In discussing syntactic features, we use a clause from Deut 7:20 for phrase marker (10.11):

---

36. Gildea and Jurafsky, "Automatic Labeling," 247 and 252.

37. For our approach to the problem of inferring semantic roles from syntactic information, the former are the dependent and the latter are the independent categories. Interestingly, Van Valin specifies algorithms for moving from syntax to semantics (§7.0.2) or from semantics to syntax (§7.0.1): R. D. Van Valin Jr., *Exploring the Syntax-Semantics Interface* (Cambridge: Cambridge University Press, 2005) 225–28.

38. See, for example, Richard O. Duda et al., *Pattern Classification* (2nd ed.; New York: Wiley-Interscience, 2000).

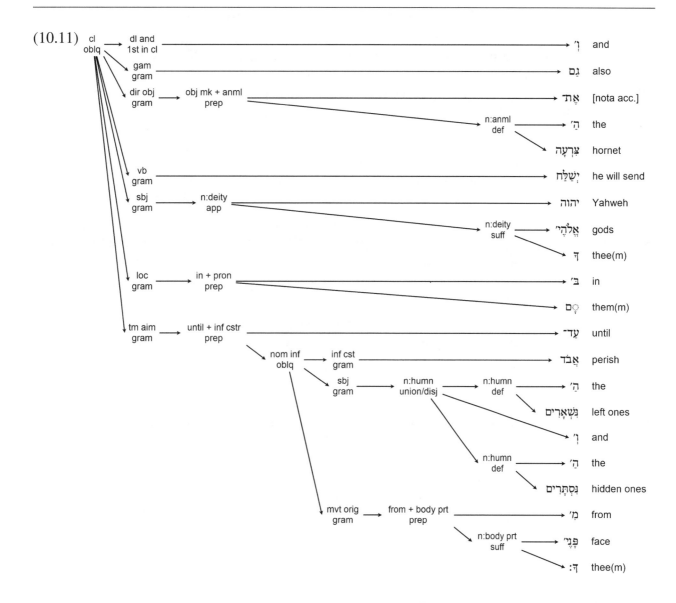

We examine GF / SR assignments for this clause considering the final three of six syntactic features proposed by Gildea and Jurafsky:[39]

1. *Phrase type.* "Different roles tend to be realized by different syntactic categories" (p. 252). In phrase marker (10.11), the <u>first CIC</u> is determined by its phrase type—actually, segment identity in this case—(dl and / 1st in cl), as are the <u>second CIC</u> (gam/gram) and the fourth CIC (vb/gram). The grammatical function of the <u>third CIC</u> is determined by its phrase type because an obj mk+anml / prep node in a clause with an active verb is, with very few exceptions, a dir obj / gram CIC. For its semantic role, one might assign *undergoer*.[40]

---

39. Regarding the first three features, Gildea and Jurafsky ("Automatic Labeling," 262) comment: "Three of our features, *position*, [*governing category*], and *path*, attempt to capture the syntactic relation between the [predicator] and the constituent to be labeled, and in particular to differentiate the subjects from objects of verbs."

40. Van Valin, *Exploring,* 54.

2. *Voice.*   "The distinction between active and passive verbs plays an important role in the connection between semantic role and grammatical function" (p. 257). We will make use of this distinction.

3. *Semantics of head word.*[41]   "[W]e expected lexical dependence to be extremely important in labeling semantic roles, as indicated by their importance in related tasks such as parsing" (p. 258).

Our preference with regard to prepositional phrases is to use as features the identity of the preposition and the grammatical features of the associated nominal. Consider the seventh CIC in phrase marker (10.11). The preposition is עַד 'until', and the nominal is a nominalized infinitive construct (nom inf / oblq). Searching our phrase markers, we find that there are 143 instances of a CIC that is a prepositional phrase consisting of עַד 'until' plus a nominalized infinitive construct predicator (nom inf / oblq). All but 11 of these (92.3%) have their dominating CIC-node classified as a tm aim / gram. Hence, a rule stating that עַד 'until' plus a nominalized infinitive construct has a *time aim* semantic role will be correct approximately 92% of the time.[42]

Other feature sets have been suggested. Grenager and Manning seek to "learn a model which relates a verb, its [accompanying] semantic roles, and their possible syntactic realizations."[43] To achieve this, they choose to "number the noun phrase (*np*), complement clause (*cl*, *xcl*), and adjectival complements (*acmpl*) appearing in an unbroken sequence directly after the verb, since this is sufficient to capture the necessary syntactic information." This approach strikes us as overly English-o-centric. Thompson, Levy, and Manning opted for a stripped-down set of features: "To simplify the model, we chose to represent each constituent by its phrasal category together with the head word of that constituent."[44] Their approach involves less work than more-expansive approaches.

Regarding the phrase marker (10.11) for Deut 7:20, we have discussed inference of grammatical functions and semantic roles for all but the fifth CIC and the sixth CIC. The fifth CIC is syntactically a masculine-singular apposition phrase having divine semantics. Because the noun phrase and predicator agree in gender and number, the noun phrase here is a candidate for filling the subject grammatical function (with semantic role of, say, *doer*).

Finally, consider the sixth CIC in phrase marker (10.11) which is shown as a loc/gram semantic role label dominating an in+pron/prep constituent. How would one use the rather sparse syntactic facts to infer the semantic role label probabilistically? The syntactic facts here are these:

- the constituent is a CIC,
- it is a prepositional phrase,
- its preposition is בְּ 'in',
- its nominal is the pronoun ם 'them'.

An attempt to assign CIC labels *purely probabilistically* relies on observed ranked frequency of occurrence. For the current instance, if we search the phrase markers of Biblical Hebrew for prepo-

---

41. The "head" is "the central element which is distributionally equivalent to the phrase as a whole" (D. Crystal, *A Dictionary of Linguistics and Phonetics* [5th ed.; Oxford: Blackwell, 2003] 215).

42. Eight of the 11 oddities have been classified as time intervals. The other 3 are in Judg 6:4, 2 Sam 5:25, and 1 Kgs 18:46, and all involve an infinitive construct having the root בא. A further instance of this sort, where the construction leads off a conjoined (union) phrase, may be found in 1 Sam 17:52.

43. Grenager and Manning, "Unsupervised Discovery," 2.

44. Thompson, Levy, and Manning, "A Generative Model," 6.

sitional phrases that are CICs consisting of "in" plus a pronoun, we find 1,349 instances distributed across 5 grammatical functions and 16 semantic roles. The distribution of the 4 most frequent (plus a residuum *other*) is as follows:

CIC Type	Incidence	Percentage
location	598	44.3
direct object	451	33.4
instrument	128	9.5
harmed one	47	3.5
other	125	9.3
Total	1,349	100.0

The table suggests that if we encounter an in+pron/prep constituent, then there is around a 50-50 chance that it is a *location*, with 3 chances in 10 that it is a direct object, and so on. For the present phrase marker, however, we know even more. Since the presence of אֵת '[object marker]' identifies a direct object CIC, we know that the constituent being classified most likely is not a direct object. Deleting that near-impossibility from the numbers yields this table of counts and adjusted percentages:

CIC Type	Incidence	Percentage
location	598	66.6
instrument	128	14.3
harmed one	47	5.2
other	125	13.9
Total	898	100.0

Given that we are not dealing with a direct object CIC, we know that the questioned constituent has a likelihood of two chances in three of being a *location*. The next most likely semantic role, *instrument*, has around one chance in ten of being correct. To improve the odds for correct assignment, one would need further information. Alternately, one might simply declare the top two or three most likely to be available and have the over-reader decide among them.[45]

This study of the role assignment possibilities for a single clause is in no way definitive. But it does provide insight into the way a more extensive study might proceed, and the results that might be achieved.[46]

Given the foregoing proposed semantic role / syntactic form correspondences and given the attributes of Biblical Hebrew, one should attempt both to infer grammatical functions and to assign

---

45. When we compare our present parsing of Deut 7:20 with the parsing of Deut 28:20 and 1 Sam 24:7, we see that our probabilistic assignment of SR to the sixth CIC in Deut 7:20 is likely incorrect: harmed one appears superior to location.

46. *Technical note.* In the exercise just completed, we obtained the needed probability estimates by surveying assignments made across all of Biblical Hebrew. In actual practice, to avoid circularity, one would manually classify a carefully designed subset of data ("the teaching data") and then use probability estimates based on outcomes in the teaching data to classify previously unseen data ("the testing data").

semantic roles to clause immediate constituents on the basis of observable characteristics of clausal constituents such as these:[47]

1. *Predicator*	2. *Noun Phrases*	4. *"Certain parts of speech"*
identity ("root")	gender	5. *"Certain set phrases"*
binyan	number	
voice	semantics	
gender	3. *Prepositional Phrases*	
number	preposition identity	
semantics	noun phrase semantics	

"Certain parts of speech" points to the fact, for example, that modals always are assigned the modal operator function. By "certain set phrases," we refer to constituents such as נְאֻם־יהוה 'oracle of Yahweh', a phrase that is invariably a label CIC.

10.3.4 The Way Forward

We have elected to attempt neither computational classification of the clause immediate constituents into the five groups introduced in chap. 9 nor computational assignment of semantic roles from the list in §10.1.2. These are challenges for another day, for us or for others.[48] Instead, in the next seven chapters, we consider the computer- and expert-assigned CIC labels to be givens and proceed as follows:

Chapter 11.   We introduce methods of displaying the composition, incidence, and ordering of CIC types.

Chapters 12–15.   We then characterize the verb corpora defined by these four high-frequency verb roots: אמר 'say', היה 'be', עשׂה 'do, make', and נתן 'give'.

Chapter 16.   Next, we investigate the way that each CIC subtype is realized *across all clauses having finite verbs*, independent of verb root.

Chapter 17.   We conclude our investigation of CICs by presenting a computational method for discovering sets of verb roots that naturally group together. Clustering verb corpora into groups allows us elegantly and informatively to represent the characteristics that they share, facilitating important generalizations.

10.4 *Brief Summary*

The semantic role of a CIC discloses "the semantic relation that a nominal bears to the rest of the clause" (Whaley). Analyses differ with regard to repertoire, taxonomy, and recognition criteria.

Semantic Role Repertoire.   After examining the SR repertoires posited by various authors, we have arrived at a set of 44 SRs, many novel to our work.

---

47. Including predicator gender / number and noun-phrase gender / number in our list of characteristics introduces a new quality into the mix: noun-verb *concord*. Noun-verb *concord* is present when a noun (phrase) and verb agree both in gender and number, allowing the noun (phrase) to be the subject of the clause under analysis.

48. The creation and assessment of carefully reasoned taxonomies is quite involved. Assessing the adequacy of our taxonomies of parts of speech and of semantic roles is an iterative process.

Semantic Role Taxonomy. As for our SR taxonomy, we have followed one standard practice and intuitively grouped our SRs into a hierarchy with eight top levels: *major participants, other participants, movement, spatial, temporal, enriching, phrasal discourse units*, and *mixed-level*.

Semantic Role Recognition Criteria. As we demonstrate, GF/SR classes are not necessarily intrinsic to specific syntactic forms; the characteristics of the clausal predicator are also critical for the classifications.

Various sets of constituent features have been proposed for computationally inferring GFs/SRs. We provide an example that illustrates how this sort of detailed computational inference might work but have not yet investigated the matter.

The present work takes as given the computer-assigned and human-adjusted GF/SR CIC label assignments and uses these to investigate CIC behaviors.

Chapter 11

Introduction to
Clause Immediate Constituent Composition,
Incidence, and Ordering

In this chapter, we take up CIC type characterization and the quantitation of CIC incidence and ordering. We introduce ways of describing the CICs in the clauses containing a given root (§11.1). We next produce *CIC-Incidence vertical bar charts* (§11.2). Finally, we study CIC ordering, displaying pairs of *CIC-Ordering horizontal bar charts* (§11.3). The purpose of this chapter is to *illustrate our methods* using the small corpus of clauses having the root חפץ 'desire' or 'delight in'.

11.1 *Clause Immediate Constituent Censuses*

11.1.1 The *Binyan* Census

In upcoming chapters, we will first provide counts of the clauses with realizations of various *binyanim*. The *binyan* census for חפץ is simplicity itself: the verbal stock for חפץ consists of 78 Qal actives.[1]

11.1.2 The CIC Subtype Census

The tally of CIC subtypes is provided as a standardized table similar to table 11.1 for חפץ. The major table headings are the five CIC subtypes introduced in §9.1 with the final subtype split into its two components. In the left two-thirds of the table, the counts specify how many times each constituent occurs as a non-GF/SR CIC. In the right-most third, we tally the GFs plus the six most frequent SRs. Based simply on the table, one may advance a few generalizations regarding the חפץ corpus: (1) as presently analyzed, the verb חפץ is transitive; (2) only 27% of the clauses have an explicit subject; (3) חפץ appears with negation 23% of the time; (4) its clauses do not involve interrogatives; (5) not very many spatial or temporal specifications appear, but aim CICs do appear. To help make these concepts more concrete, consider phrase marker (11.1) from Ezek 18:23 (p. 153). The *label* CIC contributes a count of one to the *label* entry in the left-most panel of the table. The חפץ *predicator* adds a count of one to the finite verb entry in the middle panel. The nonpredicative infinitive absolute supplies a count of one to its category in the middle panel, and the *closed interrogative* is the sole instance of its category. The remaining CIC (dir obj) is a GF. It contributes a count of one to the *direct object* GF entry in the right-most panel of the table.[2]

---

1. We never include clauses with imputed elliptic predicators in our counts (see §20.2.3). For the present root, there is a clause with an ellipted predicator in Hos 6:6. This clause is not included in our tallies. Once, in Job 40:17, a חפץ verb in a clause has the sense "cause to bend down." This clause is also excluded from our analyses.

2. In our tallies, we include *resumed* constituents, since these are genuine clause constituents. (For the חפץ corpus, the single resumed CIC is a direct object in Isa 13:17.)

Table 11.1. CIC Subtype Census for the חפץ Corpus: 78 Structures

Impermanents	Count	Predicators	Count	GFs	Count
Underspecified "and"	7	Finite verb	75	Subject	21
Lapsus calami	0	Predicative inf. abs.	0	Direct object	52
Nebulous	0	Purely verbal participle	0	Indirect object	1
Syntactic Isolates	**Count**	Noun-verb participle	3	Complement	0
Vocative	2	Infinitive construct	0	**Top Six SRs**	**Count**
Exclamative	0	Non-predicative inf. abs.[a]	2	Aim/purpose	15
Label	2	**Operators**	**Count**	Location	3
		Negative	18	Manner	2
		Closed interrogative	1	Time point	1
		Other conjunction[b]	0	Comparison	1
		Modal	1	Accompanier	1

a. To save some space, we include the aspectualizers ("nonpredicative infinitive absolute") in with the predicators.

b. "Other conjunction" includes all CIC-level conjunctions other than those classified as underspecified "and." Examples: גַם/גַּם 'also', אַף 'also', כִּי 'that', אוֹ 'or'.

(11.1)

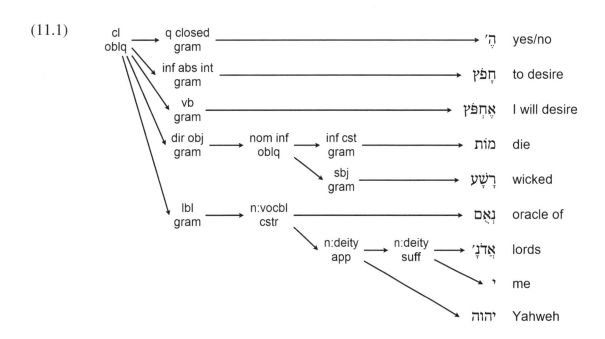

11.1.3 Survey of the Non-GF/SR Clause Immediate Constituents

While the primary focus of our examination of verb corpora is the composition, incidence, and ordering of the GF/SR items, for each verb corpus we provide a two-part survey of its non-GF/SR CICs. At each section beginning, we provide a summary of the main points of the material to be found in the remainder of the section. The main body of the survey then follows. The summary looks like this:

§11.1.3 *Main Observations.*   We note that the חפץ corpus attracts very few syntactic isolates, that in almost all חפץ clauses the predicator is a finite verb (96%), and that almost always negatives immediately precede the חפץ verb (94%) and are mostly clause initial (67%).

11.1.3.1 Impermanents

The seven *underspecified "and"* CICs represent unfinished work—CICs that one day will be promoted to discourse connectives ("cue phrases"; see §9.3.1.1).

11.1.3.2 Syntactic Isolates

There are two vocatives (clause initial in 2 Sam 24:3 and clause medial in Ps 40:9), and there are two labels (clause final in both Ezek 18:23 and 32; see §9.3.2).

11.1.3.3 Predicators

Noun-verb participles almost always precede their arguments and are viewed as anchored. The חפץ corpus has three: Ps 34:13, 35:27; and Neh 1:11. In Ezek 18:23 (see phrase marker [11.1] immediately above), we have a cognate intensifier aspectualizer. In Job 13:3, we have a noncognate amplifier aspectualizer (see §3.2.6.1).

11.1.3.4 Operators

A single closed interrogative 'הֲ 'yes or no?' appears in Ezek 18:23, and a single modal לֹ 'would that' occurs in Judg 13:23. Of the 18 negatives, 17 immediately precede their finite verb. The sole exception is in Ps 147:10, where the CIC sequence is neg . . . dir obj . . . pred ("not in the strength of the horse he will desire"). The negative CIC is clause initial in 12 clauses (67%).

11.1.4 Survey of the GF/SR Clause Immediate Constituents

The relation between the GF/SR functions and their forms, as revealed by the makeup of the CIC daughters, is a major focus of this and the following four chapters. For each verb corpus we give a two-part survey of its GF/SR CIC daughters. At each section beginning, we give a summary of the main points of the material to be found in the remainder of the section. The main body of the survey then follows. The summary looks like this:

§11.1.4 *Main Observations.*   The חפץ corpus includes very few adverbs and no clause(-like) structures. Its direct objects are often realized as prepositional phrases with 'בְּ (62%). The corpus includes an aim semantic role fairly often (20% of clauses), predominantly as a prepositional phrase with 'לְ (87%). Its bare substantive constituents almost always exercise subject or direct object grammatical functions (95%).

Table 11.2 (p. 155) tallies the forms that appear as GF/SR daughters in the חפץ corpus.

11.1.4.1 Adverbs

When describing the clause sets of frequently occurring verbs, we use tables of tallies to present the census data. With the חפץ corpus, however, the CIC daughter adverbs are so few that we simply list them, their semantic roles, and their citations.

Table 11.2. GF / SR Daughter Forms

GF / SR Daughter	*Count*
Adverb	4
Clause(-like) struct.[a]	0
Prepositional phrase	54
Noun phrase	37
Pronoun	3

[a]"Clause(-like) struct." refers to clauses, sentences, and primitive discourse structures.

Adverb		*Semantic Role*	*Citation*
הִנֵּה	'here'	location	1 Sam 18:22
מְאֹד	'very'	manner [degree]	1 Sam 19:1
אָז	'then'	time point	Ps 51:21
מְאֹד	'very'	manner [degree]	Ps 112:1

11.1.4.2   Clause(-Like) Structures

The חפץ verb corpus contains no CIC daughter clause(-like) structures.

11.1.4.3   Prepositional Phrases

There are 54 CIC daughter prepositional phrases in the חפץ corpus. The preposition incidences are:

35 בְּ׳	15 לְ׳	1 אֶל	1 כְּ׳	1 לְמַעַן	1 עִם

In studying the linkages between GF / SR functions (as disclosed by their CIC labels) and GF / SR forms (as given by the CIC daughter labels), our policy for presenting data tallies is as follows. The data tables in the text present as individually identifiable counts only the category combinations that have at least some cell counts in excess of 5% of the total number of instances under investigation. Smaller counts are consolidated under "[other]." This is intended to allow readers to grasp the major characteristics of the data without having to wade through minutiae.

The foregoing will be made clearer through examination of the tables for the frequent prepositional phrase types (PP types) of the חפץ corpus. In this and the next four chapters, readers should examine the tables, seeking generalizations that characterize the various verb corpora.

The בְּ׳ Prepositional Phrases.   The censoring threshold is 5% of the total number of PPs being considered, 35 in the case of בְּ׳. Hence, only the category combinations that have counts greater than or equal to (.05 × 35) = 1.75 are displayed in their own cells in table 11.3.

Table 11.3. 'בְּ PPs for חפץ

substantive type ↓	dir obj	[other]
[pronoun]	17	
quality	6	1
human	3	
abstract	2	
document	2	
inf. construct	2	
[other]	1	1

We observe for the חפץ corpus that: (1) any PP involving 'בְּ 'in' is most likely a direct object (94.3%); (2) around one-third of the direct objects involve 'בְּ plus a pronoun (17/52, 32.7%).

The 'לְ Prepositional Phrases. Table 11.4 provides tallies for the 15 'לְ PPs in the חפץ corpus.

Table 11.4. 'לְ PPs for חפץ

substantive type ↓	aim	dir obj	reason
inf. construct	13		
open interrog.		1	1

In the חפץ corpus, {'לְ + inf. construct} realizes an aim SR 13 times, and {'לְ + open interrogative} realizes a direct object GF once and a reason SR once.

The Remaining Prepositional Phrases. Four hapax prepositions remain to be examined. In general, we resort to simple listing when prepositions are feebly realized in a given verb corpus. In the present case, we therefore simply observe that:

- {אֶל + deity} has an *indirect object* grammatical function (GF) in Job 13:3
- {'כְּ + human} realizes a *comparison* semantic role (SR) in Isa 58:2
- {לְמַעַן + abstract} has a *direct object* GF in Isa 42:21
- {עִם + [pronoun]} realizes an *accompanier* SR in Ps 73:25

11.1.4.4 Substantives

By now we have dealt with each of the entries in table 11.2 except for the "bare" substantives: noun phrases (37×) and pronouns (3×).

The censoring threshold is 5% of the total number of bare substantives being considered, 40. Hence, only the category combinations that have counts greater than (.05 × 40) = 2.0 have their own cells in the simplified table on p. 157. We remark that the bare substantives with חפץ exercise important grammatical functions (95%).

This concludes our illustrative censuses of clause composition in the חפץ corpus. In chaps. 12–15, we will proceed along similar lines as we investigate the composition of the CICs involved in the clause corpora containing each of four frequently occurring verb roots.

substantive type ↓	dir obj	subj	[other]
human	1	11	
inf. construct	3		2
deity		6	
abstract	3		
[pronoun]		3	
thing	3		
[other]	8		

11.2 *Clause Immediate Constituent Incidence Contours*

We now turn to the visualization of the incidences of CICs in the clauses in a given verb corpus.

We are in a position to examine all of the clauses in Biblical Hebrew to see which CICs occur in verbal clauses. To visualize the relative incidences of CICs for the sets of clauses, we use a bar chart with bar heights giving the percentage incidence of the 13 constituents that occur more than 5% of the time in the full set of 45,503 clauses with Qal active predicators. To understand the bar chart, refer to the double arrows labeled a, b, c, and d below the chart (see chart on p. 158).

Important Note.   We subdivide the predicators into anchored (sequential finite verb, infinitive construct, n-v participle, and construct participle) and unanchored (non-sequential finite verb and predicative infinitive absolute) subsets. We do so because of a peculiarity of the Hebrew sequential verb forms: they are "anchored" in the clause-initial position. They thus constrain Hebrew clause configuration in a way that contrasts with the partial free CIC ordering of other kinds of Hebrew clauses. Combining the two sorts of clauses has too often led to invalid inferences.

The bar chart (p. 158) summarizes the CIC incidences across all of the Qal active verbal clauses making up Biblical Hebrew. It documents, for example, that:

1. *Unanchored predicators* are the most common type (appearing in 54% of the clauses).
2. *Anchored predicators* are in 46%, *subjects* in 38%, and *direct objects* in 48%.
3. Only the 13 CIC classes shown appear in more than 5% of Qal active clauses.

The incidence bar chart for our sample verb corpus, the חפץ corpus, appears on p. 159. We see that predicators are almost exclusively finite unanchored verbs. Subjects appear in just over one-quarter of the clauses and direct objects in nearly two-thirds. Negation is fairly common (23%), and aim/purpose appears in nearly one-fifth (19%) of the clauses.

In two clauses in the חפץ corpus, a direct object GF and an aim/purpose SR co-occur. Phrase marker (11.2) from 1 Kgs 10:9 shows one of these clauses. A nearly parallel clause is in 2 Chr 9:8.

CIC Incidence across the Qal Active Corpus

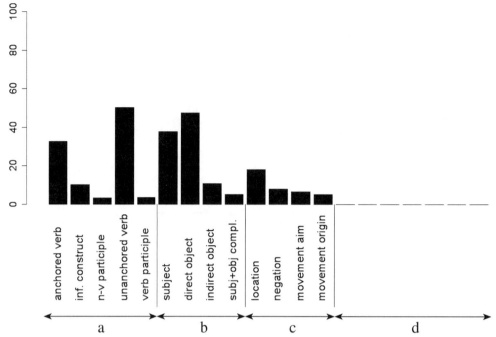

a. The first five bars from the left up to the left-most vertical line below the bars [interval a] correspond to the available choices for predicators; their percentages add up to 100.

b. The next four bars [interval b] provide the observed percentage incidences for our grammatical functions plus subject complements lumped with object complements.[3]

c. The next four bars up to the right-most vertical line [interval c] correspond to the four most common semantic roles (across all Qal active clauses) ordered from most to least frequent.

d. To the right of the right-most vertical line [interval d], we leave space to display additional CICs that occur in more than 5% of the clauses for any particular verb corpus being analyzed.

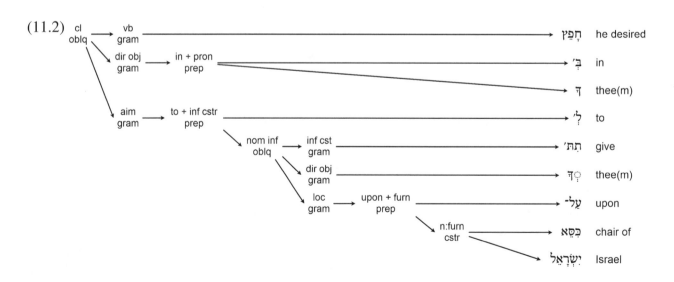

---

3. The wisdom of including subject complements and object complements in with the grammatical functions might be debated. Given the present state of our knowledge, we include them because the incidence of these complements is, in fact, a function of the verb corpus that is being examined.

CIC Incidence across the Qal Active חפץ Corpus

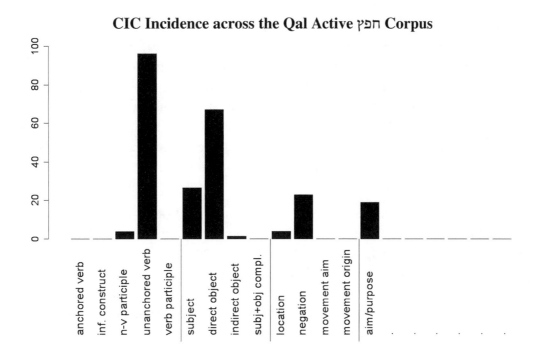

11.3 *Clause Immediate Constituent Ordering*

A significant innovation of generalized phrase structure grammar was the separation of the dominance aspects of syntax from the precedence aspects.[4] As Pollard and Sag put it:[5]

> In every human language, there are language-specific constraints upon the linear order of sister constituents which apply to all the signs of the language, and hence are to be factored out of the grammar rules.

The study of the ordering of constituents has been aptly called "positional syntax."[6] At clause level, positional syntax attempts to account for the "relative position, proximity of position, and absolute position"[7] of the CICs that make up clauses.

Here, we discuss an approach to positional syntax that some have applied to Biblical Hebrew, *fields-based positional syntax*. We then introduce and illustrate our preferred modified approach.[8]

---

4. Gerald Gazdar et al., *Generalized Phrase Structure Grammar* (Oxford: Blackwell, 1985) 44–50. As we noted in §4.1 and in our glossary, *precedence* deals with the ordering of constituents. For example, the segments making up a text occur in precedence order, which matches their physical sequence in the text.

5. Carl Pollard and Ivan Sag, *Information-Based Syntax and Semantics*, vol. 1: *Fundamentals* (Stanford, CA: CSLI, 1987) 169.

6. John H. Connolly, *Constituent Order in Functional Grammar: Synchronic and Diachronic Perspectives* (Berlin: Foris, 1991) 3.

7. Ibid., 4.

8. In appendix 3, we briefly sketch two alternate ways of investigating positional syntax that do not suit our requirements: (1) *linearization*: phrase markers mapped onto the "word order domain"; and (2) *argument structure*: valency lists ordered by "obliqueness." In appendix 3, we also introduce some factors proposed in the linguistics literature to account for CIC ordering.

11.3.1 The Fields Approach to Positional Syntax

"This approach divides a clause into several word order 'fields' . . . whose mutual position is fixed, and studies mainly the word order regularities within these 'fields.'"[9] The method has a long history, especially among German syntacticians.[10] A simplified version relies upon five fields—the forefield, left bracket, middlefield, right bracket, and postfield. "[A]ny German sentence can be divided from left to right into [these] fields whose contents will be homogeneous across sentences, despite variation in word order."[11] How the field/zone contents are determined has been specified in various ways. The following two approaches represent the extremes of complexity.

11.3.1.1 Specification by Rules

At one extreme of complexity is Connolly's approach to positional syntax. Based on an interesting taxonomy of CICs adapted and extended from the taxonomy fashioned by Dutch linguist Simon Dik,[12] Connolly goes to elaborate lengths—literally—to write a positional syntax. For example, Connolly's rule (81a) for placing "all adverbials except focusing adjuncts"[13] into a massive 17-slot template takes up just under 5 pages in his book.[14] His system is impressive in its seeming attention to coverage, but it is so complex as to be all but impossible to verify. Further, we doubt whether inferences based on it could ever attain statistical significance for our smallish corpus.

In the spirit of the functional grammar approach,[15] we wonder if some of the complexity in Connolly's approach results from trying to account for what in reality are pragmatic effects or discourse effects by enforcing (inappropriate) syntactic constraints. If this is true, then inclusion of the dimension of discourse should enable a substantial simplification of positional syntax.

11.3.1.2 Specification by Statement

Seemingly much simpler are summary statements such as the following:

> In a declarative main clause . . . , the subject occupies the forefield, the finite verb is the left bracket, and complements and modifiers typically appear in the middlefield. . . . [Alternatively] the forefield holds the direct object of the sentence. In general, the forefield may hold no more than one of the verb's arguments or modifiers; the question of which one is generally taken to be context determined.[16]

From our perspective, this sort of statement can be made, if ever, only after exhaustive research has been carefully carried out. Before we would venture this sort of summary statement, we would need to examine every verb root corpus in Biblical Hebrew. Not having done the research for Biblical Hebrew, we are not prepared to adopt the theory relied on by fields-based positional syntax.

9. Karel Oliva, "The Proper Treatment of Word Order in HPSG," *Actes de COLING-92*, 184.

10. Michael W. Daniels, *Generalized ID/LP Grammar: A Formalism for Parsing Linearization-Based HPSG Grammars* (Ph.D. diss., Ohio State University, 2005) 20. Regarding Biblical Hebrew, see Walter Gross, *Die Satzteilfolge im Verbalsatz alttestamentlicher Prosa* (Tübingen: Mohr, 1996).

11. Daniels, *Generalized*, 22.

12. Connolly, *Constituent Order*, 71–72.

13. Ibid., 87: "Focusing adjuncts, such as *only*, *merely*, or *just*."

14. Ibid., 73–77.

15. Ibid., 1: "[A]dopting a functional approach entails regarding pragmatics as the over-arching framework to which other aspects of linguistics must be related. According to this view, then, semantics subserves pragmatics, and syntax in turn subserves semantics." For us, pragmatics, semantics, and syntax do not form a strict top-to-bottom hierarchy.

16. Ibid.

11.3.2   A Descriptive Approach to Positional Syntax

The inconclusiveness of the foregoing leaves us with a question: what approach(es) to visualizing positional syntax should we use? Our approach to positional syntax is descriptive. For predicator root / *binyan* / voice combinations that occur frequently enough to allow meaningful characterization, we generate horizontal bar charts showing various patterns of CIC sequencing. Our goal is to show what is in the texts, not to account for it (at least not at this point in our investigations).

11.3.2.1   Nucleus, Core, and Periphery in Role and Reference Grammar

The basic concepts upon which our description relies have been described by Robert Van Valin, Jr.[17] Van Valin's role and reference grammar benefits greatly by being the result of his addressing the question: "What would linguistic theory look like if it were based on the analysis of languages with diverse structures such as Lakhota, Tagalog and Dyirbal, rather than on the analysis of English?"[18] In response, Van Valin introduces[19]

> a very different conception of clause structure . . . from that assumed in other approaches. . . . [T]he conception of clause structure that it posits [is] equally applicable to free-word-order, flat-syntax languages such as Dyirbal and Malayalam, to head-marking languages like Lakhota and Tzotzil . . . , and to fixed-order configurational, dependent-marking languages like English and Icelandic.

To achieve this sort of coverage, Van Valin relies on his concept of "the layered structure of the clause." Its full explication consumes much of his book. For our purposes, we need to understand only what he calls "the primary constituent units of the clause." They are (we quote):[20]

- the 'nucleus', which contains the predicate (usually a verb),[21]
- the 'core', which contains the nucleus and the arguments of the predicate,
- a 'periphery', which subsumes non-arguments[22] of the predicate, e.g., setting locative and temporal phrases.

"The universal aspects (the nucleus, core, periphery and clause) are all semantically motivated."[23] Now, here is a crucial point:[24] "Since these hierarchical units are defined semantically and not syntactically, . . . the elements in these units may in principle occur in any order, if a given language permits it." We emphasize that Van Valin's terminology relates to *semantic* definitions of nucleus, core, and periphery. Contrary to the spatial imagery that inheres in the names of the hierarchical units ("core," "nucleus," "periphery"), they do not imply a particular grouping in surface structure.

In carrying out our investigation of these matters, we will also need to be very diligent in detecting ordering constraints that have nothing to do with the semantic-to-syntactic mapping but, rather, result from other constraints.[25] For example, for presentational reasons, objects of address

---

17. R. D. Van Valin Jr., *Exploring the Syntax-Semantics Interface* (Cambridge: Cambridge University Press, 2005) 3–8.

18. Ibid., 1.

19. Ibid., 3–4.

20. Ibid., 4.

21. "Predicate" here equals "predicator" in our terminology.

22. "Non-arguments" here equals "adjuncts" in our terminology.

23. Ibid., 8.

24. Ibid., 5.

25. Note well: we are *describing* the ordering of constituents. We are not seeking to account for the ordering, although interesting—if premature in our view—efforts have been made to do so. In this connection, see Christo H. J.

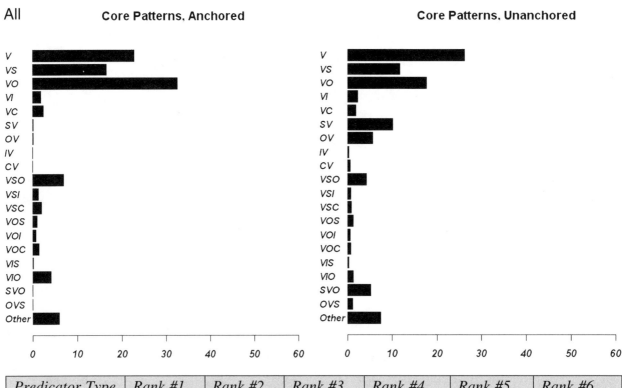

Predicator Type	Rank #1		Rank #2		Rank #3		Rank #4		Rank #5		Rank #6	
Anchored	VO	32%	V	23%	VS	16%	VSO	7%	VIO	4%	VSIO	3%
Unanchored	V	26%	VO	18%	VS	12%	SV	10%	OV	6%	SVO	5%

(i.e., speeches) overwhelmingly are clause final. This assists cognition, since for all but the shortest utterances, the processing of "and Moses said [long speech]" is far simpler than would be the processing of "and Moses [long speech] said."

11.3.2.2 The Positional Syntax of Grammatical Function CICs

The Descriptive Categories Adopted.   The number of CIC sequences attested in Biblical Hebrew is vast. The 68,089 verbal clauses exhibit 9,623 patterns. This is because we make use of so many CIC categories: three impermanent, three syntactic isolate, six predicator, four operator, four GFs, and 41 SRs—61 categories in all. To examine the positional syntax of GFs, we extract clause cores by removing from the clausal CIC sequences all non-GF/non-predicator types:

1. Each underdetermined "and" is part of a clause only because we have not promoted it to cue phrase status. The other impermanents are so few that their presence or absence can have little effect upon the results of our analysis (see §9.3.1.1).
2. The *syntactic isolates*, being isolated, are excluded from the clausal sequences (see §9.3.2). Altogether, these items account for 1.1% of the CIC population.
3. We exclude the *operators* on the grounds that 98% of them either appear immediately before the verbs that they operate upon or are clause initial.

van der Merwe and Eep Talstra, "Biblical Hebrew word order: The interface of information structure and formal features," *Zeitschrift für Althebräistik* 15/16 (2002–3) 68–107.

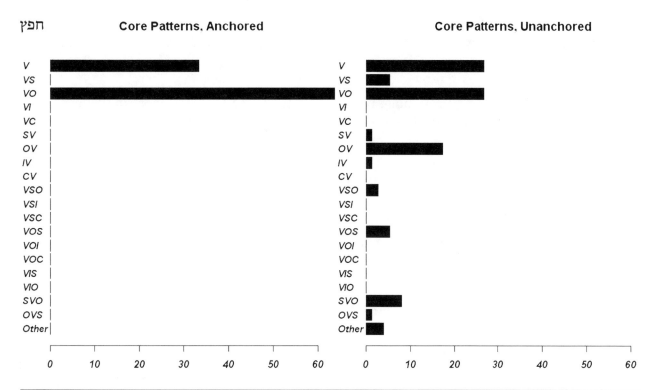

Predicator Type	Rank #1		Rank #2		Rank #3		Rank #4		Rank #5		Rank #6	
Anchored	VO	67%	V	33%	–		–		–		–	
Unanchored	VO	27%	V	27%	OV	17%	SVO	8%	VS	5%	VOS	5%

4. To reduce the repertoire of CIC sequence patterns, we delete resumed arguments.
5. For the present investigation of the positional syntax of grammatical-function CICs, we delete the SR CICs, leaving only the predicator CICs and GF CICs.

If a verbal clause has either an anchored or an unanchored predicator, and if it may have no more than one subject, direct object, indirect object, and/or complement, then one can show that there are 261 possible core sequence (GF sequence) patterns. In fact, we find 189 core sequence patterns in Biblical Hebrew. Of these patterns, 63 occur once and 23 occur twice.

11.3.2.3 Core Patterns across the Qal Active in Biblical Hebrew

We plot percentages in horizontal bar charts across all Qal active clauses with anchored or un-anchored predicators. We use 19 frequently occurring sequence patterns plus "other." Note that in all cases lacking a verb ('V') in clause-initial position, the relative frequency is higher for the unan-chored verb corpus than it is for the anchored verb corpus (for example, the SVO pattern is far more common when the Qal active verb is unanchored than when it is anchored). See chart, p. 162.

So much for core CIC sequence patterns across the Qal actives of Biblical Hebrew. We are much more interested in the comparative behavior for specific verb root corpora. In chaps. 12–15, we provide side-by-side bar charts of core CIC ordering patterns, verb corpus by verb corpus.

11.3.2.4   Core Patterns for the חפץ Corpus

In upcoming chapters, we show bar charts for clauses with anchored or unanchored predicators. By way of example, the relative frequencies for the ordering patterns in the חפץ corpus are shown in the chart above, p. 163.

The left-hand bar chart is misleading, because it presents the CIC sequences in the mere three clauses in the חפץ corpus that contain anchored predicators. Because the sample size for the anchored corpus is so small, we are well advised to avoid making comparisons between the unanchored and anchored corpora. We do observe, however, that in 32% of the חפץ corpus, the predicator is not clause initial (i.e., the sequence is OV, SVO, SV, OVS, or IV).

11.3.2.5   SRs amid GFs

There is one final matter that we investigate in chaps. 12–15: with what frequency do SR CICs appear physically amid the GF CIC constituents? We proceed as follows:

1. Divide the SR CICs into six groups. Table 11.6 shows our chosen grouping.

Table 11.6. The Six SR CIC Groups

Other Participant	Accompanier	*Movement and Spatial*	Movement aim (target)	*Manner*	Manner
	Agential		Movement bearing (direction)	*Mixed Level and Discourse Unit (DU)*	Aim / purpose
	Alternate / surrogate		Movement interval		Reason
	Beneficiary		Movement origin		Result
	Exocentric absolute		Length		Undesired outcome
	Harmed one		Location		Comparison
	Involved ones	*Enriching Constituent*	Cost		Cause
	Possessor		Instrument		Deprivation
	Ruled-over one		Material / composition		Quoter
Temporal	Time aim (goal)		Number of times		
	Time interval		Reference		
	Time origin		Resource (supply source)		For future reference, this table is reproduced inside the back cover.
	Time point		Quantity / quantifier		

2. Across each verb corpus, find all contexts where GF CICs (the predicator and its GF arguments) are not contiguous because of "interpolated" SR CICs.
3. Document these contexts using filled-in versions of table 11.7.

Table 11.7. SR Interpolations

Root	# Qal Active Clauses	Percent of SR-Groups Interpolated amid <???> GFs					
		Other Participant	Movement and Spatial	Temporal	Manner	Enriching Constituent	Mixed Level and DU

To see our perspective, consider this English clause: "Jean said 'Hello' to Mike at 6 A.M.": sbj – vb – obj addr – ind obj – time point. In this clause, the GF CICs are contiguous: sb – vb – address –

ind obj. The time point SR ("at 6 A.M.") is physically in the clause's periphery. If we had "Jean at 6 A.M. said 'Hello' to Mike": sbj – time point – vb – obj addr – ind obj, then the GF CICs would not be contiguous, the time point SR being interpolated between the subject and the predicator.

As it happens, the חפץ corpus has no interrupted GF sequences. Consequently, actual data on SR interpolations first appear in §12.6.2.

11.4   *An Aside on Valency*

11.4.1   The Perspective of Linguistics

Valency focuses on "the range of syntactic elements either required or specifically permitted by a verb or other lexical unit. . . . An element which is required is an *obligatory valent*; one which is specifically permitted but is not required is an *optional valent*."[26] "[A] given element may have different valencies in different contexts. . . . Valency deals not only with the number of valents with which a verb is combined to produce a *well formed* sentence nucleus, but also with the classification of the sets of valents which may be combined with different verbs."[27] In linguistics, the concept of valency is usually presented as less hard-edged than the concept of the obligatory complement versus the optional adjunct, but valency's utility is hindered when it relies on vague notions such as "well formedness."

11.4.2   The Perspective of Biblical Hebrew Studies

Waltke and O'Connor define valency ("valence" in their index) as "the number of links a grammatical element, especially a verb, has [with] other elements."[28] Their main treatment of the matter in their §10.2.1 demonstrates that they take a flexible-valency perspective.[29] Van der Merwe et al. have a fixed-valency perspective: "The valency of a verb refers to the number and nature of the obligatory constituents."[30] The study of valency in biblical studies is largely a European pursuit. A recent work on the subject is in German.[31]

11.4.3   Valency Cautions

We appreciate the usefulness of the concept of *valency* for pedagogy. But as a way of organizing and reporting research results, we find it to be chancy because of its operational vagueness, its risk of falling into the "translation trap," and its rather limited applicability.

11.4.3.1   Operational Vagueness

Surveying our data for frequently occurring verbs the corpora of which invariably contain obligatory constituents, we find none. Specifically, examining the 101 roots that occur more than 59 times as Qal actives (37,458 clauses), we find neither roots with their clauses always having a free-standing subject nor roots with their clauses always having a free-standing direct object. The

---

26. P. H. Matthews, *Oxford Concise Dictionary of Linguistics* (Oxford: Oxford University Press, 2005) 394.

27. David Crystal, *A Dictionary of Linguistics and Phonetics* (5th ed.; Oxford: Blackwell, 2003) 487 (italics mine).

28. B. K. Waltke and M. O'Connor, *IBHS*, 694.

29. Ibid., 163–69.

30. C. H. J. van der Merwe, J. A. Naudé, and J. H. Kroeze, *A Biblical Hebrew Reference Grammar*, 368 (cross-referencing emphases deleted).

31. Michael Malessa, *Untersuchungen zur verbalen Valenz im biblischen Hebräisch* (Assen: Van Gorcum, 2006). See also Christo H. J. van der Merwe, "Review of Malessa's *Untersuchungen zur verbalen Valenz im biblischen Hebräisch*," *Review of Biblical Literature* 4 (2007).

table shows the five roots with the largest incidence of subjects and the five with the largest incidence of direct objects.

Frequent Subjects	מלא 76.6%	כלה 68.1%	אבד 67.6%	מלך 66.7%	חרה 66.7%
Frequent Direct Objects	ירש 94.2%	אסף 94.2%	לכד 93.9%	אמר 93.9%	קרה 93.8%

Or consider the large corpus organized around Qal actives of the root נתן, a corpus of 1,896 clauses. Van der Merwe et al. cite נתן as an example of a "three-complement" verb consisting of "[v]erb + subject + object + indirect object . . . Jonathan gave his weapons to the boy (1 Sam. 20.40)."[32] Phrase marker (11.3) from 2 Kgs 22:10 provides an OVIS-instance of this prototypical "three-complement" situation.

(11.3)

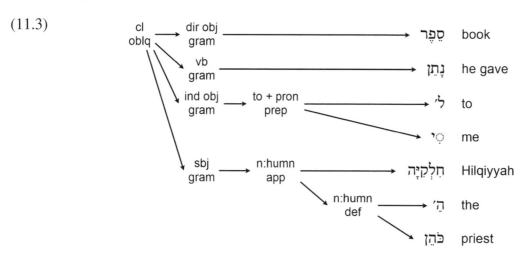

In fact, only 8% of the נתן clauses contain all three arguments, sbj – dir obj – ind obj. The table shows how often each argument actually appears in the נתן corpus.

Argument	Count	Percent Incidence
Subject	511	27%
Direct Object	1,496	79%
Indirect Object	954	50%

Looking across several languages (but not including Biblical Hebrew), Butt and King suggest "that argument drop is licensed at the level of discourse structure and that only continuing topics or background information may be omitted."[33] Research topic: Does this hold for Biblical Hebrew? It is not sufficient simply to assert that the three arguments are ontologically necessary, and so, when any are missing, they are either ellipted or are "understood." A precept that asserts that certain constituents are obligatorily present in a clause except when they are not lacks operational usefulness.

---

32. Van der Merwe, Naudé, and Kroeze, *Biblical Hebrew Reference Grammar*, 173.

33. Miriam Butt and Tracy King, "Null Elements in Discourse Structure," in *Papers from the NULLS Seminar* (ed. K. V. Subbarao; Delhi: Moti Lal Banarsi Das, 2000). Available from the Web.

11.4.3.2 The Translation Trap

If נתן in Biblical Hebrew had a semantic range analogous to 'give' in English, then the three arguments stated to be obligatory would be ontologically necessary. But, what is true of English is not necessarily true of Biblical Hebrew. The semantic range of נתן differs from the range of English 'give'. For example, in addition to the three-argument (sbj – dir obj – ind obj) sense usually translated into English by some form of 'give', there is also a three-argument (sbj – dir obj – loc) sense translated by some form of 'place'. In this circumstance, the preposition in the location CIC is עַל 'upon'.

Phrase marker (11.4) from Exod 25:30 shows an instance where נתן has this sense. Were we to distinguish this sense, the gloss would read something like 'thou(m) wilt place'. For this sense of נתן, it is reasonable to assert that loc, and not ind obj, is an argument. *Note well:* here is a context of use where what we have been considering an SR (loc) might best be considered an argument of its verb, giving it standing as a GF. When the verb corpora of Biblical Hebrew are studied in full detail, we expect that variants of this phenomenon will appear repeatedly.

(11.4)

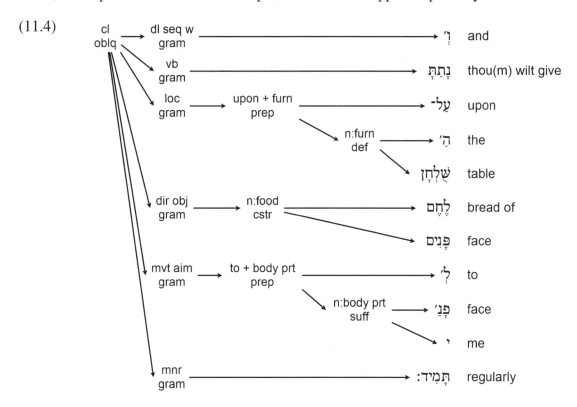

11.4.3.3 Limited Applicability

The smaller the corpus organized around a given root, the less confidence one can have in generalizations based on it. To begin with the starkest example: although we can state with certainty the valence observed for one-clause corpora involving hapax verb roots, descriptions of this sort are certainly not useful generalizations. Of the 968 Qal active verb roots attested in Biblical Hebrew, 237 occur only once (24%). There is little point in talking about the valency patterns of these verbs. To make convincing generalizations, we would need to group the roots into sets reliably.

How large should a corpus be before we seek to generalize about the quantitative and qualitative valency of its verb? In chaps. 12–15, we study verb corpora consisting of 2,000–5,000 clauses.

It should be possible to investigate valency in the 101 verbs occurring 60 times or more, but this is a mere 4% of the total verb lexeme stock.

11.5 *The Structure of Chapters 12–15*

11.5.1 The Verb Corpora Chosen for Analysis

We count 68,089 verbal clauses in Biblical Hebrew. The census of the 20 most frequent roots in predicators is as follows:

Root	Count	Root	Count	Root	Count	Root	Count	Root	Count
אמר	5,302	נתן	1,991	שמע	1,126	ידע	929	אכל	779
היה	2,817	הלך	1,497	יצא	1,034	עלה	873	מת	726
עשׂה	2,531	ראה	1,280	שׁב	1,031	שׁלח	827	קרה	719
בא	2,523	דבר	1,128	לקח	960	ישׁב	815	קם	608

These 20 roots appear in 29,496 (43.3%) of the 68,089 verbal clauses in Biblical Hebrew. In chaps. 12–15, we examine Qal active corpora for four frequent roots: אמר 'say', היה 'be', עשׂה 'do, make', and נתן 'give'. (A fifth frequent root, בא 'come', is treated with verbs of movement in §17.3.2.)

11.5.2 Reading Options

In a book such as this, there is a tension between providing too little detail and providing too much. While some readers will want access only to the main arguments and supporting data, others will want more detail. In an attempt to provide for each sort of reader, we have designed chaps. 12–15 to be read to two depths:

- Readers seeking the main points might read only the "Main Observations" previews at the beginnings of many sections. When there is no preview, our advice is to scan the section at least, studying the phrase markers along the way.
- Readers who are seeking more detail should read the chapters in toto.

11.6 *Brief Summary*

CIC Ordering.   After considering several approaches to the study of positional syntax and finding each unsuitable in some way, we opt for a softened version of the approach propounded in Van Valin's role and reference grammar, which is a descriptive approach.

Aside on Valency.   Because of its vagueness, its tendency to fall into "the translation trap," and its limited applicability, we do not use valency to organize our research or reports thereon.

The Organization of This Chapter and Chapters 12–15.   For each verb corpus in chaps. 12–15, we parallel this chapter's progression:

1. Four Censuses:
   a. *Binyanim.*   The various *binyanim* attested.
   b. *CIC Subtypes.*   Census of the five CIC subtypes.
   c. *Non-GF/SR CICs.*   Tallies of the non-GF/SR CICs encountered.
   d. *GF/SR CICs.*   How the GF/SR CICs are realized (form-to-function linking) for common prepositional phrases and bare substantives.

2. CIC Incidence Patterns: Four-part vertical-bar tables indicating predicator incidence, grammatical function incidence, most-frequent SRs, and verb-corpus-specific frequent SRs.
3. CIC Ordering ("positional syntax"):
   a. *Core Sequences.*　Pairs of fixed-format horizontal bar charts showing the incidence of various clausal GF CIC sequences for anchored and unanchored predicators.
   b. *Core "Intrusions."*　Tallies of the rate at which various SR CIC groups (defined inside the back cover) interpose into sequences of clausal GF CICs.

Chapter 12

The אמר *Corpus*

12.1 *The* Binyan *Census*

In §10.3.3, we included *binyan* in our list of grammatical features that might assist in inferring links between syntactic forms and semantic roles. For אמר, however, the census of *binyanim* is heavily concentrated in the Qal actives. The verbal stock consists of 5,277 Qal actives, 21 Niphal passives, 2 Hiphils, and 1 Qal passive. Knowledge of *binyan* assists only in the assignment of objects of address (active predicators) and subjects of address (passive predicators).

12.2 *The CIC Subtype Census*

The census of the CICs is given in table 12.1.

Table 12.1. CIC Subtype Census for the אמר Verb Corpus—5,277 Structures

Impermanents	Count	Predicators	Count	GFs	Count
Underspecified "and"	2,830	Finite verb	4,217	Subject	2,119
Lapsus calami	2	Predicative inf. abs.	1	Direct object	4,960
Nebulous	0	Purely verbal participle	51	Indirect object	1,912
Syntactic Isolates	Count	Noun-verb participle	46	Complement	2
Vocative	29	Infinitive construct	962	*Top Six SRs*	Count
Exclamative	3	Non-predicative inf. abs.	6	Manner	532
Label	10	*Operators*	Count	Time point	110
		Negative	50	Quoter	109
		Closed interrogative	20	Location	77
		Other conjunction [a]	12	Aim / purpose	56
		Modal	8	Reference	26

a. "Other conjunction" includes all CIC-level conjunctions other than those classified as underspecified "and."

12.3 *Survey of the Non-GF/SR Clause Immediate Constituents*

§12.3 Main Observations: (1) The non-GF/SR clause immediate constituents appear relatively rarely in the אמר corpus (in under 3% of the clauses). (2) The negatives immediately precede the predicators (48×) except in rhetorical questions (2×).

12.3.1   Impermanents

12.3.1.1   Underspecified "and" Cue Phrases

These impermanent CICs are excluded from the clausal analyses (see §9.3.1.1).

12.3.1.2   Indeterminate Constituents

Lapsii calami appear in Ruth 3:5 and 17, both of which are *Qere welo*ʾ *Kethiv*s. Each might eventually be restored to its *Qere* reading: אֵלַ'י 'to me'.

12.3.2   Syntactic Isolates

12.3.2.1   Vocatives

Noun phrases are formally candidates for being declared vocatives, but alternatively they may have grammatical functions and semantic roles. Of the 30 vocatives in אמר clauses, three follow exclamatives (Josh 7:8, Jer 14:13, and Ezek 21:5), almost half are clause initial (15×), and one is clause terminal (Ezek 11:5). Nearly half, all in Ezekiel, appear in the expression "Son of man, say . . ." (13×).

12.3.2.2   Exclamatives

Three exclamatives, each preceding some variant of אֲדֹנָי יהוה 'my Lord Yahweh', are in Josh 7:8, Jer 14:13, Ezek 21:5.

12.3.2.3   Labels

There are 10 set phrases: נְאֻם־יהוה 'oracle of Yahweh' or a variant.[1] Phrase marker (12.1) from Ezek 21:5 is an אמר clause containing both a vocative and an exclamative.

(12.1)

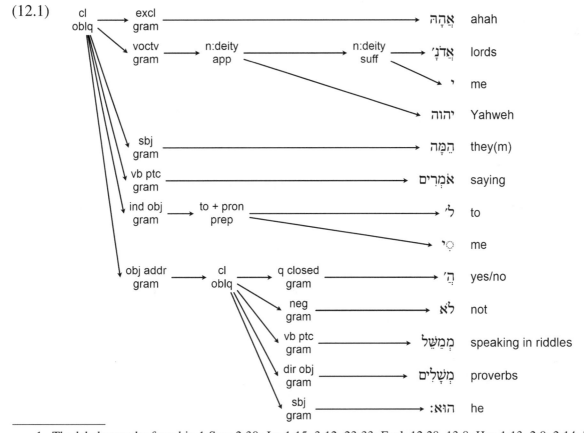

_____

1. The labels may be found in 1 Sam 2:30; Jer 1:15, 3:12, 23:33; Ezek 12:28, 13:8; Hag 1:13, 2:9, 2:14; Zech 1:3.

12.3.3 Predicators

In addition to 4,217 finite verbs and 962 infinitives construct, we find one predicative infinitive absolute (Num 6:23), 51 purely verbal participles, and 46 noun-verb participles (three-quarters in the Prophets). We find six non-predicative infinitive absolute cognate-root "intensifiers."[2]

12.3.4 Operators

12.3.4.1 Negatives

Of 50 negatives, only 2 do not immediately precede the predicator. In these cases (Gen 20:5 and 1 Chr 21:17), a rhetorical question is being posed: intrg . . . neg . . . sbj . . . vb.

12.3.4.2 Closed Interrogatives

There are 20 closed interrogatives.[3] Of these, 18 are clause initial. One follows a vocative ("son of man" in Ezek 12:9), and the other follows an indirect object (Job 34:31). Phrase marker (12.2) from 1 Chr 21:17 shows an אמר clause containing both a negative and a closed interrogative.

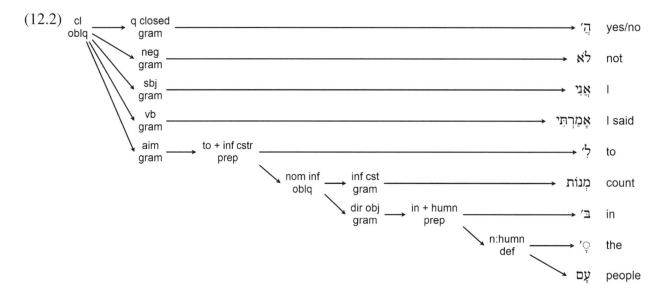

(12.2)

12.3.4.3 Other Conjunctions

There are 11 noncoordinating conjunctions, 8 instances of גַם /גֵם 'also'[4] and 3 of אַף 'also'.[5] Two are clause internal, at Esth 7:2 and Neh 3:35. The others are clause initial and might have been excluded from analysis had we done discourse analysis and declared them cue phrases.

12.3.4.4 Modals

Modals occur 8 times: כִּי 'surely' (7×) and אַךְ 'surely' (1×) (Job 33:8). Phrase marker (12.3) from Gen 3:1 shows an אמר clause containing both an includer and a modal.

---

2. They are in Exod 21:5; Judg 15:2; 1 Sam 2:30, 20:21; Jer 23:17; Ezek 28:9.

3. There are also 35 open interrogatives. Seven are phrasal: לְמָה 'to-what' = 'why?' (6×) plus עַד־מָתַי 'until when?' = 'how long?' (2 Sam 2:26).

4. These are in Judg 2:3, 17:2; 1 Kgs 1:48; Ruth 2:21; Esth 7:2; Neh 3:35, 4:16, 6:19.

5. These are all assigned to the includer CIC class and are found in Gen 3:1, 2 Kgs 5:13, and Job 35:14.

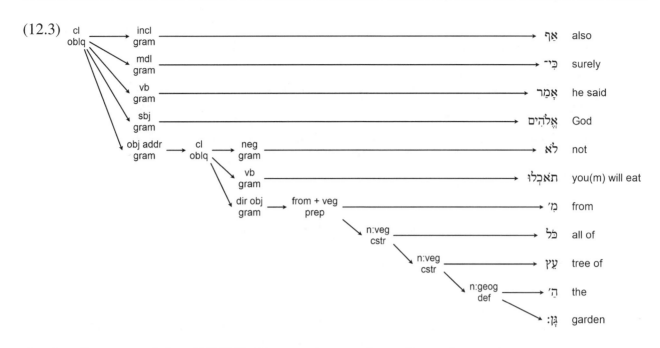

12.4   *Survey of the GF/SR Clause Immediate Constituents*

§12.4   Main Observations: (1) One adverb predominates in the אמר corpus: כֹּה 'thus' (93% of the adverbs and found in 10% of the clauses). (2) An אמר clause almost always contains a speech (94%). (3) Three kinds of GF/SR classes are determined once the semantics of the substantives in their PPs are given: time, infinitive of utterance, or pronoun. (4) The אמר corpus exhibits a strong alternation in realizing indirect objects: אל (66%) versus ל (34%). (5) Three prepositions account for 97% of the PP CICs: אל, ל, and ב. (6) The bare substantives are almost all subjects (96%).

The focus of this subsection is to investigate the linkages between the functions of the CICs (their GF/SR labels) and their forms (as provided by the CIC daughter labels). The nature of the CIC daughter raw census is given in table 12.2. Each form will be taken up in its turn.

Table 12.2. GF/SR Daughter Forms

GF/SR Daughter	Count
Adverb	548
Clause(-like) structure	4,881
Prepositional phrase	2,310
Noun phrase	2,052
Pronoun	92

12.4.1   Adverbs

The CIC daughter adverbs are subdivided into three subsets based on semantics. We distinguish adverbs having temporal semantics, adverbs having spatial semantics, and other adverbs ("adverbs

of manner"). The table tallies the adverbs in אמר clauses. Both אָז and עַתָּה have semantic role tm
pt (time point), עוֹד 'still' is a tm int (time interval), and עוֹד 'again' is a # times (number of times).

Temporal Adverbs (tm pt, tm int, or # times)		Spatial Adverbs (loc)		Adverbs of Manner (mnr)	
אָז then	7	הֵנָּה here	1	כֹּה thus	508[a]
עוֹד still [tm int]	10	שָׁם there	1	כִּי very	3
עוֹד again [# times]	4			נָא [emphatic]	16
עַתָּה now	8			פִּתְאֹם suddenly	1

    a. These appear mostly in the abundant "*Thus* said Yʜᴡʜ."

12.4.2 Clauses and Clause-Like Structures

    The vast majority of אמר clauses (93.5%) contain a speech consisting of a main clause, a sentence, or discourse unit(s). These structures exercise grammatical functions. The semantic role of the speeches is *address*. In our mixed representation, we label a speech obj addr/gram, object of address licensed by grammar, or sbj addr/gram, subject of address licensed by grammar.

    In 14 additional cases, the "speech" is preceded by a cue phrase, כִּי (8×), שֶׁ' (1×), or אֲשֶׁר (5×).[6] Under these circumstances, we label the constructions cogv cmpl/cue (cognitive complement licensed by a cue phrase). Phrase marker (12.4) from Job 36:10 shows the situation.

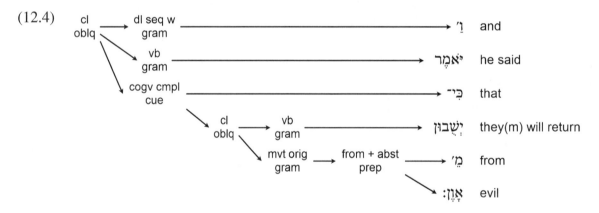

    Once, as shown in phrase marker (12.5) from Gen 12:13, we are forced[7] to declare a cogv cmpl/no cue (cognitive complement licensed without a cue phrase).

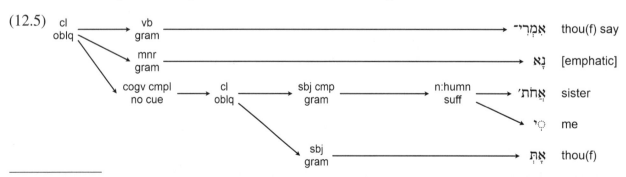

    6. For כִּי, see Judg 15:2; Isa 3:10; Ps 118:2, 3, 4; Job 36:10; Qoh 5:5; 1 Chr 21:18. For שֶׁ', see Qoh 8:14. For אֲשֶׁר, see Ezra 2:63; Neh 7:65, 13:19, 13:22; 2 Chr 21:18—Late Biblical Hebrew?
    7. "Forced" because the pronouns in the clause preclude the embedded speech from being an object of address.

12.4.2.1 Speech-less אמר Clauses

It is interesting to consider the circumstances in which an אמר clause lacks a speech, 343 clauses out of 5,277 (6.5%). Four phenomena account for the majority of these cases:

1. אמר is the predicator in a nominalized clause,
2. אמר commands aim / purpose,
3. an interrogative is used as a speech surrogate,
4. usage of אמר is akin to the use of דבר.

אמר *Is the Predicator in a Nominalized Clause.*   Sixty-three times (18.4% of the speech-less אמר clauses) the antecedent is the virtual object of אמר, as in phrase marker (12.6) from Gen 22:2.

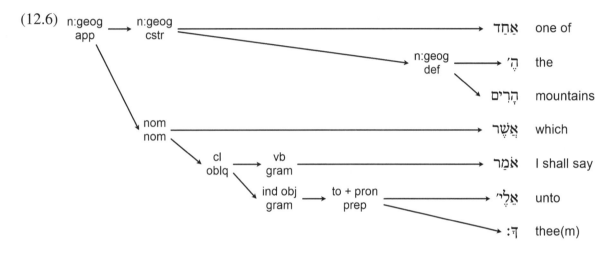

אמר *Commands Aim / Purpose.*   Forty-eight times (21.4%), we label a prepositional phrase with לְ plus an infinitive construct as an aim CIC.[8] Phrase marker (12.7) from 1 Kgs 8:12 shows the behavior.

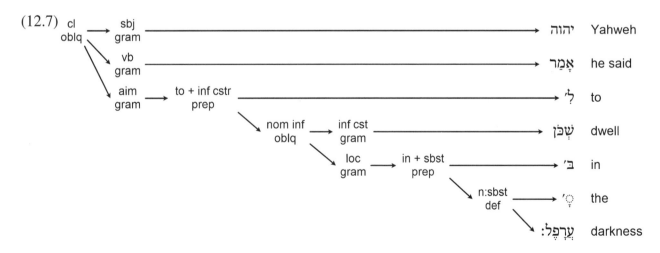

---

8. Strictly speaking, this is a misnomer. The usual aim CIC specifies the purpose of the activity portrayed by a clause's predicator. Here, "dwelling in darkness" is not the purpose of the speech act. The speech act announces this purpose.

An Interrogative Is Used as a Speech Surrogate.   Fourteen times, the open interrogative מָה 'what' is the surrogate for a speech that is being inquired about, as in phrase marker (12.8) from 1 Sam 10:15.

(12.8)

dir obj / open intrg	מָה־	what
vb / gram	אָמַר	he said
ind obj / gram → to + pron / prep	לְ	to
	כֶם	you(m)
sbj / gram	שְׁמוּאֵל:	Samuel

(cl oblq)

In phrase marker (12.9) from Lam 3:37, a demonstrative pronoun serves as the speech surrogate.

(12.9)

sbj / open intrg	מִי	who
dir obj / gram	זֶה	this
vb / gram	אָמַר	he said

(cl oblq)

Usage Is Akin to the Use of דבר.   After the foregoing explanatory mechanisms have been exploited, 220 speechless clauses remain unaccounted for. They correspond quite closely to typical patterns in דבר clauses. Phrase marker (12.10) illustrates both Exod 19:25 and 2 Sam 21:2:[9]

(12.10)

dl seq w / gram	וַ	and
vb / gram	יֹּאמֶר	he said
ind obj / gram → to + pron / prep	אֲלֵ	unto
	הֶם:	them(m)

(cl oblq)

The דבר version leads off 12 clauses. Fraternal twin–דבר (12.11) appears once, in Gen 42:24.

(12.11)

dl seq w / gram	וַ	and
vb / gram	יְדַבֵּר	he spoke
ind obj / gram → to + pron / prep	אֲלֵ	unto
	הֶם	them(m)

(cl oblq)

---

9. With a concluding explicit subject, it also appears in 2 Chr 31:10.

12.4.2.2 Deep Embedding of Speeches

Speeches embedded 5 levels deep occur 3 times, all in Jeremiah: 22:1–8, 27:2–5, and 36:28–31. Four-level embedding of speeches occurs more than 20 times. Phrase marker (12.12) for Ezek 21:14 contains 4 levels of speech embedding. The fact that the most deeply embedded speech continues on beyond the confines of the phrase marker is indicated by the rem / gram node ("remainder of address"), which hangs off the 4th obj addr / gram node.

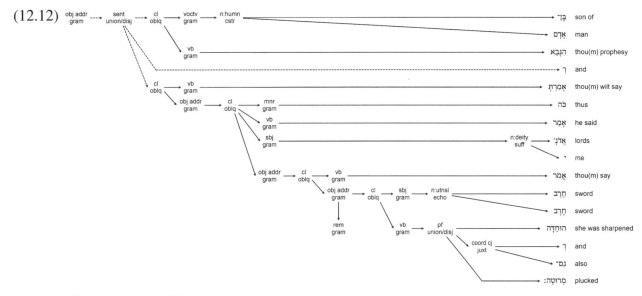

12.4.3 Prepositional Phrases

The אמר clauses contain 2,310 prepositional phrases. The incidences of 10 prepositions are tallied here:

אֶל	1,281	לְ'	835	בְּ	113	כְּ'	73	עַל	42	אַחֲרֵי	7	מְ'	6	אֶת	5	עַד	2	לְמַעַן	1

12.4.3.1 Temporal Substantive in a PP Is Part of a Time Point SR

Thirty-three times a prepositional phrase involves a noun phrase with temporal semantics. Independent of the 4 different prepositions involved, in each case the dominating CIC is a tm pt ("time point"). Trimmed phrase marker (12.13) from Ruth 2:14 shows an instance of this phenomenon (see p. 178).[10]

12.4.3.2 An Infinitive of Utterance Is Always a Quoter SR

There are 109 instances of לֵאמֹר 'to say' in אמר clauses, each assigned the CIC SR qtr ("quoter"). Phrase marker (12.14) from Zech 4:13 illustrates the construction (see p. 178).

12.4.3.3 PP with Pronoun Is Almost Always an Indirect Object

A prepositional phrase involves a pronoun 912 times. The grammatical function is ind obj ("indirect object") in all but nine cases (99%). Five of the exceptions involve עַל + [pronoun]. As we will see, עַל links fairly strongly to a refrnt ("referential") role. Phrase marker (12.14) includes an indirect object involving a preposition plus a pronoun.

---

10. To save space, we have omitted the speech in (12.13) at the end of the clause.

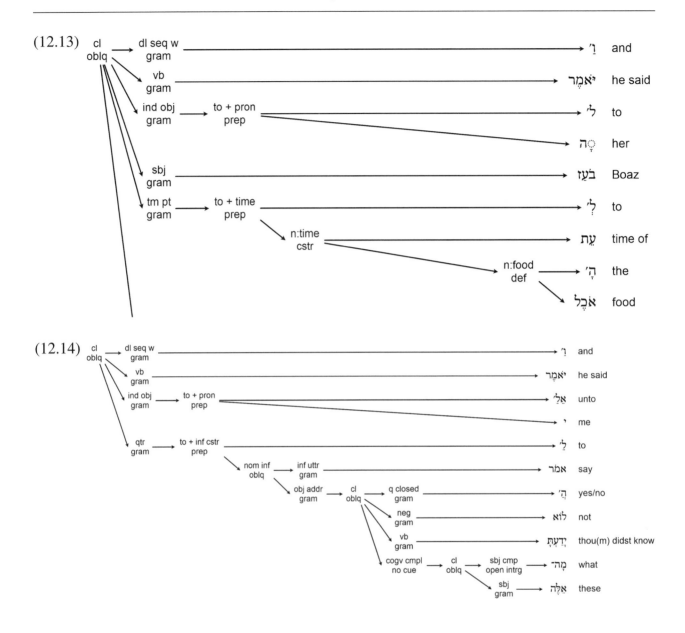

12.4.3.4 The אֶל Prepositional Phrases

The preposition אֶל is very strongly linked to the indirect object grammatical function. It occurs 1,281 times, dominated all but 5 times by an indirect object function node (99.7%). Table 12.3 reports the two main substantive types involved.

Table 12.3. אֶל-Phrase Substantive versus GFs / SRs

substantive type ↓	ind obj	[other]
human	663[a]	
[pronoun]	571	
[other]	42	5

a. Thirteen of these are distributive.

Phrase marker (12.15) from Judg 9:14 has an indirect object involving אֶל and a thornbush:

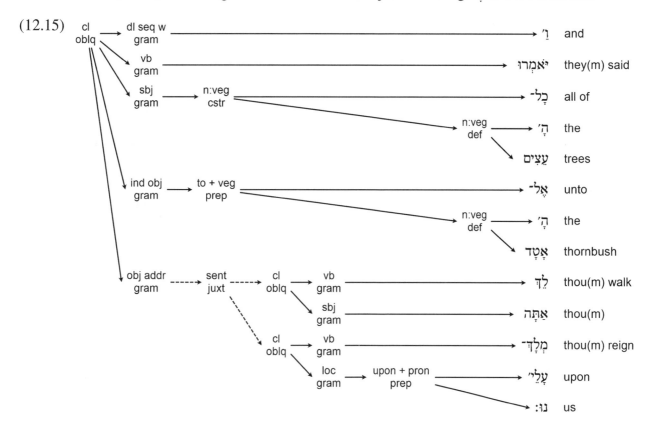

12.4.3.5 The 'לְ Prepositional Phrases

The preposition 'לְ is also strongly linked to the indirect object grammatical function. It occurs 835 times, but 109 occur with infinitives of utterance (inf utt) as just discussed in §12.4.3.2, leaving 726 instances for tabulation. These are indirect objects about 90% of the time, as table 12.4 documents.

Table 12.4. 'לְ-Phrase Substantive versus GFs / SRs

substantive type ↓	ind obj	aim	[other]
human	252		7
[pronoun]	332		1
other inf. construct	1[a]	54	
[other]	60	1	18

    a. The indirect object in Isa 49:7 consists of an infinitive construct, a noun-verb participle, and a noun phrase.

For variety, phrase marker (12.16) from Ps 139:20 shows an atypical אמר clause: (1) The indirect object is a suffixed pronoun. (2) The clause contains no object of address (no speech). (3) It contains a semantic role of aim involving a PP with a noun having mental semantics.

(12.16)

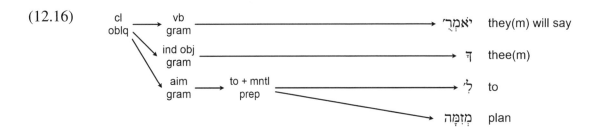

Comparing tables 12.3 and 12.4, we observe that the אמר corpus exhibits a much-discussed strong alternation in the realization of indirect objects. Indirect objects involve אֶל (66.4%) twice as often as 'לְ (33.6%). The nature of this alternation is briefly taken up in appendix 4, where we provide counterexample data suggesting that neither Jenni's "social distance" explanation nor Malessa's "separation from the predicator" explanation adequately accounts for the alternation phenomenon.

12.4.3.6   The 'בְּ Prepositional Phrases

Prepositional phrases involving 'בְּ occur 115 times in אמר clauses, never as indirect objects. They are linked to location SRs 63 times (52.9%) and to time point SRs 46 times (38.7%). These 2 SRs account for more than 90% of the instances of 'בְּ prepositional phrases in אמר clauses.

Table 12.5. 'בְּ-Phrase Substantive versus GFs / SRs

substantive type ↓	loc	tm pt	[other]
human	8[a]		
other inf. construct		17	
body part	34		
geographic	10		
temporal		27	
[other]	6		11

a. These cases involve phrases such as "in the nations," "in the people," and "in Israel," this last because we have not (yet) resolved the homography of personal names, geographical names, and so on.

The 34 location CICs involving body parts attract interest. Thirty consist of prepositional phrases of the "in my heart" variety, indicative of soliloquizing. Four involve speaking "in the ear of . . ." (Judg 17:2, Isa 49:20, Ezek 9:5, Job 33:8).

Phrase marker (12.17) from Judg 17:2 shows a clause with an SR loc involving a body part and without an object of address.

(12.17)

12.4.3.7 The Remaining Prepositional Phrases

The prepositions אֶל, לְ, and בְּ appear in 96% of the prepositional phrases, leaving 81 unlabeled prepositional phrases. These involve 6 different prepositions. We give their tallies using the condensed format:

1. כְּ—There are 31 time point (tm pt) semantic roles and 6 comparison semantic roles.
2. עַל—There are 21 refrnt (referential), 2 ind obj (indirect object),[11] and 1 loc (location)[12] semantic role.
3. אַחֲרֵי—There are 7 tm pt SRs and 1 aim SR. Three involve infinitives construct.
4. אֵת—There are 5 marked direct objects: The direct objects *refer* to utterances: "all of words of Yahweh" (1 Sam 8:10) and "this word" (Jer 13:12, 14:17, 23:38, 31:23).
5. מִ—There are 4 tm pt SRs (with temporal noun semantics: Gen 19:34, Exod 32:30, 2 Sam 15:7, and Jer 13:6) and 1 ellipted cause (mental noun semantics: Deut 28:67 2×).
6. עַד—There is 1 tm pt (2 Chr 35:25) and 1 open interrogative tm int (2 Sam 2:26).
7. לְמַעַן—There is 1 extensive aim constituent at Gen 37:22.

12.4.4 Substantives

The final constituents to be discussed are the "bare" substantives.[13] In the total 5,277 Qal active אמר clauses, there are 2,144 bare substantives. Table 12.6 provides tallies for the major categories.

Table 12.6. Substantive versus GFs / SRs

substantive type ↓	subj	[other]
human	1,166	2
deity	801	
[other]	147	28

It is natural to wonder if there are principled methods for determining which function a given substantive should have. The default rule obviously is that a bare substantive in an אמר clause is this clause's subject. This sort of blanket choice is correct 2,114 times in 2,144 rule applications (98.6%). But what about the tail of 30 substantives (1.4%) that do not function as subjects?

Possible methods of identification come to mind, none of them foolproof. Consider using number agreement as an aid. This is critical for identifying distributive subjects but fails where garden-

---

11. A standard indirect object appears in 2 Kgs 22:8; a distributive indirect object is in Jer 23:35.
12. In Ps 4:5.
13. That is, substantives that are not part of prepositional phrases.

variety subjects are concerned. Two examples should make our case. In phrase marker (12.18) from Ps 118:3, number agreement is violated since a plural verb combines with a subject currently labeled singular.[14]

(12.18)

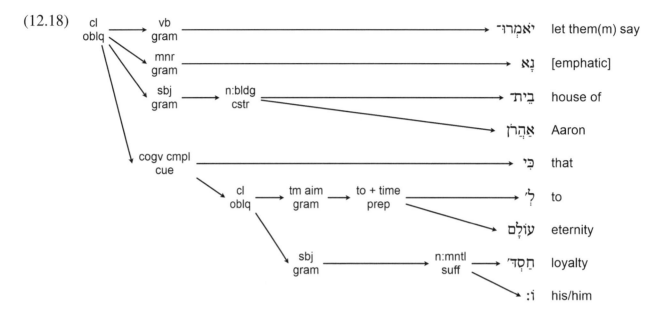

In phrase marker (12.19) from 2 Sam 17:14, number agreement is violated since a singular verb combines with a plural subject.

(12.19)

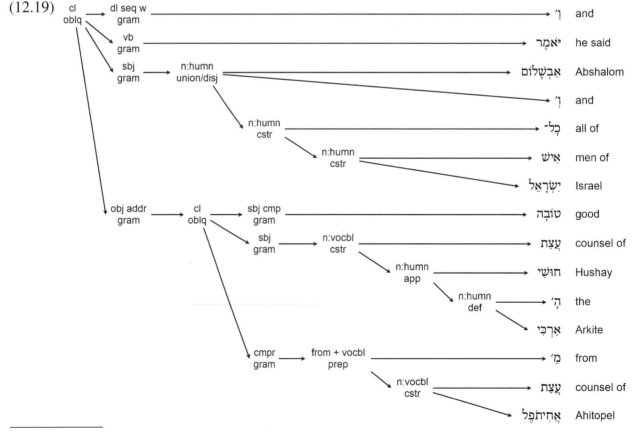

---

14. See also Exod 32:12; Deut 9:28; 1 Kgs 20:28; Ezek 12:9, and 18:29.

CIC Incidence for אמר Clauses

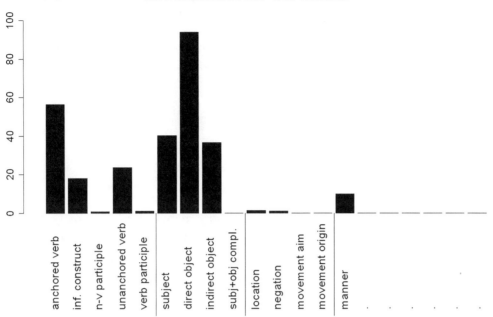

אמר

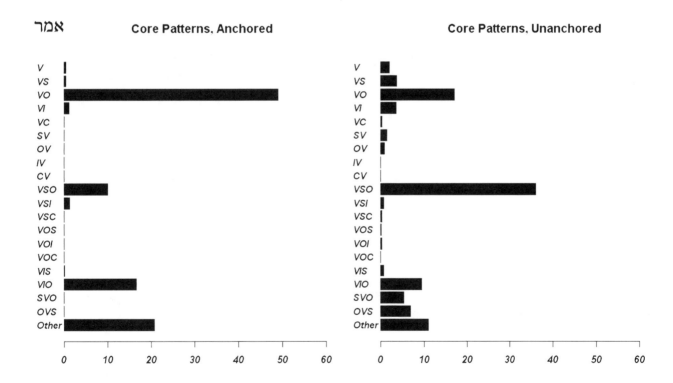

Predicator Type	Rank #1		Rank #2		Rank #3		Rank #4		Rank #5		Rank #6	
Anchored	VO	49%	VIO	17%	VSIO	16%	VSO	10%	VISO	5%	VSI	1%
Unanchored	VSO	36%	VO	17%	VIO	9%	OVS	7%	SVO	5%	VS	4%

12.5 *Clause Immediate Constituent Incidence across the* אמר *Corpus*

We next take up the incidence of CICs across the אמר corpus. Consider the bar chart at the top of p. 183 for the clauses making up the אמר corpus. Compared with the incidences of CICs across Biblical Hebrew shown in §11.2 (p. 162), אמר clauses use *unanchored verbs* half as often and *anchored verbs* twice as often. *Direct objects* (actually, *objects of address*) are twice as frequent, while *indirect object* and *manner* CICs are 4 times more frequent. Other than the formulaic *manner* CIC (כה 'thus'), few semantic role CICs are present.

12.6 *Core Constituent Ordering*

12.6.1 Core Patterns for the אמר Corpus

We plot bar charts for אמר clauses with anchored or unanchored predicators (see bottom, p. 183). The procedures for extracting the core patterns were specified in §11.3.2.2. Among the anchored predicators, the *Other* category is sufficiently large to attract scrutiny. On investigation, we find that it contains just over 20% of the corpus, its 2 largest contributors being VSIO, 15.7%, and VISO, 4.7%—both being in the top ranks.

Other for the unanchored predicators accounts for around 12% of its clauses, its 3 largest contributors being VSIO, 3.5%, SVIO, 2.7%, and IVO, 2.2%.

12.6.2 SRs amid GFs

The numerical entries in the table below disclose what percent of a given SR-group is interpolated into the GFs of the clauses making up the אמר corpus. For example, the table informs us that 4.1% of the manner SR tokens found in the אמר corpus are interpolated amid the GFs of their clauses.

Root	# Qal Active Clauses	Percent of SR-Groups Interpolated amid אמר GFs					
		Other Participant	Movement and Spatial	Temporal	Manner	Enriching Constituent	Mixed level and DU
אמר	5,277	0%	3.8%	5.0%	4.1%	12.5%	0.0%

In obtaining these figures, adjustments have been made:

- *Movement and Spatial.* Of the 78 *movement/spatial* tokens, 53 are interpolated, 67.9%. But 50 of these occur immediately before an all-but-anchored object of address, leaving 3 genuine interpolates, an incidence of 3/78 or 3.8%.
- *Temporal.* Of the 121 *temporal* SR tokens, 29 are interpolated, 24.9%. But 23 of these occur immediately before an all-but-anchored object of address, leaving 6 genuine interpolates, an incidence of 6/121 or 5.0%.
- *Manner.* Of the 532 instances of the *manner* SR, 24 are interpolated, 4.5%. But 2 of these occur immediately before an all-but-anchored object of address, leaving 22 genuine interpolates, an incidence of 22/532 or 4.1%.
- *Enriching Constituent.* Of the 64 *enriching constituent* tokens, 36 are interpolated, 56.2%. But 28 of these occur immediately before an all-but-anchored object of address, leaving 8 genuine interpolates, an incidence of 8/64 or 12.5%.

- *Mixed Level and Discourse Unit.*   Of the 176 *mixed-level/DU* tokens, 2 are interpolated, 1.1%. But both of these occur immediately before an all-but-anchored object of address, leaving no genuine interpolates.

We count 144 interpolates if the pre-speech CICs are included, 39 interpolates if the pre-speech CICs are excluded. Hence, adjuncts are not interpolated among the GFs in the אמר corpus very often. The *interpolation rate* is 39/5,277 = 7.4 interpolations per 1,000 אמר clauses.

12.7 Brief Summary

The following overview suggests that, syntactically, the אמר corpus exhibits what one might term "bureaucratic single vision."

The Censuses.   The predicators of אמר are overwhelmingly Qal actives (99.6%). Most predicators are finite verbs (80%), with "infinitive constructs of utterance" the next most common predicator (18%).

Non-GF/SR CICs are rare. Omitting impermanent "ands," they appear in 3% of clauses. Negatives are the most common, appearing in 1% of the clauses.

With regard to GFs, explicit subjects appear in 40% of the clauses, speeches appear as objects of address in 94%, and indirect objects in 36%. Indirect objects involve אל twice as often as they involve ל. There is no completely convincing explanation for this alternation.

The adverb of manner כֹה 'thus' occurs in just under 10% of the clauses. Three prepositions account for 96% of the PP CICs: ל, אל, and ב. The bare substantives are almost all subjects (97%). Bound pronouns are almost always indirect objects (97.2% of the time). Free pronouns are surprisingly rare, appearing in under 2% of the clauses, and all are subjects.

CIC Incidence.   אמר clauses use *unanchored verbs* half as often and both *anchored verbs* and *infinitive constructs* twice as often as is the case across Biblical Hebrew. *Direct objects* (actually, *objects of address*) are twice as frequent, while *indirect objects* and *manner* CICs are 4 times more frequent. The great majority of CICs exhibit grammatical functions. Other than a formulaic *manner* CIC (כֹה 'thus'), few semantic role CICs are present.

Core Patterns.   The אמר corpus has a preference for clause-initial predicators (82.1%). Of these, 91% involve anchored predicators and could not be other than clause initial, but the other 9% are unanchored. For the anchored cases, the dominant sequences are VO, followed by VIO and then VSIO. For the unanchored cases, the dominant sequences are VSO, followed by VO and then VIO. That these dominant sequences are object-of-address final is a reflex of the preference for having all but the shortest speech clause final. Intrusions of SRs into the אמר clause cores are rare, occurring at a rate of 7.4 intrusions per 1,000 clauses.

Chapter 13

The היה Corpus

13.1 Binyan *Census*

The distribution of היה *binyanim* is concentrated in the Qal: 3,546 are Qal and 19 are Niphal. Because the Niphals are so few, they are omitted from consideration here.

The root היה appears in these three very different contexts:

1. single predicators within clauses (2,798×),
2. signalers of transitions in discourse (620×),
3. auxiliary verbs in periphrastic constructions (128×).[1]

We will discuss each of these distinct uses of היה verbs, but our prime focus will be on clauses where היה is the sole predicator. Signalers in discourse will be illustrated in §13.3, but their full exposition must await our planned volume on discourse. We introduce periphrastics in §13.4.

13.2 *Single Predicators in Clauses*

13.2.1 The CIC Subtype Census

The census of the CIC subtypes is as shown in table 13.1.

Table 13.1. CIC Subtype Census for the היה Corpus: 2,798 Structures

Impermanents	Count	Predicators	Count	GFs	Count
Underspecified "and"	1,140	Finite verb	2,656	Subject	1,818
Lapsus calami	2	Predicative inf. abs.		Direct object	
Nebulous	3	Purely verbal participle	3	Indirect object	171
Syntactic Isolates	*Count*	Noun-verb participle		Complement	1,199
Vocative	25	Infinitive construct	139	*Top Six SRs*	*Count*
Exclamative	9	Non-predicative inf. abs.	11	Location	703
Label	19	*Operators*	*Count*	Possessor	570
		Negative	258	Comparison	268
		Closed interrogative	12	Time point	256
		Other conjunction[a]	18	Beneficiary	148
		Modal	8	Accompanier	134

a. "Other conjunction" includes all CIC-level conjunctions other than those classified as underspecified "and."

---

1. In one of the periphrastic constructions, both verbs have the root היה: Ps 50:21.

13.2.2   Survey of the Non-GF/SR Clause Immediate Constituents

> §13.2.2   Main Observations: (1) There are few non-GF/SR CICs in the היה corpus; 12.2% of the clauses contain them, and if the negatives are excluded, 3.3%. (2) As for the negative CICs, almost always they immediately precede the predicators (95%).

13.2.2.1   Impermanents

Underspecified "and" CICs.   Excluded from the clausal analyses.

Indeterminate Constituents.   There are two *lapsii calami*, in Jer 50:29 and Lam 5:3. Both are *Qere welo' Kethiv*s with the *Qere* readings לָהּ 'to her' and וְ 'and'.

Nebulous.   Two object markers, in 1 Kgs 11:15 and 25, and a noun phrase in Ezek 45:5.

13.2.2.2   Syntactic Isolates

Vocatives.   There are 25 vocatives. One-quarter are clause initial (6×), 2 follow exclamatives (Neh 1:5 and 1:11), and one-third are clause terminal (9×). Almost half are in the Latter Prophets (11×) and one-third (9×) in the Writings.

Exclamatives.   There are 9 exclamatives. Three are clause-initial הִנֵּה or הֵן in Gen 27:39, 30:34; and Josh 24:27; אָנָּא occurs in Neh 1:5 and 1:11.

Labels.   There are 19 set phrases: נְאֻם־יהוה 'oracle of Yahweh' or a variant. They are clause terminal 16 times and clause medial 3 times.

13.2.2.3   Predicators

Of the 11 non-predicative infinitive absolutes, there are 6 cognate-root intensifiers[2] and 5 non-cognate root amplifiers.[3]

13.2.2.4   Operators

Negatives.   Of 258 negatives, 14 do not immediately precede the predicator.

Closed Interrogatives.   There are 12 closed interrogatives.

Other Conjunctions.   Fourteen are instances of גַּם /גַם 'also', 3 of כִּי 'that' (Gen 21:30, Judg 16:25, and Jer 48:27), and 1 of אוֹ 'or', in Job 3:16.

Modals.   Modals occur 8 times: כִּי 'surely' 4×, אַךְ 'surely' 2× (1 Sam 18:17 and Hos 12:12), לוּ 'would that' 1× (Gen 30:34), and מִי־יִתֵּן, an optative-modal idiom often translated 'would that,' 1× (Deut 5:29). See §15.3.4.4.

13.2.3   Survey of the GF/SR Clause Immediate Constituents

> §13.2.3   Main Observations: (1) Adverbs are few, and none predominates. (2) The identities of two kinds of PP CICs are determined once the semantics of their substantives is given: time and infinitive of utterance. (3) The לְ-phrases are roughly equally divided among the possessor, subject complement, and "other" SRs. (4) Excluding time noun phrases, most בְּ-phrases involve locations (nearly 80%). (5) Nearly two-thirds of the bare substantives are subjects (64%), about three-tenths are subject complements (30%), and the rest are scattered over many SRs (6%).

---

2. Gen 18:18; Num 30:7; 1 Kgs 13:32; Jer 15:18; Ezek 1:3, 20:32. Each immediately precedes its predicator, except in Ezek 20:32, which has an interpolated negative.

3. 2 Sam 12:2; Qoh 2:7, 16; 11:8; and 2 Chr 32:27. All involve הַרְבֵּה 'to increase'.

This subsection investigates linkages between CIC functions (given by CIC GF/SR labels) and their forms (given by the labels on the CIC daughter nodes). The CIC daughters distribute as shown in table 13.2. Each type of form will be taken up in its turn.

Table 13.2. GF/SR Daughter Forms

GF/SR Daughter	*Count*
Adverb	164
Clause(-like) structure	3
Prepositional phrase	3,281
Noun phrase	2,524
Pronoun	191

13.2.3.1 Adverbs

The adverbs subdivide into three subsets. We distinguish adverbs with temporal semantics, adverbs with spatial semantics, and certain other adverbs ("adverbs of manner"):

Temporal Adverbs (tm pt, tm int, # times)		
אָז	then	2
כְּבָר	already	3
עֲדֶן	yet	1
עוֹד	still [tm int]	13
עוֹד	again [# times]	23
עַתָּה	now	9
טֶרֶם	not yet	1

Spatial Adverbs (loc)		
הֵנָּה	here	7
שָׁם	there	43
שָׁמָּה	thither	3

Adverbs of Manner (mnr)		
אֵפוֹא	then	1
יַחְדָּו	together	2
כֹּה	thus	3[a]
כֵּן	thus	31
מְאֹד	very	4[b]
נָא	[emphatic]	15
רַק	only [rstr]	3

a. The count includes 2 כֹּה in Gen 15:5 and Isa 24:13 and 1 כָּכָה in Neh 5:13.
b. The count consists of 3 מְאֹד and 1 כִּי (Exod 3:12).

13.2.3.2 Clause(-Like) Structures

There are three clause-like structures, each labeled a cognitive complement (cogv cmpl): Gen 21:30, Judg 16:25, and Jer 48:27.

13.2.3.3 Prepositional Phrases

The היה clauses contain 3,281 prepositional phrases that are CIC immediate daughters. Each consists of two sisters: a preposition, and a substantive or substantive-like constituent. The CIC-dominated prepositional phrase in (13.1) from Judg 11:8 illustrates the concept (see p. 189). The CIC is a beneficiary (benf) dominating the prepositional phrase (to+humn/prep), which dominates the preposition לְ 'to' and the construct chain כֹּל יֹשְׁבֵי גִלְעָד 'all of dwellers of Gilead'.

(13.1)

1,584 ל'	636 בְּ'	278 כַּ'	180 מִ'	171 עַל	168 אֶל	133 עִם	57 עַד	74 Misc.

These are the prepositions that are involved:

Temporal Substantive in PP Is Part of Time SR. Prepositional phrases involving nouns with temporal semantics occur 105 times. In all but 12 cases,[4] their dominating CICs involve time.

Infinitive of Utterance Is Always Quoter SR. The identity of the preposition is usually needed to infer the GF or SR of a prepositional phrase. If, however, an infinitive of utterance or a substantive having temporal semantics is involved, then—as was the case for the אמר corpus—the nature of the phrase of which they are part is thereby determined. There are 115 instances of לֵ'אמֹר 'to say' in היה clauses, and each is assigned the CIC label qtr (quoter). Phrase marker (13.2) from Jer 1:11 illustrates the situation:

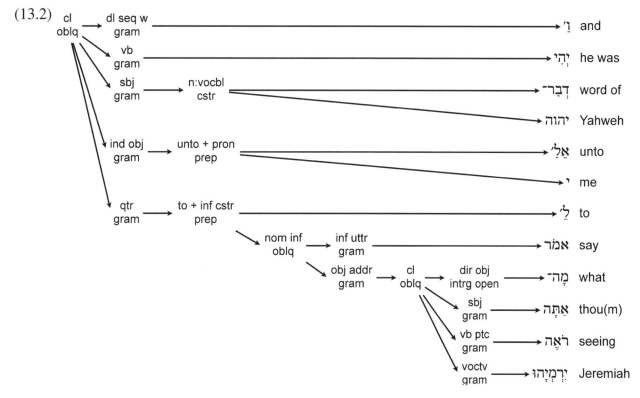

(13.2)

The ל' *Prepositional Phrases.* The CIC-dominated prepositional phrases with ל' occur 1,584 times. Table 13.3 documents how the ל' prepositional phrases are distributed across major GFs / SRs.

---

4. In 10 of these cases, some form of the preposition כְּ' 'like' is involved.

Table 13.3. 'לְ-Phrase Substantive versus GFs / SRs

substantive type ↓	poss	sbj cmp	[other]
[pronoun]	385		98
human	135	122	88
[other]	43	307	409
Total	563	426	595

The 'בְּ Prepositional Phrases.   As table 13.4 documents, prepositional phrases involving 'בְּ occur 636 times in the היה corpus. They are linked to location SRs 404 times (64%) and to time points
167 times (26%). These two SRs account for 90% of the 'בְּ prepositional phrases in היה clauses.

Table 13.4. 'בְּ-Phrase Substantive versus GFs / SRs

substantive type ↓	loc	tm pt	[other]
[pronoun]	80		10
human	53	2	8
other infinitive construct		43	1
geographic	145		1
temporal		110	10
body part	43		5
[other]	83	12	30
Total	404	167	65

Remaining Prepositional Phrases.   The 'לְ and 'בְּ PPs together account for 67.3% of the PPs.
Remaining for GF / SR specification are 1,076 PPs, involving 6 "major" prepositions:

1. 'כְּ—The next most frequent PP involves 'כְּ 'like'. We have classified these phrases as
comparisons (cmpr) 260 times out of 278 occurrences (93.5%). Twelve PPs that are not
comparisons have temporal SRs. Example: כַּיּוֹם הַזֶּה 'as is now the case', a time point
[tm pt] in Deut 4:20. In our mixed representation, 5 have the GF of subject complement
and 1 of subject. Example: וְהָיָה כַצַּדִּיק כָּרָשָׁע 'innocent and guilty fare alike' in Gen 18:25.[5]
2. 'מִ—There are 180 PPs involving 'מִ. More than half (97, 54%) are movement origins (mvt
orig). The rest scatter across 16 CIC labels.
3. עַל—Of the 171 phrases involving עַל, the substantial majority (134, 78.4%) are location
(loc) CICs. The remaining 35 appear in 8 other CIC classes.

---

5. Due to our mixed representation (§9.2), a CIC may correctly be assigned a GF in 1 context but improperly
receive an SR in another. Here, the 2 PPs have their GFs specified (sbj and sbj cmp), but we could have called each a
comparison (cmpr), albeit violating the constraint that assigning GF takes precedence over SR representation.

4. אֶל—There are 168 PPs with אֶל. Just over three-quarters are indirect objects (ind obj): pronominal 69 times, human 59 times, and divine once.[6] The remaining 39 phrases comprise 7 CIC classes, with 29 involving location or orientation.

5. עִם—There are 132 accompanier (accmp) SRs involving עִם. Twice, the preposition might be translated 'beside' (so BDB). In 2 Sam 24:16, the angel was "עִם the threshing floor," while in Deut 18:1 the priests have no territory "עִם Israel."

6. עַד—If the nonprepositional constituent is an infinitive construct (13×) or has temporal semantics (30×), then the SR is time aim (tm aim) or time interval (tm int) 1×. The SR is movement aim (mvt aim) 13×.[7]

13.2.4 Substantives

The final constituents to be considered are the 2,715 "bare" substantives.[8] Of the total 2,798 single-predicator היה clauses, 2,078 clauses (74%) contain one or more bare substantives. They distribute as shown in table 13.5.

Table 13.5. Substantives for the היה Corpus

substantive type ↓	subj	subj cmp	[other]
human	373	241	15
vocable	193	15	
[other]	1,240	492	146
Total	1,806	748	161

13.3 היה *Verbs as Discourse Transition Markers*

The discourse transition sequences וַיְהִי 'and he was' (376×) and וְהָיָה 'and he will be' (167×) are dominated by cue/cue nodes[9] in our representation, as in phrase marker (13.3) from Ruth 3:8. The two segments form a compound cue phrase.[10] We find this phenomenon 546 times (see PM (13.3), p. 192).[11] We defer discussion of the way these cue phrases function until we address discourse analysis in chap. 21. For now, we observe that in three-quarters of the contexts with these cue phrases, the first CIC in the following clause has a semantic role of time point (tm pt/gram). One of the tasks for discourse analysis will be to decide on the proper scoping of these time-specifying CICs. Over how much of a following narrative do they "hold sway"?

---

6. On this phenomenon, see F. I. Andersen and D. N. Freedman, *Hosea* (AB 24; Garden City: Doubleday, 1980) 149–51.

7. There are five exceptions: *interrog.*: Exod 10:7, Neh 2:6; *manner*: 2 Sam 2:17, 1 Kgs 18:45; *result*: 1 Kgs 17:17.

8. That is, substantives that are neither part of prepositional phrases nor nominalized entities.

9. In addition to the standard pair of markers, there are three oddities: 2 Sam 5:24, 1 Kgs 14:5, and 1 Chr 14:15.

10. Van der Merwe, Naudé, and Kroeze, *A Biblical Hebrew Reference Grammar*, 331. Also Waltke and O'Connor, *IBHS*, 54 n. 24, 634; and M. O'Connor, "Discourse Linguistics and the Study of Biblical Hebrew," in *Congress Volume: Basel, 2001* (ed. A. Lemaire; VTSup 92; Leiden: Brill, 2002) 18.

11. See C. van der Merwe, "The Elusive Biblical Hebrew Term ויהי: A Perspective in Terms of Its Syntax, Semantics, and Pragmatics in 1 Samuel," *HS* 40 (1999) 83–114. Also K. Jongeling, "'And It Came to Pass' Again,'" in *Memoriae Igor M. Diakonoff* (ed. L. Kogan et al.; Babal und Bibel 2; Winona Lake, IN: Eisenbrauns, 2005) 291–329.

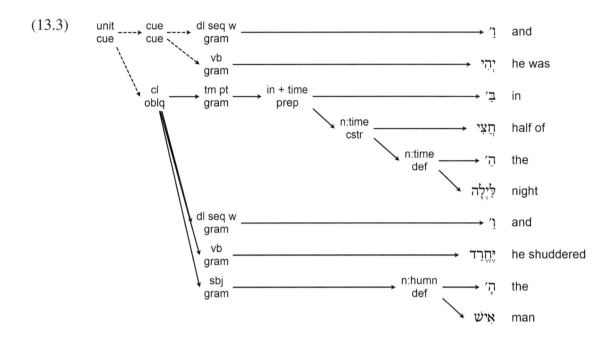

13.4 *Periphrastics*

Consider phrase marker (13.4) from Nah 3:11, where the predicator results from compounding תְּהִי נַעֲלָמָה 'do thou(m) be . . . hidden', which is licensed by the relation *inverse modification* (inv mod).

(13.4)

cl oblq	→	vb ptc gram	→	vb ptc inv mod	→	תְּהִי	do thou(f) be
					↘	נַעֲלָמָה	hidden
	↘	sbj gram	→	pers pr inv mod	→	גַּם־	also
					↘	אַתְּ	thou(f)

13.5 *Clause Immediate Constituent Incidence Contours*

Examining the bar chart for the clauses making up the היה corpus, we see that, in comparison with the overall incidences shown in §11.2, the היה clauses use *unanchored predicators* slightly more often (60% versus 54%) and use *anchored predicators* slightly less often (40% versus 46%). Explicit *subjects* are more than half-again more frequent, while *direct objects* are nonexistent. *Indirect objects* are 60% as frequent. The noun-verb participle does not occur. New to the party are *possessors, comparisons, time points,* and *beneficiaries.* The possessor semantic role occurs more than 10 times as frequently with היה as with any of the other clauses of Biblical Hebrew. Comparisons are 3 times more frequent. Time points are almost twice as frequent. Beneficiaries are nearly twice as frequent.

CIC Incidence for היה Clauses

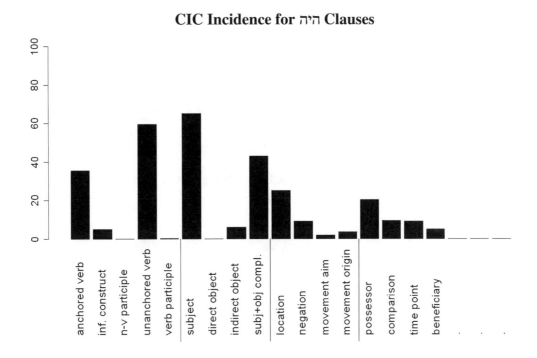

13.6 *Core Constituent Ordering*

13.6.1   Core Patterns for the היה Corpus

We plot bar graphs for היה clauses with anchored and unanchored predicators. The procedures for extracting the core patterns were specified in §11.3.2.2.

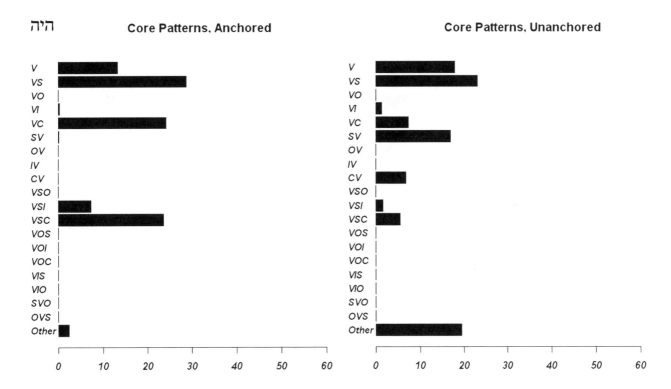

The table shows the sequence patterns for both anchored and unanchored predicators.

Predicator Type	Rank #1		Rank #2		Rank #3		Rank #4		Rank #5		Rank #6	
Anchored	VS	29%	VC	24%	VSC	24%	V	13%	VSI	7%	VCS	1%
Unanchored	VS	23%	V	18%	SV	17%	SVC	11%	VC	7%	CV	7%

13.6.2 SRs Amid GFs

The numerical entries in the table below disclose what percent of a given SR group is interpolated amid the GFs of the clauses that compose the היה corpus.[12]

Root	# Qal Active Clauses	Percent of SR-Groups Interpolated amid the היה GFs					
		Other Participant	Movement and Spatial	Temporal	Manner	Enriching Constituent	Mixed level and DU
היה	2,798	41.1%	17.8%	8.0%	21.9%	29.7%	7.3%

The specifics underlying these figures are:

- *Other Participant.* Of the 917 *Other Participant* tokens, 377 are interpolated, an incidence of 377/917 or 41.1%.
- *Movement and Spatial.* Of the 859 *Movement and Spatial* tokens, 153 are interpolated, 17.8%.
- *Temporal.* Of the 439 *Temporal* SR tokens, 35 are interpolated, 8.0%.
- *Manner.* Of the 73 instances of the *Manner* SR, 16 are interpolated, 21.9%.
- *Enriching Constituent.* Of the 155 *Enriching Constituent* tokens, 46 are interpolated, 29.7%.
- *Mixed Level and Discourse Unit.* Of 524 *aim* and *comparison* tokens, 38 are interpolated, 7.3%.

We count 665 interpolates. The "interpolation rate" is 238 interpolations per 1,000 היה clauses.

13.7 *Brief Summary*

We parse היה predicators as: single predicators in clauses (79%), discourse transition signalers (17%), and auxiliary verbs in periphrastics (4%).

The Censuses. The predicators of היה are overwhelmingly Qal actives (99.5%). When they are the sole predicators in clauses, most are finite verbs (95%), with infinitives construct next most likely (5%). Non-GF/SR CICs are uncommon (in 12% of clauses), with negatives being the most frequent (in 9% of the clauses and immediately pre-predicator in 94% of occurrences). Regarding GFs, explicit subjects are in 65% of the clauses and subject complements in 43%. SRs are common. The two most frequent (location and possessor) are in 45% of the clauses. Adverbs are SRs in 6% of the היה corpus. The most common prepositions, ל and ב, account for two-thirds of the PP SRs. The preposition ל appears in possessor (36%), subject complement (27%), and "other" (37%)

---

12. Readers wishing to be reminded of the way we group the SRs should look inside the back cover.

SRs. The preposition ב appears in locations (64%) and in time points (26%). Bare substantives are mainly subjects (67%) and subject complements (28%).

CIC Incidence. היה clauses use *unanchored verbs* slightly more often and *anchored verbs* slightly less than is the case across Biblical Hebrew. Relative to all of Biblical Hebrew, explicit *subjects* are $1\frac{1}{2}$ times more frequent, *possessors* are 10 times more frequent, *comparisons* 3 times more frequent, and *time points* and *beneficiaries* approximately 2 times more frequent.

Core Patterns. Of the 6 most frequent sequences in both anchored and unanchored היה predicators, only 2 are not predicator initial (unanchored SV, 16%, and unanchored SVC, 10%). For the anchored cases, the top 3 dominant sequences are VS, followed by VC and then VSC. For the unanchored cases, the top 3 dominant sequences are VS, followed by V and then SV. Intrusions of SRs into the היה clause cores are quite frequent, occurring at a rate of 238 intrusions per 1,000 clauses, 32 times more frequent than the rate for אמר.

Chapter 14

The עשׂה Corpus

14.1 *The* Binyan *Census*

There are 2,611 predicators with the root עשׂה in Biblical Hebrew. Of these, 80 are elliptic, leaving a total of 2,531 actual predicators. The remaining 2,531 instances involve 2,416 Qal actives, 15 Qal passives, 98 Niphal passives, and two Piel actives.[1] In this chapter, we study only the Qal actives.

14.2 *The CIC Subtype Census*

The distribution of the CICs for the 2,416 Qal active עשׂה clauses are shown in table 14.1.

Table 14.1. CIC Subtype Census for the עשׂה Corpus: 2,416 Structures

Impermanents	Count	Predicators	Count	GFs	Count
Underspecified "and"	704	Finite verb	1,966	Subject	633
Lapsus calami	2	Predicative inf. abs.	5	Direct object	1,484
Nebulous	2	Purely verbal participle	97	Indirect object	359
Syntactic Isolates	*Count*	Noun-verb participle	51	Complement	7
Vocative	20	Infinitive construct	297	*Top Six SRs*	*Count*
Exclamative	4	Non-predicative inf. abs.	11	Location	373
Label	5	*Operators*	*Count*	Comparison	304
		Negative	143	Manner	202
		Closed interrogative	13	Beneficiary	198
		Other conjunction	12	Time point	118
		Modal	9	Aim / purpose	87

14.3 *Survey of the Non-GF/SR Clause Immediate Constituents*

§14.3 Main Observations: (1) Non-GF/SR CICs are infrequent in the עשׂה corpus. They appear in 8% of the clauses, and if the negatives are excluded, in just over 2.5%. (2) As for the negative CICs, usually they immediately precede their predicator (88%).

---

1. Two Piels, in Ezek 23:3 and 8, having the sense of 'press, squeeze (unchaste act)' (BDB), are omitted.

14.3.1   Impermanents

Underspecified "and" is omitted from the analysis, as are two *lapsii calami* (in 2 Kgs 19:31 and Ezek 9:11), both *Qere welo' Kethiv*s, and two nebulous CICs, both in 2 Sam 7:23.

14.3.2   Syntactic Isolates

14.3.2.1   Vocatives

Of the 20 vocatives, 6 are clause initial, 7 clause final. There are 9 in the Latter Prophets.

14.3.2.2   Exclamatives

Clause-initial אֲהָהּ occurs before vocatives in 2 Kgs 6:15 and Ezek 11:13.

14.3.2.3   Labels

There are 5 set phrases, variants of נְאֻם־יהוה 'oracle of Yahweh'. They are clause terminal 4 times (Jer 19:12; Ezek 12:25, 36:32, 37:14) and clause medial once (Jer 5:18).

14.3.3   Predicators

Most predicators in the עשׂה corpus are finite verbs (82%), with infinitives construct second-most frequent (12%). There are 10 cognate-root infinitives absolute (intensifiers) in the עשׂה clauses. There is 1 non-cognate root infinitive absolute (amplifier), in Qoh 12:12, involving הַרְבֵּה 'to increase'.

14.3.4   Operators

14.3.4.1   Negatives

Of 143 negatives, 126 immediately precede their predicators (88%).

14.3.4.2   Closed Interrogatives

There are 13 closed interrogatives.[2]

14.3.4.3   Other Conjunctions

There are 12 noncoordinating conjunctions. Nine are גַם /גָם 'also' and 3 אַף 'also'.

14.3.4.4   Modals

There are these 9 modals: כִּי 'surely' 3×, אוּלַי 'perhaps' 4×, and אָכֵן 'surely' 2×.

14.4   *Survey of the GF/SR Clause Immediate Constituents*

> §14.4   Main Observations: (1) Adverbs are few, with כֵּן 'thus' predominating (168×). (2) The identity of one PP CIC is determined by the semantics of its substantives, time. (3) The ל-phrases are divided among the indirect object (47%), beneficiary (26%), and "other" SRs (27%). (4) Excluding time noun phrases, two-thirds of ב-phrases involve locations. (5) Of the bare substantives, 33% are subjects and 54% are direct objects.

---

2. In addition, there are 10 phrasal open interrogatives: לְ׳מָה 'to what' = 'why?' (4×) and עַד־מָתַי 'until when' = 'how long?' (3×), בַּ׳מֶה 'in what?' (2×), and תַּחַת מֶה 'under what?' (1×).

This subsection investigates linkages between CIC functions (given by GF/SR labels) and their forms (given by CIC daughter labels). The CIC daughters' distribution is shown in table 14.2.

Table 14.2. GF/SR Daughter Forms

GF/SR Daughter	*Count*
Adverb	211
Clause	7
Prepositional phrase	2,103
Noun phrase	1,594
Pronoun	291

14.4.1 Adverbs

The 211 adverbs are subdivided into 3 subsets on the basis of semantics. We distinguish adverbs having temporal semantics (temporal adverbs), adverbs having spatial semantics (spatial adverbs), and certain other adverbs (adverbs of manner). Here are the adverbs in עשׂה clauses:

Temporal Adverbs (tm pt, tm int, # times)		*Spatial Adverbs* (loc)		*Adverbs of Manner* (mnr)	
עוֹד still [tm int]	4	הֵנָּה here	9	כֵּן thus	168
עַתָּה now	4	שָׁם there	10	נָא [emphatic]	5
הָלְאָה farther[a]	1			אֵפוֹא then	2
כְּבָר already	1			מְאֹד very	3
עוֹד again [# times]	2			יַחְדָּו together	1
				פִּתְאֹם suddenly	1

a. Usually spatial, in Ezek 43:27, the sense has "leaked" into the temporal domain.

14.4.2 Clauses

There are 7 cognitive complements, each involving questioning: Gen 20:9, Exod 14:5, Num 22:28, 1 Sam 20:1, and Jer 4:30 (3×). See §8.2.2. Phrase marker (14.1) from Exod 14:5 illustrates (p. 199).

14.4.3 Prepositional Phrases

The עשׂה clauses contain 2,118 prepositional phrases involving 16 prepositions:

לְ' 727	בְּ' 436	אֵת 380	כְּ' 308	עִם 86	מִ' 67	עַל 56	לְמַעַן 16	עַד 11	תַּחַת 9	Misc. 22

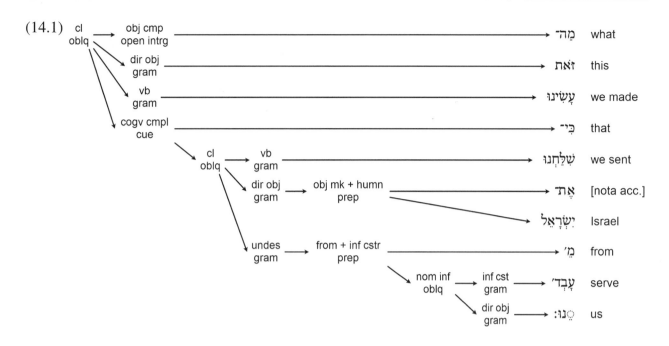

14.4.3.1   A Temporal Substantive in a PP Is Part of a Time SR

The preposition usually identifies the GF/SR of a prepositional phrase, but one of the substantive categories is determinative (temporal semantics). Prepositional phrases involving nouns having temporal semantics occur 92 times. In all cases,[3] their dominating CICs involve time.

14.4.3.2   The 'ל Prepositional Phrases

Prepositional phrases involving 'ל occur 727 times. The most common categories are indirect object (ind obj) and beneficiary (benf)—nearly three-quarters of the prepositional phrases that are CICs.

Table 14.3. 'ל-Phrase Substantive versus GFs/SRs in the עשה Corpus

substantive type ↓	ind obj	benf	[other]
[pronoun]	159	126	1
human	102	12	15
[other]	81	53	178
Total	342	191	194

It is important to understand the natures of these two categories. The first (ind obj) is a GF, while the second (benf) is an SR. They are not mutually exclusive. Indeed, in a full representation of the grammatical structure of a clause (§9.2.2), a constituent may concurrently have a GF of indirect object *and* an SR of beneficiary, as in phrase marker (14.2) from 1 Sam 19:5. The final CIC is correctly assigned the GF of indirect object. But from a semantic perspective, the constituent may well have the SR of beneficiary. Indeed, we classify the constituent לְכָל־יִשְׂרָאֵל 'to all of

---

3. The semantic roles of 3 temporal CICs are masked by the fact that, because of our mixed representation strategy, they are labeled direct objects: Exod 31:16, Deut 5:15, and Esth 9:19.

Israel' as a beneficiary in phrase marker (14.3) from 1 Chr 29:21 (p. 201). This raises an important question: did the human over-reader adhere to the mixed-representation policy of applying a GF category wherever possible in preference to the SR? Since our awareness of the distinction between grammatical and semantic functions only emerged after we were well into the process of assigning categories, the candid admission must be made that the policy could not have been adhered to strictly. This fact makes it all the more important that we implement the full representation as soon as possible.

(14.2)

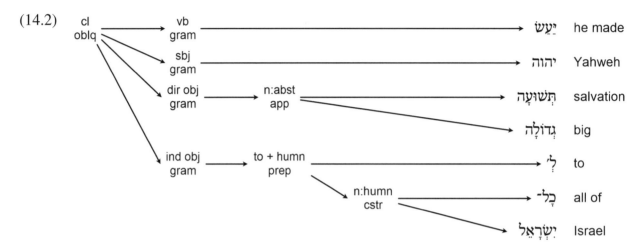

14.4.3.3 The 'בְּ Prepositional Phrases

Prepositional phrases involving 'בְּ occur 436 times in עשׂה Qal active clauses. They are linked to location SRs 259 times (59.4%) and to time SRs 70 times (16.1%). Hence, these 2 SRs account for almost 76% of the instances of 'בְּ PPs in עשׂה clauses.

Table 14.4. 'בְּ-Phrase Substantive versus GFs / SRs

substantive type ↓	loc	tm pt	[other]
body part	103		6
geographic	61		
temporal		46	
[other]	95	24	101
Total	259	70	107

This is a good place to point out a very common situation, in which information from a nearby clause is required in order properly to assign a semantic role. How does one determine the roles associated with PPs involving pronouns? Our database does not yet encode chains of referential cohesion. That is, anaphors and cataphors are not yet indicated. Hence, in an embedded obliqueness structure such as in (14.4) from Exod 35:2 (p. 202), the SR of בּוֹ 'in him' is not accessible from the clause context.

(14.3)

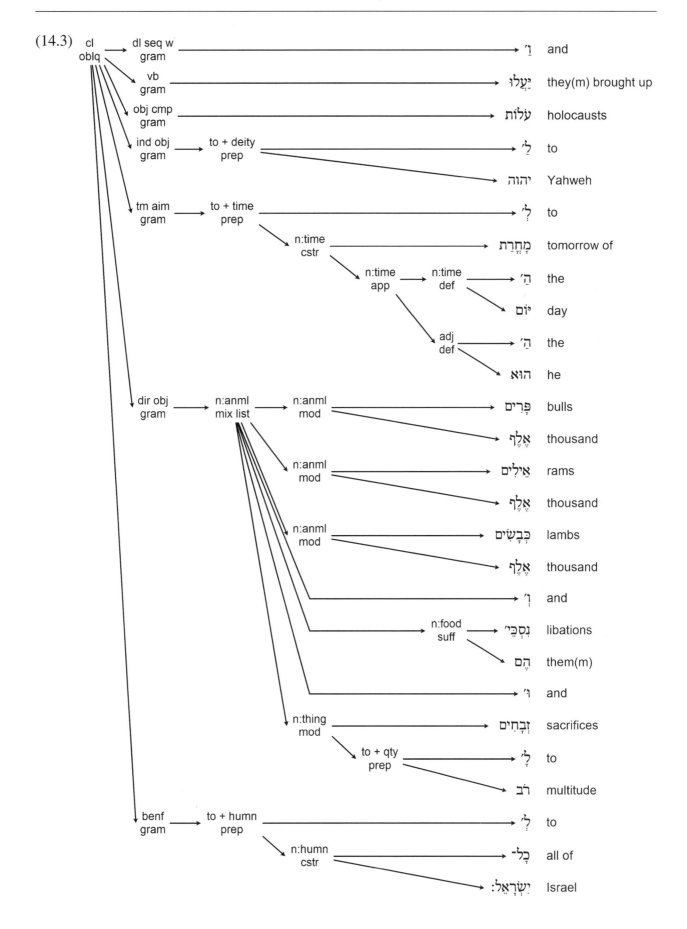

(14.4)

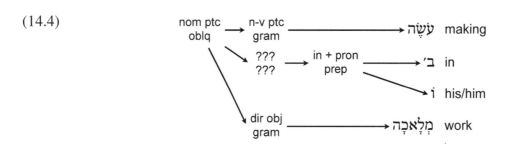

Clearly, we must work out what the anaphor (or cataphor) of 'him' is. To do this, we require access to the clause before the clause in which the nominalized participle is embedded. There, we see that the anaphor of 'him' is יוֹם הַשְּׁבִיעִי׳ 'the day the seventh'. This being the anaphor, we infer that בוֹ must have a semantic role involving time.

14.4.3.4 Nearly Invariant Prepositional Phrases

Some prepositions are predominantly associated with a single GF or SR, with very few exceptions. These are: אֶת '(object marker)' with 99.7% dir obj,[4] כְּ׳ 'like' with 97.4% cmpr,[5] and עִם 'with' with 89.5% accmp. In table 14.5, we list the prepositions and their preponderant substantive objects.

Table 14.5. Nearly Invariant Preposition GFs / SRs

substantive type ↓	אֶת dir obj	כְּ׳ cmpr	עִם accmp
[pronoun]	107	15	52
human	19	12	24
[nominalized]	17	151	
vocable	66	46	
[other]	171	84	10
Total	380	308	86

14.4.3.5 The Remaining Prepositional Phrases

To this point, we have presented the prepositional phrases associated with 5 different prepositions. These account for 91.4% of the PPs. Left for specification are 181 PPs, involving 5 "major" prepositions plus a miscellany of 6. We give their tallies in a condensed format:

1. מִ׳ —There are 67 PPs involving מִ׳ and its variants. Nearly half (28, 42%) involve position: location (loc) 5×, movement interval (mvt int) 1×, or movement origin (mvt orig) 22×. The rest are scattered across a surprising 11 CIC labels (this scattering is quite similar to what we found in the היה clauses).
2. עַל—There are 56 PPs involving עַל and variants. Most (46, 82%) involve location (loc). The other 10 involve rsn (5×), accmp (1×), refrnt (3×), and rslt (1×).

---

4. There is a subject with an object marker in Neh 9:34.
5. Seven out of the 8 noncomparatives are "approximate time" specifiers.

3. לְמַעַן—There are 16 instances of prepositional phrases involving לְמַעַן. They appear as reason (8×), result (3×), beneficiary (3×), and aim (2×).

4. עַד—There are 11 instances of prepositional phrases involving עַד.

5. תַּחַת—There are 9 instances of prepositional phrases involving תַּחַת.

6. *Miscellaneous.* The other 6 prepositions are: אֶל 'unto' (3×), אַחַר 'afterward' (2×), בֵּין 'between' (7×), בַּעַד 'through' (1×), בַּעֲבוּר 'for the sake of' (6×), לְבַד 'except' (3×).

14.4.4   Substantives

The final constituents to be tabulated are 1,885 bare substantives in the Qal active עשה clauses. Approximately two-thirds contain one or more bare substantives.

Table 14.6. Bare Substantives in the עשה Corpus

substantive type ↓	sbj	dir obj	[other]
human	316	38	5
quality	8	140	6
deity	102	17	2
pronoun	142	143	6
utensil	3	87	33
[other]	54	586	192
Total	629	1,011	245

14.5   *Clause Immediate Constituent Incidence Contours*

Below is the bar graph of CIC incidence for the Qal active עשה corpus.

CIC Incidence for Qal עשה Clauses

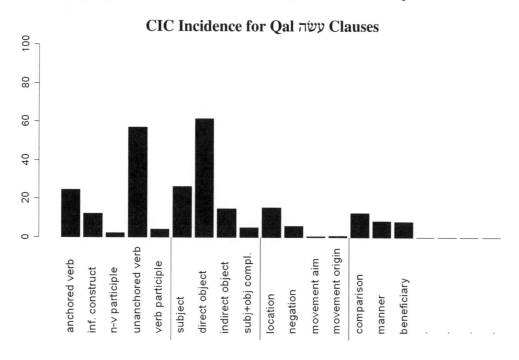

With Qal active עשׂה, unanchored finite verbs are preferred. An explicit subject occurs in one-third of the clauses, a direct object in nearly two-thirds, a location in about 15%, and movement rarely.

14.6 *Core Constituent Ordering*

14.6.1 Core Patterns for the Qal Active עשׂה Corpus

There are 940 עשׂה clauses for which the predicator is anchored. Of the 1,476 clauses with unanchored predicators, 853 are clause initial, and 623 are clause medial or final. Hence, 58% of the unanchored predicators are clause initial.

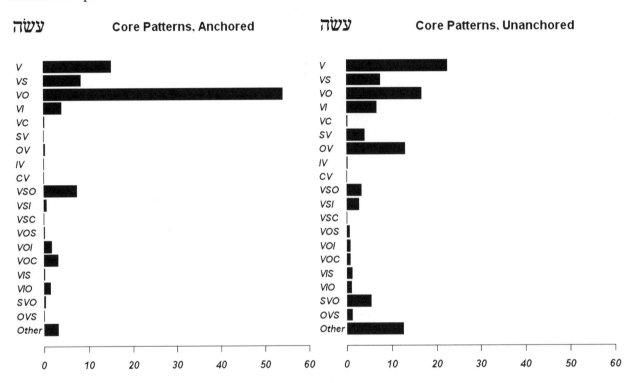

The table shows the sequence patterns for both anchored and unanchored predicators.

Predicator Type		Rank #1		Rank #2		Rank #3		Rank #4		Rank #5		Rank #6	
Anchored	940	VO	54%	V	15%	VS	8%	VSO	7%	VI	4%	VOC	3%
Unanchored	1,476	V	23%	VO	17%	OV	13%	VS	7%	VI	7%	SVO	6%

For the anchored predicators, the majority of the clauses have the VO core pattern (54%) with very few OV patterns (0.3%). Instances of the VSO pattern significantly outnumber those with the SVO pattern (7% versus 0.3%). For the unanchored predicators, many of the clauses have the VO core pattern (17%), but there also are many with the OV pattern (13%). Instances of the VSO pattern lag somewhat behind those with the SVO pattern (3% versus 6%).

14.6.2 SRs amid GFs in the Qal Active עשׂה Corpus

SRs are interpolated amid the GFs in the עשׂה corpus as shown in the table.[6]

	# Qal Active Clauses	Percent of SR-Groups Interpolated Amid עשׂה GFs					
Root		Other Participant	Movement and Spatial	Temporal	Manner	Enriching Constituent	Mixed level and DU
עשׂה	2,396	48.5%	12.1%	10.2%	16.4%	8.1%	2.6%

The specifics underlying these figures are:

- *Other Participant.*   Of the 295 *Other Participant* tokens, 143 are interpolated, an incidence of 143 / 295 or 48.5% (beneficiaries account for most of the intrusion).
- *Movement and Spatial.*   Of the 414 *Movement and Spatial* tokens, 50 are interpolated, 12.1% (location CICs account for the vast majority).
- *Temporal.*   Of the 196 *Temporal* SR tokens, 20 are interpolated, 10.2%.
- *Manner.*   Of the 201 instances of the *manner* SR, 33 are interpolated, 16.4%.
- *Enriching Constituent.*   Of the 160 *Enriching Constituent* tokens, 13 are interpolated, 8.1%.
- *Mixed Level and Discourse Unit.*   Of 426 *aim* and *comparison* tokens, 11 are interpolated, 2.6%.

We count 270 interpolations. The "interpolation rate" is 113 interpolations per 1,000 עשׂה clauses.

14.7 *Brief Summary*

The Censuses.   The predicators of עשׂה are predominantly Qal actives (95%), there being a residuum of Niphal passives (4%). Most predicators are finite verbs (81%), with infinitives construct the next most common predicator (12%). Non-GF/SR CICs are infrequent (in 9% of clauses), with negatives being the most common (in 6% of the clauses). Regarding GFs, explicit subjects appear in 26% of the clauses, direct objects in 61%, and indirect objects in 15%, mostly involving ל (95%). The adverb of manner כֵּן 'thus' occurs in 7% of the clauses. Three prepositions account for three-quarters of the PP CICs: ל, ב, and אֵת. The bare substantives are mainly direct objects (54%) or subjects (33%). Bare substantives are usually subjects when they have human semantics (88%). Bare substantives are often direct objects when they have utensil semantics (71%) or quality semantics (91%).

CIC Incidence.   Comparing relative frequencies: עשׂה clauses use *unanchored verbs* a bit more often and *anchored verbs* a bit less often than is the case across Biblical Hebrew; there are about 70% as many *subjects*, about one-quarter more *direct objects*, and 40% more *indirect objects*.

Core Patterns.   For anchored עשׂה predicators, the majority of the clauses have the VO core pattern (54%). The VSO pattern is significantly more frequent than the SVO pattern (7% versus 0.3%). For the unanchored predicators, the VO core pattern is not uncommon (17%), but OV is also not uncommon (13%).

---

6. Note: the number of clauses being considered is reduced by 20 clauses because we have excluded clauses with compound predicators to simplify the discussion.

With 113 SR intrusions per 1,000 clauses, the עשׂה corpus lies midway between the sparse intrusion occurring in the אמר corpus (7.4 / 1,000) and the rampant intrusion found in the היה corpus (238 / 1,000).

Chapter 15

The נתן Corpus

15.1 *The* Binyan *Census*

There are 1,992 instances of the root נתן: 1,896 Qal actives, 8 Qal passives, 7 Piel passives, and 81 Niphal passives. We characterize the Qal actives.

15.2 *The CIC Subtype Census*

The 1,896 clauses with Qal active נתן exhibit the distribution of CICs shown in table 15.1.

Table 15.1. CIC Subtype Census for the נתן Corpus: 1,896 Structures

Impermanents	Count	Predicators	Count	GFs	Count
Underspecified "and"	703	Finite verb	1,626	Subject	520
Lapsus calami		Predicative inf. abs.	7	Direct object	1,521
Nebulous	1	Purely verbal participle	83	Indirect object	972
Syntactic Isolates	*Count*	Noun-verb participle	22	Complement	210
Vocative	12	Infinitive construct	158	*Top Six SRs*	*Count*
Exclamative	4	Non-predicative inf. abs.	8	Location	587
Label	11	*Operators*	*Count*	Aim/purpose	146
		Negative	109	Movement aim	95
		Closed interrogative	8	Comparison	83
		Other conjunction[a]	12	Time point	75
		Modal	2	Movement origin	44

a. "Other conjunction" includes all CIC-level conjunctions other than conjunctions that are classified as underspecified "and."

15.3 *Survey of the Non-GF/SR Clause Immediate Constituents*

§15.3 Main Observations: (1) There are relatively few non-GF/SR CICs in the נתן corpus. (2) Usually the negatives immediately precede the predicators (95.2%). (3) Many negatives are clause initial or follow an underspecified "and" (69%).

15.3.1 Impermanents

Underspecified "and" is excluded from the analysis. There is one nebulous CIC, in Ezek 27:18.

15.3.2 Syntactic Isolates

15.3.2.1 Vocatives

Of 12 vocatives, 3 are clause initial, 1 postexclamative (1 Kgs 3:26), and 3 clause final.

15.3.2.2 Exclamatives

Four exclamatives appear, in 1 Kgs 3:26; Ezek 16:23, 21:20; and Hos 11:8.

15.3.2.3 Labels

There are 11 labels, 4 in Jeremiah (all are נְאֻם־יהוה 'oracle of Yahweh') and 7 in Ezekiel (all are נְאֻם אֲדֹנָי יהוה 'oracle of my Lord Yahweh').

15.3.3 Predicators

The finite verbs dominate (86%), with infinitives construct next (8%). Six infinitives absolute are cognate-root intensifiers, and 2 are noncognate root amplifiers.[1]

15.3.4 Operators

15.3.4.1 Negatives

Five of 109 negatives do not directly precede their predicators.

15.3.4.2 Closed Interrogatives

There are 8 closed interrogatives.

15.3.4.3 Other Conjunctions

There are 12 noncoordinating conjunctions. Ten are גַם /גַם 'also', 1 is אַף 'also' (Ps 89:28), and 1 is אוּלָם 'but indeed' (Job 11:5).

15.3.4.4 Modals

There is a single one-segment modal, אַךְ 'surely', in 1 Chr 22:12. More interesting are the optative modals that may be translated 'would that' in Job 6:8. Twenty of the 39 open interrogatives in the נתן corpus are instances of this modal idiom. Phrase marker (15.1) for Job 6:8 shows how we have felt forced to handle the idiomatic clause:[2]

(15.1)
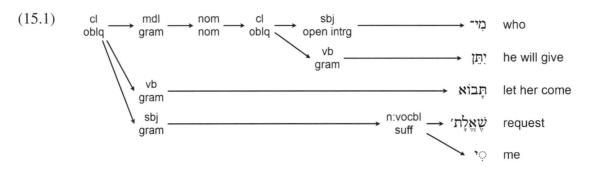

---

1. The 6 intensifiers are in Num 21:2, 27:7; Deut 15:10; Judg 8:25, 11:30; and 2 Sam 5:19. The 2 amplifiers are in 1 Kgs 5:9 and 2 Chr 25:9.

2. See C. van der Merwe, J. A. Naudé, and J. H. Kroeze, *Biblical Hebrew Grammar*, 323, where the idiom is termed an interjection; also B. Jongeling, "L'expression *my ytn* dans l'Ancien Testament," *VT* 24 (1974) 32–40.

In the clause, מִי־יִתֵּן is an embedded clause that we have marked as nominalized and called a modal.

15.4   *Survey of the GF/SR Clause Immediate Constituents*

> §15.4   Main Observations: (1) No adverb predominates in the נתן corpus. (2) The נתן corpus exhibits a mild alternation in realizing indirect objects: ל (91.4%) versus אל (4.3%). (3) Three prepositions account for 81% of the PP CICs: ל, את, and ב. (4) A bare substantive is almost twice as likely to be a direct object (864×) as to be a subject (493×).

This subsection investigates linkages between CIC functions (CIC GF/SR labels) and their forms (CIC daughter labels). The CIC daughters census is shown in the table.

Table 15.2.   GF/SR Daughter Forms

GF/SR Daughter	Count
Adverb	41
Clause(-like) struct.	2
Prepositional phrase	2,741
Noun phrase	1,272
Pronoun	368

15.4.1   Adverbs

The 41 adverbs are subdivided into temporal adverbs, spatial adverbs, and certain other adverbs ("adverbs of manner"). Here are the adverbs in נתן clauses:

Temporal Adverbs (tm pt)		Spatial Adverbs (loc)		Adverbs of Manner (mnr)	
אָז then	2	הֵנָּה here	6	כֵּן thus	5
עוֹד again (# times)	3	שָׁם there	8	נָא (emphatic)	5
עַתָּה now	6	שָׁמָּה thither	4	מְאֹד very	1
				רַק only	1

15.4.2   Clause(-Like) Structures

There are no clause-like structures. The 20 cases of מִי־יִתֵּן are not CIC daughters in נתן clauses.

15.4.3   Prepositional Phrases

The נתן clauses contain 2,763 CIC daughter prepositional phrases involving 19 prepositions:

1,262 לְ	516 אֵת	464 בְּ	194 עַל	100 מְ	85 כְּ	75 אֶל	16 תַּחַת	16 עַד	10 עִם	26 Misc.[a]

a. Eight different prepositions make up this miscellany.

15.4.3.1 Nearly Invariant Prepositional Phrases

The preposition identifies the GF/SR of the PP in 3 instances. All CIC-daughter PPs:

- with אֵת '(obj marker)' (516×)—except 1 in 1 Kgs 11:35, obj cmp—are *direct objects*;
- with 'כַּ 'like' (85×)—except in Exod 31:18, tm pt, and Gen 42:30, obj cmp—are *comparisons*;
- with עִם 'with' (10×) are *accompaniers*.

The other PPs manifest 36 GFs/SRs.

15.4.3.2 Prepositional Phrases with Temporal Semantics

Prepositional phrases with temporal nouns occur 59 times. Their dominating CICs involve time (47×). Of 12 nontemporal CICs, 8 are comparisons involving time. For example, Jer 11:5 has: לָתֵת לָהֶם אֶרֶץ זָבַת חָלָב וּדְבַשׁ כַּיּוֹם הַזֶּה, which NJPS translates 'to give them a land flowing with milk and honey, as is now the case'.

15.4.3.3 The 'לְ Prepositional Phrases

The 1,262 CIC daughter phrases involving 'לְ have the distribution shown in table 15.3.

Table 15.3. 'לְ-Phrase Substantive versus GFs/SRs

substantive type ↓	ind obj	aim	obj cmp	[other]
[pronoun]	498			5
human	280		33	32
other infinitive construct		137		7
[other]	110	4	69	87
Total	888	141	102	131

Clearly 'לְ + [pronoun] or 'לְ + human mostly link to an *indirect object* GF (91%), while 'לְ + infinitive construct almost always links to an *aim/purpose* SR (97%).

15.4.3.4 The 'בְּ Prepositional Phrases

PPs involving 'בְּ occur 464 times in נתן clauses (see table 15.4).

Table 15.4. 'בְּ-Phrase Substantive versus GFs/SRs

substantive type ↓	loc	tm pt	[other]
body part	176		20
geographic	63		2
human	29		11
temporal		28	2
(other)	67	14	52
Total	335	42	87

The prefix 'בְּ + geographic usually links to a location SR, as does 'בְּ + body part.

15.4.3.5 The עַל Prepositional Phrases

Prepositional phrases involving עַל occur 194 times in נתן clauses (table 15.5).

Table 15.5. עַל-Phrase Substantive versus GFs / SRs

substantive type ↓	loc	ind obj	[other]
body part	53		7
(pronoun)	34	15	6
human	14	1	2
geographic	13		1
(other)	42		6
Total	156	16	22

The עַל phrases are linked to location SRs 156 times (80.4%) and to indirect objects 16 times (8.0%), accounting for almost 89% of the instances of the עַל PPs in נתן clauses.

15.4.3.6 The Remaining Prepositional Phrases

To this point, we have presented the prepositional phrases associated with 6 different prepositions. Together these account for 95.6% of the total number of CIC-daughter prepositional phrases in נתן clauses. Remaining for GF / SR specification are 122 prepositional phrases, involving 4 "major" prepositions plus a miscellany of 26 more. We give their tallies in a condensed format.

1. 'מִ—There are 100 prepositional phrases involving 'מִ and its variants. Over half (54) involve position: location (loc) 10× and movement origin (mvt orig) 44×. The rest are scattered across 11 CIC labels (this scattering is quite similar to that of היה clauses).
2. אֶל—There are 75 instances of prepositional phrases involving אֶל. There are 42 indirect objects, 27 involving movement, plus 6 others.
3. תַּחַת—There are 16 instances of prepositional phrases involving תַּחַת. They appear as location (6×) and surrogate (10×).
4. עַד—There are 16 instances of prepositional phrases involving עַד. Nine are time aims, 6 are movement aims, and 1 (Deut 2:5) is an area!
5. *Miscellaneous.* We list the 8 prepositions with their counts (or references):

בֵּין	'between' (9×)	בִּגְלַל	'on account of' (1 Kgs 14:16, Jer 15:4)
לְמַעַן	'for' (5×)	לְבַד	'except' (Gen 32:17, 2 Sam 20:21)
אַחֲרֵי	'after' (4×)	אַחַר	'afterwards' (Num 6:17)
אֵצֶל	'near' (2 Kgs 12:10, Ezek 43:8)	בְּעַד	'through' (Job 2:4)

15.4.4 Substantives

The final constituents to be discussed are the 1,640 "bare" substantives.[3] Of the single-predicator נתן clauses, 1,388 (69%) contain at least 1 bare substantive.

---

3. That is, substantives that are not part of prepositional phrases.

Table 15.6. Substantives for the נתן Corpus

substantive type ↓	sbj	dir obj	[other]
human	151	68	25
deity	207		1
[pronoun]	92	269	7
geographic	11	69	19
substance	5	77	2
body part		62	4
abstract	1	64	7
food		27	1
vocable		44	2
[other]	26	284	115
Total	493	964	183

We observe that in the נתן corpus, a bare substantive is twice as likely to be a direct object as to be a subject (see table 15.6). If the substantive has deity semantics, it is a subject (99.5%). If a substantive is not a pronoun or has semantics other than human or deity, then it is often a direct object (76.5%).

15.5 *Clause Immediate Constituent Incidence Contours*

Consider the bar chart for the clauses making up the נתן cohort.

CIC Incidence for Active נתן Clauses

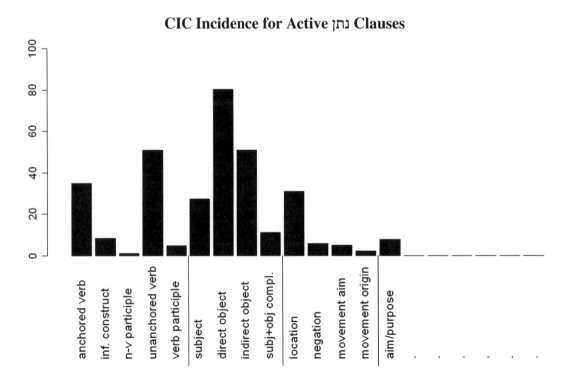

The incidence of the various kinds of predicators is very similar to the incidence for the average clause. Across Biblical Hebrew, we find 46% of predicators are anchored and 54% are unanchored; for the נתן corpus, the percentages are 45% and 55%. Comparing relative frequencies, there are about three-quarters fewer *subjects*, about three-quarters more *direct objects*, and nearly 5 times more *indirect objects*. There are two-thirds more location SRs and somewhat fewer movement origins and movement aims (12% versus 7%).

15.6   *Core Constituents and Their Ordering*

15.6.1   Core Patterns for the נתן Corpus

We plot the horizontal bar charts for נתן clauses with anchored and unanchored predicators.[4]

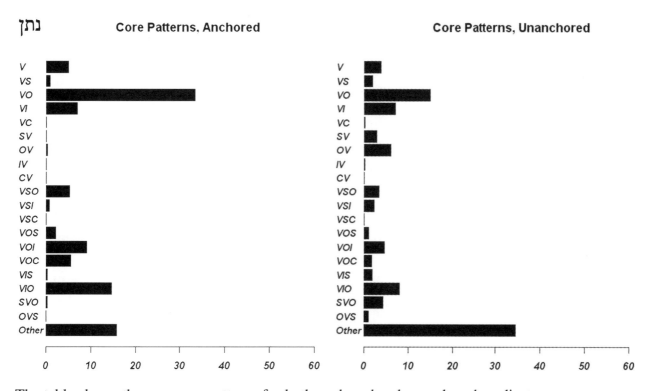

The table shows the sequence patterns for both anchored and unanchored predicators.

Predicator Type		Rank #1		Rank #2		Rank #3		Rank #4		Rank #5		Rank #6	
Anchored	844	VO	33%	VIO	15%	VOI	7%	VI	7%	VOC	6%	VSO	5%
Unanchored	1,052	VO	15%	VIO	8%	OVI	8%	VI	7%	OV	6%	VOI	6%

These are spread-out distributions. For the anchored predicators, the "other" category includes 25% of the clauses. Its top few contributors are V, 5%; VSIO, 3%; VSOI, 2%; VISO, 2%; and VOIC, 1%. For the unanchored cases, the "other" category is very large, 51%. It scatters across many CIC sequence patterns. Its top 4 contributors are SVO, 4%; SVI, 4%; V, 4%; IVO, 4%. Note that almost 62% of the clauses with unanchored predicators are not predicator initial.

---

4. The procedures for extracting the core patterns were specified in §11.3.2.2.

15.6.2 SRs amid GFs in the Qal Active נתן Corpus

Peripheral constituents interpose into the GF cores of clauses having נתן as predicators fairly frequently, as is shown in the table:

| | *# Qal* | Percent of SR-Groups Interpolated amid the נתן GFs | | | | | |
Root	*Active Clauses*	*Other Participant*	*Movement and Spatial*	*Temporal*	*Manner*	*Enriching Constituent*	*Mixed level and DU*
נתן	1,896	19.6%	15.1%	15.5%	35.0%	10.0%	4.0%

The specifics underlying these figures are:

- *Other Participant.* Of the 51 tokens, 10 are interpolated, an incidence of 10/51 or 19.6%.
- *Movement and Spatial.* Of the 710 tokens, 107 are interpolated, 15.1%.
- *Temporal.* Of the 103 tokens, 16 are interpolated, 15.5%.
- *Manner.* Of the 20 instances of the *Manner* SR, 7 are interpolated, 35.0%.
- *Enriching Constituent.* Of the 80 *Enriching Constituent* tokens, 8 are interpolated, 10.0%.
- *Mixed Level and Discourse Unit.* Of the 249 *Mixed Level and DU* tokens, 10 are interpolated, 4.0%.

We count 158 interpolations. The "interpolation rate" is 83.3 interpolations per 1,000. *We see that several kinds of adjunct significantly interpose into clause cores in the* נתן *corpus and that the interpolation rate is closer to the rate found for* עשׂה *than the rate found for* אמר *or* היה.

15.6.3 The Dative Shift

At this point, we encounter the *dative shift*. The dative shift is the much-studied "phenomenon by which an underlying dative (indirect object) is realized as a direct object, the underlying direct object being realized as some sort of peripheral element."[5] Consider first an example from English. The clause "Bill gave the book to Mary" (sbj – vb – dir obj$_i$ – ind obj$_j$) can be recast as "Bill gave Mary the book" (sbj – vb – dir obj$_j$ – 2nd obj$_i$). The indirect object in the first clause is the direct object in the second clause; the direct object in the first is the *second object* in the second. This phenomenon occurs 10 times in the נתן corpus. As an example, compare the "standard" V-I-O phrase marker (15.2) from Josh 15:19 with shifted-dative O2-V-O phrase marker (15.3) one clause earlier.

(15.2)

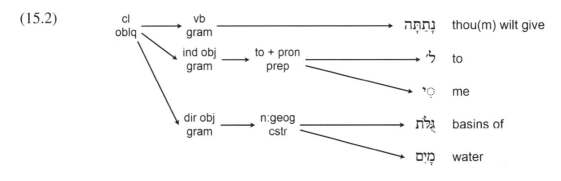

---

5. R. L. Trask, *A Dictionary of Grammatical Terms* (London: Routledge, 1993) 71.

(15.3)

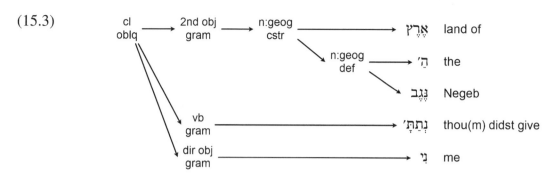

The 10 instances of the dative shift in the נתן corpus are found in Gen 15:10; Josh 15:19; Judg 1:15; Isa 27:4; Jer 9:1; Ezek 16:7, 38; Job 9:18; Dan 1:9; and Neh 1:11.

15.7   *Verb Corpora Overview*

15.7.1   CIC Incidence across Four Qal Active Verb Corpora

The consolidated CIC incidences observed for the four sets of clauses investigated in chaps. 12–15 are documented in table 15.7.

Table 15.7. CIC Incidence Percentages for Four Qal Active Verb Corpora

CIC Types		CIC Label	All	אמר	היה	עשׂה	נתן
Predicators		anchored verb	32.7	56.3	35.5	24.5	35.0
		infinitive construct	10.3	18.2	5.0	12.4	8.3
		noun-verb participle	3.2	0.9	0.0	2.1	1.2
		unanchored verb	50.3	23.6	59.4	56.9	50.7
		verb participle	3.5	1.0	0.1	4.2	4.7
Gramatical Functions		subject	37.7	40.1	65.0	26.2	27.4
		direct object	47.5	94.1	0.0	61.4	80.2
		indirect object	10.7	36.5	6.1	14.7	50.7
		sbj / obj complement	5.2	0.0	42.9	5.0	11.1
Main Semantic Roles		location	18.2	1.5	25.1	15.4	31.0
		negation	8.0	0.9	9.2	5.9	5.7
		mvt aim	6.7	0.0	1.9	0.5	5.0
		mvt origin	6.2	0.0	3.5	0.9	2.3
Other Semantic Roles (in >5%)		manner	-	10.1	-	8.4	-
		possessor	-	-	20.3	-	-
		comparison	-	-	9.6	12.6	-
		time point	-	-	9.1	-	-
		beneficiary	-	-	5.0	8.2	-
		aim (purpose)	-	-	-	-	7.7

The 4 major Qal active verb corpora here studied account for almost one-fifth of the verbal clauses in Biblical Hebrew. Overall, anchored predicators appear in 46% of these Qal active verbal clauses, while unanchored predicators appear in 54%. While subjects occur in a bit over one-third of all verbal clauses (38%) and almost two-thirds of היה clauses (65%), they only appear in one-quarter of עשׂה (26%) and נתן (27%) clauses. Half of the verbal clauses in this Qal active corpus contain direct objects (48%). They are almost always found in אמר clauses (94%) and never found in היה clauses. Indirect objects occur in around one-tenth of all verbal clauses (11%), one-third of the time in אמר clauses (37%), and half the time in נתן clauses (51%). Subject and object complements appear in one-twentieth of Qal active verbal clauses (5%) but four-tenths of היה clauses (43%).

15.7.2   SR Interpolations for Four Verb Corpora

Table 15.8 consolidates the CIC interpolation data observed for the four major verb corpora studied in chaps. 12–15. The results are ordered by increasing interpolation rate. The results for the complete Qal active corpus have also been introduced. (In all cases, clauses with compound predicators have been excluded.)

Table 15.8. CIC Intrusion Percentages for Four Verb Corpora

Root	# Qal Active Clauses	Core Intrusion Rate (per 1,000)	Percent of SR-Groups Interpolated amid GFs					
			Other Participant	Movement & Spatial	Temporal	Manner	Enriching Constituent	Mixed Level & DU
אמר	5,277	7	0%	13.0%	3.9%	1.7%	12.2%	0.0%
All	44,915	81	32.8%	11.4%	7.6%	14.4%	14.4%	5.3%
נתן	1,896	83	19.6%	15.1%	15.5%	35.0%	10.0%	4.0%
עשׂה	2,416	113	48.5%	12.1%	10.2%	16.4%	8.1%	2.6%
היה	2,798	305	41.1%	17.8%	8.0%	21.9%	29.7%	7.3%

The mapping from SR-groups to individual SRs may be found inside the back cover.

Regarding the phenomenon of SR interpolation, a few observations are in order:

- Qal active אמר clauses usually have their SRs outside their GF cores.
- The discourse-unit CICs remain outside GF cores to a large extent.
- The "other participant" CIC group appears more likely to be interpolated into a core than any other group (to judge from the evidence for these four major roots and overall).
- Verbs in Biblical Hebrew lie along a *core-interpolation-rate* cline. Of the frequently attested verbs, we conjecture that אמר and היה are at or near the cline extremes.
- Within a given verb corpus, does interpolation exhibit significant variation and, if so, what factors influence this variation?

15.8   *Brief Summary*

The Censuses.   The predicators of נתן are strongly Qal actives (95.2%). Most predicators are finite verbs (85.8%), with infinitives construct the next–most common predicator (8.3%). Non-

GF / SR CICs are uncommon (in 8% of clauses) with negatives being the most frequent (in 6% of the clauses). Usually the negatives immediately precede the predicators (95.4%). There are few adverbs; they appear in 2% of the clauses. With regard to GFs, direct objects appear in 80% of the clauses, explicit subjects in 27%, and indirect objects in 51%. With regard to SRs, 3 prepositions account for 76% of the PP CICs: ל, את, and ב. The prefix ל plus an infinitive construct is almost always an *aim* SR (95%), while any other substantive with ל is typically an indirect object (79.4%). The preposition את essentially always marks a direct object (99.8%). The prefix ב plus a temporal substantive is usually a time point SR (93.3%), while any other substantive with ב tends to be a location SR (77.2%). The bare substantives are usually direct objects (59%) or subjects (30%).

CIC Incidence.   Across Biblical Hebrew, we find 46% of predicators are anchored and 54% are unanchored; for the נתן corpus, the percentages are 45% and 55%. There are about three-quarters fewer *subjects*, about three-quarters more *direct objects*, and nearly 5 times more *indirect objects*. There are two-thirds more location SRs and somewhat fewer movement origins and movement aims.

Core Patterns.   The נתן corpus has one-quarter more unanchored predicators than anchored. For the anchored predicators, the "other" category includes 25% of the clauses. Its top few contributors are V, 5%; VSIO, 3%; VSOI, 2%; VISO, 2%; and VOIC, 1%. Among the unanchored cases, "other" is very large, 51%. It comprises many CIC sequence patterns. Its top 4 contributors are SVO, 4%; SVI, 4%; V, 4%; IVO, 4%. Note that almost 62% of the clauses with unanchored predicators are not predicator initial. Intrusions of SRs into the נתן clause cores are fairly frequent, occurring at a rate of 83.3 intrusions per 1,000 clauses.

Chapter 16

Makeup of
Clause Immediate Constituent Subtypes

In this chapter, we examine the way that each CIC subtype is realized (as a CIC daughter) *across all of Biblical Hebrew*, independent of verb root. *We include all CICs in all clauses.* We visualize the data using tables and / or shaded bar charts. The tables characterize each CIC subtype by:

- CIC incidence (labeled "Overall Token Count" in the tables)
- CICs realized by noun phrases
  - Percentage that are noun phrases (labeled "Noun Phrase / Token %")
  - Number of semantic classes found (labeled "Noun Phrase / Semantic Classes")
- CICs realized by prepositional phrases
  - Percentage that are prepositional phrases (labeled "Prepositional Phrase / Token %")
  - Number of preposition lexemes (labeled "Prepositional Phrase / Preposition Lexemes")
  - Number of distinct semantic classes (labeled "Prepositional Phrase / Semantic Classes")
- CICs realized by other types of constructions (labeled "Other / Token %")

The shaded bar charts graph the tallies of the various realizations of CICs.

CIC Subtype: All inclusive	Overall Token Count	Noun Phrase		Prepositional Phrase			Other
		Token %	Semantic Classes	Token %	Preposition Lexemes	Semantic Classes	Token %
All CICs	241,553	27%	32	26%	12	39	47%

This tells us that the 241,553 CICs found in Biblical Hebrew consist of slightly over one-quarter *noun phrases*, one-quarter *prepositional phrases*, and about half *other* entities. The NPs occupy 32 semantic classes. The PPs involve 12 different prepositions (1 of them being a miscellany class). The substantives in prepositional phrases divide among 39 semantic classes. The "other" category consists of various kinds of particles plus clauses and sentences. Throughout this chapter, shaded cells contain the dominant row percentage.

16.1 *The Impermanent CIC Subtype*

In §9.3.1, we identify 3 sorts of "impermanent" CICs. The first sort ("underspecified 'and' cue phrases") is highly homogeneous in that its members are always and only realized as clause-initial coordinating conjunctions. They constitute a transitory CIC category, since they will eventually be promoted into discourse level. The other 2 impermanent sorts (*lapsus calami* and nebulous) are each very heterogeneous, the former because we do not know how they function and the latter because the great majority represent gaps in the texts filled by *Qere* readings.

CIC Subtype: Impermanent	Overall Token Count	Noun Phrase		Prepositional Phrase			Other
		Token %	Semantic Classes	Token %	Preposition Lexemes	Semantic Classes	Token %
'And' cue phrases	25,812	0	–	0	–	–	100%
Lapsus calami	24	?	?	?	?	?	?
Nebulous	35	60%	9	29%	5	9	11%

One reads the table for the structures of the impermanent CICs as follows: the 25,812 "underspecified 'and' cue phrases" are neither NPs nor PPs but are clause-initial coordinating conjunctions (and therefore appear in the table only under "other"). The nebulous CICs, excluding 4 "other" realizations (11%),[1] have 60% realized by 21 NPs assigned to 9 different semantic classes. The remaining 29% are realized by 10 PPs involving 5 different prepositions and 9 different semantic classes. The 24[2] *lapsii calami* CICs are indeterminate, hence the "?" entries. Three tokens are garbled words: Gen 30:11; Ps 10:10, 55:16. The other 21 tokens are *Qere welo' Kethiv*s.

16.2 The Syntactic Isolate CIC Subtype

In §9.3.1, we identified 3 sorts of syntactic isolates. These are tallied in the table and commented on in the subsequent paragraphs, each of which comments on one row of the table.

CIC Subtype: Syntactic Isolate	Overall Token Count	Noun Phrase		Prepositional Phrase			Other
		Token %	Semantic Classes	Token %	Preposition Lexemes	Semantic Classes	Token %
Vocative	1,589	100%	22	0%	–	–	0%
Exclamative	344	37%	7	0%	1	1	63%
Label	683	89%	10	11%	2	4	0%

Vocative Specifics. 45% of the vocatives have the semantic category *human*, 36% have the semantic category *deity*, 7% have the semantic category *geographic* (when a city is personified), and the remaining 12% are scattered over 19 semantic classes, for a total of 22 semantic classes for the noun phrases. Three instances involve "all of you," each referring to the semantic category *human*. These are found in Judg 20:7, Isa 48:14, and 50:11.

Exclamative Specifics. 63% (217/344) of the exclamative CICs are single segments classified as exclamatives ("other"). Another 19% are noun phrases with the semantic category *medical*, 13%

---

1. These may be found in 2 Sam 14:26, 19:7; 2 Kgs 9:25; and Isa 51:19.

2. In §3.2.1.1, we give the locations of 32 *lapsii calami*; here we tally only 24. Why this discrepancy of 8 instances? There are 8 places where a *lapsus calami* is not the daughter of a laps CIC. Six are located within phrases: 1 Sam 4:13, 2 Sam 8:3, 1 Kgs 12:33, 2 Kgs 4:7, Job 26:12, and Lam 4:3. Two are CIC daughters, but in the version of our database here used, we failed to assign them laps tags: Deut 33:2 (sbj) and 2 Chr 34:6 (loc).

are noun phrases with the semantic category *quantity*, and 2% are noun phrases with the semantic category *mental*, plus 4 additional semantic classes. The single PP is in Gen 30:13 ("in my happiness"). Since it is presently a unique realization of an exclamative, one might well examine its context to see if an alternate CIC assignment might be more appropriate.

Label Specifics. 71% are vocable noun phrases (נְאֻם־יהוה 'oracle of the Lord'); 12% are nebulous noun phrases (סֶלָה 'Selah'); and 11% (72/683) are PPs with ל 'to' plus a noun with human (93%), place, or other semantics (such as מִזְמוֹר לְדָוִד 'psalm of/to David').

16.3 *The Predicator CIC Subtype*

Predicators are realized by various predicator subtypes (the rows in the table). The column entries rank common verb forms (*binyan* + voice) from most-frequent ("Rank one") to fourth–most frequent ("Rank four"). The percentages are percentages of the associated "Token Counts."

Predicator Subtype	Token Count	Rank one Form		Rank two Form		Rank three Form		Rank four Form	
Infinitive absolute	195	Q A[a]	66%	H A	18%	P A	9%	N P	5%
Infinitive construct	6,722	Q A	70%	H A	14%	P A	11%	N P	2%
Noun-verb/noun participle	109	Q A	61%	H A	28%	P A	6%	N P	3%
Noun-verb participle	2,336	Q A	61%	H A	11%	N P	8%	Q P	7%
Verbal participle	2,787	Q A	40%	compound	23%	H A	6%	P A	6%
Unanchored finite verb	35,447	Q A	65%	H A	14%	P A	10%	N P	6%
Anchored finite verb	20,735	Q A	73%	H A	13%	P A	7%	N P	4%
Quasiverbal[b]	1,255	אֵין	47%	הִנֵּה	28%	יֵשׁ	11%	עוֹד	7%

a. Binyan: Q = Qal; P = Piel; H = Hiphil; N = Niphal. Voice: A = active; P = passive.
b. The quasiverbals are the subject of chap. 18.

16.4 *The Operator CIC Subtype*

The 6 CIC types that we define to be operators were described in §9.3.4. Since they are realized neither by noun phrases nor by prepositional phrases, we simply list their characteristics.

- *Negation operator* (5,954×).   85% are לֹא 'not', 12% are אַל 'do not', and 3% are בַּל '[negation]'.
- *Closed interrogative* (876×).   87% are הֲ- 'yes/no?', and 13% are אִם '[question]'.
- *Clausal* גַם/גַם *'also'* (326×).   Always the segment that provides the name of this subtype. Most of the גַם/גַם 'also' segments (58%) are supra-clausal.
- *Includer* (84×).   These are all clausal אַף 'also'.
- *Restricter* (29×).   These are רַק 'only' and many instances of אַךְ.
- *Modal* (265×).   The modals are listed in §3.2.2.1, with the idiom type discussed in §15.3.4.4.

16.5   *The Grammatical Function CIC Subtype*

16.5.1   Subjects

At the start of §9.3.5.1, we pointed to examples of various kinds of subjects: the standard subject (of which, we find 33,572, with 310 being distributive),[3] the Janus subject complement / subject (of which we presently have declared 107), and the subject of address (of which we find 22), yielding a grand total of 33,701. These are tallied and characterized below.

CIC Subtype: Subjects	Overall Token Count	Noun Phrase		Prepositional Phrase			Other
		Token %	Semantic Classes	Token %	Preposition Lexemes	Semantic Classes	Token %
Subject	33,572	99%	44	0.3%	8	24	0.7%
Janus sc / sb	107	100%	15	0%	—	—	0%
Subject of address	22	0	—	0%	—	—	100%

Subject Specifics.   The main semantics labels for the NPs are 36% human, 10% deity, and 4% each for body part and geographic. In addition, 11% of the subjects are free pronouns and 4% are suffixed pronouns.

Distributive Subject Specifics.   92% of the distributive subjects have human semantics.

Janus sc / sb Specifics.   34% have human semantics, and 26% have abstract semantics.

Subject-of-Address Specifics.   All 22 of the subjects of address consist of single clauses.

16.5.2   Objects

The characteristics of the various sorts of objects are as shown:

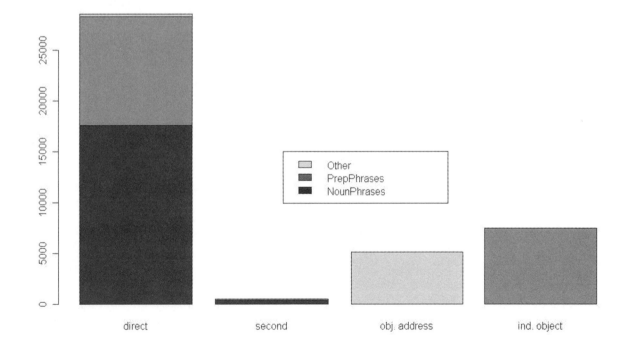

---

3. Suspended and resumed subjects are included.

CIC Subtype: Objects	Overall Token Count	Noun Phrase		Prepositional Phrase			Other
		Token %	Semantic Classes	Token %	Preposition Lexemes	Semantic Classes	Token %
Direct object	28,517	62%	29	37%	9	33	1%
Second object	502	76%	28	24%	6	22	0%
Object of address	5,134	0%	—	0%	—	—	100%
Indirect object	7,466	0%	6	99%	9	31	0%

Only 37% of the direct objects and only one-quarter of the second objects are prepositional phrases. All of the objects of address have been parsed as clauses, sentences, or discourse structures (are "other"). And essentially all of the indirect objects are realized as prepositional phrases.

Direct Object Specifics.   The leading semantic labels for the noun phrases are 16% human, 7% body part, and 6% vocable. In addition, 19% (5,395×) are suffixed pronouns. Free pronoun objects are rare (0.4% [107×], all but 2 are demonstratives). With regard to the prepositional phrases, the most common involve the object marker[4] plus: a human noun (26% of occurrences), a suffixed pronoun (19%), a place (9%), a body part (7%), or a vocable (6%).

Distributive-Object Specifics (18×).   21% of the distributive objects have human semantics, 14% are utensils, and 10% are numbers.

Second-Object Specifics.   The makeup of the second objects is remarkably diverse. The most frequent realization is the human NP with 13%. Following along behind are the place, utensil, and substance NPs, each with around 4%. And so on, and so on.

Object-of-Address Specifics.   57% of the objects of address involve sentences, while 43% are single clauses. Lost in the rounding off of these percentages are 27 instances (0.5%) that are discourse units.

Indirect-Object Specifics.   The indirect objects are overwhelmingly realized by prepositional phrases. The preposition is ל in 58.4%, אֶל in 37.3%, and עַל in 3.2%. The remaining 1.1% are scattered among 7 other prepositions.

Distributive-Indirect-Object Specifics (40×).   All are realized as prepositional phrases. 65% are אֶל + human, and 30% are ל + human.

16.5.3 Complements

The characteristics of the various sorts of complements are as shown:

CIC Subtype: Complements	Overall Token Count	Noun Phrase		Prepositional Phrase			Other
		Token %	Semantic Classes	Token %	Preposition Lexemes	Semantic Classes	Token %
Subject complement	7,053	87%	30	9%	7	29	4%
Object complement	1,237	64%	29	35%	6	22	0%
Cmpl. aspect.	442	17%	1	82%	2	1	1%
Cogn. cmpl.	829	0%	—	0%	—	—	100%

---

4. Of 10,705 direct objects realized by PPs, 83% involve the object marker, 12% בְּ 'in', and 3% ל 'to'.

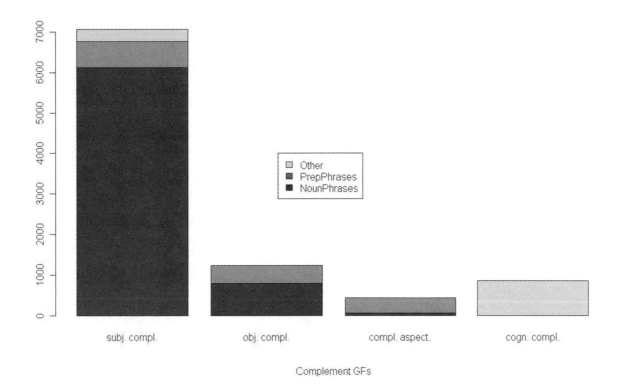

Complement GFs

Subject Complement Specifics. Nearly 90% of subject complements are bare nominals (87%). These are scattered across a large number of semantic classes. As for the prepositional-phrase realizations (631×), the most common preposition is ל 'to' (86%).

Object Complement Specifics. Regarding substantives, the most common semantic label is human, 20%. Next most frequent are noun-verb participial constructions, 10%. The dominant prepositional lexeme is ל 'to', 92%.

Complement of Aspectualizing Verb Specifics. Almost all of the nominal phrases (91% of them) involve a nominalized infinitive construct. The nominalized infinitives construct account for 17% of this class of CICs. By far the most common realization among the PPs (362×) involves ל 'to' + infinitive construct (98%).

Cognitive Complement Specifics. In 16 instances, a compound cognitive complement is present. Phrase marker (16.1) from Gen 29:12 provides an instance of this phenomenon (see p. 224). A non-compound complement clause may (81%) or may not (19%) have an associated cue phrase. In (16.1), the cue phrases are homographs of כִּי/כִּי, here glossed 'that'.

16.6   *The Semantic Role CIC Subtype*

We divide the semantic role CICs into the seven subgroups listed inside the back cover. Some of the subgroup assignments may arguably have been made differently.

16.6.1   Other Participants

The characteristics of the various sorts of "other participant" CICs follow PM (16.1):

(16.1)

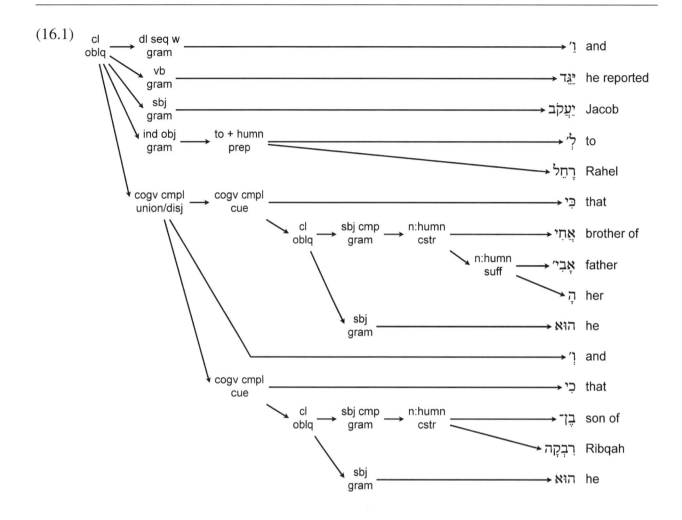

CIC Subtype: Other Participants	Overall Token Count	Noun Phrase		Prepositional Phrase			Other
		Token %	Semantic Classes	Token %	Preposition Lexemes	Semantic Classes	Token %
Accompanier	1,668	1%	10	99%	9	30	0%
Agential	229	3%	3	97%	5	15	0%
Alternate / surrogate	180	0%	–	100%	5	18	0%
Beneficiary	2,097	1%	8	99%	5	31	0%
Harmed one	261	1%	2	99%	7	17	0%
Involved one	80	1%	1	99%	3	8	0%
Possessor	1,623	2%	5	98%	4	27	0%

With very few exceptions, "other participants" are realized by prepositional phrases. Across all 7 "other participant" CIC types (table rows), only 4 instances of the "other" class occur.

Accompanier Specifics. By far the most common preposition lexeme is some form of עִם 'with', which appears in 1,501 (90%) of these CICs. With regard to the semantics of the nominals in the prepositional phrases, by far the most frequent are the pronoun suffixes (58%) and nominals having human semantics (26%). While it is unusual to see so many different semantic classes associated with a CIC class (10 in all), they do seem bona fide.

Agential Specifics. The most common agential expression translates as 'in hand of <X>'. This sort of construction accounts for 51% of the agential realizations. The runners-up involve some form of בְּ 'in' plus either a suffix pronoun (16%) or a deity (8%).

Alternate/Surrogate Specifics. These are all prepositional phrases, the vast majority (93%) involving תַּחַת 'underneath'; 53% involve pronoun suffixes, while 22% involve nominals having human semantics.

Beneficiary Specifics. By far the most common preposition is לְ 'to' (90%). The associated nominal is a pronoun suffix (61%), has human semantics (16%), and divine semantics (5%).

Harmed-One Specifics. The distribution of the prepositions is less concentrated than for the CICs examined above. The data are: בְּ 'in' 38%, עַל 'upon' 41%, and לְ 'to' 10%. The harmed ones involve pronoun suffixes 43% of the time, humans 36% of the time, and deities 8% of the time.

Involved-One Specifics. With one exception (Qoh 7:27), this CIC involves prepositional phrases. The preposition is בֵּין 'between' in 87% of cases. The nominal is a pronoun suffix 45% and a human 36% of the time. The typical formula is 'between X and between Y'.

Possessor Specifics. The preposition is לְ 'to' in 97.4% of the cases. The nominal is a pronoun suffix 58% of the time, has human semantics 25% of the time, and divine semantics 4% of the time.

16.6.2 Movement, Actual and Notional

The characteristics of the movement CICs are as shown (with table following on p. 226).

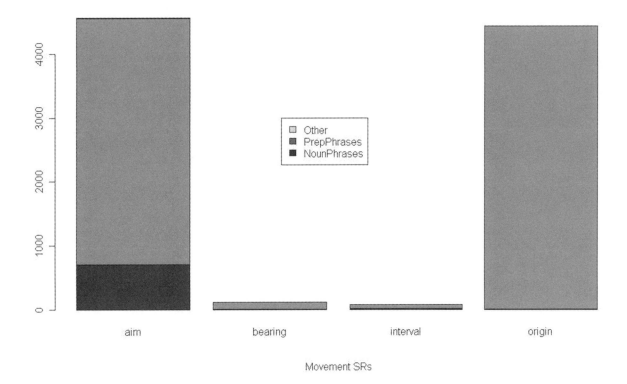

Movement SRs

Movement Aim Specifics. This CIC type exhibits 126 prepositional phrase patterns. The preposition is אֶל 54% and לְ 27% of the time. The 4 most frequent realizations are: אֶל + place, 12%; אֶל + human, 10%; place nominal, 11%; אֶל + pronoun suffix, 9%.

CIC Subtype: Movement SRs	Overall Token Count	Noun Phrase		Prepositional Phrase			Other
		Token %	Semantic Classes	Token %	Preposition Lexemes	Semantic Classes	Token %
Movement aim	4,538	15%	15	84%	8	35	1%
Movement bearing	139	12%	3	88%	4	12	0%
Movement interval	80	29%	5	70%	3	9	1%
Movement origin	4,308	0%	8	100%	5	31	0%

Movement Bearing Specifics. 81% of the prepositions are לְ. The associated nominals are: suffix pronoun, 42%; deity, 26%; human, 17% (nominals of place only occur in 3% of the PPs!).

Movement Interval Specifics. 11% of these CICs involve a bare spatial noun, 9% a place noun. For the PPs, the preposition is some form of מִן 'from' 91% of the time. The most popular associated nominal semantic labels are: place, 30%; human, 20%; spatial, 18%.

Movement Origin Specifics. Although 5 different preposition lexemes are attested, מִן 'from' is the overwhelming favorite, 99%. The most popular associated nominal labels are: place, 25%; body part, 17%; pronoun suffix, 13%; human, 12%.

16.6.3 Spatial

The characteristics of the various sorts of spatial CICs are as shown.

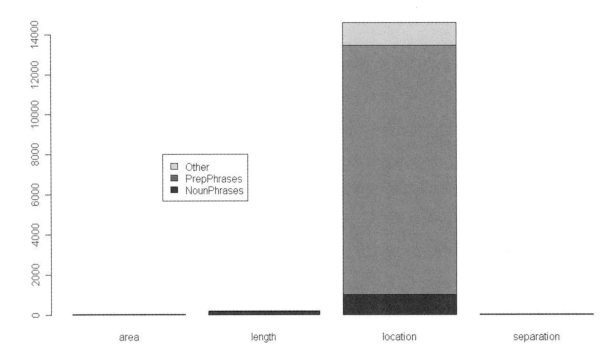

Spatial SRs

CIC Subtype: Spatial SRs	Overall Token Count	Noun Phrase		Prepositional Phrase			Other
		Token %	Semantic Classes	Token %	Preposition Lexemes	Semantic Classes	Token %
Area	33	30%	2	70%	4	5	0%
Length	189	92%	3	8%	4	7	0%
Location	14,557	7%	21	85%	9	34	8%
Separation	23	0	–	100%	2	11	0%

Area Specifics.   48% of the area specifics are complex geographical specifications (as in Exod 23:31); 21% are echo noun phrases found only in Ezekiel:[5] סָבִיב סָבִיב 'all around' (NJPS).

Length Specifics.   This is usually realized as a nominal headed by סָבִיב 'around'.

Location Specifics.   The noun phrases are fairly sparsely attested, accounting for 7% of the location CICs. Place nouns make up 4% of the overall total. The prepositional phrases occur in almost 150 patterns. The "other" category includes 1,024 adverbs of space (53 being locatives).

Separation Specifics.   A small, scattered class. The sole CIC assigned to "other" is in Ps 34:14.

16.6.4   Time

The characteristics of the various sorts of time CICs are as shown.

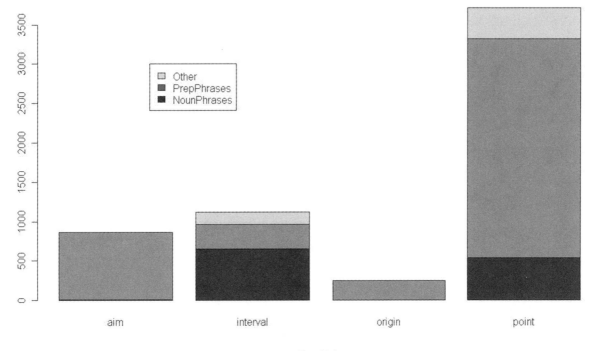

Time SRs

---

5. See Ezek 37:2; 40:5, 16; 41:9, 15, 19; 43:12.

CIC Subtype: Temporal SRs	Overall Token Count	Noun Phrase		Prepositional Phrase			Other
		Token %	Semantic Classes	Token %	Preposition Lexemes	Semantic Classes	Token %
Time aim	869	1%	2	99%	5	18	0%
Time interval	1,124	57%	8	28%	7	21	14%
Time origin	249	0%	1	100%	4	15	0%
Time point	3,708	15%	9	75%	9	29	10%

Time Aim (Goal) Specifics. Three prepositional-phrase shapes outnumber all of the others: ל + time, 38%; עַד + time, 34%; עַד + infinitive construct, 17%.

Time Interval Specifics. Nominals having temporal semantics constitute the largest group, 57% overall. The second most common pattern involves temporal adverbials, 14%. Among the prepositional phrases, time nominals are the most common, being 38% of the nominals in prepositional phrases. There are 3 curious prepositional phrases involving the object marker: Exod 13:7, Deut 9:25, and Ezek 16:22. The "other" entry (161×) consists almost entirely of the temporal adverbs.

Time Origin Specifics. The most common pattern is some form of מִן + time nominal, 59%. Forms of מִן are the most common preposition, 81%. The lone noun phrase occurs in Isa 40:21.

Time Point Specifics. The most common shape is forms of בְּ + temporal noun phrase, 35%, followed by forms of בְּ + infinitive construct, 19%. Next are the time noun phrases, at 13%, followed by temporal adverbs, at 10%. The most common preposition is בְּ, which accounts for 76% of the prepositions.

16.6.5 Enriching Constituent

The characteristics of the various sorts of enriching constituent CICs are as follows.

CIC Subtype: Enriching Constituent	Overall Token Count	Noun Phrase		Prepositional Phrase			Other
		Token %	Semantic Classes	Token %	Preposition Lexemes	Semantic Classes	Token %
Cost	106	4%	2	96%	5	17	0%
Instrument	2,485	8%	24	89%	8	32	3%
Manner	2,457	10%	20	16%	8	27	74%
Material / composition	91	93%	4	7%	2	2	0%
Number count	1	100%	1	0%	–	–	0%
Number of times	360	34%	4	4%	4	2	62%
Reference	1,109	4%	19	95%	9	32	0%
Resource (source of supply)	248	3%	5	97%	2	19	0%
Ruled-over one	45	4%	2	96%	3	7	0%
Quantity / quantifier	50	68%	2	32%	3	6	0

Cost Specifics. The surprise here is that only 4 costs involve bare noun phrases (Num 18:21, 31; Deut 15:18; Isa 5:23). The prime preposition is בְּ, 79% of the prepositions. The nominals in the prepositional phrases are scattered. The top few are: human, 19%; valuables, 18%; and substance, 13%.

Instrument Specifics. The most common bare nominal semantics is substance, 2%. The most common preposition is בְּ, 83% of the prepositions. The most common nominal constituents of the prepositional phrases have semantics: utensil, 23%; body part, 14%; abstract, 11%; substance, 10%.

Manner Specifics. 72% of these CICs are adverbial. The top performers are the various forms and congeners of כֵּן/כֹּה 'thus', 39%; מְאֹד 'very', 8%; various forms of יַחְדָּו 'together', 6%.

Material/Composition Specifics. Two-thirds of these CICs are bare nominals having substance semantics (66%). Vegetation nouns account for another 14%, and utensil nouns for an additional 10%.

Number Count Specifics. This class of CICs is a place saver. The single instance is at Josh 5:2.

Number of Times Specifics. The 223 CIC instances classified as "other" involve the temporal adverb עוֹד 'again' and account for 62% of the instances. Bare temporal nominals account for 34%.

Reference Specifics. This class is the "when-all-else-fails" category. Consequently, its semantic role is vague, and its makeup is quite disparate, because there are over 100 different patterns attested. The predominant referent pattern involves לְ 'to' + human, 21%. The runner-up is עַל 'upon' + pronoun suffix, 12%. Five interrogative CICs have been assigned to "other" (0.4%).

Resource (Source of Supply) Specifics. The 2 prepositions involved are forms of מִן 'from' (94%) and forms of בְּ 'in' (6%). Such a construction is usually termed a partitive מִן. The majority of the nominals in the prepositional phrases have human semantics (56%); 8% are pronoun suffixes.

Ruled-over-One Specifics. At present, this class is incompletely marked up; 58% of its instances involve עַל 'upon' + human, and 18% involve עַל + pronoun suffix.

Quantity/Quantifier Specifics. 66% of these are numbers.

16.6.6 Phrasal Discourse Unit

The characteristics of the various sorts of phrasal discourse unit (phrasal DU) CICs are as follow.

CIC Subtype: Phrasal DU	Overall Token Count	Noun Phrase		Prepositional Phrase			Other
		Token %	Semantic Classes	Token %	Preposition Lexemes	Semantic Classes	Token %
Comparison	2,682	1%	7	99%	7	35	0%
Cause	63	3%	21	97%	5	13	0%
Deprivation	69	1%	1	99%	4	21	0%
Quoter	925	0%	–	100%	1	1	0%

Comparison Specifics. Naturally, the most common preposition is כְּ 'like' and its congeners, 89%. The top 4 semantic categories for the nominals found in the prepositional phrases are: nominalized clause, 21%; human, 11%; vocable, 7%; creature, 7%.

Cause Specifics. This CIC type is feebly realized at phrase level; it will loom much larger once we classify supra-clausal discourse units. The leading prepositional phrases are some form of מִן + body part, 17%; forms of בְּ + abstract noun, 13%; and מִן + mental, 10%.

Deprivation Specifics.   Deprivation is most often expressed by some form of מִן + human, 14%, or some form of מִן + number, 7%.

Quoter Specifics.   All of these are לְ + infinitive of utterance (לֵ'אמֹר).

16.6.7 Mixed Level

The characteristics of the various sorts of mixed-level CICs are as follows:

CIC Subtype: Mixed Level	Overall Token Count	Noun Phrase		Prepositional Phrase			Other
		Token %	Semantic Classes	Token %	Preposition Lexemes	Semantic Classes	Token %
Aim / purpose	2,996	1%	4	99%	6	20	0%
Reason	804	4%	6	83%	9	26	13%
Result	93	10%	2	90%	5	9	0%
Undesired outcome	171	1%	1	99%	3	11	0%

We have omitted 3 mixed-level "place saver" categories[6] from this table:

- But rather: only so labeled in Deut 4:12 and 1 Kgs 12:20.
- Concessive: only so labeled in Ezek 32:30.
- Condition: only so labeled twice, in Gen 4:7 and Job 4:2.

Aim / Purpose Specifics.   The vast majority consists of לְ + infinitive construct, 93%.

Reason Specifics.   This highly diffuse type most often occurs as the prepositional phrase מִן + body part, only 16%. The 106 instances of "other" are overwhelmingly interrogatives (101×).

Result Specifics.   Mostly prepositional phrases, this CIC type is most often realized by לְ + infinitive construct, 39%, and לְ + quality / quantity, 14%.

Undesired Outcome Specifics.   Almost entirely prepositional phrases, the 3 top contributors are מִן + infinitive construct, 74%, לְ + infinitive construct, 6%, and מִן + human, 6%.

16.7 *Brief Summary*

Procedures.   Across all of the clauses of Biblical Hebrew, we have examined CIC subtype makeup in terms of whether and when the CICs are realized by noun phrases, by prepositional phrases, or by other entities. The presentation consists of: (1) table entries for CICs that are primarily of one sort and / or (2) bar charts when there is significant variety.

Impermanent, Syntactic Isolate, Predicator, and Operator CICs.   The *impermanent subtype* provides little of interest, because it is a "ragbag." *With regard to the syntactic isolates*, vocatives are almost always realized by NPs (100%), about half of them having human semantics and about one-third having divine semantics. The exclamatives are realized by exclamative POSs 63% of the time and otherwise by NPs involving 8 different semantics classes 37% of the time. Labels are realized by NPs 89% of the time. *Predicators* are most frequently realized by Qal actives. *With regard to the operators*, each kind is realized by lexemes of the relevant POS. For example, the 5,943 closed interrogatives are 89% -הֲ 'yes / no?' and 11% אִם '[question]'.

---

6. That is, we have not yet assigned these categories systematically.

Grammatical Function CICs. Subjects are overwhelmingly NPs (99%); direct objects are 62% NPs and 37% PPs; objects of address are 100% clauses, sentences, or discourse structures; and indirect objects are essentially 100% PPs. *Complements*, a mélange that we smuggle in among the grammatical functions because of their importance for the היה-corpus and verbless clauses, consist of subject complements (89% NPs and 9% PPs), object complements (64% NPs and 35% PPs), complements of aspectualizing verbs (17% NPs and 82% PPs), and cognitive complements (100% clauses, sentences, or discourse structures).

Semantic Roles. *With regard to Other Participant SRs*, essentially 100% are PPs. *With regard to Movement SRs*, movement aim is mixed (15% NPs and 84% PPs) as is movement interval (29% NPs and 70% PPs), bearing is mixed (12% NPs and 88% PPs), while origin is essentially 100% PPs. *With regard to Spatial SRs*, location is mixed (7% NPs, 85% PPs, and 7% adverbs of space). The location SR (14,557×) dwarfs the other spatial SRs: area (33×), length (189×), and separation (23×). *With regard to the Time SRs*, time aim is 99% PPs, time interval is significantly mixed (58% NPs, 28% PPs, and 14% temporal adverbs), time origin is 100% PPs, and time point is mixed (15% NPs, 75% PPs, and 10% temporal adverbs). *With regard to Enriching Constituent SRs*, material, number count, and quantity are basically NPs; cost, instrument, reference, resource, and ruled-over one are basically PPs; manner SRs are usually adverbs (74%), as are number of times (62%). *With regard to Phrasal Discourse Units*, all (comparison, cause, deprivation, and quoter) are essentially 100% PPs. *With regard to Mixed-Level SRs*, all (aim/purpose, reason, result, undesired outcome) are around 90% PPs.

Chapter 17

Computing the Distances between Verb Corpora

In this chapter, we introduce methods for computing and representing the distances between verb corpora. Knowing these distances allows us to cluster the verb corpora into natural affinity groups. This, in turn, permits us to build up a powerful generalization storehouse, the hierarchical lexicon. While the ideas underlying all this are not simple, their grasp should reward perservering readers.

17.1 *The Hierarchical Lexicon, Verb Classes, and Inter-Clause Distance*

17.1.1 The Hierarchical Lexicon

Grammarians are ever on the prowl for generalizations about the languages that they study. The hierarchical lexicon is a construct that is designed to make certain language generalizations explicit. In a traditional lexicon, each entry contains the particular information that pertains to the lexeme being described. There is much redundancy, wasted space. In a hierarchical lexicon, each lexeme is positioned in a hierarchical structure. It inherits many of its characteristics from its "ancestors."

When viewing the lexicon from the syntactic perspective, one works in terms of syntactic categories. One may then observe that the characteristics of *Nouns* are inherited by *CommonNouns* (in other words, *CommonNouns* are daughters of *Nouns*). Similarly, *ProperNouns* inherit properties from *Nouns* of which they also are daughters. Getting even more specific, the lexeme *Book* inherits characteristics from the *CommonNouns*, so we may write:

$$Substantive > Noun > CommonNoun > Book$$

The > symbol can be read "contains."

When viewing the lexicon from the semantic perspective, one uses a hierarchy of semantic categories. One much-used hierarchy[1] allows us to assert that:

$$Entity > Physical > Object > SelfConnectedObject > CorpuscularObject > Artifact > Text > Book$$

In practice, matters are more complicated, as Forbes has discussed.[2] The main point of all this, for our purposes, is that the formation of a hierarchy involves the making of useful generalizations.

---

1. Ian Niles and Adam Pease, "Towards a Standard Upper Ontology," *Proc. 2nd Int. Conf. on Formal Ontology in Info. Sys. (FOIS-2001)*, www.ontologyportal.org. The building of taxonomies and their very useful extensions, ontologies, is notoriously labor intensive.

2. A. D. Forbes, "How Syntactic Formalisms Can Advance the Lexicographer's Art," in *Foundations for Syriac Lexicography III* (ed. Janet Dyk and Wido van Peursen; Piscataway, NJ: Gorgias, 2009) 150–55.

17.1.2   Verb Classes

Linguists find it useful to think in terms of "verb classes." Once verb classes are created, one can seek generalizations class by class rather than verb by verb. Beth Levin has classified the English verbs, producing a four-level hierarchy: Verb > VerbClass [49 in all] > SubClass > SubSubClass.[3] The subsubclasses become awesomely specific. Example:

Verbs > VerbsOfExistence > VerbsOfGroupExistence > SwarmVerbs >

{abound, bustle, crawl, creep, hop, run, swarm, swim, teem, throng}[4]

17.1.3   Inter-Clause Distance

17.1.3.1   The Distances between Sets of Clauses

We seek to group verb corpora, based (for starters) on clause immediate constituent incidence. Consider the pair of "stripped" CIC incidence plots[5] for the sets of clauses involving אמר and היה shown below. Clearly, the two sets of clauses characterized are quite different. For example, in the seventh bar position (direct-object incidence / object-of-address incidence), the two bars in the two charts are very different in height. While אמר clauses almost always have a direct object (actually, object of address), the היה clauses have none.

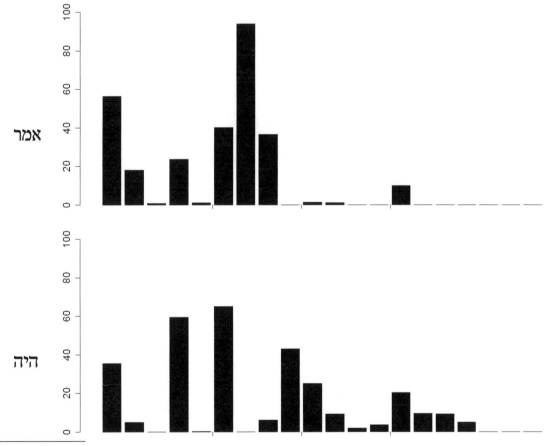

3. Beth Levin, *English Verb Classes and Alternations: A Preliminary Investigation* (Chicago: University of Chicago Press, 1993).

4. Ibid., 253.

5. By "stripped," we indicate that bar labels have been removed.

We ask: "With regard to CIC incidence, what is the specific distance between the אמר corpus and the היה corpus?"

Or consider these CIC-incidence plots for the sets of clauses involving בא and עלה. Clearly, these two sets of clauses are quite similar. But how far apart are the corpora that they describe?

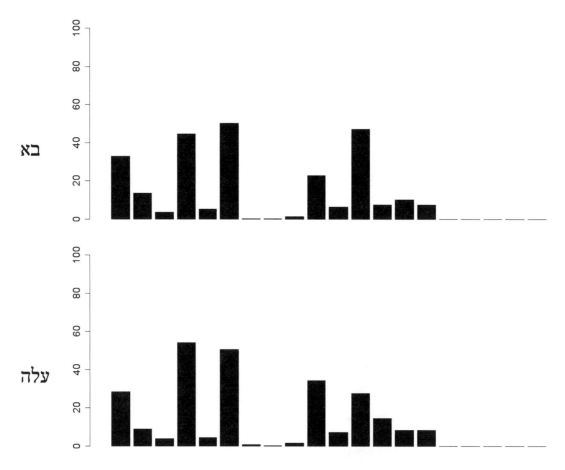

If we call the unit of inter-clause distance the *lambdin* (or *lam*), in memory of the Harvard professor, then the אמר and היה sets of clauses are 17.42 *lams* apart, while the בא and עלה clauses are 1.72 *lams* apart, 10 times closer together. They are the closest together of Qal active verbs occurring more than 60 times. Next, we informally sketch the way that we obtained these distances.

17.1.3.2 The Estimation of Inter-Clause Distances

Estimation of inter-clause distances involves analytical subtlety. In particular, one must:

- Specify the sample space (our data lie in a *23-simplex*),
- Transform the data (via the *closure operation*),
- Remove the sampling zeros (via *multiplicative replacement*),
- Select the proper distance measure (the *Aitchison metric*).

If this sounds fairly technical, this is because it is. The details (with references) are given in appendix 5. But we can provide a sense of what is involved in layperson's prose:

One decides which incidences to use. The resulting CIC incidence data require special handling for three reasons: (1) When the predicator incidences are expressed as fractions, they add to unity. (2) The incidences all lie between zero and one. (3) A few of the incidences may happen to be precisely zero. Each peculiarity must be addressed as one devises the distance-estimation process. The first issue is addressed by selecting an appropriate space in which to situate the data points, the second by appropriately normalizing the data, and the third by adjusting the data so that any zero values are replaced by appropriate tiny values with the other values suitably compensated. Once all this is done, the statistical literature supplies an appropriate formula for the distances sought.

CIC Incidences Used. Any book on pattern recognition devotes considerable space to the problem of *feature selection*. This is because, when one is building a pattern recognizer, the use of too many features can lead to very brittle systems that do not classify never-before-seen data accurately. Because we are not attempting pattern recognition but, rather, are merely seeking to infer the affinities exhibited within the data at hand, we can afford to be rather blasé in regard to feature selection. Consequently, we elect simply to use as our features a subset of the incidences associated with the most frequently attested CICs. We use the incidences of all of the CICs that occur more than 1,500 times in Biblical Hebrew, 23 CICs in all. Included are the 17 CICs listed in the CIC incidence plot for היה in §13.5 plus aim, instrument, closed interrogative, manner, accompanier, and vocative.

CIC Incidence Adjustments. By constraining the fractional predicator incidences associated with each verb corpus to sum to unity, we make them consistent with the required sample space, a simplex.[6] The distance metric suited to such a space (the so-called Aitchison metric) involves the logarithms of each of the CIC incidences. If an incidence is zero, then the distance involves an infinite value. We, therefore, must adjust the zero entries appropriately in order to avoid all these sorts of infinities. Precisely how this is done is explained in §A5.2.4.

17.1.4 A Simple Example Involving Four Clause Sets

In chaps. 12–15, we presented the CIC-incidence bar charts for clauses built around four very frequently attested Qal active verbs: אמר 'say', היה 'be', עשׂה 'make', and נתן 'give'. These proved to be quite disparate in their behaviors. Proceeding along the lines just outlined (executing the specifics given in appendix 5), we estimate the inter-clausal distances for the four sets of clauses as follows:[7]

Aitch	אמר	היה	עשׂה
היה	17.0		
עשׂה	9.6	12.4	
נתן	9.4	13.5	5.0

We see that אמר and היה are the farthest apart (17 *lams*), while עשׂה and נתן are the closest together (5 *lams*). We note also that עשׂה and נתן are nearly equidistant from אמר (~9.5 *lams*) and also from היה (~13 *lams*). Given these few sets of clauses, we might use the six distances to produce a two-

---

6. A three-simplex is better known as an equilateral triangle. A four-simplex is better known as a tetrahedron or pyramid.

7. The abbreviation "Aitch" is a reminder that the table holds distances computed using the Aitchison metric.

dimensional map having the verb corpora as its "cities." The distances, however, only determine the relative positions of the corpora and not the orientation of the map. This, of course, is true of the mileage chart on a map. From an appropriate mileage chart, we find that Paris is 342 kilometers from London, but we cannot discover that Paris is southeast of London.

17.2 *Inter-Clause Clustering*

17.2.1 Options for Inter-Clause Representation

Just how the four sets of clauses are positioned with respect to each other is not immediately obvious from the table of distances, but there are well-understood ways of producing displays showing how objects are positioned relative to each other on the basis of tables portraying the distances between them. There are two basic approaches, geometrical and clustering.[8]

17.2.2 The Geometrical Approach to Representation

In the geometrical approach, one attempts to project data from a high-dimensional space onto a lower-dimensional space and then leave it to observers to infer which projected objects "go together" to form clusters that have a great deal in common. Ideally, one would project the data onto a two-dimensional space (a plane). We have done this sort of thing in the context of the analysis of Hebrew spelling practices.[9] As usual, there is a possible hitch: if the data being represented "fully inhabit" the high-dimensional space,[10] then projecting them onto a low-dimensional space will distort the distance relations, perhaps catastrophically. There are ways of assessing the adequacy of a given projection, but they are too technical to be included here.[11] For our situation, suffice it to assert that projections onto lower-dimensional spaces are too distortive, making the geometrical approach less than appealing.[12]

17.2.3 The Clustering Approach to Representation

The inference of the verb class clusters remains to be considered. Clustering has long been a staple of taxonomists. Attention to it accelerated after Sokal and Sneath published *Principles of Numerical Taxonomy* in 1963.[13] In recent years, interest has been intensified because of its growing usefulness in "data mining" and "bioinformatics."

---

8. For an accessible discussion of these options in the context of biblical studies, see chap. 8 ("Choice of Statistical Methods") of D. N. Freedman, A. D. Forbes, and F. I. Andersen, *Studies in Hebrew and Aramaic Orthography* (Biblical and Judaic Studies from UCSD 2; Winona Lake, IN: Eisenbrauns, 1992) 93–110.

9. Ibid., 104–10.

10. As an example, consider two classes of data—the members of one class being constrained to lie within a sphere and the members of the other lying within a spherical shell concentric to the sphere holding the members of the first class. Projecting this three-dimensional configuration onto two dimensions will overlap the two clusters badly. In three-dimensional space, the separation of the classes is trivial. If a point is within the sphere, it is a member of the first class; otherwise, it is a member of the second class. No such (perfect) decision rule can hold for the two-dimensional projection.

11. *Technical note.* They assess the fraction of the total variance accounted for by various projections and involve ratios of linear combinations of the squares (or absolute values) of the eigenvalues of the principal components. See for example, Brian Everitt, *An R and S-Plus® Companion to Multivariate Analysis* (Berlin: Springer, 2005) 46–47.

12. *Technical note.* Put more concisely and technically, our eigenvalues asymptote to zero too slowly. For the movement verbs discussed in §17.3.2, the two-dimensional projection includes only 55% of the total variance, the three-dimensional projection only 68%, and the four-dimensional projection only 77%.

13. R. Sokal and P. Sneath, *Principles of Numerical Taxonomy* (San Francisco: Freeman, 1963).

Of the several approaches to clustering, we prefer *agglomerative* (or "bottom-up") *clustering*. In this variant, one initially considers each object being classified to be a (singleton) cluster. One then proceeds as follows:

- *Step A.*   Based on the estimated distances between the various objects, one combines the two closest objects to form a cluster.
- *Step B.*   Then, using one of several available rules,[14] one computes the distances from the just-formed cluster to all of the other clusters.
- *Step C.*   One returns to Step A until there is only one cluster, at which point the clustering has been completed.

The outcomes of this process are represented by a tree structure, or a "dendrogram." Here is the dendrogram for our four verb corpora.

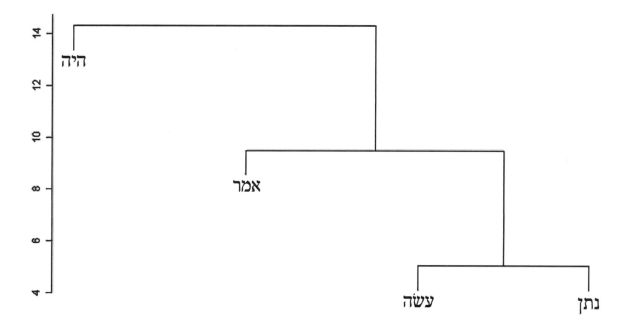

The tree makes explicit the similarities among its four corpora. The היה corpus is very different from the others, since it is a bit over 14 *lams* from the cluster consisting of the other three corpora.[15] The verbs עשׂה and נתן are two to three times closer to each other than to the others, being separated from each other by 5 *lams*.

---

14. Among the options are: (1) the "complete link" (or "furthest neighbor") distance, wherein the distance from one cluster to some other cluster is the distance between the two furthest neighbors out of each of the clusters; (2) the "single link" (or "nearest neighbor") distance, wherein the distance from one cluster to some other cluster is the distance between the two nearest neighbors out of each of the clusters; and (3) the "average" (or "unweighted pair-group method using arithmetic averages" = UPGMA) distance, wherein the distance from one cluster to some other cluster is the average of all distances between pairs of objects out of each cluster. On (1) and (2), see D. J. Hand, *Discrimination and Classification* (Chichester: Wiley, 1981) 164–69. On (3), see H. C. Romesburg, *Cluster Analysis for Researchers* (Belmont, CA: Lifetime Learning, 1984) 15–23. We use the "average" distance.

15. The distance between clusters is the level of the horizontal line joining them as read from the scale on the left.

17.2.4 A Measure of Dendrogram Adequacy

One more task is required. We need to indicate how well the dendrogram shown reflects the facts contained in the distance chart upon which it is based. There is a much-used statistic designed to do just this, the *cophenetic correlation coefficient* (CCC).[16] Its name makes it sound more arcane than it actually is. Its computation involves three simple steps:

1. Recover the distances among the clustered objects as encoded in the dendrogram and form a distance table (the "cophenetic matrix"). This is done by "walking" from one object node to another, with the largest distance encountered along the way recorded as the distance.
2. Lay out the original distances (the "Aitchison distances") and the distances represented in the dendrogram as two parallel lists.
3. Compute the correlation between the two lists, the cophenetic correlation coefficient (CCC).

The closer the CCC is to 1.00, the greater the fidelity of the dendrogram to the original distances. The usual threshold of acceptability is CCC ≥ 0.80.[17]

17.3 *Affinities for Two Large Collections of Verb Corpora*

17.3.1 Clauses Involving the Twenty Most Frequent Qal Active Verbs

Late in chap. 11, we tabulated the 20 most-frequent verb roots, including all of their *binyanim*, along with their incidence counts. Here are the 20 most-frequent *Qal active verb roots* along with their incidence counts:[18]

Root	*Count*	*Root*	*Count*	*Root*	*Count*	*Root*	*Count*	*Root*	*Count*
אמר	5,295	בא	1,975	לקח	960	אכל	726	עלה	590
היה	2,944	הלך	1,372	יצא	827	שׁב	670	שׁלח	550
עשׂה	2,492	ראה	1,114	ידע	816	קרא	661	נשׂא	545
נתן	2,007	שׁמע	1,024	ישׁב	778	שׂם	624	מת	521

Applying the methods sketched above in this chapter, we obtain the dendrogram for verb corpora containing the 20 most-common Qal active roots shown on p. 239. What does this dendrogram tell us at first glance?

- The fairly low value of the CCC (0.84) tells us that there are relations among the verb corpora that are not fully represented by the cluster diagram (the clustering is more distortive than we could wish).
- The fact that היה 'be' and מת 'die' are located very high in the diagram tells us that these 2 roots are quite atypical among these frequent verbs in the way that they make use of the CIC repertoire.
- Of the 20 verb corpora analyzed, the בא corpus and the עלה corpus are most similar, joining as they do at the smallest distance apart (~1.7 lams).

---

16. The best treatment of which we are aware is Romesburg, *Cluster Analysis*, 24–27. For one recent example of its use, see E. E. Kuramae et al., "Cophenetic correlation analysis as a strategy to select phylogenetically informative proteins: An example from the fungal kingdom," *Bio-Med Central Evolutionary Biology* 7 (2007) 134–44.

17. Romesburg, *Cluster Analysis*, 27.

18. Note that דבר and קם are no longer present, while קרא and נשׂא now are.

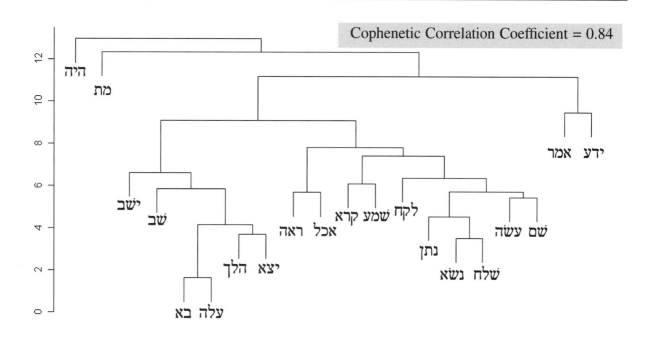

There is more to be said, but first we must extract the clusters.

17.3.1.1 Isolating Clusters

We need to explain how the dendrogram allows one to define verb corpora clusters. Since one does not know *ab initio* how many clusters there are, one usually tries out several sets to see if any groupings of the objects seem superior to others. This is done by drawing horizontal lines at various levels across the dendrogram, all edges having been notionally extended to the zero level by pulling each leaf down to the zero level. Each sub-tree below the cut-level is then a cluster.

The classification tree below (p. 240) should help make this clear. Each corpus-identifying Hebrew root is a leaf on the classification tree. Before isolating clusters, we (notionally) drag each corpus label down to the zero level of the scale, lengthening the branch connecting to it. If a horizontal threshold drawn across the diagram intersects a branch connecting to a leaf or cluster of leaves, then the dangling cluster (or leaf) is a cluster as defined by that threshold level. At the far right of the classification tree is a pair of corpora, אמר and ידע. When the cut threshold is set at 8 *lams* (dotted line), each of the 2 corpora occupies its own (singleton) cluster. But when the cut threshold is set to 10 *lams* (dashed line), then the 2 corpora are parts of the same cluster. For this dendrogram:

- A cut-level at 10 *lams* (dashed line) delimits 4 verb-corpus clusters. Two are strongly idiosyncratic corpora. These corpora do not fit in anywhere, at least as far as the present set of 20 verb corpora is concerned.
  - Cluster 1 (היה 'be')
  - Cluster 2 (מת 'die')
- Cluster 3 consists of אמר 'say' and ידע 'know'.
- Cluster 4 contains 16 verb corpora. It divides into 2 major clusters if the cut-level is reduced to 8 *lams* (dotted line):
  - a 6-corpus cluster containing a 5-corpus "movement cluster," labeled "M"
  - a 10-corpus cluster containing a 6-corpus "transitive cluster," labeled "T"

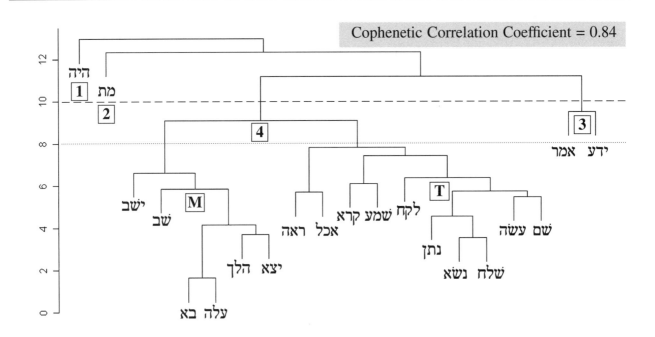

17.3.1.2 The "Mindless" Clustering Algorithm

The principle invoked for considering these clause types together ("frequently attested") in no way ensures that they fall into natural subgroups. And, in the event, they do not cluster into neat, highly compact and well-isolated clusters. Rather, several of the verb corpora just noted are strongly idiosyncratic. Further, the fairly low value of the cophenetic correlation coefficient (0.84) indicates that the dendrogram has done only a fair job of accounting for the distances separating the "top 20."

This points to a characteristic of the clustering algorithm that can lead to false inferences if one ignores the results-check provided by the cophenetic correlation coefficient (CCC): *no matter what distances are supplied to the clustering algorithm, a dendrogram will be built.*

To make our point concretely, consider the sets of clauses containing one or the other of the 2 Qal active verbs (occurring more than 60 times) that are farthest from each other, טמא 'be unclean' (75×) and חפץ 'desire' (78×). The CIC incidence bar chart for טמא is shown at the top of p. 241. The CIC incidence bar chart for חפץ is shown at the bottom of p. 241.

Across the 103 sets of clauses having Qal active verbs and at least 60 clauses each, the average distance separating the corpora is 13 *lams*. The distance separating the טמא and חפץ clause types is 22 *lams*, approaching double the average. Hence, the cluster of the 2 sets that would be formed by supplying only their incidences to the clustering algorithm would lack compactedness. Saying that the 2 sets are in the same cluster would be akin to placing an elephant and a sardine, say, in the same taxonomic cluster. While both are animals, on the surface they have little in common.

17.3.2 Clauses Involving Frequent Verbs of Movement

17.3.2.1 Qal Active Verbs of Movement

When we clustered the 20 most-common Qal active roots in §17.3.1, the affinities among the verb corpora resulted by happenstance. In this subsection, we consider verb corpora involving 17 Qal active verbs (each occurring more than 60 times) that we independently marked as having

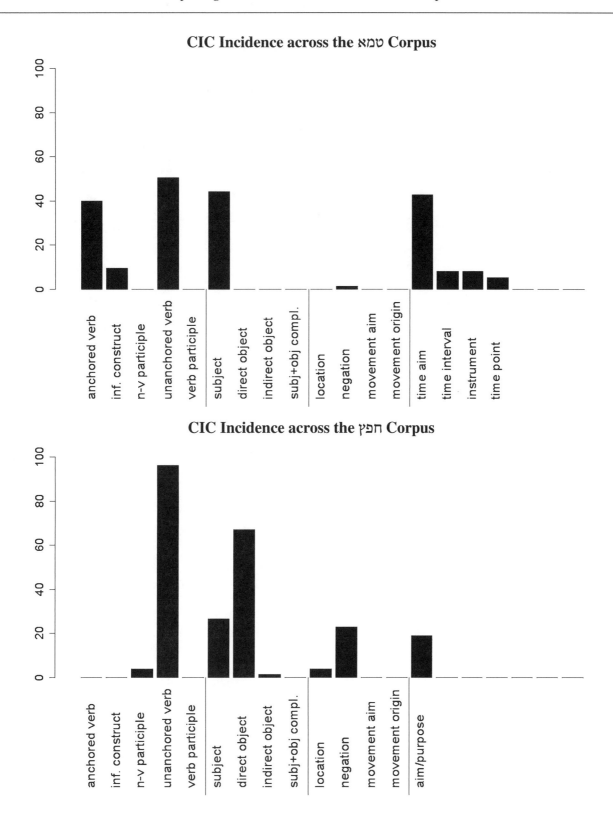

CIC Incidence across the טמא Corpus

CIC Incidence across the חפץ Corpus

simple movement semantics. To the extent that our assignments were valid, we expect the sets to form illuminating clusters.

Root	*Gloss*	*Count*	*Root*	*Gloss*	*Count*	*Root*	*Gloss*	*Count*
בא	go in	1,975	עמד	stand	435	נס	flee	148
הלך	walk	1,368	נפל	fall	356	נסע	break camp	136
יצא	go out	827	ירד	go down	289	פנה	turn	116
שב	return	670	שכב	lie down	191	גר	sojourn	76
עלה	go up	590	עזב	leave	182	רץ	run	73
קם	arise	449	סר	turn aside	175			

When we submit the distances between the corpora of the foregoing 17 Qal active roots to the clustering algorithm, we obtain the following dendrogram:

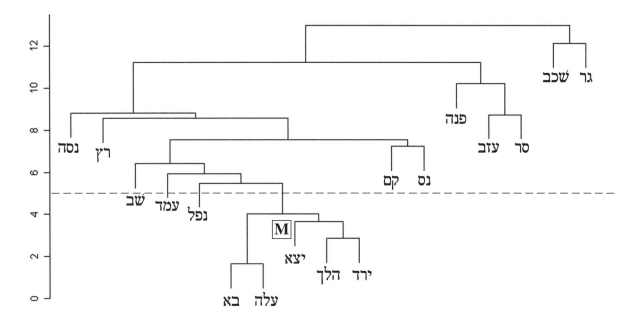

The cophenetic correlation coefficient (CCC) is gratifyingly large (0.91), indicating that the dendrogram reflects the computed distances rather well.

When the cut-level is at 5 *lams*, we obtain a prototypical 5-corpus movement cluster ("**M**") consisting of בא 'go in', עלה 'go up', יצא 'go out', הלך 'walk', and ירד 'go down'. Because the algorithm has identified a cluster, the next step would be to investigate which properties these verb corpora have in common, which would be the beginnings of producing a hierarchical lexicon of verbs.

With regard to other aspects of the dendrogram, we note, among other things, that:

- The words שכב 'lie down' and גר 'sojourn' are not prototypical movement verbs. A complete analysis would seek the sources of their peculiarity.
- We see that פנה 'turn', עזב 'leave', and סר 'turn aside' form a loose cluster, being separated by about 10 *lams*. These are not movement verbs of the sort in the prototypical cluster (which involve an agent's moving from A to B). Rather, they involve an agent's changing orientation (signaled by the mvt dir CIC).

- The other singleton clusters merit examination to identify the idiosyncrasies that lead to their relative isolation with respect to the prototype clause sets.

In §17.2.2, we referred to geometrical methods of clustering but opted to use the clustering approach relying on dendrograms. In this case, however, we now use a geometrical method[19] to check our results. When we plot the data for eight selected clause sets, the following diagram is the result:

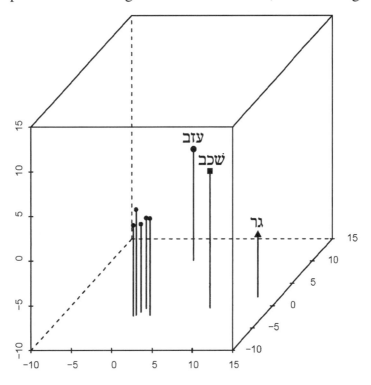

The five smaller dots (●) above the origin of the horizontal (x-y) plane correspond to the "M" cluster for בא 'go in', עלה 'go up', יצא 'go out', הלך 'walk', and ירד 'go down' in the dendrogram. The larger dot (●) is עזב 'leave', the square (■) is שכב 'lie down', and the triangle (▲) is גר 'sojourn'.

17.3.2.2 Hiphil Active Verbs of Caused Movement

We previously and independently found 2,347 Hiphil active verbs of caused motion. To allow for them to cluster differently from the Qal actives, we segregated them from the Qals. Thirteen of the Hiphil active forms appear more than 30 times (in 2,288 clauses, 97.5% of the total):

Root	Gloss	Count	Root	Gloss	Count	Root	Gloss	Count
בא	bring in	559	קם	raise up	146	נפל	make fall	61
שב	bring back	353	שלך	throw	111	הלך	make walk	46
יצא	bring out	286	עמד	stand	90	גלה	deport	35
עלה	bring up	273	עבר	make cross	76			
קרב	present	185	ירד	bring down	67			

---

19. *Technical note.*   We used classical multidimensional scaling to project the data into three-space. Just over two-thirds of the variance is preserved in the plot. See Mark Davison, *Multidimensional Scaling* (New York: Wiley, 1983).

When we submit the distances among the corpora containing the foregoing 13 Hiphil active roots to the clustering algorithm, we obtain the following dendrogram:

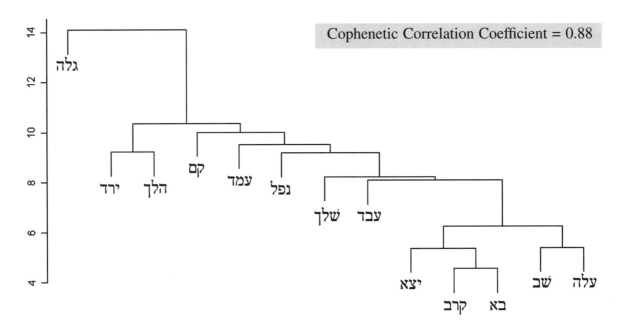

The cophenetic correlation coefficient is slightly less than that of the Qal active movement verbs.

17.4 *Affinities for Corpora Based on Single* Binyanim, *Etc.*

As our final probe of verb corpora affinities in this chapter and as preparation for taking up quasiverbal-predicator clauses (QVCs) in chap. 18 and verbless clauses (VLCs) in chap. 19, we next present a gallery of 7 large-corpora CIC-incidence bar charts for self-study. We then display a dendrogram that portrays the affinities among these corpora.

17.4.1 A Gallery of CIC Incidence Bar Charts

Here, we present a CIC-incidence bar chart for the sets of clauses based on:

- The Qal active verbs
- The Qal active verbs without היה

We omit the היה clauses because of the strong difference between היה and other verbs (see pp. 245ff.). The main difference between these charts is the diminution of subject complement incidence in the lower chart.

As the bar chart of CIC incidence for verbless clauses clearly reveals, they lack predicators (p. 247).

Our glossary defines the quasiverbal as "a segment that does not have verb morphology but functions as a predicator. Included are: *behold!* (הִנֵּה), *exists* (יֵשׁ), *still* (עוֹד), *not-exists* (אֵין) and, strictly speaking, *where?* (אַיֵּה)." Because of their novel status, we have not included them among the predicators in our bar charts. Instead, they are treated in their own right in chap. 18.

CIC Incidence for Qal Actives

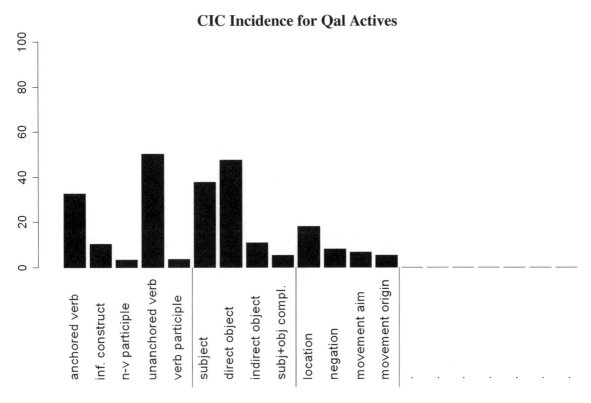

CIC Incidence for Qal Actives without היה

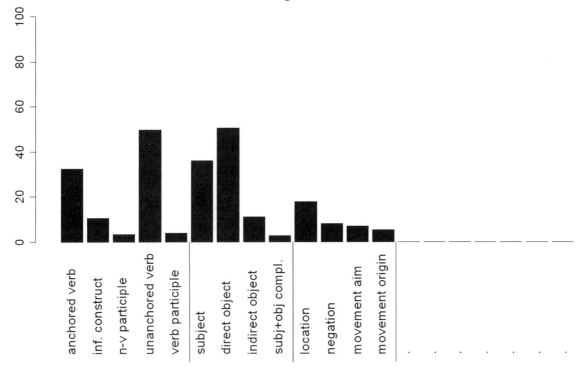

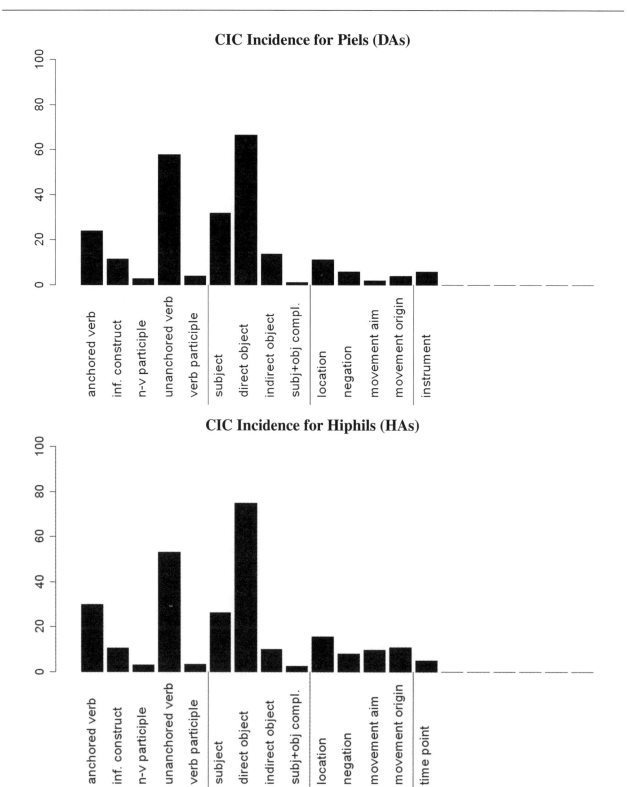

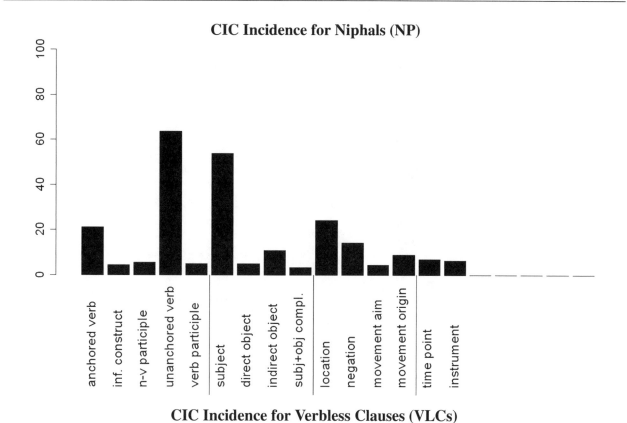

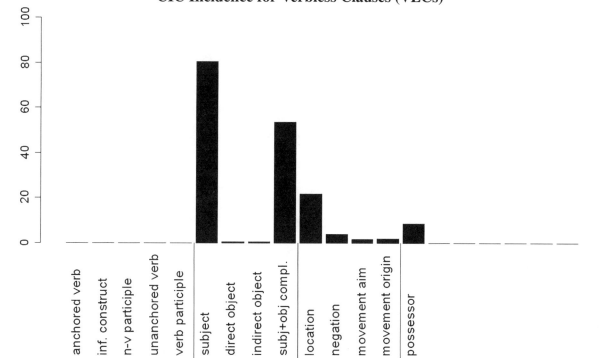

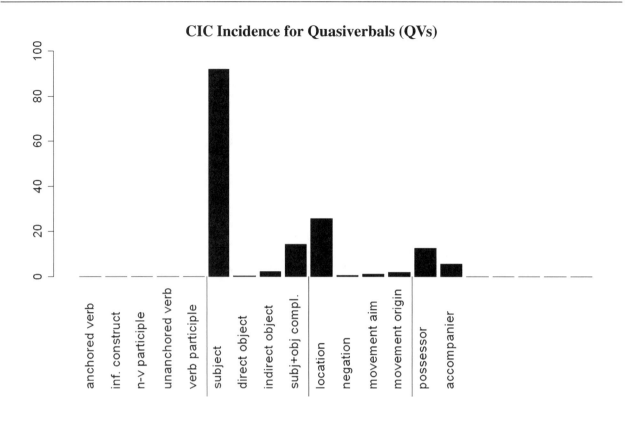

CIC Incidence for Quasiverbals (QVs)

17.4.2 Dendrogram Based on CIC Incidences

The table gathers the top 13 CIC incidences for the verb corpora that we have studied.

	Qal Act.[a]	*Piel*	*Hiphil*	*Niphal*	היה	*VLC*	*QV*	*Qal Act.*
anchored verb	32.5%	24.1%	29.8%	21.2%	35.5%	–	–	32.7%
inf. constr.	10.6%	11.4%	10.5%	4.5%	5.0%	–	–	10.3%
participle	3.4%	2.8%	3.1%	5.6%	–	–	–	3.2%
unanchored	49.7%	57.7%	53.1%	63.6%	59.4%	–	–	50.3%
verb particip.	3.7%	4.0%	3.4%	5.0%	–	–	–	3.5%
subject	35.9%	31.9%	26.3%	53.8%	65.0%	80.4%	91.9%	37.7%
direct object	50.6%	66.4%	74.8%	4.9%	–	0.6%	0.3%	47.5%
indirect object	11.1%	13.6%	10.1%	10.8%	6.1%	0.6%	2.3%	10.7%
sbj/obj compl.	2.8%	1.0%	2.4%	3.2%	42.9%	53.7%	14.2%	5.2%
location	17.8%	11.1%	15.5%	24.2%	25.1%	21.7%	25.8%	18.2%
negation	7.9%	5.8%	8.0%	14.3%	9.2%	3.8%	0.6%	8.0%
mvt aim	7.1%	1.9%	9.7%	4.6%	1.9%	1.5%	1.1%	6.7%
mvt origin	5.3%	4.0%	10.7%	8.8%	3.5%	1.8%	2.0%	5.2%

a. The first column is for the Qal actives without היה.

17.4.2.1   Clause Set Affinities, All CIC Incidences Included

When we carry out our standard clustering on 7 of the sets of clauses in the gallery above,[20] we obtain this dendrogram:

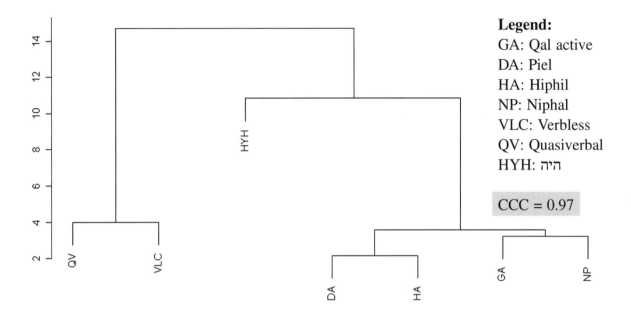

Legend:
GA: Qal active
DA: Piel
HA: Hiphil
NP: Niphal
VLC: Verbless
QV: Quasiverbal
HYH: היה

CCC = 0.97

This dendrogram does an excellent job of characterizing the distances separating the verb corpora, because its cophenetic correlation coefficient is 0.97.

We see that the Piel (DA) and Hiphil (HA) corpora are closest to each other, with the Qal active and Niphals joining in a bit farther away. As usual, the היה clauses "have a mind of their own." The verbless clauses and the quasiverbal clauses have affinities, being closer to each other than they are to the other sets of clauses.

17.5   *Brief Summary*

Generalization and the Hierarchical Lexicon.   One path to useful generalizations regarding the verb stock of Biblical Hebrew is to locate each verb corpus in a taxonomy containing all verb corpora ("the hierarchical lexicon"). Statements made about any group of verb corpora ("verb classes") may then be powerful generalizations regarding its members.

Inter-Clause Distance.   We construct our hierarchical lexicon using the CIC incidence patterns associated with each verb corpus. This requires that we carefully define the distance between pairs of verb corpora, a technically demanding task.

Inter-Clause Clustering.   Given the table of distances separating the verb corpora, we are in a position to form groups of verb corpora using agglomerative clustering techniques. These methods find the hierarchy of verb corpora that best fits the table of distances. There is a statistic that then allows us to judge how well the hierarchy incorporates the distances on the basis of which it has been produced (the "cophenetic correlation coefficient").

---

20. We do not include the full set of Qal active clauses but, rather, separate the CIC incidences for היה from them.

Clustering the Top Twenty Qal-Active Verb Corpora.   We cluster the corpora associated with the 20 most frequent Qal active verbs and then show how the resulting tree can be used to group the corpora.

Clustering Verbs of Movement.   We carry out analogous operations for the 20 most frequent verbs of movement, first using Qal actives and then using Hiphil actives.

A Gallery of CIC Incidence Bar Charts.   For reader study, we display an instructive gallery of CIC incidence bar charts: Qal actives, Qal actives without the היה-corpus, Piels, Hiphils, Niphals, verbless clauses, and quasiverbals. We use these CIC incidences to cluster the *binyanim*, verbless corpus, and quasiverbal corpus. We find, for example, that the verbless corpus has much in common with the quasiverbal corpus, that the היה corpus stands alone, and that the Piels and Hiphils have more in common with each other with regard to CIC incidence than they do with the Qal actives and Niphals.

Chapter 18

The Five Quasiverbals

In this chapter, we examine characteristics of the five lexemes that we grouped under the heading *Quasiverbals* in our tables of parts of speech in §3.2. This list is reordered from §3.2.5:

יֵשׁ *exists*   אֵין *does not exist*   עוֹד *still*   הִנֵּה *behold*   אַיֵּה *where?*

Approximately 720 of these lexemes combine with verbal elements to produce compound predicators. Because 75% of these involve the phenomenon of discontinuity, we discuss them in chap. 20. Here we deal with the 1,213 clauses in which these items appear as simple predicators.

In this chapter, we address three issues: (1) the way the five lexemes are characterized in standard reference works, (2) the patterns of CIC usage exhibited by each, and (3) the affinities that the five exhibit.

18.1   *Standard Biblical Hebrew References on the Five Lexemes*

18.1.1   How They Are Described

יֵשׁ *exists*.   The lexeme יֵשׁ has received several classifications:[1]

- Lambdin: "predicator of existence"[2]
- *IBHS*: "quasi-verbal indicator" and "predicator of existence"[3]
- Van der Merwe et al.: "predicator of existence"[4]
- Joüon / Muraoka: "adverb of existence"[5]
- Williams: "existential particle"[6]

The fact that יֵשׁ takes suffixes is frequently noted.[7]

אֵין *does not exist*.   This lexeme[8] has also received diverse classifications:

---

1. The homograph involving יֵשׁ occurs once, in Prov 8:21. There, יֵשׁ is a noun that is glossed 'substance'.

2. Lambdin, 165 (all references to Hebrew grammars in this chapter are by author's name or by acronym only; consult the bibliography for full information).

3. *IBHS*, 72 and 623.

4. Van der Merwe et al., 320.

5. Joüon / Muraoka, 541.

6. Williams, 170–71.

7. BDB, 441; Lambdin, 165; Blau, 78n; Joüon / Muraoka, 320; Williams, 170–71.

8. Homographs: Seven times אַיִן is classified as a noun, glossed 'nothing'. Once אַיִן (Isa 40:23) is a noun, also glossed 'nothing'. Forty-one times אֵין is a construct noun, glossed 'nothing of'.

251

- BDB: "particle of negation"[9]
- Lambdin: "predicator of non-existence"[10]
- *IBHS*: "clausal adverb" and "predicator of non-existence"[11]
- Van der Merwe et al.: "negative adverb"[12]
- Joüon/Muraoka: "negative adverb" and "adverb of non-existence"[13]
- Williams: "[t]he negative"[14]

The fact that it takes suffixes is frequently noted.[15]

עוֹד *still.*   The classifications of עוֹד[16] are less scattered than those of several of the other lexemes here considered. We find:

- BDB: "used mostly as adv. acc. still, yet, again, besides . . ."[17]
- Lambdin: "In verbal sentences, עוֹד is used as a simple adverb in the sense of 'again, still, yet, once more'."[18]
- *IBHS*: "constituent adverb, qualifying the time extent of the predicate."[19]
- *HALOT*: "[substantive] repetition, duration [develops into] adv. again, still (with fluid transition) from one to the other."[20]
- Van der Merwe et al. as well as Joüon/Muraoka: "adverb."[21]

The fact that the lexeme can take a pronoun suffix is repeatedly asserted.[22]

הִנֵּה *behold.*   The lexeme[23] has also received several distinct classifications:

- BDB: "demonstrative particle."[24]
- Lambdin: "predicator of existence emphasiz[ing] immediacy, the here-and-now-ness of the situation."[25]
- *IBHS*: "particle," "demonstrative adverb," "deictic particle," and "presentative."[26]
- *HALOT*: "deictic and interrupting interjection."[27]
- Van der Merwe et al.: "discourse marker."[28]

---

9. BDB, 34.
10. Lambdin, 165.
11. *IBHS*, 623.
12. Van der Merwe et al., 318.
13. Joüon/Muraoka, 306 and 541.
14. Williams, 146–48. Williams specifies eight different uses of the lexeme.
15. BDB, 34; Lambdin, 165; *IBHS*, 661; Williams, 146. Also, J. Blau, *A Grammar of Biblical Hebrew* (2nd ed.; Wiesbaden: Harrassowitz, 1993) 78n.
16. We have divided this form into three homographs: two are temporal adverbs, one durational (glossed 'still', 317×) and the other repetitive (glossed 'again', 60×). The rest are classified as quasiverbals (116×).
17. BDB, 728.
18. Lambdin, 171.
19. *IBHS*, 657.
20. *HALOT*, 796.
21. Van der Merwe et al., 308, and Joüon/Muraoka, 307.
22. BDB, 728–29; Lambdin, 171; Blau, 78n; *HALOT*, 796; Joüon/Muraoka, 307.
23. We split the forms into three homographs: a spatial adverb (glossed 'here', 268×), an exclamative (glossed 'behold!' 19×), and a quasiverbal (glossed 'behold', 912×).
24. BDB, 243.
25. Lambdin, 168.
26. *IBHS*, 300, 307, 635, and 675.
27. *HALOT*, 252.
28. Van der Merwe et al., 328.

- Joüon/Muraoka: "presentative adverb."[29]
- Andersen: "positive perspectival presentative predicator."[30]

Most resources note that this lexeme can and does take pronoun suffixes.[31]

אַיֵּה *where?*   It is typically stated or implied that אַיֵּה is an interrogative or interrogative adverb.[32] That it can take suffixes is commonly noted.[33] It is asserted that it is not used with verbs:

- BDB: "used of both persons and things (but never with a *verb* [contrast אֵיפֹה])."[34]
- *IBHS*: "not used with verbs."[35]
- *HALOT*: "never before verbs, always in direct questions."[36]

Against these assertions, we find the lexeme in five verbal clauses: Gen 16:8, 2 Sam 1:3, Jer 5:7, Job 2:2, and Qoh 11:6. In these, we recognize a pure interrogative.

18.1.2 Verb-Like Behavior

In the foregoing, the notion of the lexemes' exhibiting predicative function appeared for יֵשׁ 'exists', אֵין 'does not exist', and הִנֵּה 'behold'. Indeed, the concept of "quasi-verbal indicators" even appeared, in the Waltke and O'Connor *IBHS* discussion of יֵשׁ 'exists'. Along these lines, Lambdin remarks that יֵשׁ and אֵין "approximate a verbal function in Hebrew, serving almost as tenseless forms of the verb 'to be'."[37] He further comments that "עוֹד, like הִנֵּה, may be inflected and used as a predicator of existence, with the nuance of 'to still be, to yet be.'. . . עוֹד, like הִנֵּה, may be extended from purely existential predication to use in other types of non-verbal sentences."[38] We are aware of only a single dissenting voice, GKC:[39]

> The usual explanation of [adverbial] suffixes (especially of the forms with *Nûn energicum*) as verbal suffixes, which ascribes some power of verbal government even to forms originally substantival (e.g., יֶשְׁנוֹ *there is, he is*), is at least inadmissible for forms . . . which are evidently connected with noun suffixes; even for the other forms it is questionable.

No evidence for the final assertion is provided.

18.2 *Existentials*

18.2.1 Biblical Hebrew Background

The lexemes יֵשׁ and אֵין are typically referred to as *existentials*. In Biblical Hebrew reference works, there is general agreement about the verb-like behavior of these lexemes. We find:

---

29. Joüon/Muraoka, 351.

30. F. I. Andersen, "Taxonomy and Translation of Biblical Hebrew הִנֵּה," in *Hamlet on a Hill: Semitic and Greek Studies Presented to Professor T. Muraoka on the Occasion of His Sixty-Fifth Birthday* (ed. M. F. J. Baasten and W. T. van Peursen; Leuven: Peeters, 2003) 56.

31. BDB, 243; Lambdin, 168; Blau, 78n; *IBHS*, 675; *HALOT*, 252; Joüon/Muraoka, 307.

32. BDB calls it an "interrogative adverb," 32, as do Joüon/Muraoka, 306. *HALOT*, 39, calls it an interrogative; this is implied by *IBHS*, 328, and by van der Merwe et al., 326.

33. Lambdin, 172; Blau, 78n; *HALOT*, 39. It is suffixed in 9 of 83 occurrences.

34. BDB, 32.

35. *IBHS*, 328.

36. *HALOT*, 39.

37. Lambdin, 165.

38. Ibid., 171.

39. GKC, §100o, 297.

- As noted earlier, van der Merwe et al. assert that יֵשׁ and אַיִן function as "predicators of existence."[40]
- BDB comments that יֵשׁ 'exists' "asserts *existence*, and so corresponds to the verb *substantive*, is (are, was, were, will be). . . . On this word, see esp. [Nöldeke], who exemplifies its different constructions in Semitic, and [shows] how it tends to pass into a verb."[41]

18.2.2 General Linguistics Background

In general linguistics, there is a surprisingly substantial literature on existentials. Central to this literature are the concepts of *pivot*[42] and of a *definiteness effect*.[43] Careful study of pivots indicates that the distinction between *subjects* and *pivots* is not valid for Biblical Hebrew. Nor do we see any need for a definiteness effect, an impression reinforced by Francez, who refers to "languages like Hebrew that do not exhibit a definiteness effect."[44] Nonetheless, there are some observations in the literature that are relevant to Biblical Hebrew:

- "By far the most common answer to the question of the semantic structure of existentials in the literature is that existentials are semantically locative predications."[45]
- "[I]n many, and perhaps in all, languages existential and possessive constructions derive (both synchronically and diachronically) from locatives. . . . [I]t might appear reasonable to say that all existential sentences are at least implicitly locative (the term 'locative' being taken to include both temporal and spatial reference)."[46]
- Most Biblical Hebrew grammarians, we daresay, would agree with Falk's assertions:[47]

[Y]eš is often analyzed as if it were a verb, either the present of *haya* or something essentially similar. . . . While the motivation is clear (the paradigmatic relation between *haya* and *yeš*), it is also obviously the case that *yeš* is not a verb. It appears to be a noun, as does its negative *eyn*. . . . In all their uses, *yeš* and *eyn* conform to our claim that they are categorically nouns but functionally verb-like.

- Falk also observes that "*yeš* is used in locative, existential, and possessive constructions."[48]

---

40. Van der Merwe et al., 318. In addition, אַיִן "[n]egates events to which a participle refers."

41. BDB, 441.

42. David Beaver et al., "Bad Subject: (Non-)canonicality and NP Distribution in Existentials," *Semantics and Linguistic Theory* 15 (2005), www.linguistics.ucla.edu/salt/.

43. E. L. Keenan, "The Definiteness Effect: Semantics or Pragmatics?" *Natural Language Semantics* 11 (2003) 187–216.

44. Itamar Francez, "Semantic structure and argument realization in (mostly Hebrew) existentials," 2006. On the web at: http://home.uchicago.edu/~ifrancez/IATL07.pdf. Note that *Modern* Hebrew is involved here.

45. Ibid., 3. Precisely for this reason, these sorts of location CIC might be considered core, not only in predicates in verbless clauses, but also in היה clauses.

46. John Lyons, "A note on possessive, existential, and locative sentences," *Foundations of Language* 3 (1967) 390.

47. Yehuda N. Falk, "The Hebrew Present-Tense Copula as a Mixed Category," in *Proceedings of the LFG04 Conference* (ed. M. Butt and T. H. King; Stanford, CA: CSLI, 2004) 229 and 241. *Note well* that this essay deals with *Modern* Hebrew. Some of its assertions are incorrect for Biblical Hebrew. For example, it refers to "the impossibility of [*yeš*] appearing with the negative *lo*" (p. 231), but see Job 9:33, where we find: לֹא יֵשׁ־בֵּינֵינוּ מוֹכִיחַ.

48. Ibid., 236. Compare Williams, 170–71.

18.2.3   CIC Incidences for Existentials in Biblical Hebrew
18.2.3.1   יֵשׁ

The CIC-incidence bar chart documents that clauses containing יֵשׁ commonly include a subject CIC (almost 90% of the time) and include locations (about one-third of the time), possessors, and interrogatives (each about one-fifth of the time), and accompanier, and aim/purpose CICs (9% and 6% of the time).

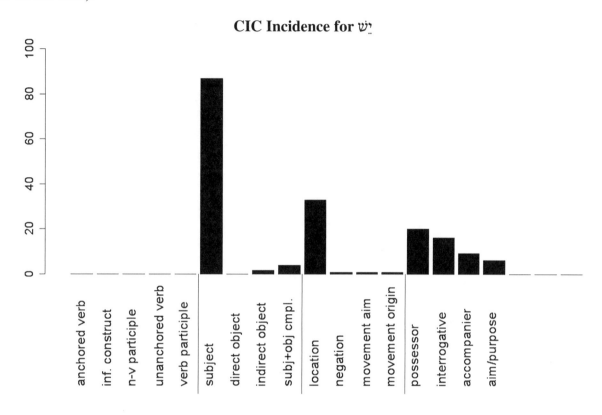

CIC Incidence for יֵשׁ

It is useful to proceed further and observe the way that these CICs co-occur.[49]

- There are 3 contexts (4 instances) where יֵשׁ occurs alone, always in answers.[50]
- There are 38 two-CIC clauses involving יֵשׁ.[51] More than half of these simply consist of a QV sbj.[52]
- There are 47 יֵשׁ-clauses with 3 noncoordinating conjunction CICs. Closed interrogatives occur 3 times, always in lead position: interrog QV. Five additional times, יֵשׁ is not in lead position. Three of the CIC sequences following the 37 clauses with initial יֵשׁ exhibit alternating CIC order:

| sbj loc | 8 | poss sbj | 6 | sbj acc | 3 |
| loc sbj | 8 | sbj poss | 1 | acc sbj | 1 |

---

49. *Note*: The Aramaic equivalent of יֵשׁ, אִיתַי 'exists', is included in these tallies. In passing, we observe that the Aramaic form is preceded by לָא 'not' six times: Dan 2:10, 11 (2×); 3:29; 4:32; Ezra 4:16.

50. 1 Sam 9:12, 2 Kgs 10:15 (וְיֶשׁ שׁ), Jer 37:17, and Dan 3:1.

51. Two of these involve ellipted יֵשׁ: Jer 5:1 and Prov 13:7. Eight have an introductory "and" (7×) or "also" (1×).

52. Sbj QV order occurs once, in 1 Sam 21:5.

- Thirty-nine יֵשׁ-clauses consist of 4 CICs, with 38 containing a subject CIC. Fourteen begin with the sequence interrog QV, and a closed interrogative is used in all 14 of these.
- Six clauses consist of 5 or more CICs, too few clauses for useful generalizing.

18.2.3.2   אַיִן

We turn next to the negative polarity existential, אַיִן 'does not exist'. This lexeme appears in compound verbal structures 129 times. We focus here on its 594 appearances as a clausal CIC in its own right. The CIC incidence bar chart reveals the sorts of CICs that appear along with it. We see that clauses containing אַיִן commonly include a subject CIC (about 90% of the time) and include locations (26% of the time), possessors (18% of the time), and aim / purpose and accompanier CICs (each around 6% of the time). Note that, unlike the situation with יֵשׁ (21.1%), there are fairly few interrogatives with אַיִן (3.4%).

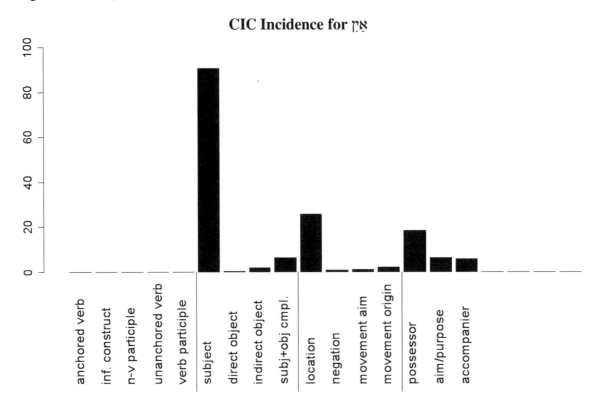

CIC Incidence for אַיִן

It is interesting to observe how these CICs co-occur.

- There are 18 contexts where אַיִן occurs alone in a clause. Six of these involve אַיִן־אֹם,[53] and 2 involve כִּי־אַיִן.[54]
- There are 204 two-CIC clauses involving אַיִן.[55] More than 85% of these simply consist of QV sbj.
- There are 255 אַיִן clauses with 3 noncoordinating conjunction CICs. The existential is in lead position 71% of the time. Two CIC sequences following the 179 clauses with initial אַיִן exhibit alternating CIC ordering:

---

53. Exod 17:7, 32:32; Judg 9:15, 9:20; 2 Sam 17:6; 2 Kgs 2:10.
54. 1 Sam 10:14; Job 35:15.
55. Two of these involve ellipted יֵשׁ: Jer 5:1 and Prov 13:7. Eight of these have an introductory "and" (7×) or "also" (1×).

| sbj loc | 41 | poss sbj | 31 |
| loc sbj | 22 | sbj poss | 15 |

- 95 אֵין-clauses consist of 4 CICs, with 91 of these (96%) containing a subject CIC.
- 20 clauses consist of 5 or more CICs, each exhibiting a unique sequence of CICs.

18.3 עוֹד

The CIC-incidence bar chart for עוֹד highlights the range of CICs observed in its 86 appearances as a noncompounded clausal predicator.

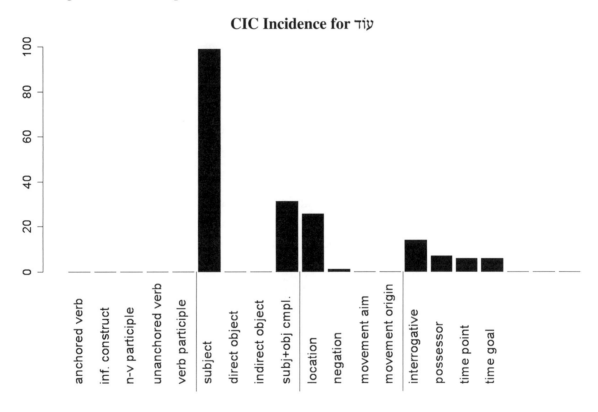

CIC Incidence for עוֹד

It is interesting to observe how these CICs co-occur:

- There are no QV-only clauses.
- Two-CIC clauses occur 22 times, 19 (86%) being QV sbj.
- There are 41 three-CIC clauses. These are QV-initial 90% of the time.
- There are 22 four-CIC clauses. Five (23%) are interrog QV sbj sbj-cmp.
- The 6 clauses having 5 CICs share little with regard to CIC sequencing.

18.4 הִנֵּה

This CIC-incidence bar chart for הִנֵּה highlights the limited range of CICs observed in its 350 appearances as a noncompounded clausal predicator.

CIC Incidence for הִנֵּה

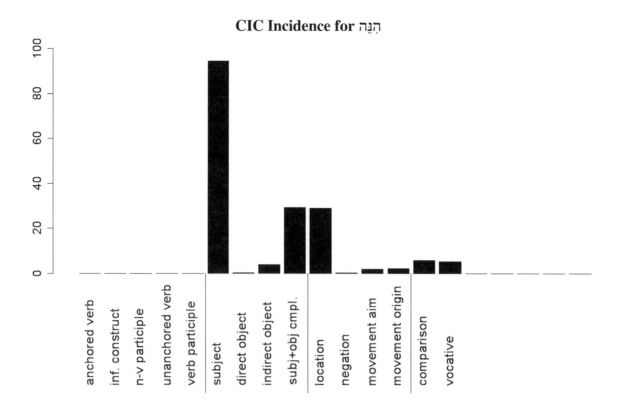

A subject appears in 92% of the clauses, while subject complements and locations appear in almost 30%. Comparison and vocative CICs each appear in slightly over 5% of the clauses.

As for the co-occurrence patterns of the CICs, we find:

- There are no QV-only clauses.
- There are 107 two-CIC clauses, all but 1 being QV-initial. The preponderant sequence is QV sbj (81%).
- There are 140 three-CIC clauses, all but 3 being QV-initial (98%). For the 137 QV-initial clauses, the patterns of the final 2 CICs primarily are:

sbj sbj-cmp	39	sbj loc	33
sbj-cmp sbj	12	loc sbj	9

- There are 74 four-CIC clauses exhibiting around 50 patterns.
- There are 19 five-CIC clauses, 3 six-CIC clauses, and 1 seven-CIC clause.[56]

18.5   אַיֵּה

This CIC-incidence bar chart for אַיֵּה highlights the limited range of CICs observed in its 59 appearances as a noncompounded clausal predicator.

---

56. The clause is in Ps 123:2. Four of its CICs are "pulled up" from the following clause.

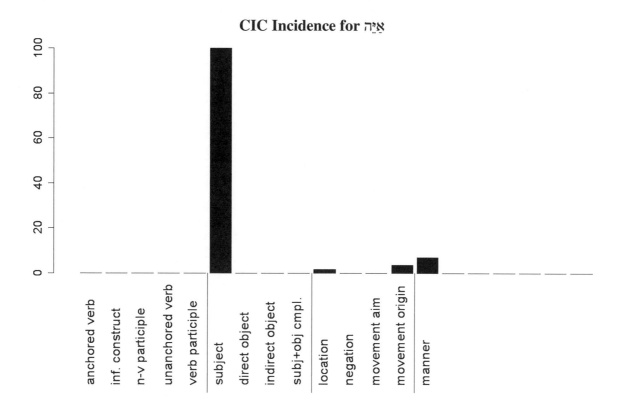

CIC Incidence for אַיֵּה

The CIC co-occurrence patterns are:

- There is 1 context where אַיֵּה occurs alone in a clause: Job 15:23. All but 2 of the clauses contain a subject.
- There are 48 two-CIC clauses involving אַיֵּה, all consisting of QV sbj.
- There are 8 אַיֵּה clauses with 3 noncoordinating conjunction CICs. The lexeme is in lead position in all but one, Zech 1:5.
- One אַיֵּה clause consists of 4 CICs: Jer 5:7.

18.6   *Affinities among the Five Lexemes*

We naturally wonder what affinities exist among the quasiverbals. Following the procedures explained in chap. 17 and more rigorously in appendix 5, we can use the CIC incidences for the 5 quasiverbal lexemes to compute the distances separating the lexemes and then use these to perform hierarchical clustering. We obtain the dendrogram shown on p. 260. The cophenetic correlation coefficient for the tree is 0.94, indicating an excellent fit to the data. Note that the 2 existentials are closest together, being separated by 5 *lam* units. To this prototypical cluster, הִנֵּה joins in; then comes עוֹד, followed by אַיֵּה. Put differently, *the existentials are the most prototypical of the quasiverbals, while* אַיֵּה *is the least.*

18.7   *Brief Summary*

Standard Treatments of Quasiverbals.   For some of the items that we group as quasiverbals, the standard Biblical Hebrew literature recognizes predicative functions. This is especially true of

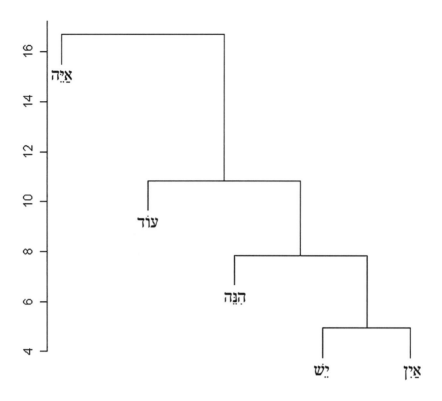

the existentials. But the 5 lexemes are not standardly grouped into a family. As far as we know, our work is the first time that these 5 lexemes have been grouped together as a distinct part of speech.

Patterns of Quasiverbal Usage.   When we examine its CIC incidence bar charts, we find that the quasiverbal corpus is uniform in its preference for explicit subjects. While the location SR is fairly frequent, explicit negation is rare. Subject complements occur fairly frequently with עוֹד 'still' and הִנֵּה 'behold', but not with the other 3.

Quasiverbal Affinities.   When we cluster the quasiverbals, we find that יֵשׁ 'exists' and אֵין 'does not exist' (the existentials) are most similar, with הִנֵּה 'behold' more distant, עוֹד 'still' even more distant, and אַיֵּה 'where?' the mixed lexeme, most idiosyncratic of all.

Chapter 19

Verbless Clauses

We here discuss the major issues pertaining to *clauses having neither verbals nor quasiverbals.*[1]

19.1 *Verbless/Nominal Clauses*

19.1.1 Naming Conventions

The special kinds of clausal entity that we are about to consider have two naming conventions based on the characteristics of their clausal predicates:

- The older convention focuses on what the predicates supposedly contain, following Albrecht in calling the clauses *Nominalsatzen* ("nominal sentences") or *nominal clauses.*[2]
- The more recent convention emphasizes what the predicates lack, following Andersen in calling the clauses *verbless clauses* or *nonverbal clauses.*[3]

The former convention is preferred by scholars in the European tradition, the latter by those in the North American tradition. In a survey volume on our topic containing essays by 12 contributors, 5 of 6 European contributors refer to the clauses as *nominal*, while 5 of 6 North American contributors refer to the clauses as *verbless.*[4] The reference works fluctuate in use between "nominal clause" and "verbless clause":

- Gesenius/Kautzsch uses "die Nominalsätze,"[5] which Cowley translates "noun-clause."[6]
- For Joüon's "Proposition nominale,"[7] Muraoka adopts the English term "nominal clause" and retains Joüon's mention of both conventions: "The category of nominal clause includes every clause the predicate of which is a noun or the equivalent of a noun, i.e., a participle, a preposition with a noun or pronoun, etc.; or, put negatively, every clause the predicate of which is not a verb . . . is a nominal clause."[8]

---

1. We might write *predicator-less structures* rather than *verbless clauses*, since a few of the structures to be considered are not clauses, in that they lack predicates. These structures are dealt with in §19.9. For definitions of *clause*, see §7.1. From our four types of participles (§3.2.4.2), *we include only the pure noun participles.*

2. C. Albrecht, "Die Wortstellung im hebräischen Nominalsatze," *ZAW* 7 (1887) 218–24; 8 (1888) 249–63.

3. F. I. Andersen, *The Hebrew Verbless Clause in the Pentateuch* (Nashville: Abingdon, 1970).

4. Cynthia L. Miller, ed. *The Verbless Clause in Biblical Hebrew: Linguistic Approaches* (Linguistic Studies in Ancient West Semitic 1; Winona Lake, IN: Eisenbrauns, 1999).

5. W. Gesenius and E. F. Kautzsch, *Hebräische grammatik* (27th ed.; Leipzig: Vogel, 1902) 458. On the Web at books.google.com.

6. GKC, 451.

7. Joüon, 466.

8. Ibid., 528.

- Waltke and O'Connor have a chapter on verbless clauses.[9]
- Van der Merwe et al. opt for "nominal clause" defined by what is absent: "Nominal clauses refer to clauses in [Biblical Hebrew] that do not contain a finite form of the verb."[10]
- In his index under "nominal clause," Williams has "See verbless clause."

Name choices are nearly equally divided between the two names. Where do we come down? We agree with Baasten:

> [T]he predicate of a non-verbal clause is not necessarily a noun phrase. As no-one seems to deny, the predicate of such clauses may also be, among other things, a prepositional phrase or an adverbial phrase, constituents that cannot properly be called 'nominal.'[11]

Dryer states that "there are three types of clauses with nonverbal predicates whose properties vary considerably across languages. These are adjectival predicates, nominal predicates, and locative predicates."[12] Biblical Hebrew includes these three sorts of nonverbal predicates, and more. Hence, we will continue to gather every kind of clause that lacks a verbal or quasiverbal predicator under the term *"verbless clause."* We will sometimes abbreviate "verbless clause" as VLC ("vᵊlick").

Cameron Sinclair sees introduction of the nominal / verbless clause type as unnecessary. He seeks a "single unified description of the syntax of clauses employing the copula הָיָה and of nominal clauses."[13] To achieve this goal, Sinclair identifies and provides examples of a range of constituent types that are "complements both in clauses with הָיָה and in verbless clauses."[14] Based on these parallels, he asserts that הָיָה clauses and nominal clauses "are really not two clause-types at all but, rather, variants of a single type in which the verb occurs when it is needed . . . but is otherwise simply omitted." The fact that a set of constituents can be defined as appearing both in הָיָה clauses and in verbless clauses is not a sufficient condition for declaring the two "variants of a single type." To make this declaration, one must show in full detail that they are typological siblings.

19.1.2 Accepted Properties of Verbless Clauses

Although the choices of name for the clause type are nearly evenly divided, there is near universal agreement regarding several characteristics of VLCs:[15]

1. *Most VLCs contain two CICs.* The orthodox view is that verbless / nominal clauses are *bipartite.* Something like this is assumed in most reference works. A few references deal with tripartite verbless clauses, a controversial topic touched on in §19.11.[16] As for

---

9. *IBHS*, 125–35. Waltke and O'Connor are aware of the multiplicity of possible predicators that appear in verbless clauses (pp. 72–73).

10. Van der Merwe et al., 361. Several times they include both terms, "nominal clause (or verbless clause)," for example, on p. 63.

11. Martin F. J. Baasten, *The Non-Verbal Clause in Qumran Hebrew* (Ph.D. diss., Leuven University, 2006) 14–15.

12. Matthew S. Dryer, "Clause Types," in *Language Typology and Syntactic Description*, Vol. 1: *Clause Structure* (2nd ed.; ed. Timothy Shopen; Cambridge: Cambridge University Press, 2007) 224.

13. Cameron Sinclair, "Are Nominal Clauses a Distinct Clause Type?" in *The Verbless Clause in Biblical Hebrew* (ed. C. Miller; LSAWS 1; Winona Lake, IN: Eisenbrauns, 1999) 52.

14. Ibid., 75.

15. When checks of the asserted properties of verbless clauses are easily feasible, our results appear as underlined text.

16. *IBHS*, 131; van der Merwe et al., 252; Joüon/Muraoka, 538–43; Williams, 50.

non-two-CIC VLCs, the literature is basically silent.[17] We break the silence in §19.9 and §19.11–12. In our mark-up of the verbless clauses, 57% (5,453/9,500) have only two CICs.

2. *Analysis is formulated in terms of subjects and predicates.* This is the reigning paradigm.[18]

3. *The subject of a VLC is "generally" a substantive or pronoun.* Typically, a writer provides a few examples of the major constituents and then of the less common constituents.[19] We find that 56.4% of the subjects of VLCs are phrasal substantives, 14.7% are segmental substantives, and 28.0% are pronouns, leaving 0.9% for all other kinds of constituents.

4. *The predicate of a VLC can be any of several constituent types.* The predicate may be a substantive, adjective, participle, numeral, pronoun, adverb, or prepositional phrase specifier of time, place, quality (according to GKC).[20] We agree with this assertion for reasons that will become clear in §19.9–§19.11.

5. *Substantive-substantive VLCs identify or classify*[21] *their subjects.* This distinction originated independently with Andersen and Muraoka[22] and has been universally adopted.[23] A clause of identification tells who or what is the subject, while a clause of classification specifies an attribute or a relationship of the subject.[24]

6. *Identification clauses tend to be S + P, while classification clauses tend to be P + S.* In these assertions, much hinges on the specifics of "tend."[25] Various factors can affect the ordering of the two major constituents.[26] See §19.10.2.4.

7. *Other testable generalizations are found.* We check these two generalizations:

   a. "The subject usually stands first in the clause."[27] Across all of the structures without predicators, this is not true. Only 43% of them lead off with their subject.

---

17. Regarding monopartites, see the very brief passing references in Joüon/Muraoka, 528, 529, 537. There is a three-page chapter on quadripartite nominal clauses in Wido van Peursen, *Language and Interpretation in the Syriac Text of Ben Sira* (Leiden: Brill, 2007) 306–9.

18. So GKC, 450; *IBHS*, 130; van der Merwe et al., 252; Joüon/Muraoka, 528; Williams, 206.

19. So GKC, 451 ("may be substantive or pronoun") and Joüon/Muraoka, 528. Joüon, in the first edition, comments: "De plus, le sujet peut être: (1) Une préposition avec son nom (ou pronom). . . . (2) Un infinitif construit. . . . (3) Raremont un infinitif absolu: Pr 25,27" (pp. 466–67).

20. GKC, 451–52; van der Merwe et al., 248, 275; Joüon/Muraoka, 529, add infinitive construct; Williams, 199–200.

21. Muraoka refers to "description" rather than classification.

22. Francis I. Andersen, *The Syntax of Biblical Hebrew* (Ph.D. diss., Johns Hopkins University, 1960). The chapter on verbless clauses in Genesis was expanded and published as *The Hebrew Verbless Clause in the Pentateuch*. Takamitsu Muraoka, *Emphasis in Biblical Hebrew* (Ph.D. diss. Hebrew University, Jerusalem, 1969). Published as *Emphatic Words and Structures in Biblical Hebrew* (Jerusalem: Magnes / Leiden: Brill, 1985).

23. So *IBHS*, 130; van der Merwe et al., 248; Joüon/Muraoka, 530; Williams, 198, 206.

24. *IBHS*, 130 and 132.

25. *IBHS*, 130–35; Williams, 207; Baasten, *Non-Verbal Clause*, 72–79.

26. Ordering is said to be conditioned on *emphasis* or *prominence* (notoriously elastic concepts) in both GKC, 454 ("*predicate–subject . . . must* be used when emphasis is laid on the predicate") and Joüon/Muraoka, 532–36. This explanation goes back to Albrecht, well summarized by Baasten, *Non-Verbal Clause*, 63–66. We read: "A personal pronoun tends to occupy the second slot when no prominence is intended to be given to it" (Joüon/Muraoka, 532).

27. Van der Merwe et al., 248.

b. "In purely statistical terms, the *word order* within the nominal clause is often S-P, which is true in roughly two out of every three cases."[28] <u>As stated, this is a weak assertion. Working only with structures having adjacent subjects and subject complements, we find that the order is S-P in 58% of cases.</u>

19.2 *The Layered Structure of Verbless Clauses*

One may probe verbless clauses using ideas from Van Valin's role and reference grammar (RRG):

[RRG] posits three main representations: (1) a representation of the syntactic structure of sentences, which corresponds closely to the actual structural form of utterances [the layered structure of the clause], (2) a semantic representation representing important facets of the meaning of linguistic expressions, and (3) a representation of the information (focus) structure of the utterance, which is related to communicative function.[29]

Van Valin's "layered structure of the clause" was devised to describe *verbal* clauses:

On this view, the primary constituent units of the clause are the 'nucleus', which contains the [predicator] (usually a verb), the 'core', which contains the nucleus and the arguments of the [predicator], and a 'periphery', which subsumes non-arguments of the [predicator], e.g., setting locative and temporal phrases.[30]

The layered structure may be schematized as followings:

Clause				
	Core			Periphery (Adjuncts)
Lead Zone	Prenucleus Zone	Nucleus (Predicator)	Postnucleus Zone	

We have extended the structure by converting the argument slot into a prenucleus zone and a postnucleus zone and by changing "precore slot" to a less theory-specific "lead zone" and "argument" to "zone." We introduce the layered structure model here because it approximates the sort of model assumed in the traditional verb-centric Biblical Hebrew literature. We will see that this model is of limited usefulness when verbless clauses are being described.

According to orthodoxy, in this representation the subject of an identification clause is in the prenucleus zone, while the subject of a classification clause is in the postnucleus zone. To maintain contact with the linguistics literature, we have kept the left-to-right ordering of the zones, even though for Biblical Hebrew texts the zones are ordered right-to-left, and for our phrase markers, top-to-bottom.

A VLC may differ from other VLCs with regard to the contents of any of its constituents: (1) lead zone, (2) prenucleus zone, (3) nucleus (predicator) zone, (4) postnucleus zone, and (5) pe-

---

28. Joüon / Muraoka, 531.

29. Robert D. Van Valin Jr., *Exploring the Syntax-Semantics Interface* (Cambridge: Cambridge University Press, 2005) 1. See also our §12.5.1.

30. Van Valin, *Exploring*, 4. We have adjusted terminology to comport with our usage.

riphery. The number of possible combinations of these elements in verbless clauses is enormous, and their communicative functions are myriad. When clauses contain neither verbal nor quasiverbal constituents, these zonal distinctions are neither very helpful nor very convincing. Consider:

- *Nucleus.* The linchpin nucleus is no longer identifiable on the basis of morphology. It must be identified with reference to its surroundings, be they local—using relative definiteness clues within the structure, or more remote—using "topic" (old information) and "comment" (new information) distinctions based on surrounding discourse.
- *Arguments.* It makes little sense to refer to "the arguments of the predicator" when said predicator is, say, a noun phrase.
- *Periphery.* While Van Valin specifies that locative and temporal phrases are in the periphery, Dryer states that nonverbal clauses can have "adjectival predicates, nominal predicates, and locative predicates."[31] So, should locatives in verbless clauses be assigned to a periphery, or to a core, or now to one and then to the other?

19.3 *Elliptic Verbal Clauses*

Before examining the verbless clauses, we touch on clauses that masquerade as verbless. The representation of many of these involves non-tree phrase markers, so they are treated in chap. 20.

19.3.1 Adjacent Ellipted Predicators

Many of these sorts of clauses are "completed" by pulling in a nearby ellipted predicator. Phrase marker (19.1) from Isa 64:9 illustrates the sort of behavior involved:

(19.1)

sent juxt	cl oblq	sbj gram	צִיּוֹן	Zion
		sbj cmp gram	מִדְבָּר	desert
	cl oblq	vb gram	הָיָתָה	she was
		sbj gram	יְרוּשָׁלַם	Jerusalem
		sbj cmp gram	שְׁמָמָה:	devastation

As represented, the first clause "pulls in" its verb from the second clause. The NJPS puts the verb in the first clause: "Zion has become a desert, Jerusalem a desolation." In both analyses, these sorts of clauses require non-tree representations (since some nodes have more than one mother) and so are discussed in §20.2.3.

19.3.2 Nearby Predicators

There are clauses whose completion depends not on a nearby predicator—typically concordant—but rather on a more remote—typically discordant—predicator. This phenomenon often occurs in conversation. In phrase marker (19.2) from 1 Kgs 20:14, the predicator in the question (יֶאְסֹר 'he will bind') suggests an (ellipted) predicator for the answer ('thou[m] wilt bind') in (19.3):

---

31. Dryer, "Clause Types," 224.

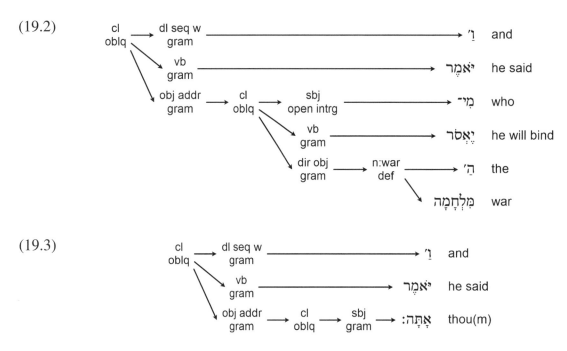

19.4 *Dealing with Rare CICs and Syntactic Isolates*

For our analyses, we set aside clauses containing any CIC that occurs fewer than 30 times and also ignore all instances of syntactic isolate CICs, retaining the reduced clauses. For the record, we here report on rare CICs and syntactic isolates in clauses without predicators.

19.4.1 Instances of Rare CICs

The table (see p. 267, top) provides a census of the 24 CIC types that occur fewer than 30 times in the 9,500 VLCs. The 223 rare CICs identify 221 clauses for exclusion (they appear in 2.3% of the VLCs).

19.4.2 Instances of Syntactic Isolates

Syntactic isolates are simply removed from the clauses in which they appear, leaving the clauses in play unless a "clause" consists of syntactic isolate(s) and, possibly, a coordinating conjunction. There are 344 structures that consist of a single syntactic isolate (110 solo exclamatives, 201 solo labels, and 33 solo vocatives). Eighty-two structures consist of 2 syntactic isolates. In 3 cases, a single isolate follows a coordinating conjunction.[32] Three syntactic isolates make up 2 structures, in Isa 30:1 (containing an extended vocative having 22 segments) and in Jer 23:1 (containing a vocative having 8 segments). A coordinating conjunction plus 2 labels appears in 1 Chr 26:25.

To see what these clauses are like, consider phrase markers (19.4) [solo exclamative] from Num 5:22, (19.5) [solo label] from Isa 13:1, and (19.6) [solo vocative] from 1 Sam 3:16.

Of the 214 exclamatives in verbless clauses, 205 are initial, 5 are medial,[33] and 4 are final.[34] Of the 364 labels in these clauses, only 8 are medial.[35] The 297 vocatives are much less positionally concentrated, with 33 solo, 52 initial, 164 final, and 48 medial.

---

32. Num 2:14 ("and" + lbl), 26:4 ("and" + lbl); and Prov 8:32 ("and" + excl).

33. Gen 20:12; Ps 8:2, 10; Prov 15:23; 16:16.

34. 1 Sam 25:26; Ps 84:13, 137:8; Prov 29:18.

35. While 201 are solo, 62 are initial, and 93 are final. All of the initial and final instances might well have been made solo. The 8 medial instances are in Exod 34:14; Jer 1:19, 30:11; Ps 51:1, 52:1, 54:1, 56:1, 60:1.

CIC Type	*Count*
Undesired outcome	20
Exocentric absolute	20
Involved ones	16
Movement bearing	16
Quantity	16
Composition	15
Agential	14
Quoter	12
Cost	12

CIC Type	*Count*
Includer	11
Nebulous	11
Object of address	10
Movement interval	9
Area	7 [e]
Ruled-over one	7 [g]
Result	6 [i]
Alternate / surrogate	6 [j]
Deprivation	4 [k]

CIC Type	*Count*
Lapsus calami	3 [a]
Number of times	3 [b]
Restricter	2 [c]
Cause	1 [d]
Condition	1 [f]
Separation	1 [h]

a. Found in Gen 30:11, Ps 55:16, and Prov 27:24.
b. A curious form, subj CIC plus "number of times" CIC, occurs in 1 Kgs 7:4.
c. Found in Deut 4:6 and Judg 19:20.
d. There is a phrasal *cause* in 2 Chr 29:25b.
e. Found in Num 35:4; Judg 1:36; Ezek 40:16; 41:9, 15; 43:12; Zech 9:10.
f. There is an embedded conditional finite-verb clause ("if you-do-right") in Gen 4:7.
g. Solo in Gen 43:16; initial in 1 Kgs 16:9; final in 1 Chr 9:31, 33; 23:28; 26:29, 30.
h. Found in 2 Sam 3:28.
i. Found in Isa 56:7; Ezek 17:9; Prov 14:23, 17:21; Song 5:9; 2 Chr 26:18.
j. Found in Gen 30:2, 50:19; Josh 2:14; Isa 61:7; Zeph 2:10; Prov 21:18.
k. Found in Deut 3:5, 4:12; Jer 51:5; and Job 21:9.

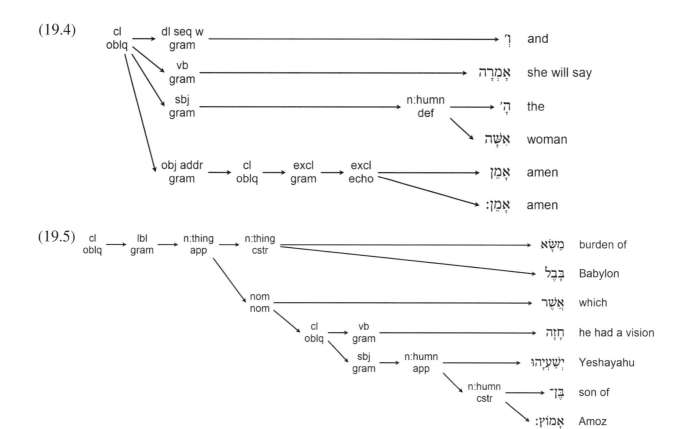

(19.6)
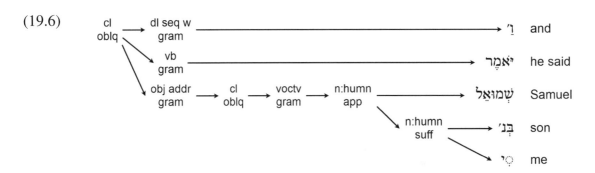

19.4.3   Tally of Censored VLCs

After we set aside clauses that contain rare CICs, ignore syntactic isolates, and suppress coordinating conjunctions, the CIC census of the 8,850 remaining VLCs is as follows.

Number of CICs	Verbless Clause Tally		Number of CICs	Verbless Clause Tally	
1	1,462	16.5%	6	11	
2	5,424	61.3%	7	1	
3	1,534	17.3%	8	3	0.3%
4	349	3.9%	9	8	
5	55	0.7%	10	3	

19.5   *Atypical Subjects and Subject Complements in Verbless Clauses*

By a sizable margin, the two most frequently occurring CICs in verbless clauses are subjects (7,348×) and subject complements (5,016×).[36] Only 66 of the subjects (0.9%) are nonsubstantives, being prepositional phrases. Only 52 of the subject complements (1.0%) are nonsubstantive, also prepositional phrases. As the table documents (see p. 269, top), 5 main prepositions are involved.

The 12 instances of a CIC consisting of a prepositional phrase involving the *nota accusativi* make up a puzzling cohort. Consider the example shown in phrase marker (19.7) from Judg 20:44.

(19.7)
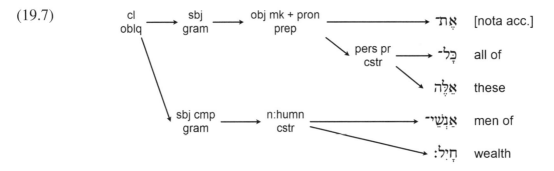

We accept the use of אֵת '(nota acc.)' in this context as real, uncorrupted Biblical Hebrew.

---

36. Data are for the 8,850 censored VLCs (§19.4.3). The next most frequent CICs are location (2,022×) and possessor (788×).

	אֶת	בְּ	+ לְ (inf. constr.)	+ לְ (other)	מִן	(miscellany)
Sbj	13 [a]	5 [b]	22 [c]	7 [d]	16 [e]	3 [f]
Sbj cmp	4 [g]	6 [h]	—	23 [i]	18 [j]	1 [k]

a. Exod 1:14; Num 22:6; 35:6; Josh 22:17; Judg 9:29; 20:44, 46; 1 Kgs 7:45; Ezek 47:19; Zech 8:17; Qoh 4:3; 2 Chr 31:10, 17.

b. Exod 13:2; Isa 26:4; Hos 13:9; Mal 1:10; Ezra 3:3.

c. Exod 8:22; 9:28; Josh 24:15; 1 Sam 15:22; 2 Sam 13:16; 18:11; Jer 40:4; Amos 6:10; Ps 92:2; Prov 21:9; Qoh 5:17; 7:2, 5; 11:7; Esth 5:8; 6:6; Ezra 4:3; Neh 13:13; 2 Chr 20:17; 25:9; 26:18; 29:10.

d. Gen 47:26; Num 26:45; 2 Sam 16:2; Ps 69:23; Song 1:3; Qoh 9:4; 1 Chr 26:21.

e. Gen 40:17; Exod 9:28; Num 26:4; Ezek 7:11(3×); 43:14; Neh 11:36; 13:28; 1 Chr 5:18; 9:28, 30, 32; 12:30; 2 Chr 20:1; 34:13.

f. 1 Kgs 3:18, Job 41:3, Prov 6:26.

g. Num 35:6; Jer 23:33, 45:4; 1 Chr 2:9.

h. Exod 18:4; Ps 118:7, 146:5; Job 23:13, 34:35, 37:10.

i. Exod 16:32; Lev 3:6; 11:39; Isa 26:8; Jer 3:23; Nah 1:7; Hab 1:11; Zech 4:7; Ps 4:3; 37:26; 69:23; Job 6:26; 13:12, 16; Lam 4:3; Dan 9:16; 1 Chr 9:23; 21:3, 12; 29:11; 2 Chr 23:4; 28:21; 29:32.

j. Gen 17:12; Exod 2:6; 30:2; Num 17:5; Judg 19:12; 1 Kgs 7:34, 35; 8:41; 11:14; 20:41; Isa 41:24; 44:11; Hab 1:13; Ps 45:14; Ruth 2:20; Esth 6:13; 1 Chr 8:40; 2 Chr 6:32.

k. Prov 6:26.

One of the 11 instances of a CIC within a VLC consisting of a prepositional phrase involving בְּ 'in' has a ב of specification.[37] A few others involve *beth essentiae*.[38] The single instance of the former is shown in phrase marker (19.8) from Exod 13:2.

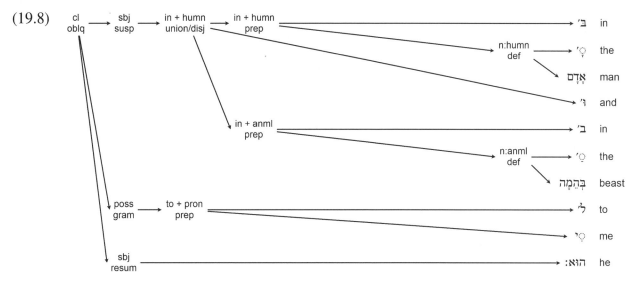

(19.8)

In VLCs, the 22 instances of a subject CIC consisting of a prepositional phrase involving לְ 'to' plus an infinitive construct are well documented.[39]

---

37. Once, as per Williams, 100, who cites Exod 13:2.

38. The literature on this topic is sparse. GKC, 379, cite Ps 146:5 and Job 23:13 as examples but deprecates Isa 26:4 as "textually very uncertain." Williams, 100, provides Exod 18:4 as one of two examples. Joüon/Muraoka, 458, assert that the *beth essentiae* is "used to indicate the predicate" and cite Exod 18:4; Ps 118:7, and 146:5.

39. See, among others, Joüon/Muraoka, 401–2. Three of their examples are in our list (Josh 24:15; 1 Sam 15:22; 2 Sam 18:11). We classify the three examples not in our list (Gen 23:8, 31:29; Esth 4:2) as quasiverbal clauses.

There are 30 cases where ל 'to' appears with a sister other than an infinitive construct. The significance of this configuration remains to be worked out.[40] Phrase marker (19.9) from Job 13:12 shows a case where parallel subject complements appear first without a 'ל and then with a 'ל:

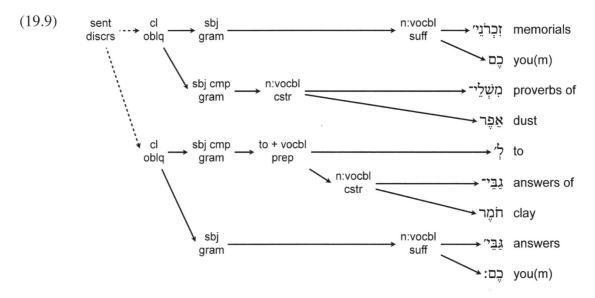

The 34 cases of a subject CIC or subject complement CIC consisting of a prepositional phrase involving some form of מִן 'from' are instances of partitive-מ that make a semantically nominal phrase.[41] In a full representation (§9.2.2), the CICs would also have the SR of "resource" (rsrc). Phrase marker (19.10) from 1 Chr 9:30 illustrates the partitioning phenomenon:

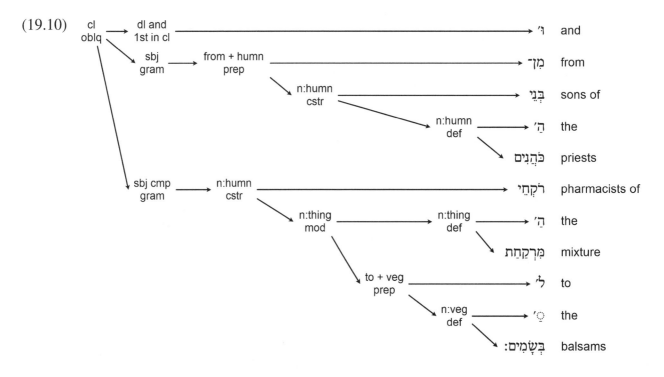

---

40. There is evidence that in the configuration under consideration the preposition ל saliently marks a subject complement as the result of a process. See Job 37:10, Lam 4:3, and Dan 9:16, among others.

41. GKC, 382; Williams, 122–23; *IBHS*, 213–14; van der Merwe et al., 289; Joüon/Muraoka, 460.

19.6 *Operators and the Lead Zone*

Although we do not put much store in the details of the role and reference grammar (RRG) layered structure of the clause where verbless clauses are concerned, we do take seriously the idea that certain constituents tend to occur, or perhaps are constrained to occur, in the lead zone or—as RRG would have it—in the "precore slot." Van Valin sees the lead zone as "the position in which question words appear in languages in which they do not appear *in situ* . . . ; it is also the location in which the fronted element in a sentence . . . appears."[42] We will show that the lead zone is the preponderant locus of the *operators* in verbless structures. We use the operators identified in §9.3.4 but have set aside, as before, clauses containing the infrequent operators: includer (11×) and restricter (2×) (see the table in §19.4.1, p. 267).

19.6.1 Clause-Level גַּם 'also'

After we remove clauses containing rare CICs, the residuum of verbless clauses (8,850×) contains 40 instances of גַּם 'also'. Thirty-five of these are clause initial, and 3 follow an interrogative in the lead zone.[43] Two occur in sbj/susp – sbj cmp/gram – gam/gram – sbj/resum clauses.[44] Overall, at least 95% of the clausal גַּם s occur in the lead zone.

19.6.2 Modals

There are 46 modals, of which 45 are in the lead zone (98%).[45]

19.6.3 Clause-Level Negatives

The reduced corpus of verbless clauses includes 349 negatives. Of these, 216 are clause initial, and 91 follow other operators (88 follow a closed interrogative,[46] and 3 in Qoh 9:11 follow גַּם 'also'). This leaves 42 instances that occur outside the lead zone. Hence, 88% of the negatives are in the lead zone. The identities of the CICs preceding the 42 seeming-outlier negatives are interesting.

Predecessor Sequence		*Count/Cite*		*Predecessor Sequence*		*Cite*
Subject		25 [a]		Time point		Zech 8:11
Suspended subject		4 [b]		Time aim		1 Chr 15:13
Possessor		3 [c]		Time origin		2 Chr 30:26
Suspended subject	Closed interg.	2 [d]		Location		Isa 63:9
Closed interg.	Subject	Jer 23:23		Manner		Job 36:4
גַּם 'also'	Time point	Prov 19:2		Comparison	Manner	Prov 26:1

a. Nineteen of these involve VLCs having the form sbj/gram – neg/gram – sbj cmp/gram. We should consider whether the negatives might be parsed as inverted modifiers of the constituents making up the subject complements.
b. Deut 11:10; 2 Sam 21:2; Prov 24:23, 28:21.
c. Isa 53:2 (2×); Job 18:19.
d. Gen 34:23; Jer 5:3.

---

42. Van Valin, *Exploring*, 5.

43. Follow an open interrogative: 1 Kgs 14:14 and Mal 1:10; follows a closed interrogative: Esth 7:8.

44. Prov 17:15, 20:10. Both instances of גַּם might be identified as inverted modifiers of the following שְׁנֵיהֶם 'two of them' and hence phrasal operators.

45. The odd locus is in Job 12:2, where a manner CIC ("truly") precedes the modal ("surely").

46. For the distinction between closed and open interrogatives, see §9.3.5.2.

If we declare suspended subjects to inhabit the lead zone, declare the various time margins to be fronted in the lead zone, and absorb the 19 negatives positioned between subjects and subject complements into the subject complements, then 97% of the negatives are in the lead zone.

19.6.4 Closed Interrogatives

There are 206 closed interrogatives in the reduced set of verbless clauses. All but four are clause initial (98%). Two are preceded by a suspended subject (Gen 34:23 and Jer 5:3), one by a movement origin (2 Sam 23:19), and one is between a subject and a subject complement (Jer 31:20).

19.6.5 Overall Results

Our results show that operators do gravitate strongly to the lead zones of verbless clauses.

Operator	*Percent in Lead Zone*
גַּם 'also'	95%
Modal	98%
Negative	88% / 97%
Closed Interrogative	98%

19.7 *Embedding and Verbless Clauses*

In this section, we examine how the embeddedness status of a verbless structure relates to its organization. We distinguish 9 kinds of embeddedness by their parent identity. Their incidence across the reduced set of 8,850 verbless clauses in Biblical Hebrew is given in the count-column in the table. (The final two rows report statistics for rare parental entities and will not be discussed.)

Identity of Parent	*Count*	*Average # of CICs*	*Percent with Sbj*	*Percent with Operator*
All Censored VLCs	8,850	2.1	80.3	6.2
No parent (matrix structure)	3,969	2.3	94.5	3.6
Sentence	1,900	2.3	89.0	11.5
Nominalized structure	1,323	1.3	23.4	1.7
Discourse unit with cue phrase	848	2.2	85.7	5.7
Object of address	491	2.1	77.2	11.0
Discourse unit without cue phrase	260	2.1	77.7	22.3
Paradoxical discourse unit	20	2.0	95.0	—
Miscellany	39	1.7	61.5	—

Three of the identity labels include the phrase "discourse unit," a topic that we do not take up until chap. 21. For our present purposes, suffice it to (1) remark that the non-paradoxical discourse units tend to dominate subordinated clauses, and (2) provide an example of each. Phrase marker (19.11) from Mal 3:6 shows a *reason* discourse unit with the cue phrase כִּי 'because':

(19.11)

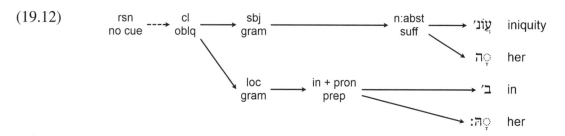

Phrase marker (19.12) from Num 15:31 shows a *reason* discourse unit that lacks a cue phrase.

(19.12)

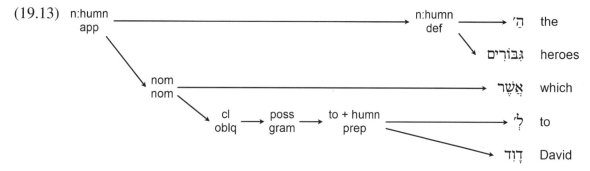

Among the frequently occurring parents, nominalized clauses attract attention. Compared with the other frequently occurring parents, they have a low average CIC count (1.3), are much less likely to contain an overt subject (23% versus the overall average of 80%), and are unlikely to have an operator (1.7%). Phrase marker (19.13) from 1 Kgs 1:8 shows a complex noun phrase containing a nominalized clause:

(19.13)

The form לְדָוִד 'to David' is a prepositional phrase, and calling it a possessor CIC is reasonable. Having the possessor CIC as the sole clause immediate constituent may seem odd, but it is eminently justifiable, as we will show in §19.9.6.

Were there no nominalizer אֲשֶׁר 'which', the prepositional phrase likely would have been combined directly with הַגִּבּוֹרִים 'the heroes' and would have been licensed by "modification." Phrase marker (19.14) from 1 Chr 18:2 illustrates a similar situation:

(19.14)

Since nominalization is forced by the presence of אֲשֶׁר, and since we have declared that it is a *clause* that is nominalized by אֲשֶׁר, we have been constrained to create a sizable set of one-CIC verbless clauses. There are 978 of these one-CIC nominalized clauses; 65% of them consist of location CICs, 16% of possessor CICs, 9% of accompanier CICs, and 10% other CICs.

19.8   *Indeterminacy in CIC Enumeration*

When dealing with verbless clauses, one finds complicating factors. The nature and number of CICs making up a verbless clause are often uncertain. This is because syntactic ambiguity is ever with us. To illustrate what we mean by this, consider the following pair of phenomena.

19.8.1   Combine Constituents or Not?

Consider phrase-marker (19.15) from Jer 1:1, where we have dominated the two in+geog/prep constituents with an in+geog/superset node. In this representation, the embedded clause is a one-CIC (location) verbless clause:

(19.15)

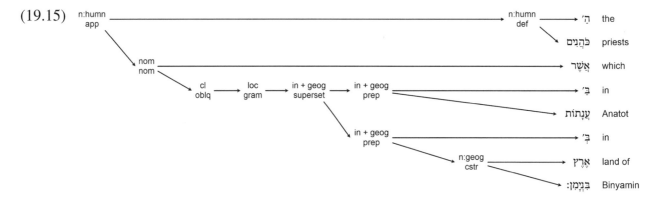

In an earlier version of our database, the embedded clause consisted of two location CICs. Given our repertoire of licensing relations, the combining of the original pair of constituents was proper. However—and this is the critical point—whether constituents should be combined is not always so clear. Syntactic ambiguity is common. Consider phrase marker (19.16) from Song 2:14:

(19.16)

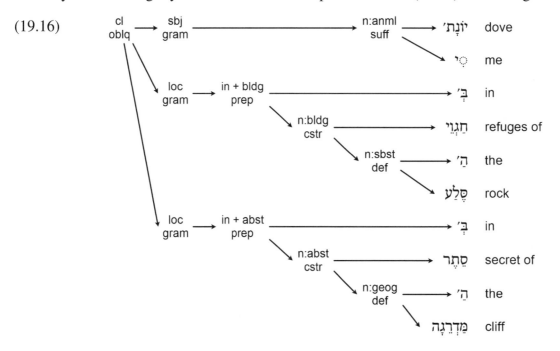

Is this a three-CIC verbless clause, or should the location constituents be combined, giving a two-CIC verbless clause? The answers involve interpretive, exegetical decisions.

19.8.2 Absorb Constituents or Not?

Or consider phrase marker (19.17) from Ezek 32:2. Here the debate is whether "in the seas" should be a CIC that locates the subject "in the seas," as shown, or better, should modify "the dragon." Opinions may differ in cases such as this.

(19.17)

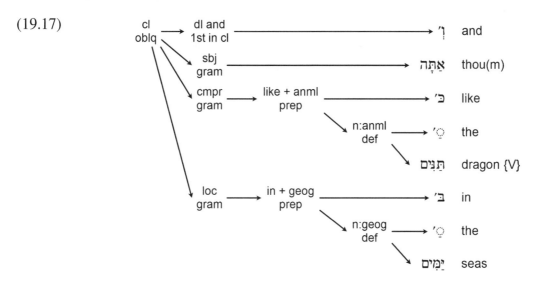

Because of these phenomena, the grouping of verbless clauses by number of CICs is not precise.

19.9 *One-CIC Verbless Structures and Clauses*

19.9.1 Impermanents and Isolates in One-CIC Structures

As documented in §19.4, we set aside structures[47] that consist solely of single, rare CICs or single syntactic isolates, which leaves us with 1,466 one-CIC verbless structures to consider.

19.9.1.1 Impermanent CICs

There are 8 instances where we cannot determine the status of a one-CIC structure. One is a *lapsus calami*, a one-segment utterance in Gen 30:11. The other 7 CICs are labeled nebulous: 1 Kgs 8:31, Isa 8:6, Jer 8:15 (2×), Mic 6:12, Ps 68:14, and Qoh 5:6.

19.9.1.2 Syntactic Isolate CICs

Syntactic Isolate CICs are numerous. In §9.3.2, we provided arguments that syntactic isolates are not syntactic constituents of clauses. For Biblical Hebrew, we nominated three sorts of CIC for membership in this CIC subtype: *exclamative*, *label*, and *vocative*.

Exclamatives.   There are 110 exclamatives among the one-CIC structures. Of these, 37 involve an oath formula. Phrase marker (19.18) provides an example from 2 Sam 22:47:

(19.18)

cl → excl → n:med → חַי־   life of
oblq   gram   cstr
                    ↘ יהוה   Yahweh

---

47. We write "structures" rather than "clauses" in this subsection because the items under discussion have little claim to be clauses. But see §19.9.6, where one-CIC covert-subject verbless clauses are taken up.

Labels.   There are 201 labels. Consider, for example, phrase marker (19.19) from Isa 15:1:

(19.19)

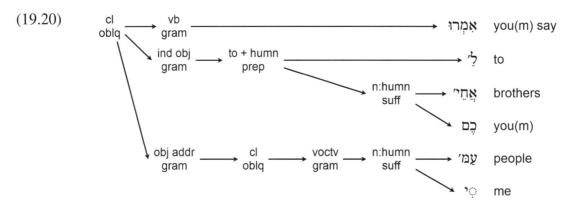

This lbl constituent is really only a label, a title actually. That the CIC is dominated by a clause node reflects our hesitancy to introduce a non-clausal node for these structures.

Vocatives.   Our repertoire of one-CIC structures includes 33 vocatives. Eight are in oracles, and 25 are in speeches. Phrase marker (19.20) from Hos 2:3 provides an example, a one-CIC speech.

(19.20)

19.9.2   Operators in One-CIC Structures

Of the 6 operator CICs presented in §9.3.4, only 1 appears in one-CIC structures: *negative* (41×). The negatives are in speeches / oracles or in discourse units. Phrase marker (19.21) from Num 22:30 shows a negative-in-a-speech:

(19.21)

Phrase marker (19.22) from 1 Sam 2:16 shows a negative in a one-CIC condition:

(19.22)

19.9.3 The Influence of Context on One-CIC Clause Makeup

We do not engage in discourse analysis at this stage of our analysis, but we will informally examine the incidence of the GFs and SRs in terms of "the grammatical function of the clause in its linguistic context [with f]our relationships distinguished: independent, coordinate, subordinate, nominalized."[48] We identify the final three relationships on the basis of any preposed *cue phrase*.[49] When neither cue phrase nor other identifying clue(s) is/are present, the relation of *independence* is posited. Modifying Andersen, we abbreviate the four relationships as Asyndetic ("unconnected"), Syndetic ("connected"), Subord, and Nomin, respectively.[50]

We group the SRs in one-CIC VLCs into the six groups detailed inside the back cover.

Six Semantic Role Groups			
PR	Other Participant	MN	Manner
SP	Movement and Spatial	EN	Enriching Constituent
TM	Temporal	DU	Mixed-Level and Phrasal Discourse Units[a]

> [a.] Since our focus is on the verbless clause, we have assigned "time point" to the temporal superset.

Using the GFs and SR groups and the four context relationships, we tabulate CIC incidence in one-CIC verbless clauses.

	Asyndetic	*Syndetic*	*Subord*	*Nomin*	*All*
sbj	100	7	19	9	135
dir obj	8	1	2	—	11
ind obj	1	—	—	—	1
cmp	67	2	40	10	119
operator	38	1	12	—	51
PR	23	2	5	254	284
SP	16	1	7	679	703
TM	30	2	5	15	52
MN	14	—	4	—	18
EN	23	3	10	3	39
DU	23	5	14	11	53
total	343	24	118	981	1,466

Patterns emerge more clearly when we convert the columns into percentages.

---

48. Andersen, *The Hebrew Verbless Clause*, 25.
49. On cue phrases, see §8.2.1, §8.3, §9.3.1.1, and §21.3.2. A cue phrase is part of a discourse, not part of a clause.
50. Andersen, *The Hebrew Verbless Clause*, 109.

	Asyndetic	*Syndetic*	*Subord*	*Nomin*	*All*
sbj	29.1%	29.2%	16.1%	0.9%	9.2%
dir obj	2.3%	4.2%	1.7%	—	0.7%
ind obj	0.3%	—	—	—	0.1%
cmp	19.5%	8.3%	33.9%	1.0%	8.1%
operator	11.1%	4.2%	10.2%	—	3.5%
PR	6.7%	8.3%	4.2%	25.9%	19.4%
SP	4.7%	4.2%	5.9%	69.2%	47.9%
TM	8.7%	8.3%	4.2%	1.5%	3.5%
MN	4.1%	—	3.4%	—	1.2%
EN	6.7%	12.5%	8.5%	0.3%	2.7%
DU	6.7%	20.8%	11.9%	1.1%	3.6%

The table enables us to refine our observations regarding one-CIC VLCs. For example, almost half of the CICs making up one-CIC VLCs have spatial SRs (far right column), but it is far more revealing to observe that, while spatial SRs account for approximately 5% each of the asyndetic, syndetic, and subordinated one-CIC VLCs, they account for more than two-thirds of the nominalized one-CIC VLCs. Or, note that, while subject complements (cmp[51]) are fairly common in subordinated clauses (33.9%), they are very rare in nominalized clauses (1.0%).

When the sole predicative CIC is a spatial or temporal CIC—as obtains in 51% of the tabulated cases—then Van Valin's notion (quoted in §19.2) that "the primary constituent units of the clause [include] . . . a 'periphery', which subsumes non-arguments of the predicate, e.g., setting locative and temporal phrases,"[52] seems inappropriate. These CICs are the *only* explicit predicative constituents and hence can hardly be considered "peripheral." Surely they are nuclei.

19.9.4 Grammatical Functions in One-CIC Clauses

Our repertoire of GFs was presented in §9.3.5.1. We next discuss each with regard to one-CIC VLCs.

19.9.4.1 Objects

There are only 10 direct objects.[53] Six are in answers to questions (Deut 10:12, 20:11; Jer 24:3; Amos 7:8, 8:2; Ps 120:4). Phrase marker (19.23) from Amos 7:8 supplies the elliptical answer "[I see] tin" to the question מָה־אַתָּה רֹאֶה עָמוֹס 'What are you seeing, Amos?'

(19.23)

The remaining 4 instances of a sole direct object are not as clear-cut:

---

51. One of the complements is not a subject complement, the cognitive complement (!?) in Neh 10:31.

52. Van Valin, *Exploring*, 4.

53. Additionally, among the one-CIC VLCs, we find no indirect objects and no distributive indirect objects.

- *Gen 49:25.* The constituent is marked with an object marker, so we hesitate to force it to be the subject of the following clause contra NJPS.
- *Num 21:14.* About which, the NJPS has this footnote: "The quotation that follows is a fragment; text and meaning are uncertain." We agree.
- *1 Sam 19:3.* The "what" that will be seen.
- *Ps 136:23.* A baffler . . .

19.9.4.2   Subjects

Among the one-CIC VLCs, we find no subjects-of-address, no distributive subjects, and no Janus sbj-cmp/sbj constituents. We do find 135 subject CICs. These are a motley lot. Just over one-third (53×) are in speeches, and just over one-third (51×) are fragments that we called "subjects" (by default) rather than "fragments" or "nebulous," leaving a residue one-fifth (31×) of miscellaneous wannabe clauses.

Phrase marker (19.24) from 2 Kgs 9:19 shows speech (within a speech) consisting of a single subject CIC:

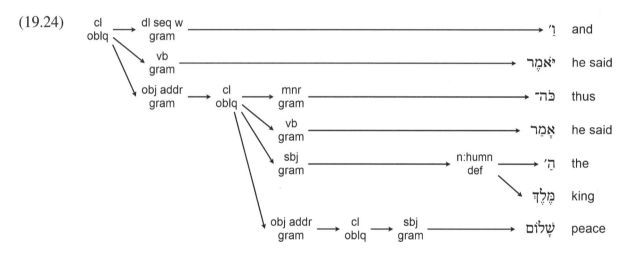

19.9.5   Subject Complements and Semantic Roles in One-CIC Clauses

When we remove from further consideration all of the CICs discussed in §19.9.1–§19.9.2 and the subjects and objects of §19.9.4, we are left with 1,266 one-CIC VLCs that overtly consist only of subject complements[54] or predicates with SRs already assigned—loc, poss, and so on. For the census of these CICs, see the table:

Clause Immediate Constituent	Count	Clause Immediate Constituent	Count
Location	653	Aim/purpose	29
Possessor	167	Beneficiary	20
Subject complement	118	Movement origin	20
Accompanier	86	Comparison	19
Time point	36	Other	118

---

54. Predicates, the semantic roles of which have yet to be assigned.

The first three CIC types account for about two-thirds of the total of all one-CIC verbless clauses.[55] These predicate CICs populate the VLC nuclei. No subject CICs *overtly* combine with the nuclei to form fully fledged clauses. But, as we will see in the next section, there are *covert* subjects nearby or inferable. *These one-CIC VLCs actually involve two CICs, a predicate and a* covert *subject.*

19.9.6   Covert-Subject Verbless Clauses

We begin with a concrete example of the phenomenon that we are about to investigate. Our database includes many phrase markers such as the construction from Ruth 3:15 seen in (19.25). Considered by itself, it is impossible to make sense of it. *What* is "upon thee"?

(19.25)

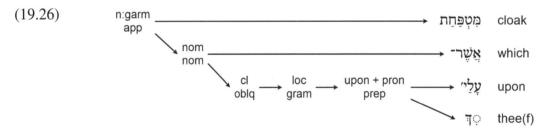

Here we have labeled a location-CIC as being a clause. That the actual subject of the clause is nearby can be seen by examining the nominalized construction in its larger context. The noun phrase of which it is a part has phrase marker (19.26). It is (the) *cloak* that is *upon thee*. The covert subject of the embedded clause is "cloak."

(19.26)

This sort of behavior is common. When we examine all 9,500 verbless clauses, we find that 2,224 lack a subject (23.4%). That is, almost a quarter of the structures that we have classified as verbless clauses lack an overt subject. Among the 1,466 one-CIC VLCs, 1,327 lack subjects (91%). But these verbless clauses do have a covert or linked subject, as the notion of *control* describes.

19.9.6.1   Kinds of Control in Biblical Hebrew

According to Jaworska:

> There is a range of subject-predicate constructions where the subject appears to be missing. Yet, it is quite easy to interpret the missing element correctly as either coreferential to some other noun phrase (NP) within the same sentence or as having arbitrary reference.[56]

---

55. As predicate, almost 52% of the clauses have a location CIC, 13% have a possessor CIC, and 9% have a subject complement. The overwhelming majority of the location CICs are in nominalized clauses (642/655 or 98%).

56. E. Jaworska, "Control," in *Concise Encyclopedia of Grammatical Categories* (ed. Keith Brown and Jim Miller; Amsterdam: Elsevier, 1999) 107. For a presentation of the two main theories of control, see Richard Hudson, "Con PRO, or the virtues of sharing," *University College London Working Papers in Linguistics* 7 (1995) 277–96.

Note that it is a lacking *subject* in the embedded clause that is usually supplied by an NP in the matrix clause or some prior clause.[57] This noun phrase is called the *controller*.

In Biblical Hebrew, we have found these four common kinds of control:

- *Head control.* The covert subject is the head of the embedding noun phrase. In (19.27) from 1 Chr 22:2, we see *head control*, a very common phenomenon. The n:humn/app noun phrase head, הַגֵּרִים 'the sojourners', is the subject of the embedded nominalized clause.

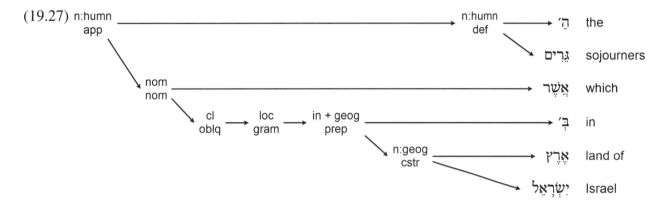

- *Discourse control.* The covert subject is found in the preceding discourse. Phrase marker (19.28) (see p. 282) from 2 Chr 20:31 shows *discourse control*. The subject of the first clause is the covert subject of the second clause.[58]
- *Object control.* The covert subject is the object in the matrix clause. Phrase marker (19.29) (see p. 282) from Gen 1:4 shows *object control*. "The light" is the direct object in the matrix clause and the subject in the embedded clause.
- *Arbitrary control.* The covert subject must be inferred. Phrase marker (19.30) (p. 283) from Gen 7:23 illustrates *arbitrary control*. The covert subject of the nominalized clause is supplied by the NJPS: "Noah . . . and *those* with him in the ark."

The foregoing are the main kinds of control but are not the only kinds.

We have seen that the one-CIC VLCs are not somehow deficient but, rather, exhibit the phenomenon of control. Hence, we augment our glossary definition of clause by adding "*possibly covert*" to yield:

clause — Typically, a syntactic unit that includes a predicator and the clause immediate constituents that accompany it. In Biblical Hebrew, a *possibly covert* subject plus some other constituent(s) can constitute a clause that has no predicator (a "verbless" or "nominal" clause).

---

57. See also D. Crystal, *A Dictionary of Linguistics and Phonetics*, 107; P. H. Matthews, *Oxford Concise Dictionary* (Oxford: Oxford University Press, 2005) 74; R. L. Trask, *A Dictionary of Grammatial Terms* (London: Routledge, 1993) 62.

58. We do not call this "subject control" because the second clause is not embedded in the first clause.

(19.28)

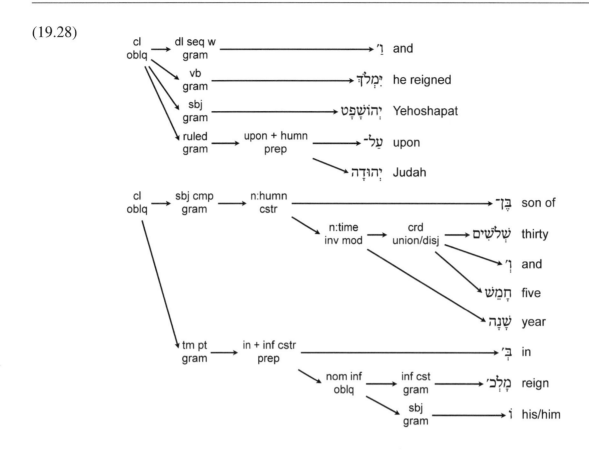

(19.29)

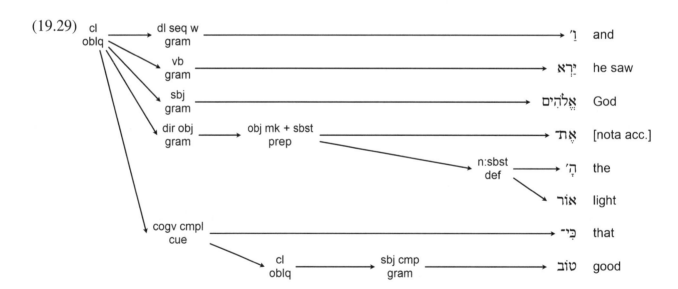

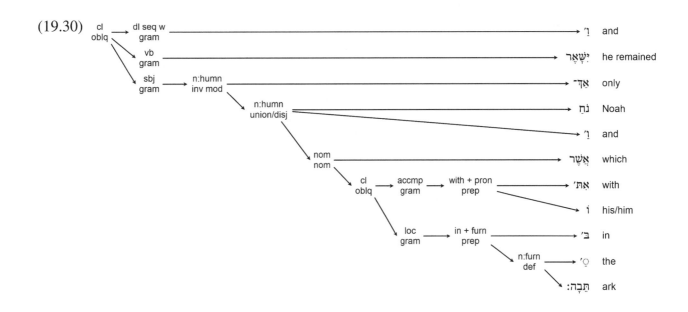

(19.30)

19.10   *Two-CIC Verbless Clauses*

When we shunt aside 100 two-CIC VLCs that involve a Janus subject complement-subject,[59] set aside all clauses that contain any "rare CIC," and omit empty clauses that result when syntactic isolates are ignored, then we are left with 5,320 clauses for study.

19.10.1   Operators in Two-CIC Clauses

Only two of the operators listed in §9.3.4 occur in significant numbers: *negative* (57×) and *closed interrogative* (29×). All but five of the negatives are clause initial.[60] The closed interrogatives are all clause initial. Hence 94% of the operators in two-CIC VLCs are clause initial. As is the pattern across all VLCs, operators in two-CIC VLCs strongly tend to appear at the beginning of the clauses.

19.10.2   The Influence of Discourse Context on Two-CIC Clause Makeup

19.10.2.1   Two-CIC VLC Contexts

As with one-CIC VLCs, we identify the four clause contexts exemplified below.

1. *Asyndetic.*   This context type consists of seemingly freestanding clauses, as in phrase marker (19.31) from Song 1:15:

(19.31)

---

59. These verbless sentences are addressed in appendix 6.

60. The five clause-final negatives are in Gen 24:21, 27:21, 37:32; Judg 14:15; and 2 Kgs 20:19. Each is preceded by a closed interrogative.

None of the freestanding clauses is shown as part of some larger (discourse) unit only because we have not yet advanced much into discourse relations (see chap. 21).

2. *Syndetic.*   Phrase marker (19.32) from Ps 73:22 shows this type of context:[61]

3. *Subordinated.*   Phrase marker (19.33) from Lev 5:11 is illustrative:

4. *Nominalized.*   Phrase marker (19.34) from Gen 1:11 shows nominalization:

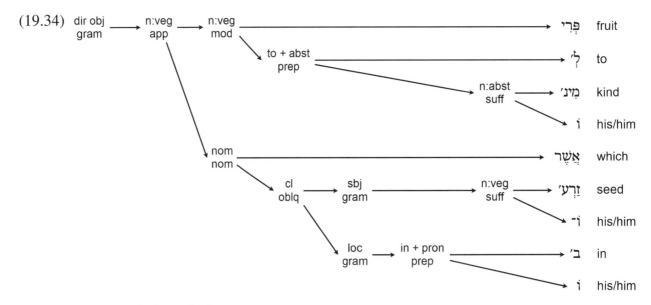

19.10.2.2 Two-CIC VLC Supersets

We group the SRs in two-CIC VLCs into the six groups detailed inside the back cover.

Semantic Roles			
PR	Other Participant	MN	Manner
SP	Movement and Spatial	EN	Enriching Constituent
TM	Temporal	DU	Mixed-Level and Phrasal Discourse Units[a]

a. Since our focus is on the verbless clause, we have assigned "time point" to the temporal superset.

61. At first glance, this VLC has three CICs. But the coordinating conjunction is impermanent. It awaits promotion into discourse. It connects the clause with its prior context.

19.10.2.3   Incidence as a Function of Context

We first look at simple CIC incidence as a function of context. We use the GFs and six SR groups along with the four context relationships introduced in §19.9.3.

	Asyndetic	*Syndetic*	*Subord*	*Nomin*	*All*
sbj	3,563	459	782	257	5,061
dir obj	4	–	2	–	6
ind obj	2	1	–	–	3
cmp	2,541	266	576	148	3,531
operator	62	12	8	8	90
PR	376	70	74	41	561
SP	537	108	86	132	863
TM	70	15	46	–	131
MN	26	2	4	1	33
EN	64	17	8	1	90
DU	227	24	14	6	271
Total	7,472	974	1,600	594	10,640

Patterns emerge more clearly when we convert the *columns* into percentages.

	Asyndetic	*Syndetic*	*Subord*	*Nomin*	*All*
sbj	47.7%	47.1%	48.9%	43.3%	47.6%
dir obj	0.1%	–	0.1%	–	0.1%
ind obj	0.0%	0.1%	–	–	0.0%
cmp	34.0%	27.3%	36.0%	24.9%	33.2%
operator	0.8%	1.2%	0.5%	1.3%	0.8%
PR	5.0%	7.2%	4.6%	6.9%	5.3%
SP	7.2%	11.1%	5.4%	22.2%	8.1%
TM	0.9%	1.5%	2.9%	–	1.2%
MN	0.3%	0.2%	0.2%	0.2%	0.3%
EN	0.8%	1.7%	0.5%	0.2%	0.8%
DU	3.0%	2.5%	0.9%	1.0%	2.5%

The table enables us to make some observations regarding two-CIC VLCs: (1) Almost half of the CICs in two-CIC VLCs are subjects. Hence, an overt subject is present in most of the two-CIC VLCs.[62] (2) A subject complement represents about one-third of the CIC total.[63] (3) Spatial SRs in

---

62. There are 5,320 two-CIC VLCs (and hence 10,640 CICs). There are 5,061 subjects. Hence, 95% of the two-CIC VLCs contain overt subjects. It might be instructive to examine the 40 nominalized clauses lacking overt subjects (297 − 257 = 40) to ascertain whether covert subjects are in their picture.

63. One of the complements is not a subject complement, the cognitive complement (!?) in 2 Chr 10:16.

Nomin clauses are two times more common than in Syndetic clauses and 3½ times more common than in Asyndetic or Subord clauses.

19.10.2.4 Sequence as a Function of Context

Given 4 types of contexts and the 11 CIC groups, there are roughly 500 possible sequence patterns to keep track of in two-CIC VLCs. In practice, however, only 66 patterns are realized, and many of these are realized feebly. Rather than document all of the patterns, we present in table form only the 3 most common patterns for each context.

	Asyndetic			*Syndetic*			*Subord*			*Nomin*		
Rank #1	sbj+cmp	1,533	41%	sbj+cmp	173	36%	cmp+sbj	357	45%	sbj+cmp	105	35%
Rank #2	cmp+sbj	929	25%	cmp+sbj	82	17%	sbj+cmp	211	26%	sbj+SP	51	17%
Rank #3	sbj+SP	322	9%	sbj+SP	67	14%	sbj+SP	56	7%	cmp+sbj	40	13%
Fraction included			75%			67%			78%			65%

(1) The top three sequences account for around 70% of the clauses in each context type. (2) Unlike the situation in the other contexts, subordinated two-CIC VLCs prefer the cmp+sbj order. (3) Note that "setting locatives" (SP) fairly often are the sole predicative constituents and hence constitute their clause's nucleus rather than periphery.

19.10.3 Grammatical Functions in Two-CIC Verbless Clauses

19.10.3.1 Objects and Complements

There are only 6 direct objects. In 4 cases, a verb may have been dropped out: Exod 32:29, 2 Sam 23:17, 2 Kgs 4:14, and Isa 66:18. One is in an answer to a question, 1 Sam 6:4. One is very strange: Deut 11:2.

There are 3 indirect objects. Twice, they are contained in questions (Num 14:27 and Jonah 1:6). Once, ellipsis is involved (Hos 3:3).

With regard to complements, there are 3,530 subject complements and 1 cognitive complement (2 Chr 10:16).

19.10.3.2 Subjects

There are 259 two-CIC VLCs with no overt subject indicated: 173 asyndetic, 28 syndetic, 18 subordinated, and 40 nominalized. When there is no overt subject in a two-CIC VLC, the covert subject may be:

1. *Quite nearby.* This is the case for 33 of the 40 nominalized two-CIC VLCs lacking overt subjects. Consider, for example, phrase marker (19.35) from Zech 14:4 (see p. 287). Here, the subject of the nominalized clause is just the head of the apposition phrase.
2. *Remote from the clause under study.* Consider phrase marker (19.36) from Isa 53:3 (see p. 287). In searching for an explicit constituent that can serve as the subject of this clause, we are forced to go back five verses, to Isa 52:13, where we encounter עַבְדִּי 'my servant'.
3. *Not a simple constituent.* Consider phrase marker (19.37) from Gen 48:18 (see p. 287). Here, the subject might be said to be the action of Jacob's putting his hand upon Ephraim's head.

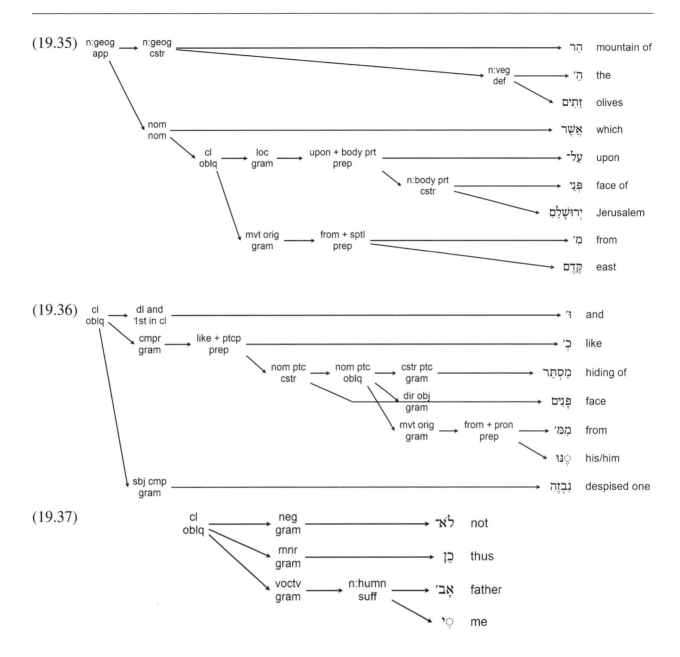

19.11 *Three-CIC Verbless Clauses*

Together, the one-CIC and two-CIC VLCs account for over three-quarters of the verbless clause stock (78%). The three-CIC VLCs account for nearly another one-fifth (17%). After carrying out our usual reduction procedures, we have 1,534 three-CIC verbless clauses. These we subdivide into four major types:

1. Subject and subject complement (**sbj** and **sbj cmp**) plus one different CIC (56%)
2. Subject (**sbj**) plus two non-**sbj cmp** CICs (29%)
3. Three non-subject (**non-sbj**) CICs (5%)
4. Suspended and resumed subject (or distributive subject) plus one CIC (10%).

Before examining types 1–3, we separate off the type 4 clauses, since they overlap with other types.

19.11.1 Subject and Subject Complement plus One CIC

The following table documents how three-fifths of the three-CIC VLCs (61%) consist of a sbj CIC and a sbj cmp CIC, plus *one* additional CIC.

CIC Sequence			Incidence	Most Frequent "???" CIC					
sbj	sbj cmp	???	263	loc	80	benf	36	refrnt	31
sbj cmp	sbj	???	275	loc	69	tm pt	43	benf	28
???	sbj	sbj cmp	88	intrg	15	gam	15	loc	13
???	sbj cmp	sbj	91	intrg	28	neg	25	mdl	10
sbj	???	sbj cmp	95	loc	21	neg	20	poss	13
sbj cmp	???	sbj	52	loc	11	benf	10	comp	10
Total			864						

19.11.2 Subject plus Two CICs

Approximately one-third of the three-CIC VLCs have a sbj CIC plus *two* more CICs, neither being a sbj cmp.

CIC Sequence			Incidence	Most Frequent "??? + ???" CIC Pairs					
sbj	???	???	168	loc + aim	12	loc + loc	10	loc + poss	7
???	sbj	???	170	neg + loc	17	neg + poss	13	intrg + poss	7
???	???	sbj	94	neg + poss	9	cmpr + mnr	10	intrg + neg	5
Total			440						

19.11.3 Subject-less VLC: Three-CIC No-Subject VLCs

Of the 1,534 three-CIC verbless clauses, 74 (5%) lack a subject. There are few repeated patterns. Seventy-seven patterns are *hapax*, 14 are *dux*, 7 are *tris*, 1 occurs 4 times, one occurs 6 times (all in Numbers 29),[64] and 1 occurs 12 times (all in Psalms).[65]

19.11.4 Suspended and Then Resumed Subject plus One Different CIC

The sbj-susp sbj-resum variant accounts for about 10% of the three-CIC VLCs.

CIC Sequence			Incidence	Most Frequent "???" CIC					
sbj-susp	sbj-resum	???	86	sbj cmp	73	loc	3	cmpr	2
sbj-susp	???	sbj-resum	79	sbj cmp	57	poss	11	loc	5
Total			165						

---

64. These are actually all mismarked elliptic clauses: Num 29:17, 20, 23, 26, 29, and 32.
65. These are all labels (titles): Psalm 5:1, 8:1, 9:1, 12:1, 22:1, 53:1, 55:1, 62:1, 67:1, 76:1, 77:1, and 80:1.

The phenomena of suspension and resumption of constituents were introduced in §9.3.5.2 above. An example should recall the idea of suspension/resumption. Consider phrase marker (19.38) from 1 Kgs 20:3.

(19.38)

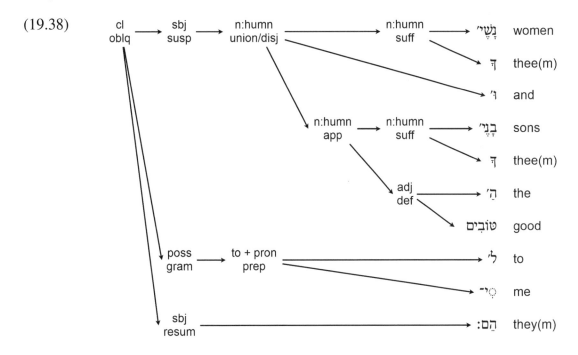

The clause-initial CIC is the subject of the clause. Its susp licensing relation makes sense in light of the resum relation at the end of the clause. The referents of נָשֶׁיךָ וּבָנֶיךָ הַטּוֹבִים and הֵם are identical. We say that the pronoun הֵם *resumes* the *suspended* subject נָשֶׁיךָ וּבָנֶיךָ הַטּוֹבִים. Note the attachment ambiguity in this clause. The NJPS translates this: "your beautiful wives and children are mine." We parse it as 'your wives and your good sons are mine'. Take your pick.

A three-CIC VLC is said to be a tripartite verbal or nominal clause when "one of the three components is a third-person independent personal pronoun. One of the remaining two components may not be a noun phrase (NP) but an adverbial or a prepositonal phrase."[66] We leave the theory of tripartites to others.[67]

There are also structures containing three CICs that we call *Janus sentences*. These are briefly treated in appendix 6. There, we analyze certain trios of CICs as sentences consisting of a pair of linked two-CIC verbless clauses, the middle CIC performing double duty in the first and second clause.

---

66. T. Muraoka, "The Tripartite Nominal Clause Revisited," in *The Verbless Clause in Biblical Hebrew: Linguistic Approaches* (ed. C. L. Miller; Linguistic Studies in Ancient West Semitic 1; Winona Lake, IN: Eisenbrauns, 1999) 188.

67. Those interested in the details of tripartite verbless clause analysis will do well to consult W. van Peursen, "Three Approaches to the Tripartite Nominal Clause in Syriac," in *Corpus Linguistics and Textual History* (ed. P. S. F. van Keulen and W. T. van Peursen; Assen: Van Gorcum, 2006) 157–73. The references in this paper provide entrée to the literature of this topic. See also in this volume the responses by Gideon Goldenberg (pp. 175–84), by Jan Joosten (pp. 185–88), and by Takamitsu Muraoka (pp. 189–96) along with van Peusen's re-response (pp. 197–204).

A somewhat related phenomenon is worth noting. There are three places where a subject is immediately followed by a distributive subject followed by some other distributive CIC: Exod 25:20, 37:9; and Num 16:17.

19.12 *Multi-CIC Verbless Clauses*

Together, the one-, two-, and three-CIC VLCs account for 95% of the VLCs, leaving the four-CIC through ten-CIC VLCs to account for the final 5%.

19.12.1 Four-CIC Verbless Clauses

We count 349 four-CIC VLCs.[68] These subdivide into four major types:

1. Subject and subject complement (sbj and sbj cmp) plus two other CICs (50%)
2. Subject (sbj) plus three non-sbj cmp CICs (22%)
3. Suspended and later resumed subject plus two CICs (15%)
4. Four non-subject (non-sbj) CICs (8%)

We do not go into detail. Phrase marker (19.39) from Deut 14:19 is an example of type #3:

(19.39)

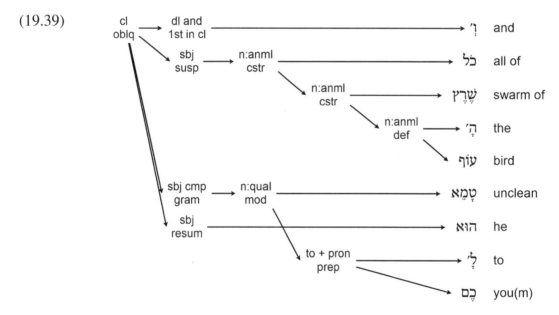

19.12.2 Five-CIC and Longer Verbless Clauses

The 81 verbless clauses having 5 or more CICs account for 0.9% of the VLCs. We do not investigate them. Here, however, are the CIC sequences and references for the 12 longest. Note the similarities exhibited by 8 of the 10 clauses in Numbers 1.

---

68. When we ignore syntactic isolates and operators, 267 four-CIC VLCs are unchanged while 7 five-CIC VLCs and 5 six-CIC VLCs reduce to four-CIC VLCs.

# CICs	CIC Sequence										Reference
9	obj	poss	loc	obj cmp	loc	loc	area	loc	obj cmp		Ezek 41:15
9	poss	refrnt	refrnt	—	instr	rsrc	sbj-susp	sbj-resum	poss	sbj cmp	Num 1:24
9	poss	refrnt	refrnt	—	instr	rsrc	sbj-susp	sbj-resum	poss	sbj cmp	Num 1:26
9	poss	refrnt	refrnt	—	instr	rsrc	sbj-susp	sbj-resum	poss	sbj cmp	Num 1:28
9	poss	refrnt	refrnt	—	instr	rsrc	sbj-susp	sbj-resum	poss	sbj cmp	Num 1:30
9	poss	refrnt	refrnt	—	instr	rsrc	sbj-susp	sbj-resum	poss	sbj cmp	Num 1:34
9	poss	refrnt	refrnt	—	instr	rsrc	sbj-susp	sbj-resum	poss	sbj cmp	Num 1:36
9	poss	refrnt	refrnt	—	instr	rsrc	sbj-susp	sbj-resum	poss	sbj cmp	Num 1:38
9	poss	refrnt	refrnt	—	instr	rsrc	sbj-susp	sbj-resum	poss	sbj cmp	Num 1:40
10	poss	refrnt	refrnt	refrnt	instr	rsrc	sbj-susp	sbj-resum	poss	sbj cmp	Num 1:32
10	sbj-susp	sbj-resum	refrnt	refrnt	instr	rsrc	refrnt	refrnt	poss	sbj cmp	Num 1:42
10	sbj	poss	loc	mvt aim	sbj cmp	mvt aim	loc	loc	mvt aim	poss	Ezek 48:21

19.13   *Insufficiently Investigated Problems in Verbless Structures*

To conclude this chapter, we provide a list of some problems associated with VLCs that await proper investigation.

1. The binarism of the prevailing definitions of VLC as S and (nonverbal) P has neglected or overlooked VLCs with more than two CICs. We have seen, however, that Biblical Hebrew contains VLCs with as many as ten CICs.
2. The proposal to treat VLCs as היה clauses with the equative verb ellipted is part of a larger and more general question of possible verb ellipsis in clauses that contain no verbal or quasiverbal predicator. Diagnostics are needed for telling the difference between a true VLC and a pseudo-VLC with verb ellipsis.
3. A verbal or quasiverbal predicator is not the only kind of CIC that may be ellipted from a VLC.
4. In the literature, the categories used to describe the syntax of VLCs are a mixture of grammatical, semantic, logical, pragmatic, and rhetorical functions and relations. For progress to be made, these dimensions need to be distinguished in a principled way.
5. The differing functions of VLCs in discourse constitute a parameter, the variables of which are formal, modal, semantic, and functional. Formally, a VLC may be asyndetic, syndetic,

subordinated, or nominalized. The possible correlation of the prototypical discourse functions of these types of VLCs with their distinct forms invites systematic investigation. Considerations of discourse coherence and cohesion may involve tendencies to ellipsis. This is evident in the abundant control involved with nominalized VLCs. While modality may be indicated by some operator, it can also be the result of discourse coherence. Polarity is another variable that has not been taken into account.

6. The relative definiteness of the two constituents making up a standard two-CIC VLC assists in sorting out their functions. What differs among the researchers who pursue this notion is the fineness of the distinctions with regard to relative definiteness that they work with.[69] When binary distinctions are involved, we find assertions such as: "In an *identifying clause* both the subject and predicate are definite. . . . In a *classifying clause* the subject is definite and the predicate indefinite."[70] Finer distinctions with regard to definiteness have been investigated but not fully worked out.[71]

19.14 *Brief Summary*

Naming Conventions and Agreed Characteristics.   Surveying the evidence for terming these predicator-less structures *nominal clauses* versus *verbless clauses*, we retain our preference for *verbless clauses* (VLCs). There is substantial agreement in the literature regarding many characteristics of the verbless corpus, and we agree with almost all of this material.

The Structure of VLCs.   We see models of clauses such as the model advanced by Role and Reference Grammar as having limited usefulness where VLCs are concerned. Working in terms of information structure probably has much more to offer.

Elliptic Verbal Clauses.   These masquerade as verbless, usually having their predicators in adjacent clauses or at least nearby.

Removing Marginal VLCs and CICs.   In order to discern patterns the better, we drop from consideration verbless clauses that contain globally rare CICs. In the remaining corpus, we delete all syntactic isolates. For most studies, we also delete clause-initial coordinating conjunctions.

Operators.   Study of the positioning of operator CICs discloses that they strongly prefer to be clause initial (around 97%).

One-CIC Verbless Clauses.   After winnowing out rare CICs and isolated CICs, we obtain a one-CIC VLC corpus of 1,466 clauses. When we examine the distribution of one-CIC VLCs across four kinds of contexts, we find that spatial SRs occur in about 5% of the asyndetic, syndetic, and subordinated contexts but in 69% of the nominalized contexts. Furthermore, while subject complements are fairly common in subordinated clauses (34%), they are very rare in nominalized clauses (1%). Many one-CIC VLCs involve the phenomenon of *control*, whereby a "missing" subject is actually to be found in an embedding noun phrase, nearby in discourse, as the object of a matrix clause, or in world knowledge. Control situations might well be considered a subclass of ellipsis.

---

69. But, it should be noted, very few investigators work, even in part, with definiteness.

70. Van der Merwe et al., 248–49.

71. For a reliable survey of Andersen's notions regarding definiteness and a trial of relative definiteness for Judges, see Kirk Lowery, "Relative Definiteness and the Verbless Clause," in *The Verbless Clause* (ed. C. L. Miller; Winona Lake, IN: Eisenbrauns, 1999) 251–72.

Two-CIC Verbless Clauses.   This is the largest group of VLCs, 5,320 in all, omitting Janus clauses. The few operators found in two-CIC VLCs are predominantly clause initial (94%). An overt subject is present in most two-CIC VLCs (95%). Subject complements are one-third of the CICs. Spatial SRs in nom clauses are two times more common than in syndetic clauses and 3½ times more common than in asyndetic or subord clauses.

Three-CIC Verbless Clauses.   In the text, we have only briefly summarized this class of 1,534 VLCs. They almost always contain a subject (95%). More than half of them consist of a subject, a subject complement, and one different CIC. This "different CIC" has a location SR more often than any other (29% of the three-CIC VLC corpus).

Multi-CIC Verbless Clauses.   Four- through 10-CIC VLCs make up the final 5% of the corpus. For details, consult the text.

Chapter 20

Non-Tree Phrase Markers

Until now, with a few exceptions, our phrase markers have been labeled, directed *trees*. Being trees, the phrase markers have obeyed these three constraints, briefly introduced in §4.2:

Non-tangling Condition—Edges may not cross.
Single-Mother Condition—Any non-root node has only one mother.
Single-Root Condition—There is only one root node.

As we will see below: Multiple Roots → Multiple Mothers → Tangling. For example, a phrase marker having multiple roots must also have multiple mothers and exhibit tangling.

In this chapter, we examine the circumstances where syntactic structure requires violation of tree constraints. When this occurs, the resulting phrase marker is a graph, not a tree.

20.1 *Tangled Edges: Discontinuity*

20.1.1 An Instance of a Tangled Edge

Tangling occurs when there is no way to lay out a phrase marker so that no edge crosses another.[1] When this occurs, there is discontinuity, which is "the splitting of a constituent by the intrusion of another constituent."[2] For the present, we seek simple discontinuity without attendant violation of either the single-mother or single-root conditions. Consider phrase marker (20.1) from Deut 23:16 (see p. 295). Here, the subject is the segment עֶבֶד 'servant' in discontinuous apposition with an extended nominalized clause providing a central characteristic of the servant. There is no way for these two constituents to be joined without having a crossing edge.

20.1.2 The Incidence of Discontinuity as a Function of Licensing Relation

It is interesting to study how the incidence of discontinuous constructions varies from one licensing relation to another. Some licensing relations are of a sort that never occurs with discontinuity. For a few, discontinuity is common. For each licensing relation *encountered in the daughters of CICs*, the following table presents the percent of occurrences that involve discontinuity.

---

1. Because of layout engine inadequacies, a phrase marker may exhibit edge crossing that is avoidable. An egregious example was shown in §6.4.2.2, phrase marker (6.18). That phrase marker involves no intrinsic edge crossing.
2. From our glossary.

294

(20.1)

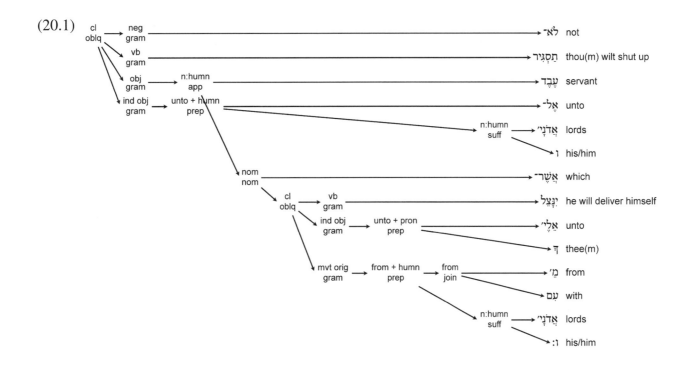

Licensing Relation	*Percent Discontinuous*	*Count Discontinuous*	*Incidence Count*
Definite	0.0%	0	4,062
Prepositional	0.0%	0	58,420
Suffixation	0.0%	1	7,285
Construct	0.1%	9	9,175
Union	4.4%	319	7,316
Apposition	8.2%	529	6,454
Joined	8.5%	125	1,466
Subsetted	8.8%	18	204
Echoed	8.9%	14	157
Modified	14.1%	195	1,380
Nested	14.3%	2	14
Supersetted	27.9%	51	183
Inverted Modification	28.5%	591	2,072
Bonded	40.3%	23	57
Distributed Apposition	74.0%	37	50

Discontinuous Suffixation.   The single instance of discontinuous suffixation and the 9 instances of discontinuous constructs immediately attract our interest. The discontinuous suffixation is in Ps 89:3. Since it involves a violation of the single-mother constraint, we take it up in §20.2.3.4.

Discontinuous Construct.   The 9 discontinuous constructs are a fascinating lot. They may be found in: Exod 26:2, 26:8, 36:9; 2 Sam 1:9; Isa 10:5; Jer 50:5; Hos 6:9, 14:3; Job 27:3. The construction in phrase marker (20.2) from Jer 50:5 is especially curious:

(20.2)
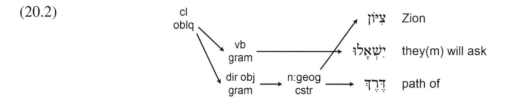

Discontinuous Union / Disjunction, Apposition, Join.   These are not infrequent, occurring in 4% to more than 8% of instances. Phrase marker (20.3) from Nah 1:2 provides a simple example:

(20.3)
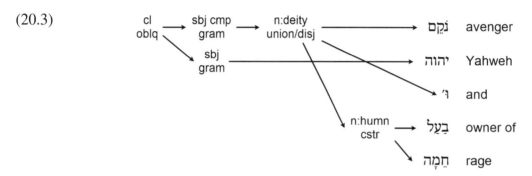

Discontinuous Echo.   This category may seem strange until one considers the alternatives. Consider phrase marker (20.4) from Josh 19:32 (see p. 297). If we do not call the second לִבְנֵי נַפְתָּלִי 'to sons of Naptali' an echo, what do we do with it? To avoid the tangling (discontinuity), some syntacticians might designate the first instance a "suspended beneficiary" and the second a "resumed beneficiary." But the idea of a constituent that is left hanging as being reactivated or completed by a later constituent hardly applies when the constituents are identical. Since we do not avoid discontinuity, we are happy with our solution. It seems to us to be less of a representational stretch.

Discontinuous Modification.   We have identified a fair number (195×) of these. That a later constituent in a clause often discontinuously modifies an earlier constituent in a clause is not in any doubt. Consider, for example, phrase marker (20.5) from 1 Sam 17:23:

(20.5)
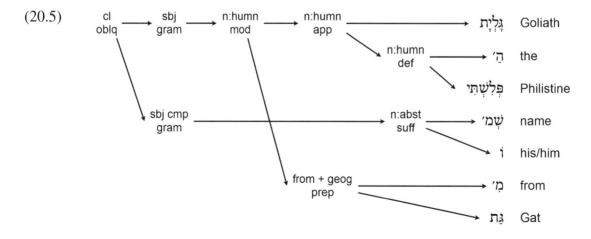

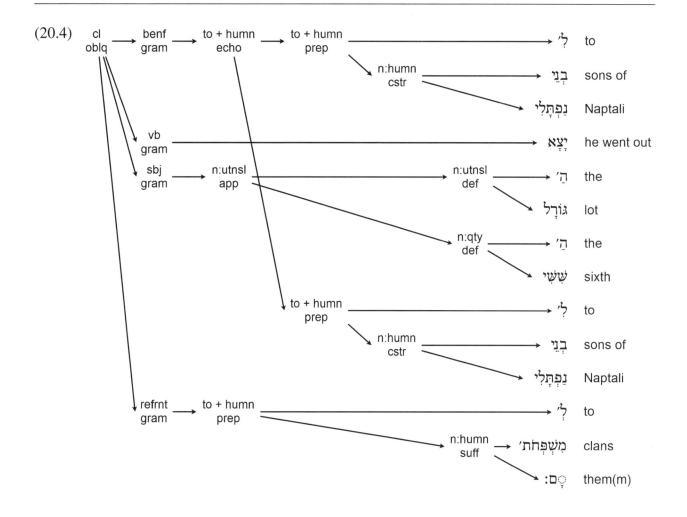

Would anyone be comfortable arguing that the prepositional phrase combines with anything in the clause other than the apposition phrase?

But matters are not always so clear-cut. Constituent attachment ambiguity is often a real problem. Consider the parsing represented in phrase marker (20.6) from Gen 37:3:

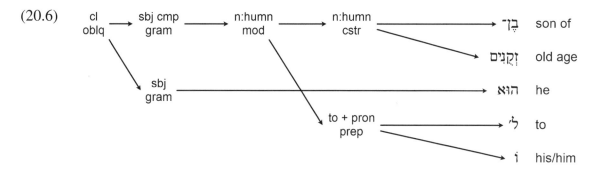

In this verbless clause, should the prepositional phrase be a beneficiary CIC in its own right? A case for this parse certainly can be made. Ideally, and eventually, both possibilities should be represented. As we will show in a very limited way in §20.3, our representational apparatus is designed to allow for multiple parses. But, for our initial pass through the corpus, we decided to represent only the "salient reading," as judged by our human "oracle" (Francis I. Andersen). So, we select the preferred parsing and represent it only at this point.

Subsetting, Supersetting, and Nesting.   Identifying and representing these three kinds of semantics-based structures is unfinished work. There surely are many more instances in which these sorts of structures might be usefully marked. In spite of the provisional status of these construction types, it nonetheless is interesting that such a large proportion (almost 28%, 51 out of 183) of the superset constituents are discontinuous. More than 60% of the discontinuous constituents involve the statement of a subject, an intervening CIC, and then the expansion of the subject, usually with a pronoun in a coordination phrase. Phrase marker (20.7) from 2 Chr 32:26 is a typical example:

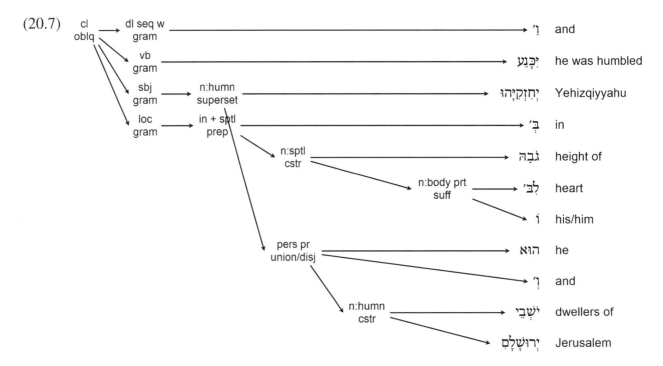

Discontinuous Inverted Modification.   Approximately 29% (591 / 2,072) of the instances of inverted modification involve discontinuity. Discontinuous inverted modification involving nonverbal constituents is rare. We find eight instances in CIC daughter constituents.[3] Rather than display one of these, we prefer to show a wonderful non-CIC daughter instance in phrase marker (20.8) from Song 6:8 (see p. 299). Here we have discontinuous inverted modification in the first conjunct as well as a discontinuous coordination phrase.

The vast majority of instances of discontinuous inverted modification in CIC daughters involve compound predication of a quasiverbal plus a verbal participle or a finite verb. A full discussion of compound predication will be provided in our volume on discourse analysis when we deal with tense, aspect, mood, and voice as *properties of clauses.* For now, we represent a quasiverbal plus a verbal participle (or finite verb) by combining them into a verbal-participial phrase (502×) or finite-verb phrase (80×), as in phrase marker (20.9) from Esth 3:8. The predicator is doubly compounded.

---

3. See Gen 31:41, 42:32; Exod 9:6, 27:15; Josh 11:21; 1 Chr 12:15, 23:4, 27:8.

(20.8)

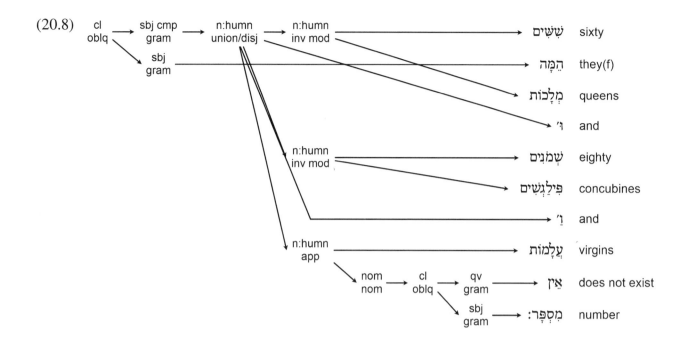

(20.9)

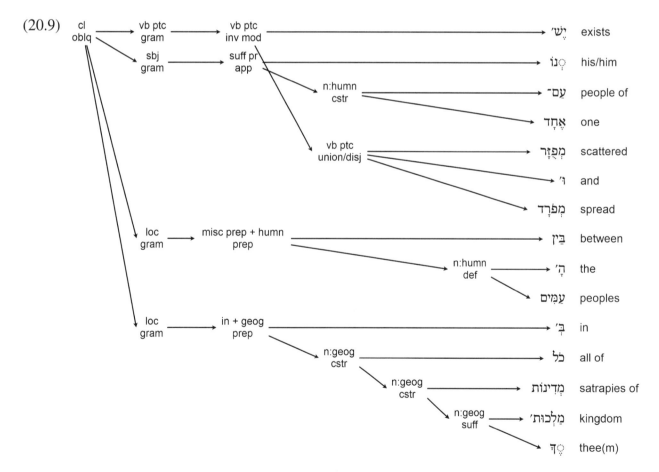

Discontinuous Bonding. The bonding relation is rare (57×). It licenses constructions "X, but not Y," or "not X, but Y." Nearly half involve discontinuity, as in phrase marker (20.10) from Job 32:13:

(20.10)

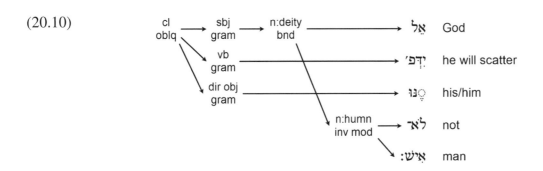

Discontinuous Distributed Apposition. This licensing relation involves multiple mothers. See §20.2.

20.1.3 The Incidence of Discontinuity as a Function of CIC Type

We next document how the incidence of discontinuous constructions varies across CIC types (see table, p. 301). Another table gives the incidence of construction types across *semantic roles* (p. 302). Of the frequently occurring semantic roles, these most commonly exhibit discontinuity:

CIC Type	Percent Discontinuous
Purely Verbal Participle	20.3%
Subject Complement	3.9%
Subject	1.2%
Vocative	1.1%
Direct Object	1.0%

In the 504 discontinuous verbal participial phrases, the "interpolate" is the subject 470 times (93%).

With regard to the elevated frequency of other discontinuous CIC types (subject complement, subject, vocative, and direct object), we conjecture—but do not prove—that the discontinuous CICs are more complex (or as the literature has it, "heavier") than their continuous brothers.

20.2 *Multiple Mothers: Construct Participles, Distributed Apposition, and Ellipsis*

We utilize multiple-mother constructions when we represent these three phenomena:

- the triple nature of construct participles (109×),
- distributed apposition (388×),
- ellipsis without resorting to empty categories (1,186×).

Since they violate the single-mother condition, the resulting phrase markers are not trees but are graphs. We shall take up each phenomenon in its turn.

20.2.1 The Triple Nature of Construct Participles

A few participles (109×) have construct morphology and also have a predicative function. We call them *noun-verb/noun participles*, indicating that they are nominal "up front" and *both* verbal

CIC Type	Segmental	Continuous Phrase	Discontinuous Phrase	Clause and "Above"
Impermanent				
Lapsus Calami	24			
Nebulous	9	26		
Syntactic Isolate				
Vocative	600	971	18	
Exclamative	220	122	2[a]	
Label	88	595		
Predicator				
Inf. Absolute	191	4[b]		
Ptcp: N-V/N	109			
Ptcp: N-V	2,327	9		
Ptcp: V	1,858	125	504	
Unanch. Finite V	35,098	218	130	
Anch. Finite V	20,725	9	1[c]	
Inf. Construct	5,756	1[d]		
Inf. Utterance	965			
Quasiverbal	1,224	31		
Grammatical Function				
Subject Address				22
Subject	15,705	17,470	396	
Obj. of Address				5,134
Direct Object	10,174	18,044	299	
Second Object	211	288	3[e]	
Indirect Object	15	7,412	39	
Subject Cmpl	2,677	4,094	278	
Object Cmpl	386	838	13	
Cognitive Cmpl				859
Cmpl Aspect	7[f]	435		
Operator				
Negative	5,954			
Closed Interg.	876			
Modal	236	29		
Includer	84			
Restricter	29			

a. See Jer 4:31 and Amos 8:14.

b. Each is a coordinated phrase with two infinitive absolute conjuncts: Deut 9:21, Jer 9:23, Ezek 1:14, 2 Chr 31:10.

c. See the compound construction in Ezek 25:7.

d. In Exod 32:6, we find a coordination phrase with infinitive construct and infinitive absolute conjuncts.

e. Deut 8:16, Isa 48:6, 2 Chr 24:14.

f. These are "bare" infinitives construct: Exod 2:18; Isa 47:12; Jer 6:11, 15:18, 20:9; Amos 5:2; Ps 77:3.

Semantic Role CIC	Segmental	Continuous Phrase	Discontinuous Phrase	Clause and "Above"
Other Participants				
Accompanier	3	1,657	8	
Agential	3	225	1[a]	
Alternate / Surrogate		180		
Beneficiary	2[b]	2,083	12	
Exocentric Absolute	17	43		
Harmed One		260	1[c]	
Involved Ones		80		
Possessor	16	1,597	10	
Aspectualizer				
Infinitive Intensifier	483	19	1[d]	
Infinitive Amplifier	44	13		
Movement				
Aim (Goal)	369	4,152	17	
Direction (Bearing)	11	126	2[e]	
Interval		80		
Origin	24	4,272	12	
Space				
Area		33		
Length	100	87	2[f]	
Location	1,431	13,057	69	
Separation		23		
Time				
Point	535	3,144	27	
Aim (Goal)	4	863	2	
Interval	367	828	4	
Origin		252	1[g]	
Enriching Constituents				
Cost		106		
Instrument	132	2,335	18	
Manner	1,980	476	1[h]	
Material	46	45		
Number Count	1[i]			
Number of Times	267	91	2[j]	
Reference	21	1,076	12	
Resource	2	241	5[k]	
"Ruled"		45		
Quantity	1	49		
Phrasal "Discourse Units"				
Cause		63		
Comparison	4	2,662	16	
Deprivation		69		
Quoter		925		

Semantic Role CIC	Segmental	Continuous Phrase	Discontinuous Phrase	Clause and "Above"
Mixed-Level Constituents				
Aim/Purpose	2[a]	2,989	9	
"But-Rather"		1[m]		1[n]
Concessive		1[o]		
Reason	106	695	3	
Result		93		
Undesired Outcome		171		

a. Gen 28:14.
b. Zeph 3:19, Job 34:10.
c. 2 Chr 32:25.
d. Ps 126:6.
e. Josh 18:13, Isa 2:8.
f. Judg 11:33, Ezek 46:23.
g. Prov 8:23.
h. Isa 10:7.

i. Josh 5:2.
j. Exod 23:14; Deut 16:16.
k. Deut 32:42; Lev 1:10; Num 31:28, 30, 42.
l. Isa 35:4; Amos 5:16.
m. 1 Kgs 12:20.
n. Deut 4:12.
o. Ezek 32:30.

and nominal "out back." Rather than ignore the construct morphology, we choose to represent both the construct behavior and the verbal behavior as is shown in phrase marker (20.11) from Gen 4:15:

(20.11)

The left-most node encodes the fact that a construct relation is present. A sequence of three edges runs along the top of the diagram from this node to the *nomen regens* segment; a single edge runs from the left-most node to the *nomen rectum* segment. Hence, the *nomen rectum* segment has two mother nodes, making the structure a graph rather than a tree.

The next node to the right indicates that predicative behavior is present. A predicator (n-v ptc/gram) and a direct object (dir obj/gram) are both daughters of the nom ptc/oblq node.

20.2.2 Distributed Apposition

To quote our glossary, "distributed apposition licenses the assembly of apposition constructions wherein a later constituent is in apposition to two or more earlier constituents considered *together*. The resulting construction exhibits multidominance and discontinuity." Previously, we mentioned "distributed apposition" in passing (§5.4 and §6.4) and provided two incidental examples while discussing other phenomena: in §7.2.2 (1 Sam 31:2, two segments in distributed apposition with a final phrase) and in §8.1.3.4 (1 Chr 22:13, two basic phrases in distributed apposition with a lengthy nominalized clause). These phrase markers should be examined afresh.

Distributed apposition occurs in these kinds of constructions:

- Rare are segments and phrases in distributed apposition with a final *segment*:

    1. Two segments: Exod 37:25, Ezek 40:47
    2. Nine segments: Ezra 8:16
    3. Two phrases: Exod 38:1, Lev 9:3, Ezek 42:5
    4. Three phrases: Num 28:14

- Less rare are segments in distributed apposition with a final *phrase*:

    1. Two segments: 41 instances
    2. Three segments: Exod 32:13, Num 32:34, Josh 15:14, 1 Sam 31:2, Zech 6:10, 1 Chr 10:2
    3. Five segments: Num 31:8, Josh 13:21
    4. Ten segments: Esth 9:7–10
    5. Fifteen segments: 2 Chr 11:6–10

- More common are phrases in distributed apposition with a final *phrase*:

    1. Two phrases: 94 instances
    2. Three phrases: Lev 9:10, 20:25; Deut 7:11, 14:6, 16:11; Jer 8:2, 24:8; Neh 1:7, 2 Chr 23:9
    3. Four phrases: Lev 23:38; Deut 16:14, 28:27; Jer 27:19–20, 29:1; 1 Chr 22:16
    4. Five phrases: Jer 27:9
    5. Six phrases: Ezek 36:4

- Mixed constituents occur 15 times:

    1. with a final segment:
        a. Phrase and segment: Lev 9:2
    2. with a final phrase:
        a. Segment and phrase: Deut 4:47; 2 Sam 4:9; Jer 49:28; Zech 1:12; Ps 26:9, 95:8–9, 147:7–9; Song 8:14
        b. Phrase and segment: Jer 10:9, Ezek 36:5, Nah 3:17, Qoh 12:1
        c. Phrase, segment, phrase: 2 Chr 20:10
        d. Segment, Segment, Segment, Phrase, Segment, Segment, Segment, Segment: Num 32:34

20.2.3 Ellipsis

20.2.3.1 The Traditional Definition of Ellipsis

Here is a traditional definition of ellipsis, from Trask:

Any construction in which some material which is required for semantic interpretation and which could have been overtly present is absent but immediately recoverable from the linguistic context, particularly when that material is overtly present elsewhere in the sentence.[4]

---

4. R. L. Trask, *A Dictionary of Grammatical Terms* (London: Routledge, 1993) 89.

Most of the time, this definition suffices. But, as we shall see, there are contexts in which it is too simplified, since "[e]llipsis is a discourse phenomenon, in the sense that the interpretation of the missing constituent sometimes depends on something said in an earlier sentence—possibly even by another speaker."[5] Indeed, the interpretation of the missing constituent may lie even further afield.

20.2.3.2 Standard Biblical Hebrew Reference Works on Ellipsis
The standard reference works have little to say regarding ellipsis:

- GKC[6] has a few brief references to the topic:

  1. §117*f* gives eight instances of omitted pronominal objects.
  2. §116*s* takes up omitted personal pronouns in participial clauses.
  3. §134*n* asserts that "[c]ertain specifications of measure, weight, or time, are commonly omitted after numerals."

- Waltke and O'Connor touch lightly on ellipsis in a three-page discussion of some uses of prepositions.[7]
- In van der Merwe et al., ellipsis appears only in a footnote: "The complement of a verb may be omitted, but then only when it can be inferred from the context of the sentence."[8]
- Joüon/Muraoka have scattered passing references to the ellipsis of: objects, subjects, time words, measure words, participles, protases, and apodoses.[9]
- Williams has a three-and-one-half page concluding section on ellipsis.[10] It is only slightly generalized from what Joüon/Muraoka have.

All in all, these reference works "address" ellipsis in a perfunctory, echo-chamber sort of way.

20.2.3.3 Our Approach to Representing Ellipsis
In deciding how to represent ellipsis, we began with the traditional definition. If it was true that the missing material was overtly present nearby, then why not represent this fact by joining the "external material" to the clause exhibiting ellipsis, running an edge from the shortened clause to the external material? Resolving ellipsis explicitly required having nodes with multiple mothers, but we already had introduced them for dealing with construct participles and distributed apposition.

Forward Ellipsis.   Phrase marker (20.12) from Isa 34:13 illustrates our representational strategy for the usual (forward) ellipsis (also known as "analipsis"). We draw an edge from the second clause's root node up to the predicator node in the first clause, indicating that the predicator does service in both clauses. The more common way of representing ellipsis is to have an empty node[11] in the second clause and to co-index it with the predicator in the first clause.

---

5. I. A. Sag, T. Wasow, and E. M. Bender, *Syntactic Theory: A Formal Introduction* (2nd ed.; Stanford, CA: CSLI, 2003) 416.

6. B. T. Arnold and J. H. Choi (*A Guide to Biblial Hebrew Syntax* [Cambridge: Cambridge University Press, 2003] 192) repeat the GKC observations, adding that "[e]llipsis also occurs frequently with negatives." Where Arnold and Choi see ellipsis of negatives, we see scoping of negatives (see §9.3.5.1).

7. Waltke and O'Connor, *IBHS*, 222–25.

8. Van der Merwe et al., 241.

9. Joüon and Muraoka, passim (14 articles).

10. Williams, 208–11.

11. The empty node occupies the place where the ellipted constituent "should be." This sort of locus is known as a *gap*, "a location in a sentence in which no element is overtly present even though some element appears to be in some

(20.12)

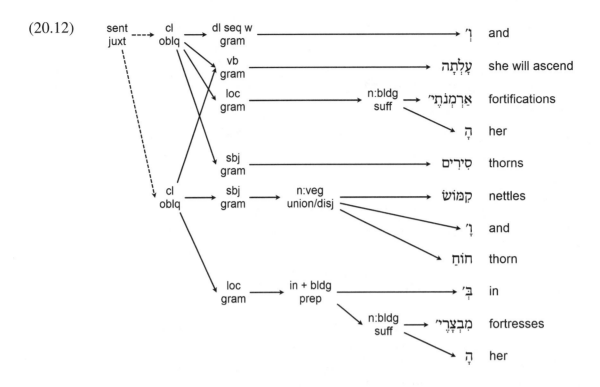

The verb in the first clause does "double duty," being the explicit predicator in the first clause and the ellipted predicator down in the second clause. We find 1,135 instances of forward verb ellipsis.

Backward Ellipsis.   A verb may be missing in a first clause, being supplied in a second clause. This situation involves backward ellipsis, also known as "catalipsis." Phrase marker (20.13) from Ps 70:2 illustrates the phenomenon. We have found 51 instances of backward verb ellipsis.

(20.13)

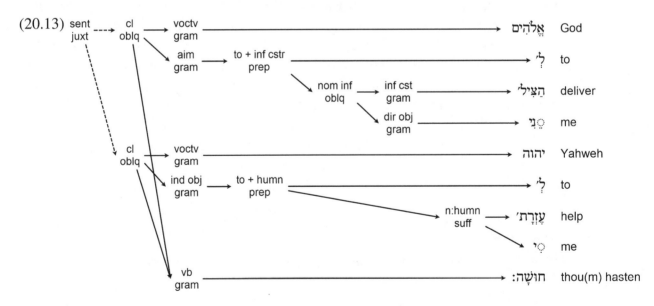

---

sense grammatically required" (Trask, *A Dictionary*, 114).

20.2.3.4 Miller on Verbal Ellipsis

In an ongoing series of papers, Cynthia Miller has been investigating and characterizing the various kinds of ellipsis. In this subsection, we comment on her generalizations regarding verb ellipsis.[12] We are not yet in a position to assess Miller's work for two reasons: (1) we have not yet carried out consistency checking on our own ellipsis markup;[13] (2) as Miller demonstrates,[14] the parsing of clauses that *may* involve ellipsis often involves resolution of ambiguity.

To understand the second point, consider phrase marker (20.14) from Nah 3:10, where we have parsed the two asyndetic clauses as involving ellipsis. The first clause, however, might be a verbless clause. The NJPS renders the clause as though it were verbless: "Yet even she was exiled," as does the NRSV: "Yet she became an exile." Nonetheless, we are comfortable with our parsing for reasons that might be adduced. Both interpretations are defensible. As we will glimpse in §20.3, we are able to represent both parses. But, for now, we show only our preferred parse.

(20.14)

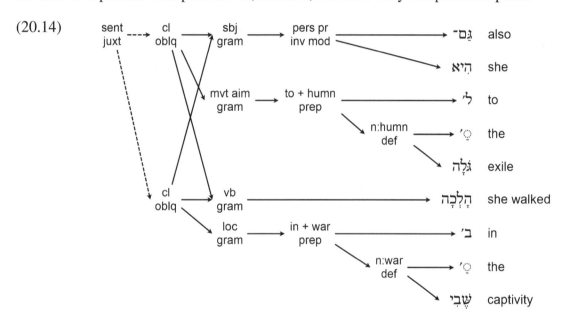

Miller's Three Universal Conditions[15] *("must be present for ellipsis to operate")*:

1. "[E]llipsis operates on coordinate structures [be they syndetic or asyndetic]."
2. "[T]he two halves of the coordinate sentence must . . . match exactly."[16]
3. "[T]he verb that is present and the verb that is deleted must be lexically identical. . . .
   However, the two verbs need not be identical in person, gender, or number."

---

12. C. L. Miller, "A Linguistic Approach to Ellipsis in Biblical Poetry (Or, What to Do When Exegesis of What Is There Depends on What Isn't)," *BBR* 13 (2003) 251–70. On another kind of ellipsis, see idem, "Ellipsis Involving Negation in Biblical Poetry," in *Seeking Out the Wisdom of the Ancients: Essays Offered to Honor Michael V. Fox on the Occasion of His Sixty-Fifth Birthday* (ed. R. L. Troxel, K. G. Friebel, and D. R. Magary; Winona Lake, IN: Eisenbrauns, 2005) 37–52.

13. Consistency checking is an area that we are only beginning to enter. See A. D. Forbes, "The Challenge of Consistency," *Computer Assisted Research on the Bible in the 21st Century: Proceedings of the Eighth AIBI Conference, El Escorial, Madrid, June 2008* (ed. L. Vegas, G. Seijas, and J. del Barco; Piscataway, NJ: Gorgias, 2010) 99–115.

14. Miller, "A Linguistic Approach," 255–60.

15. Ibid., 260–62.

16. In her n. 30, Miller specifies two situations in which this condition may be violated.

These conditions have great merit, but they are more "rules-of-thumb" than laws. Our parse of Nah 3:10, for example, disobeys condition #2. Consequently, we are more inclined to say that the conditions are very useful generalizations than to use them to exclude certain parses.

Distinctively Hebrew Features of Ellipsis:

1. "[E]llipsis may occur in the first line, a situation known as backwards ellipsis."
2. "Ellipsis may occur when the verb is in initial, medial, or final position with respect to the other clausal constituents."
3. "[B]ackwards ellipsis only occurs when the verb is in final position."
4. "The order of constituents may be chiastic, unless the verb is in final position."[17]

As statements of realized possibilities, the first, second, and fourth features are demonstrably true. Examples illustrating each statement lie ready to hand. It is the third assertion that gives us pause. We must question it on two grounds: cross-linguistic and empirical.

Cross-Linguistic.   Miller tells us that "this observation about backwards ellipsis corresponds to what we know about ellipsis cross-linguistically."[18] We find contrary evidence. Using Sanders's six-type classification of ellipsis patterns, Haspelmath asserts that "no ellipsis type is universally impossible, but there are strong restrictions on which combinations of ellipsis types a language can have."[19] He even cites one language that allows all six types of ellipsis: Tojalabal.

Empirical Evidence.   More convincing is the empirical evidence. Consider phrase marker (20.15) from Ps 77:2 in which the verb is second-clause *initial*, contrary to Miller's feature #3:

(20.15)
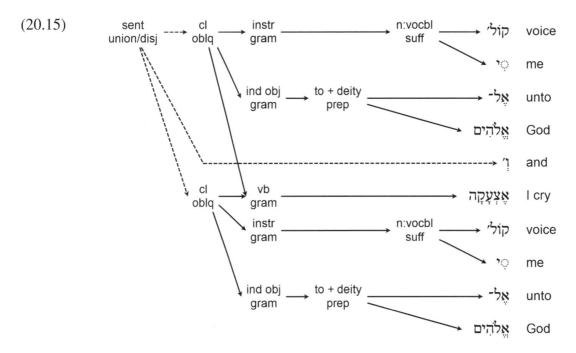

17. Ibid., 262–65.
18. Ibid., 264.
19. Martin Haspelmath, "Coordination," in *Language Typology and Syntactic Description*, vol. 2: *Complex Constructions* (2nd ed.; ed. Timothy Shopen; Cambridge: Cambridge University Press, 2007) 44–45. Haspelmath is describing ellipsis in general.

The NJPS translates: "I cry aloud to God; I cry to God." Parsing the first clause as verbless seems forced to us, given that the two clauses are identical except for the verb. Other examples of backward ellipsis where the predicator is not second-clause final do exist. See, for example, Gen 14:23; 2 Kgs 7:18, 25:15 (= Jer 52:19b); Isa 3:8–9; Jer 6:20b.

Multiple Ellipsis. It is fairly common for multiple items to be ellipted. An example is shown in phrase marker (20.16) from Gen 28:20, where both the verb and the indirect object are ellipted.

(20.16)

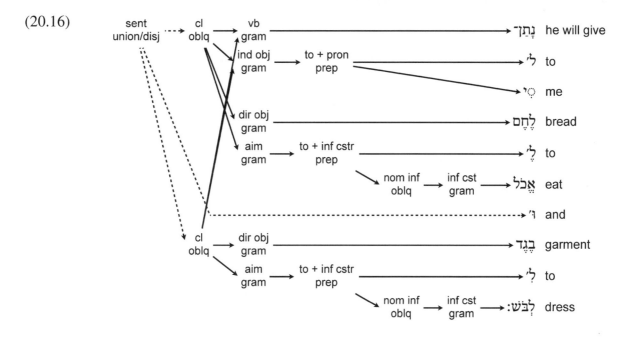

Some of our clause pairs marked as containing ellipsis involve not a little exegesis and may be analyzed along more conventional lines upon further consideration. Phrase marker (20.17) from Ps 89:3 shows what we are talking about.

(20.17)

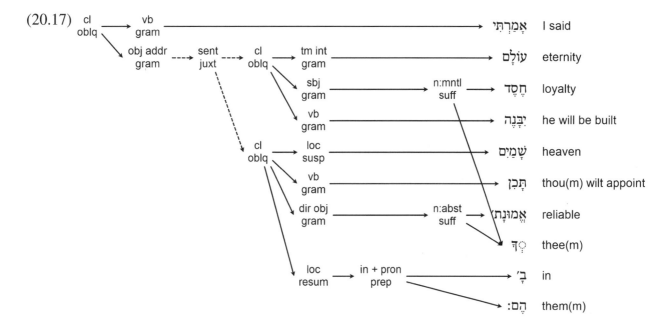

This is the only instance in the MT where a pronoun suffix has two mothers. . . . A bridge too far?

20.3   *Multiple Roots: Ambiguity and Multiple Parses*

Elsewhere in this book, we have discussed lexical ambiguity (§1.1.3.3 and appendix §A1.3.3), structural ambiguity (§1.1.3.4), and clause-boundary ambiguity (§2.2.2). We have also published two papers addressing the problems of ambiguity, especially structural ambiguity.[20]

In this subsection, we will use a simple example to illustrate how our representation can depict structural ambiguity. Consider the parsing(s) of Amos 1:2a:

יהוה מִצִּיּוֹן יִשְׁאָג

Taken in isolation, this clause is ambiguous.[21] The ambiguity is explicit in that the clause can be rendered by two translations, involving different CICs:

> *Yahweh, from Zion, has roared* (sbj loc pred).
>
> *Yahweh-from Zion has roared* (sbj pred).

Suppose that we wish to visualize both parses. We might show two separate parses, or we might combine the possibilities as is shown in phrase marker (20.18).

(20.18)

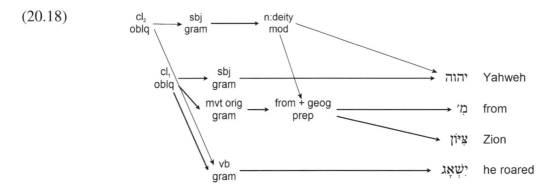

Here cl₁ and its offspring represent the first parse (involving three CICs). Cl₂ and its offspring embody the second (involving two CICs). The phrase marker has two roots. Two of its nodes have two mothers, and it exhibits tangling. Clearly, this phrase marker is not a tree.

20.4   *Brief Summary*

Discontinuity.   We investigate parses in which phrase marker edges unavoidably must cross. *Regarding licensing relations*, some licensing relations essentially disallow discontinuity: definite, prepositional, suffixation, and construct. With the other licensing relations, there is discontinuity. Its frequency can range from rather rare (union, 4%) to predominant (distributed apposition, 74%). The largest counts are for inverted modification (591×) and apposition (529×). *Regarding CIC subtype*, verb participles in periphrastics exhibit the most discontinuity (504×, 20%). Regarding

---

20. F. I. Andersen and A. D. Forbes, "Syntactic Ambiguity in the Hebrew Bible," in *Proceedings of the Fourth International Colloquium: Bible and the Computer—Desk and Discipline* (Paris: Honoré Champion, 1995) 356–67; idem, "Attachment Preferences in the Primary History," in *Proceedings of the Sixth International Colloquium: From Alpha to Byte* (Leiden: Brill, 2002) 167–86.

21. The next clause is not ambiguous and drives the parse toward the first interpretation: וּמִירוּשָׁלַ͏ִם יִתֵּן קוֹלוֹ. This is the parse opted for in our disambiguated current rendering of the text.

GFs, subjects have the largest number of discontinuities, albeit resulting in a low overall percentage (396×, 1.2%). Regarding SRs, discontinuity is quite rare, perhaps because these constituents typically follow the core constituents. The location SR is discontinuous more often than any other SR (69×, 0.5%).

Multiple Mothers. Constituents have multiple mothers in our representations of construct participles (109×), distributed apposition (388×), and ellipsis (1,186×). After examining treatments of ellipsis in the reference works, we provide examples of forward and backward ellipsis. We then examine Cynthia Miller's approach to verbal ellipsis, finding her "universal conditions" and "distinctive features" illuminating but treating them as rules-of-thumb rather than strict constraints. (We do take issue with one of her features, finding exceptions to her assertion that "[b]ackwards ellipsis only occurs when the verb is in final position.")

Multiple Roots. We show how we have made provisions for handling ambiguity and multiple parses. To date, we have nowhere relied upon our ability to have phrase markers with multiple roots.

Chapter 21

Discourse Analysis and Supra-Clausal Structures

Our primary goals in this chapter are first to provide an outline of our planned approach to discourse analysis (§21.1) and then to illustrate how our barely begun work on discourse analysis has affected the structure of the current phrase markers (§21.2). We will also note two additional respects in which our phrase markers represent "work in progress." We will then introduce the supra-clausal constituents (SCCs) and cue phrases that appear in our supra-clausal representation (§21.3). Finally, we will expose the problem of "paradoxical intra-clausal discourse units" (§21.4).

21.1 Introduction to Our Perspectives on Discourse Analysis

We touched on discourse analysis very briefly in §1.2.3.3, on the supra-clausal "level" in §5.1, and on one kind of discourse construction, the adverbial subordinated clause, in §8.3. We now turn to a more detailed introduction to our approaches to discourse analysis. In this subsection, we will sketch our approach to discourse analysis (DA), an approach that we hope to develop in detail in a later volume.

21.1.1 Definitions of Discourse Analysis

Introducing *The Handbook of Discourse Analysis*, Schiffrin et al. observe that "[s]o abundant are definitions of discourse that many linguistics books on the subject now open with a survey of definitions."[1] They comment that the many definitions of discourse fall into one of three super-classes: "(1) anything beyond the sentence, (2) language use, and (3) a broader range of social practice that includes nonlinguistic and nonspecific instances of language." We focus on linguistics-based approaches to super-class (1).

The terminology of DA is chaotic. Different analysts use terms in different ways. Kruijff-Korbayová and Steedman write of the need to "transcend the difficulties caused by proliferating terminologies."[2] Here, we will attempt to define our own terms clearly and use them consistently, indicating how others use these terms differently or use different terms roughly equivalent to ours. Our emphases in analyzing texts are on *communication* (not acquisition) and on *recognition* (not generation). These emphases affect our assessment of the approaches taken by discourse analysts.

---

1. Deborah Shiffrin et al., *The Handbook of Discourse Analysis* (Oxford: Blackwell, 2001) 1.
2. Ivana Kruijff-Korbayová and Mark Steedman, *Information Structure, Discourse Structure, and Discourse Semantics: Workshop Proceedings* (13th European Summer School in Logic, Language and Information, 2001) v.

21.1.2 Eight Aspects of Discourse Analysis

We will now explain our approach to discourse analysis in terms of these eight aspects:

1. interface with syntax
2. text types analyzed
3. primary foci
4. basic units of analysis
5. dimensions of discourse
6. representation(s)
7. analytic procedures
8. rule and knowledge bases

21.1.2.1 Interface with Syntax

Webber et al. describe three stances regarding the relation of sentence syntax and DA: *narrow-focus*, *disjoint*, and *unified*.[3]

Those who take the *narrow-focus* stance try to represent discourse phenomena within sentence-level grammar. We know of no successful narrow-focus analyses. Those who take the *disjoint* approach seek to "use a completely different approach to discourse-level syntax and semantics than to sentence-level syntax and semantics, combining (for example) a definite clause grammar with rhetorical structure theory."[4] Those who adopt the *unified* stance "recognize the overlapping scope and similar mechanisms [at sentence and discourse levels] and simply extend a sentence-level grammar and its associated semantic mechanisms to discourse."[5] Both disjoint and unified approaches continue to be researched. Our hunch is that the way forward will combine both disjoint and unified approaches, relying more on the latter.

21.1.2.2 Text Types Analyzed

As can be seen from appendix §A7.3, even setting aside the poetry/prose distinction, text type assignment can become quite elaborate. We distinguish these four rough-and-ready text types:

1. exposition ("an explanation")
2. narration ("a story")
3. indirect speech ("he said that . . .")
4. dialogue

21.1.2.3 Primary Foci

Linguistics-oriented discourse analysis focuses on one or more of the following:

1. information structure
2. discourse cohesion
3. discourse structure
4. discourse semantics[6]

---

3. Bonnie Webber et al., "Anaphora and Discourse Structure," *Computational Linguistics* 29 (2003) 572.
4. Ibid.
5. Ibid.
6. For good or ill, these terms are often not truly mutually exclusive.

Information Structure. "Information Structure is a [Clause] Internal partition of the informa-tion in an utterance according to its relation to the discourse context under dichotomies such as topic/comment, theme/rheme, given/new, focus/background etc. Such categories are essentially Referential in nature."[7]

Discourse Cohesion. Halliday and Hasan "designed [discourse cohesion] to move beyond the structural resources of grammar and consider discourse relations which transcend grammatical structure. . . . [Cohesion is achieved via] reference, ellipsis, substitution, conjunction, and lexical cohesion."[8]

Discourse Structure. "Discourse Structure concerns the Inter-clausal relations of explana-tion, elaboration, exemplification, and illocutionary force that hold between successive utterances of a discourse or dialog, supporting inference about the domain and purposes of the discourse."[9] "[Discourse Structure] thus subsumes notions such as [discourse] segmentation, relations between [discourse] segments (informational and intentional), anaphoric relations, modal subordination, dis-course topic, thematic progression, etc."[10]

Discourse Semantics. "Discourse Semantics centrally concerns the nature of the contextual model, and the entities in it to which Information Structure categories relate. . . ."[11]

21.1.2.4 Basic Units of Analysis

We refer here to the problem of *discourse* segmentation. Or, as Polanyi asks: "what are the atomic units of discourse?"[12] For most researchers, a starting point is the main clause. One variable is whether the basic units include or exclude cue phrases.[13] Discourse units can be:

1. clauses with any preposed cue phrase included as part of the basic unit
2. clauses with any preposed cue phrase external to the basic unit
3. certain phrases
4. certain fragments "[whose] full interpretation remains unrecoverable from surrounding context."[14]

Discourse units are assigned various names. The most common terms are *discourse unit (du)*, *el-ementary discourse unit (edu)*, and *elementary discourse constituent unit (e-dcu)*.

---

7. Kruijff-Korbayová and Steedman, *Information Structure*, 1; emphasis in original.

8. James R. Martin, "Cohesion and Texture," in *The Handbook of Discourse Analysis* (ed. D. Shiffrin et al.; Oxford: Blackwell, 2001) 36. According to Martin, later work recast "non-structural" cohesive phenomena as discourse semantic structures.

9. Kruijff-Korbayová and Steedman, *Information Structure*, 1.

10. Ibid., v.

11. Ibid., 1.

12. Livia Polanyi, "The Linguistic Structure of Discourse," in *The Handbook of Discourse Analysis* (ed. D. Shiffrin et al.; Oxford: Blackwell, 2001) 265.

13. Cue phrases are linking words such as *if, because, since*. They are also called *discourse markers* (quite com-mon), *discourse items* (R. L. Trask, *Dictionary of Grammatical Terms* [London: Routledge, 1993] 84), and *extrapropo-sitional discourse operators* (Polanyi, "Linguistic Structure of Discourse," 265). See §21.3.2.

14. Livia Polanyi et al., "A Rule Based Approach to Discourse Parsing," *Proceedings of the 5th SIGdial Workshop on Discourse and Dialogue* (2004) 111.

21.1.2.5   Dimensions of Discourse

The relations among the discourse segments can be described in terms of multiple concurrently valid dimensions. What we call *dimensions*, most analysts call *levels*. Levels imply mutual exclusivity and hierarchy. To avoid this unwanted implication, we introduce the notion of dimensions.

The following dialogue between speakers A and B illustrates our point on concurrent validity:

(1)   A: George collects coins.
(2)   B: No he doesn't.
(3)   A: He has examples of every kind of U.S. dollar coin.

Statement (2) purports to be a <u>correction</u> of statement (1). Statement (3) is an <u>elaboration</u> of statement (1), but it also is <u>counterevidence</u> against statement (2).[15] Thus, statement (3) is concurrently in two different relations to two different statements.

Four dimensions have been proposed for carrying out discourse analysis. Our preferred terminology for them is as follows:

1. *Informational.*[16]   Relations that convey information advancing the discourse (example: elaboration).
2. *Intentional.*[17]   Relations that describe attempts to alter behavior, beliefs, feelings (example: motivation).
3. *Textual.*[18]   Relations involving adjacencies that are simply imposed by the presentation medium (example: presentational sequence).[19]
4. *Exchange.*[20]   Relations in dialogue that involve turn-taking stimulus and response (example: question-answer).

There are situations in which all four dimensions are relevant. Consider this dialogue:

(4)   A: Why doesn't the engine work?
(5)   B: You need to buy a new fuel filter, and you need clean gas.

Discourse analysts would all agree that we have three discourse units here: one clause uttered by speaker A and two clauses uttered by speaker B.

The Standard Analysis.   The *exchange relation* between A and B is <u>question-answer</u> (B answers A's question). There is a <u>conjunction</u> *textual relation* between the two clauses uttered by B (the ordering of the clauses in B's response could be reversed, but both are required to answer the question fully). The *intentional relation* between A and B is <u>motivation</u> (B wants A to purchase the items needed to repair the engine). The *informational relation* between A and B is (indirect) <u>cause</u> (apparently, dirty gas has fouled the fuel filter; these factors together cause the engine not to function).

---

15. In this subsection, the names of discourse relations are underlined (e.g., <u>justify</u>).
16. Also called *semantic*, *subject-matter*, and *ideational*.
17. Also called *presentational* and *interpersonal*.
18. Also called *presentational*. This is similar to what some refer to as *schema*.
19. This numbered list (*informational, intentional, textual, exchange*) exhibits an arbitrary presentational sequence.
20. We use *exchange* rather than the usual *adjacency pairs*, since the related segments may be neither adjacent nor pairs.

What about categories?   The foregoing analysis makes no attempt to distinguish between categories of discourse units and the relations among them. All of the analytical weight is borne by relations. In clause-level syntax, we identify the classes that entities belong to, and we then investigate the relations that can hold among them. Must discourse-level syntax be different?

Consider the exchange dimension. In their analysis of the exchange dimension (which they term *adjacency pairs*), Stent and Allen distinguish 11 different relations: greeting-response, summons-response, question-answer, question-no answer, assertion-acknowledge, assertion-modify, assertion-reject, assertion-hold, proposal-accept, proposal-modify, and proposal-reject.[21] This list is woefully incomplete. For example, one might well observe greeting-no answer ("How are you?" [*silence*]), greeting-modify ("Hello, Bob." "Bill, actually."), or greeting-reject ("Good to see you." "Who you kidding?"), and so on. By our analysis, 30 relations are possible.

Each of Stent's and Allen's relations can be viewed as consisting of 1 of 5 stimulus acts hyphenated with 1 of 7 response acts. If we collapse response into answer and replace no answer with silence in the list of responses, then we have 5 stimuli and 6 responses, yielding 30 possible exchange (i.e., adjacency pair) relations. It is more parsimonious to distinguish 5 stimulus and 6 response exchange "parts of discourse" than to have 30 exchange relations. This leads one to ask if the category of the exchange might not be viewable as one feature (partially) defining a *part of discourse* analogous to a part of speech (POS) in clause-level syntax.

Or, consider the intention dimension. In "The Standard Analysis" above, we asserted that the *intentional relation* between A and B is motivate. But we might say that the *intention feature* on part of discourse (5) has the value motivate. In general, our preference is to assign dimensional features to parts of discourse rather than to identify the relations between them. As in our approach to clause syntax, we adopt a constituent perspective rather than a dependency perspective.

Modern syntacticians view grammatical classes as *bundles of features.* "Treating categories as bundles of features makes it possible to represent large numbers of grammatical categories quite compactly, since every different combination of features and values is a different category."[22]

21.1.2.6 Representation(s)

Several methods of representing discourses have been used. Shorn of their particularities, they fall into these four major types:

1. Text descriptions—exemplified by the paragraph "The Standard Analysis" above.
2. Trees (indented lists, labeled trees)—introduced in §1.3.2.
3. Labeled graphs—taken up in chap. 20.
4. Discourse representation structures—"an intermediate level of semantic representation . . . , derived by an algorithm from the syntactic structure of sentences."[23] This method is quite beyond the scope of the present survey.[24]

---

21. Amanda J. Stent and James F. Allen, *Annotating Argumentation Acts in Spoken Dialog*, 27 (Technical Report 740; Rochester, NY: University of Rochester, Department of Computer Science, 2000).

22. Thomas Wasow, "Generative Grammar," in *The Handbook of Linguistics* (ed. Mark Aronoff and Janie Rees-Miller; Oxford, Blackwell, 2001) 304.

23. D. Crystal, *A Dictionary of Linguistics and Phonetics* (5th ed.; Oxford: Blackwell, 2003) 142–43.

24. For an older but useful introduction, see L. T. F. Gamut, *Logic, Language, and Meaning*, vol. 2: *Intensional Logic and Logical Grammar* (Chicago: University of Chicago Press, 1991) 271–77. See also Nicolas Asher and Alex Lascarides, *Logics of Conversation* (Cambridge: Cambridge University Press, 2003) 39–48.

21.1.2.7   Analytic Procedures

Analysts rely on one of the following four procedures:

1. "expertise" (decided by a human expert)
2. directives from annotation manual (decided by an analyst following a protocol)
3. syntactic, semantic, and pragmatic rules (via hard logic, heuristically weighted evidence, or probabilistic discrimination)
4. evidence fusion across multiple knowledge bases

Early discourse analysis relied on the intuitions of its practitioners. Seeking predictability, analytic protocols were written and used. Some have sought to remove the human analyst from the process by defining sets of objective rules and devising schemes for combining evidence. Others have relied on computational manipulation of multiple knowledge bases.

21.1.2.8   Rule and Knowledge Bases

Evidence for analysis is extracted from several kinds of sources:

1. clausal syntactic and semantic information
2. semantic networks
3. cognitive models
4. world knowledge

Traditional syntactic and semantic information has been exploited to make robust analyses. For tracking discourse lexical cohesion, "lexical reference resources" have proved very useful.[25] In an effort to infer information regarding intentions, various analysts have exploited cognitive models. When nothing else has sufficed, they have resorted to world knowledge.

21.1.2.9   Summary Matrix

Each of the foregoing eight characteristics of approaches to discourse analysis can take on one or more values out of three or four available values. Therefore, corresponding to any given approach to DA a summary matrix will be provided, an unspecified version of which is shown below. If an approach exploits a particular item, then this item will receive a check mark in the descriptive DA matrix (see table, top of p. 318). The matrix includes two additional specifications in its leftmost column:

1. If the approach relies on punctuation in defining its basic analytical units, then the "punctuation feature" (first column, fourth row) will be set to +punct; if punctuation is not relied upon, then the feature value will be set to –punct.
2. If the approach allows multiple dimensions to be concurrently active, then the "concurrency feature" (first column, fifth row) will be set to +conc; if concurrency is not allowed, then the feature will be set to –conc.

21.1.2.10   Ideal Characteristics of Discourse Analysis of the Hebrew Bible (DAHB)

We populate a DA matrix with the constellation of check marks that corresponds to ideal discourse analysis for the Hebrew Bible (DAHB), as we envision it (see table, bottom of p. 318).

---

25. Christiane Fellbaum, ed., *WordNet: An Electronic Lexical Database* (Cambridge, MA: MIT Press, 1998) 7.

Unspecified Discourse Analysis Matrix

Interface with Syntax	Narrow-Focus	Disjoint	Unified	
Text Types Analyzed	Exposition	Narration	Indirect Speech	Dialogue
Primary Foci	Information Structure	Discourse Cohesion	Discourse Structure	Discourse Semantics
Basic Units (±punct)	Clauses incl. Cue Phr.	Clauses excl. Cue Phr.	Certain Phrases	Certain Fragments
Dimensions of Discourse (±conc)	Informational	Intentional	Textual	Exchange
Representation(s)	Text	Tree	Graph	DRS[a]
Procedures	"Expertise"	Annotation Manual	Rules and Logic	Evidence Fusion
Rule and Evidence Bases	Clausal Information	Semantic Networks	Cognitive Models	World Knowledge

a. DRS = Discourse Representation Structure.

Andersen-Forbes Proposed DAHB Matrix

Interface with Syntax	Narrow-Focus	Disjoint	Unified	
			✓	
Text Types Analyzed	Exposition	Narration	Indirect Speech	Dialogue
	✓	✓	✓	✓
Primary Foci	Information Structure	Discourse Cohesion	Discourse Structure	Discourse Semantics
	✓	✓	✓	✓
Basic Units (–punct)	Clauses incl. Cue Phr.	Clauses excl. Cue Phr.	Certain Phrases	Certain Fragments
		✓	✓	✓
Dimensions of Discourse (+conc)	Informational	Intentional	Textual	Exchange
	✓	✓	✓	✓
Representation(s)	Text	Tree	Graph	DRS
			✓	✓
Procedures	"Expertise"	Annotation Manual	Rules and Logic	Evidence Fusion
			✓	✓
Rule and Evidence Bases	Clausal Information	Semantic Networks	Cognitive Models	World Knowledge
	✓	✓	✓	✓

The matrix discloses that our approach to discourse analysis:

1. seeks a unified interface with syntax,
2. analyzes all four major text types,
3. focuses on the four traditional foci (downplaying information structure to some extent),

4. does not rely on punctuation clues,
5. considers clauses (without cue phrases) to be the basic units (with certain phrases and certain fragments as basic units as well),
6. uses all four of the dimensions of discourse that we have identified (allowing concurrent realization),
7. uses graphs and the DRS for representation,
8. relies on rules and logic as well as evidence fusion, and
9. extracts evidence (to varying extents) from each of the four identified sources.

21.2 *Our Phrase Markers as a "Work in Progress"*

Our phrase markers are incomplete in these respects:

1. Assembly and labeling of discourse structures have scarcely begun.
2. Some of our analytical categories have not yet been propagated through the database.
3. The representation is mixed (see §9.2.1).
4. Constituent features are insufficiently propagated up through the phrase markers.
5. Errors and inconsistencies in the phrase markers are continually being corrected.

21.2.1 Provisional Representation of Discourse Form and Function

21.2.1.1 The Sancta Clause Parade

Our original intention was for our phrase markers to consist only of main clauses, saving indication of all discourse structures for much later. Based on this plan, the phrase marker for Sisera's speech in Judg 4:20 would consist of seven or eight isolated clauses (depending on how we handled וְהָיָה).

21.2.1.2 Gathered Speeches

In practice, the resulting display of isolated clauses was disconcertingly "jerky." And so, we tried simply binding embedded speeches together using dashed edges. Based on this plan, the phrase marker for Sisera's speech looks like (21.1) (see p. 320).[26] In this display, each clause is identified, and the speech is gathered under one obj addr node in the phrase marker. The dashed edges indicate that the analysis is provisional. The phrase marker does not show how the clauses are related. For example, the presence of the cue phrase אִם 'if' implies that one of the two subsequent ו-segments is likely a "*waw* of apodosis."[27] But the phrase marker shown does not indicate which ו is the "*waw* of apodosis."

21.2.1.3 Skeletal Indication of Discourse Structure

In light of our preliminary work on discourse, we have decided at this stage to indicate how some clauses interrelate with regard to the *form* of the discourse. Much less frequently, we represent

---

26. This display can be obtained with the Logos Research Systems program by bringing up our phrase markers, selecting the phrase marker window, clicking on Display, and then *deselecting* "Supra-Clausal Structures."

27. That is, one of the ו-segments is the cue phrase indicating the onset of the apodosis (the "then-unit") corresponding to the protasis (the "if-unit") cued by the אִם. See P. Joüon and T. Muraoka, *A Grammar of Biblical Hebrew* (rev. Eng. ed.; Rome: Pontifical Biblical Institute, 2006) 607–10.

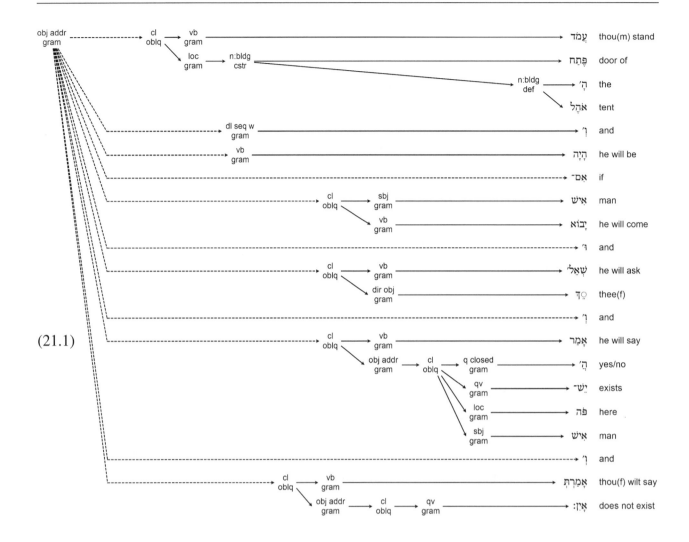

(21.1)

discourse *function*. For Judg 4:20, the interim phrase marker[28] is (21.2) (see p. 321). We make four observations regarding the structure of this phrase marker:

1. The three main clauses making up the protasis are gathered into a (supra-clausal) sentence licensed by the union relation. The sent / union / disj node specifies the *form* of the discourse unit. This node is dominated by a cond / cue node which tells the *function* of the discourse unit (cond = *condition* = *protasis*) and dominates both the sentence and cue phrase, אִם 'if'.
2. The segment sequence וְהָיָה is dominated by a cue / cue node. The two segments together form a compound cue phrase, referred to variously as a *text-deictic* or *macro-syntactic sign*.[29] Regarding compound cue phrases, see §21.3.2.3.

---

28. Strictly speaking, a *phrase marker* discloses the structural representation of a *clause consisting of phrases*. What we have here might more precisely be termed a *clause marker* since it discloses—albeit in incomplete form—the structure of a *discourse consisting of clauses*. In the interests of simplicity, for now we will retain the less precise terminology.

29. *Cue phrase*: C. H. J. van der Merwe, J. A. Naudé, and J. H. Kroeze, *A Biblical Hebrew Reference Grammar* (Sheffield: Sheffield Academic Press, 1999) 331; *text-deictic*: Bruce K. Waltke and M. O'Connor, *IBHS*, 54 n. 24, 634; *macro-syntactic sign*: M. O'Connor, "Discourse Linguistics and the Study of Biblical Hebrew" in *Congress Volume: Basel, 2001*) VTSup 92; Leiden: Brill, 2002) 18.

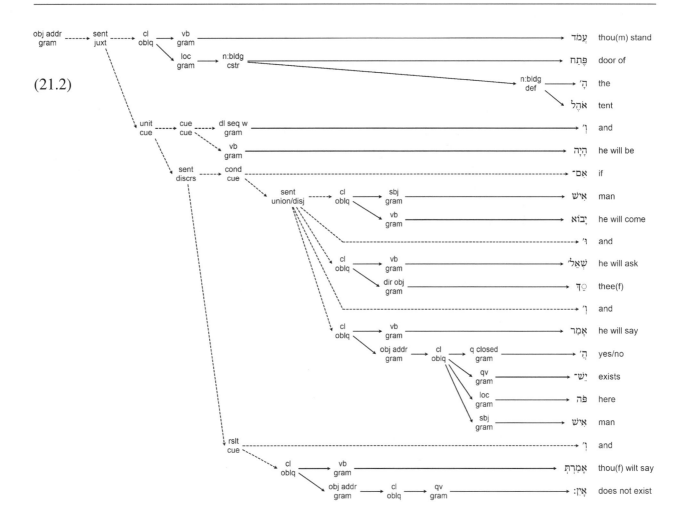

3. The apodosis is labeled as being a *result* licensed by the cue phrase וְ. Other discourse units and relations in this complex verse are not yet specified.

4. In addition to the use of dashed edges, the provisionality of the present analysis is shown by discourse units that are often labeled with the indeterminate labels unit / cue and unit / no cue.

21.2.2   Partially Installed Categories

In our glossary, an obelisk (†) identifies these categories that have not yet been completely marked:

condition	exocentric absolute	ruled-over one
cue phrase	janus sb / sc	separation
discourse unit	material	

There are also five incompletely assigned licensing relations:

| cue phrase absent | paradoxical discourse relation | strictly supersetting constituents |
| nested constituents | strictly subsetting constituents | |

The meaning of each of the foregoing CIC labels and licensing relations is given in the glossary.

Early on, we debated whether to disclose these categories now or to supply them only when they were completely in place. We decided to follow the former course so that users of our data would know the direction(s) that we are taking and so that they would be able to find instances of each, even if they could not undertake exhaustive analyses.

21.2.3 Errors and Inconsistencies

If we decided to withhold the data until "all" errors were discovered and expunged, users would never have access to our data. The phrase markers have already been checked for legality of representation, and we have begun searching for and correcting inconsistencies.

21.3   *Supra-Clausal Constituents*

21.3.1 Discourse Unit Stand-Ins

In interim phrase marker (21.2) for Sisera's Judg 4:20 speech shown in §21.2.1.3, there are seven non-leaf nodes that make up the scaffolding of the speech's supra-clausal structure. Both the incoming and outgoing edges of these nodes are dashed, reminding users of their provisionality. Each sentence node (sent) is licensed in one of two loosely held ways:[30]

1. by a bottom-up "syntactic" structural relation (juxt, union/disj, mixed) related to form,
2. by a top-down discourse relation (discrs) related to discourse function.

In addition to the various sentence nodes, the phrase marker contains two nodes that specify the functions of two discourse units: cond/cue and rslt/cue.[31]

At present, the supra-clausal structures may contain any of these seven node labels:

| sent = sentence | cond = condition | undes = undesirable outcome | tm pt = time point |
| unit | rslt = result | rsn = reason | |

When present in the supra-clausal domain, these labels do not name clause immediate constituents (CICs). Rather, they label what might be termed *supra-clausal constituents*. Note, however, that— with the exceptions of sent and unit—each of these labels can also appear as a CIC label.

21.3.2 Cue Phrases

Already in this volume, we have repeatedly referred to the cue phrase. In each context, we have provided readers with simple examples of the concept and/or referred them to the glossary. In this

---

30. The distinction here between syntactic bottom-up licensing and discourse top-down licensing is, in fact, rather forced. In practice, the gathering of sentences into primitive discourse units depends on both sorts of analysis.

31. *Note well*: not all instances of any given discourse function have yet been marked.

subsection, we will take up the cue phrase in a little more detail.[32] Note, however, that where cue phrases in Biblical Hebrew are concerned, there are still many unanswered questions.

Cue phrases are linking words. In the literature, they are also called *discourse markers* (quite common), *discourse items*,[33] and *extrapropositional discourse operators*.[34]

21.3.2.1   Many Frequently Used Cue Phrases Are Polysemic

It is useful to distinguish "monosemic cue phrases" (or, "strong cue phrases") from "polysemic cue phrases" (or, "weak cue phrases"). Summarizing two Hebrew grammars,[35] Lowery classified 45 Biblical Hebrew cue phrases based on whether they were monosemic or polysemic and which of 15 kinds of discourse units they marked.[36]

He found 31 monosemic cue phrases in Biblical Hebrew. He included in this subset such segments as: עַד 'until' (temporal), טֶרֶם 'before' (temporal), בַּעֲבוּר 'for the sake of' (telic), יַעַן 'because' (causal), עֵקֶב 'because' (causal), and אֲבָל 'but' (adversative).

Lowery also found 14 polysemic segments. The 3 most polysemic "segments" are:

Segment	No. of Polysemes
Ø	6
כִּי	7[a]
וְ	9

> a. We distinguish the seven meanings by glosses, which read: 'because', 'but', 'that', 'although', 'when', 'if', 'surely'.

Deciding the meaning of a polysemous cue phrase in a given context is a major problem for discourse analysis (and exegesis).

21.3.2.2   Cue Phrases as Scoping Operators

Cue phrases also exercise scope. The scope of an operator (segment) is "[t]hat portion of a sentence which is interpreted as being affected by an operator present in that sentence, such as a quantifier or a negative,"[37] or—we add—a cue phrase.

Thus, for example, in phrase marker (21.2) above, the scope of the אִם cue phrase is taken to be the sentence made up of the three coordinated clauses following it. The וְ immediately following the coordinated clauses is taken to be the "*waw* of apodosis." But there are two other "and"s between the אִם and the final וְ. Taking either of these to be the *waw* of apodosis would shorten the scope of the אִם. In a proper discourse analysis, the scope adopted must be justified. This example, by the way, illustrates how the resolution of polysemy and the determination of operator scope often are intimately related.

---

32. Cue phrases are treated thoroughly from the perspective of general linguistics in Kerstin Fischer (ed.), *Approaches to Discourse Particles* (Bingley, UK: Emerald Group, 2008).

33. Trask, *A Dictionary*, 84.

34. Polanyi, "The Linguistic Structure of Discourse," 265.

35. These are: R. J. Williams, *Hebrew Syntax: An Outline* (Toronto: University of Toronto Press, 1967); and GKC.

36. Kirk E. Lowery, *Toward a Discourse Grammar of Biblical Hebrew* (Ph.D. diss., UCLA, 1985) 185–86.

37. Trask, *A Dictionary*, 248.

21.3.2.3 Simple and Compound Cue Phrases

There is another complication to the analysis of cue phrases. They are of two sorts: simple and compound. A *simple cue phrase* is just a single-segment cue phrase. The אָם and various "and"s in Sisera's speech above are simple cue phrases. But cue phrases can also be multi-segmental. Multi-segmental cue phrases can be *compound* or *separate-level*. Consider the cue phrase below from Exod 21:11. The mini-discourse leads off with the segments וְאִם 'and-if' dominated by a cue/cue node. Phrase marker (21.3) shows how we represent a compound cue phrase. A compound cue phrase consists of more than one segment but operates upon a single discourse unit. In our example, the "and-if" compound cue phrase is shown operating only on the following clause, together making a condition (protasis) discourse unit (cond/cue).

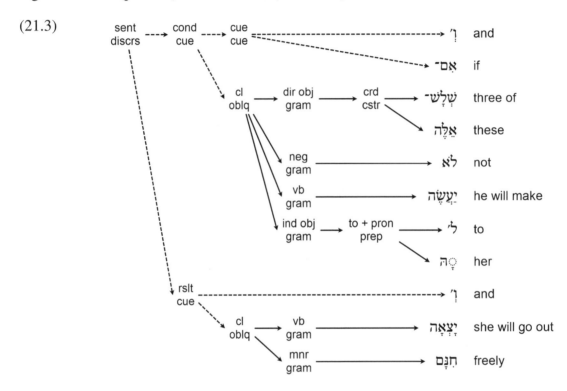

But there is another possibility. The different segments might be operating on different (nested) discourse units. This is in fact what we have here: a pair of adjacent cue phrases actually operate on different levels. The analysis of situations involving adjacent non-compound cue phrases is very complex.[38] The present representation does not show the multi-level analysis. The proper two-level structure will be made explicit when a full discourse analysis is implemented.

21.4 *Paradoxical Intra-Clausal Discourse Units*

There is a limited set of constructions in Biblical Hebrew that involves the embedding of small discourse units within small phrases. Consider phrase marker (21.4) from Isa 60:9 (see p. 325). The rsn ("reason") CIC is licensed by the relation pdox ("paradox"). At issue is where the rsn CIC

---

38. Sarah L. Oates, "Multiple Discourse Marker Occurrence: Creating Hierarchies for Natural Language Generation," *Proceedings of the ANLP-NAACL 2000*, 41–45.

(21.4)

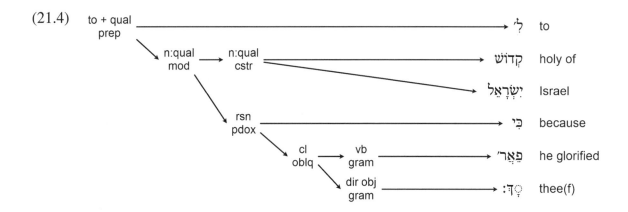

attaches. In our provisional analysis, Isa 60:8–9 constitutes a discourse. We view the embedded reason as somehow modifying the preceding construct phrase (קְדוֹשׁ יִשְׂרָאֵל). But just how the constituents combine and to what effect are unclear to us. Hence our introduction of the paradoxical licensing relation, pdox.[39]

21.5 *Brief Summary*

Aspects of Discourse Analysis.   We approach discourse analysis via eight aspects:

1. interface with syntax: we adopt the *unified approach*,
2. text types analyzed: we work in terms of four text types—exposition, narration, indirect speech, and dialogue,
3. primary foci: we rely on discourse cohesion, structure, and semantics, with a reduced emphasis on information structure,
4. basic units: for us, cue phrases are not parts of clauses,
5. dimensions of discourse: we work in terms of informational, intentional, textual, and exchange dimensions,
6. representation: we rely on graphs (nodes and edges) and the discourse representation structure,
7. procedures: we exploit rules and logic plus evidence fusion,
8. rule and evidence bases: we accept all comers—clausal information, semantic networks, cognitive models, and world knowledge.

Representation of Discourse Form and Function.   We illustrate the "clause marker" portion of a representation of the fiendishly complex Judg 4:20.

Our Present Supra-Clausal Representation.   We briefly discuss provisional structures in our phrase markers. Cue phrases, both simple and compound, are also introduced in an elementary way.

---

39. The NJPS attaches the constituent where we have attached it, but it treats the embedded phrase as nominalized, translating it as "the Holy One of Israel, who has glorified you."

Appendix 1

Text Choice, Corrections, and Reductions

A1.1 *The Choice of a Manuscript*

A1.1.1 Attitudes toward Texts in Antiquity

All scholars of Biblical Hebrew would like to think that they are working with the Masoretic Text (the MT). But, strictly speaking, there is no such thing as "the MT," as Harry M. Orlinsky never tired of pointing out.[1] All one can hope for is to have a text that is "Masoretic" in some sense. Historically, this means any text of Biblical Hebrew that has come down through Jewish channels. All these are Masoretic. What we need is a Masoretic text of the best attainable quality. Opinions likely will differ as to whether this or that available working edition in fact represents the "best attainable quality."

As far as Biblical Hebrew is concerned, the way the texts were treated during the Second Temple Period shows very clearly that those who used them did not feel that they were under any obligations not to tinker with the text. Portions of Biblical Hebrew repeated in more than one manuscript among the Dead Sea Scrolls exhibit differences that can be quite extensive, even substantial. Apparently these differences did not worry the Qumran community. There is no evidence that they ever debated the merits of competing texts.

We cannot claim that studying the Leningrad Codex (**L**) will give us the grammar of Biblical Hebrew. It is only one manuscript in the Masoretic tradition, and its being the oldest known complete תנ״ך does not make it the best (see §A1.1.4). Strictly speaking, Biblical Hebrew is the language found in all copies of the תנ״ך, including Palestinian, Babylonian Masoretic traditions, as well as pre-Masoretic Hebrew Bible texts. There are 222 of these documents among the Dead Sea Scrolls, and they have just as much right to be considered evidence for Biblical Hebrew as the later Bible of the rabbis.[2] Indeed, it has been claimed that they should be placed side by side with the ancestors of the later Masoretic texts, to make up the corpus of Biblical Hebrew as it existed in the time of the Second Commonwealth.[3] For fuller coverage of the syntax of Biblical Hebrew, we suggest that others analyze these texts along the lines we report here. Including the texts of pre–Common Era inscriptions would enlarge the corpus to include all of the available evidence for "ancient" Hebrew.

---

1. See, for example, Harry M. Orlinsky, "The Masoretic Text: A Critical Evaluation," in *Introduction to the Mass-oretico-Critical Edition of the Hebrew Bible* (ed. C. D. Ginsburg; New York: KTAV, 1966) ix and xviii.

2. James VanderKam and Peter Flint, *The Meaning of the Dead Sea Scrolls* (San Francisco: Harper, 2002) chap. 6.

3. Lawrence F. Schiffman, Emanuel Tov, and James C. VanderKam, eds., *The Dead Sea Scrolls Fifty Years after Their Discovery* (Jerusalem: Israel Exploration Society, 2000) chap. 1.

A1.1.2   The Masoretic Traditions

The labors of the Ben Asher family are recognized as the culmination of the Masoretic movement. The "crown" is the Aleppo Codex (**A**).[4] We accept the identification without further ado. Nor do we dispute the recognition of Aaron Ben Asher as the scholar finally, perhaps entirely, responsible for its production. The inherent qualities of **A** give it sufficient claim to be the best available specimen of the Ben Asher Masoretic tradition. This conclusion still leaves open the assessment of the claims of its nearest rival, the Ben Naphtali tradition, and also the Babylonian tradition. But whether the Ben Asher tradition deserved to win out or not, it did outclass its rivals, with the result that comparatively little evidence of these other Masoretic streams has survived. As a result, the task of making the best possible critical edition of the Hebrew Bible amounts to coming as close as possible to what the Aleppo Codex represents.

A1.1.3   Option Not Taken: "Restore" the Material Lost from Aleppo

Setting dreams aside and instead agreeing that we are studying the Bible of the rabbis, we must realize that the claims of **A** are weakened by the tragic fact that it is incomplete.[5] The loss of most of the Torah is particularly distressing. A case can be made for using the best source for each portion of the Hebrew Bible: British Library Or 4445 for what **A** lacks of the Torah,[6] **L** (the Leningrad Codex, B19a)[7] for the other pieces missing from **A**, and a third source for Josh 21:36–37, missing from both **A** and **L**. Most scholars agree that this sort of patchwork would not be very satisfactory. There is a consensus that it is better simply to go with **L** in its entirety.

Even if we had **A** intact, it could not be accepted blindly as immaculate, ignoring all other textual evidence. One would still be obliged to prepare a critical edition, using all of the appropriate tools on the available evidence. Hence the Jerusalem Hebrew University Bible project, while using a diplomatic edition of **A**, also provides an apparatus of variants from other manuscripts, the Dead Sea Scrolls, Versions, and so on. It refrains from conjectural emendation.

A1.1.4   Option Taken: Use the Leningrad Codex

A case can be made for preparing a conservatively eclectic edition, "correcting" **L** where it would be pedantic to reproduce its readings when they are palpably inferior. After all, **L** is nearly a century later than **A**, and is already divergent from **A**, assuming that **A** lies behind **L**. It is not likely that **A** immediately outclassed and eliminated all other copies. There was no imprimatur to make it the only authorized copy. It had to make its way by its intrinsic merit and by the prestige of the Ben Asher family. **L** shows a mixture of drift from **A** and the influences of other traditions including that of Ben Naphtali. It exhibits divergence in the use of *matres lectionis*, in vocalization, in the repertoire of *Qere / Kethiv*, in cantillations, and in the marginal Masora.

In addition, L itself has been "corrected." Text criticism must decide whether deviations from **A** and later corrections in **L** were warranted and should be allowed to stand or whether they were misguided and should be "uncorrected" and replaced by the reading of the first hand. The state-of-

---

4. Moshe H. Goshen-Gottstein, ed., *The Aleppo Codex* (Jerusalem: Magnes, 1976).

5. Here we might mention Nahum Ben Zvi, ed., *Jerusalem Crown* (Jerusalem: Ben Zvi, 2000), an attempt to use the principles laid down by M. Breuer to produce a "reconstructed" Aleppo Codex.

6. This was G. E. Weil's proposal, gently communicated verbally to Dean Forbes in 1985.

7. D. S. Loewinger, ed., *Pentateuch, Prophets and Hagiographa: Codex Leningrad B 19^A* (Jerusalem: Makor, 1971). David N. Freedman et al., eds., *The Leningrad Codex: Facsimile Edition* (Grand Rapids, MI: Eerdmans, 1998).

the-art photography behind *Biblica Hebraica Leningradensia* (*BHL*)[8] permits recovery of original readings not visible to the naked eye in the manuscript itself. Dotan has used this and other evidence to justify some 800 adjustments in his edition of *BHL*.

So we are left with **L** in some form or another. For the purposes of our computer-assisted research, we note that there are layers of scribal activity in which **L** is flawed or inferior to **A**.[9] There is not much wrong with the basic layer of consonants. All the words are there. There could be dispute over the use of *maqqep*, which the crowded writing of **L** makes hard to detect in some instances. But this hardly matters. There have been complaints about the deviation of **L** from **A** in the use of vowel letters (*matres lectionis*), but this does not matter either since the vowels themselves are shown by the points, so that the identity of the words is not affected. The same is true for the divergence of **L** from **A** (perhaps toward Ben Naphtali) in the use of *ḥateps*. We took comfort from the fact that none of these uncertainties makes any difference to our main ongoing research interests: syntax and discourse. So, finally, we decided that it was best to use **L**.

A1.2 Correcting "Obvious Errors" in L

A1.2.1 Adjusting the Majority of the "sic L" Readings

We depart from readings provided by the Leningrad Codex when we and, often, Dotan judge these readings to be simple errors, such erroneous readings being signaled in the apparatus of BHS by "sic **L**." Our responses, and those of Dotan, in the 36 places in Genesis where BHS has "sic **L**" are shown in the next subsection. We each replace the "sic **L**" readings in Genesis about two-thirds of the time. As it happens, the per-word incidence of "sic **L**" notes in Genesis is among the highest in the Hebrew Bible, as the following table demonstrates.

"sic L" Count per 10,000 Words	*Portion*	*"sic L" Count per 10,000 Words*	*Portion*	*"sic L" Count per 10,000 Words*	*Portion*
5.02	Lev	8.53	Num	14.42	Ezek
5.97	Josh	9.06	2 Sam	15.17	Judg
6.62	Ezra-Neh	10.24	1 Chr	16.42	Esth
6.79	1 Sam	10.52	2 Chr	17.46	Gen
6.87	Jer	10.59	2 Kgs	18.11	Minor Prophets
7.70	Deut	11.81	Isa	27.56	Job
8.17	Ps	13.76	Exod	30.37	Prov
8.37	1 Kgs	14.14	Megillot	33.79	Dan

Across the whole of BHS, we count 368 "sic **L**" notes. We change an erroneous reading 216 times, 58%, quite similar to our rate for Genesis, as is documented in the next subsection.

When a correction alters the part-of-speech assignment of a word, then we must change our syntactic analysis. For example, in Exod 10:28 **L** has this strange sequence:

---

8. Aron Dotan, ed., *Biblica Hebraica Leningradensia* (Peabody, MA: Hendrickson, 2001).
9. M. Breuer, *The Aleppo Codex and the Accepted Text of the Bible* (Jerusalem: Mossad Harav Kook, 1976).

אַל־תֹּסֶף רְאוֹת פָּנַי

We replace אֶל by אַל, changing the part of speech of the word from preposition to negative so that our text reads:

אַל־תֹּסֶף רְאוֹת פָּנַי

Fortunately, very few of the adjustments that we make force us to change our syntactic analysis.

Examining the ranked list above, it is interesting to ponder possible causes of the different incidences of anomalous readings as judged by the editors of BHS. Does the rank in the list of a book or section provide a relative measure of transmission damage, a measure of BHS editor diligence, or what?

A1.2.2   Readings Adopted by Andersen-Forbes (A-F) and Dotan in Genesis

Our responses, and those of Dotan, in the 36 places in Genesis where BHS has "sic **L**" are gathered in the table. An equal-sign bridges adjacent columns that agree, cantillations aside.

Citation	L	A-F	Dotan	*Citation*	L	A-F	Dotan
Gen 2:18	אֶעֱשֶׂה =	אֶעֱשֶׂה	אֶעֱשֶׂה	Gen 32:18	וּשְׁאֵלְךָ =	וּשְׁאֵלְךָ	וּשְׁאֵלְךָ
Gen 6:16	תְּכַלֶּנָּה	תְּכַלֶּנָּה =	תְּכַלֶּנָּה	Gen 32:24	לוֹ	לוֹ =	לוֹ
Gen 7:23	וַיִּשָּׁאֶר	וַיִּשָּׁאֶר =	וַיִּשָּׁאֶר	Gen 34:11	אָבִיהָ	אָבִיהָ	אָבִיהָ
Gen 14:10	הַשִּׂדִּים	הַשִּׂדִּים =	הַשִּׂדִּים	Gen 34:28	חֲמֹרֵיהֶם	חֲמֹרֵיהֶם	חֲמֹרֵיהֶם
Gen 15:10	הַצִּפֹּר	הַצִּפֹּר =	הַצִּפֹּר	Gen 35:1	בְּבָרְחֲךָ =	בְּבָרְחֲךָ =	בְּבָרְחֲךָ
Gen 16:2	מִמֶּנָּה =	מִמֶּנָּה	מִמֶּנָּה	Gen 36:13	אֵלֶּה	אֵלֶּה =	אֵלֶּה
Gen 19:2	וַהֲלַכְתֶּם =	וַהֲלַכְתֶּם	וַהֲלַכְתֶּם	Gen 38:9	לֹא =	לֹא =	לֹא
Gen 19:5	הָאֲנָשִׁים	הָאֲנָשִׁים =	הָאֲנָשִׁים	Gen 38:16	לִּי =	לִּי =	לִּי
Gen 22:12	מְאוּמָה =	מְאוּמָה	מְאוּמָה	Gen 38:26	לְדַעְתָּה	לְדַעְתָּה =	לְדַעְתָּה
Gen 24:36	לוֹ	לוֹ	לוֹ	Gen 39:19	עָשָׂה =	עָשָׂה	עָשָׂה
Gen 26:1	אֲבִימֶלֶךְ	אֲבִימֶלֶךְ =	אֲבִימֶלֶךְ	Gen 40:3	הַטַּבָּחִים	הַטַּבָּחִים =	הַטַּבָּחִים
Gen 26:29	תַּעֲשֵׂה	תַּעֲשֵׂה	תַּעֲשֵׂה	Gen 41:24	הַשִּׁבֳּלִים =	הַשִּׁבֳּלִים	הַשִּׁבֳּלִים
Gen 27:29	וְיִשְׁתַּחֲווּ	וְיִשְׁתַּחֲווּ =	וְיִשְׁתַּחֲווּ	Gen 41:26	הַשִּׁבֳּלִים	הַשִּׁבֳּלִים =	הַשִּׁבֳּלִים
Gen 30:19	לְיַעֲקֹב =	לְיַעֲקֹב	לְיַעֲקֹב	Gen 41:46	וַיַּעֲבֹר	וַיַּעֲבֹר =	וַיַּעֲבֹר
Gen 31:51	הַמַּצֵּבָה	הַמַּצֵּבָה =	הַמַּצֵּבָה	Gen 43:7	וַנַּגֶּד	וַנַּגֶּד =	וַנַּגֶּד
Gen 32:5	עֲבְדְּךָ	עֲבְדְּךָ	עֲבְדְּךָ	Gen 43:28	וַיִּשְׁתַּחֲווּ	יִשְׁתַּחֲווּ	וַיִּשְׁתַּחֲווּ
Gen 32:16	וְעָיְרִם =	וְעָיְרִם =	וְעָיְרִם	Gen 45:6	וְקָצִיר =	וְקָצִיר	וְקָצִיר
Gen 32:18	יִפְגָּשְׁךָ =	יִפְגָּשְׁךָ	יִפְגָּשְׁךָ	Gen 49:8	יִשְׁתַּחֲווּ	יִשְׁתַּחֲווּ =	יִשְׁתַּחֲווּ

Overall, readings judged noteworthy by the editor of Genesis in BHS are dealt with by us and by Dotan as follows:

	A-F kept L	**A-F changed L**	
Dotan kept L	11%	14%	25%
Dotan changed L	28%	47%	75%
	39%	61%	

We see that Dotan changed three-fourths of the **L** oddities in Genesis, while we changed about three-fifths of them (61%). We and Dotan jointly changed about half of the designated oddities (47%) and jointly kept about one-tenth of them (11%).

A1.2.3 Other Departures from **L**

Our three changes that are not signaled in BHS by a "sic **L**" note are:

Citation	*L*	*A-F*	*Dotan*
Lev 19:1	לֵאמֹר	לֵאמֹר׃ =	לֵאמֹר׃
2 Sam 20:8	לְבֻשׁוֹ	לְבֻשׁוֹ =	לְבֻשׁוֹ
2 Chr 29:34	וַיְחַזְּקוּם	וַיְחַזְּקוּם	וַיְחַזְּקוּם

A1.3 *Reducing the Text*

A1.3.1 Omission of Cantillations

We could be faulted for ignoring the cantillations in our work, because they ostensibly enshrine rabbinic traditions about grammatical structure implicit in rhapsodic composition. We did not make this decision lightly, even though we confess that the initial task of transcribing the text into machine-readable form would have been daunting and beyond our resources in the early developmental stages of our work if we had included the cantillations.[10] We experimented with the *athnāḥ* as the most likely to assist in the mapping of clause boundaries, since at least in poetic texts it divided many one-bicolon verses into two clauses. But even then, there could be one-clause verses and one-verse tricolons. And with prose texts, it soon became evident that even the *athnāḥ* would not yield results worth the labor of installing it.

But those who come after us and who have fully cantillated texts prepared by others are certainly encouraged to discover how much grammatical information might be extracted from the additional data that the cantillations provide. As far as we know, only four researchers[11] have tried to use the cantillations in a disciplined way for syntax.

In practice, we did use the cantillations in marking up the text, as for instance in the laborious task of resolving homographs such as מֶלֶךְ 'king', which can be normal or construct. The MT al-

---

10. In our earliest work (in 1970) and for some years, our input device was a teletype that had only uppercase alphanumerics, severely constraining the repertoire of items encodable by single key strokes.

11. Lars Lode, "A discourse perspective on the significance of the Masoretic accents," in *Biblical Hebrew and Discourse Linguistics* (ed. Robert D. Bergen; Dallas: Summer Institute of Linguistics, 1994) 155–72; Matthew P. Anstey, "The Grammatical-Lexical Cline in Tiberian Hebrew," *JSS* 51 (2006) 59–84. Kirk Lowery, in a presentation at the 2007 SBL meeting, indicated that his group had successfully used cantillations in phrase-level parsing. Michael Seleznev, "Syntactic Parsing behind the Masoretic Accentuation (I)," *Babel und Bibel* 3 (2006) 353–70.

ways has connecting accents for these well-formed phrases. Prosody matches grammar, at least for short phrases, so we could exploit the cantillations in deciding how to label words.

The accents serve two purposes. First, they join or divide. But they constitute a gradient, because "join" and "divide" are relative. Ultimately, every word as a prosodic unit (orthography encodes prosody) is both divided (hence the spacers) and joined to its neighbors as part of a running text. The reason that we do not gain much mileage out of these cantillations is that they correspond to syntactic structures only accidentally, being only phonological.

Second, the accents sometimes show which syllable of a word is stressed, and so they resolve the ambiguity of words that differ only in stress position. We have made use of this information abundantly, if not completely, to distinguish sing. fem. participles from the perfect in verbs with a two-consonant root. For example, we thereby resolve בָּאָה 'she is coming' from בָּאָה 'she came'.

A1.3.2 *Kethiv* Readings Used

We adopted the vocalized *Kethiv* readings of L to obtain our basic text. Representing the *Qere* text should be straightforward once the *Kethiv* text is dealt with adequately.

We accept L's repertoire of *Qere / Kethiv* readings.[12] We have done this so that we can read the text either with the *Kethiv* readings or the *Qere* readings. We are not completely comfortable about this acceptance, but where would we find a more authoritative list? Gordis? Ginsburg? We excuse ourselves from searching for alternates on the grounds that few of the *Qere / Kethiv* pairs make a difference to the questions of syntax that we are investigating.

To make the *Kethiv* readings compatible with the rest of the text, we supply vocalizations from Gordis.[13] Some may object to this choice, but it is for practical purposes, and we make no claim for the correctness of the vocalizations. They are, however, adequate for grammatical study.

A1.3.3 Lexical Ambiguity Resolved

Choosing a manuscript is only the first step in specifying a text. Because of the *Qere / Kethiv* choice and because of intrinsic ambiguities, a manuscript actually corresponds to many possible texts. The following English sentence has been crafted to illustrate four kinds of linguistic ambiguity:[14]

The mime, who plans to marry a clown, saw her duck, ready to eat, under the table.
The four kinds of ambiguity are:

1. *Deep Structure.*   Is the referent-of-*her* ready to eat, is the duck ready to eat, or is the duck ready to be eaten?
2. *Semantic.*   Is the identity of the clown already known or is it yet to be determined? We don't know the gender of the mime and clown, except that at least one of them is female.

---

12. We note that the presentation in BHS differs from that in BHK by attempting harmonization with the Masoretic annotations, which do not always match the actual text. Because of this, the statement that we "accept L's repertoire" is not strictly true if one relies on BHS, which has made some adjustments in an attempt to overcome the deficiencies of L in this matter. See the caveat in William S. Morrow, "Kethib and Qere," *Anchor Bible Dictionary* 4:26b.

13. Robert Gordis, *The Biblical Text in the Making: A Study of the Kethib-Qere* (Jersey City, NJ: Ktav, 1971).

14. The sentence is from F. I. Andersen and A. D. Forbes, "Attachment Preferences in the Primary History," in *Bible and Computer* (ed. Johann Cook; Leiden: Brill, 2002) 167–86. See also F. I. Andersen and A. D. Forbes, "Syntactic Ambiguity in the Hebrew Bible," in *Proceedings of the Fourth International Colloquium: Bible and the Computer, Desk and Discipline* (Paris: Honoré Champion, 1995) 356–67.

If the clown is female, she owned the duck or she was the one the mime saw duck under the table. If the mime is female, she owns the duck.

3. *Lexical.*　　Is *duck* a noun or a verb?

4. *Structural.*　　What is *under the table*—the seeing, her ducking, or the duck?

Any representation of the grammatical structure of a text must deal with these sorts of ambiguity.

Ambiguity resolution is one part of the specification of the text, and so its discussion fits in here nicely. Ambiguity resolution presupposes a fully developed taxonomy of parts of speech of the sort that we present in §3.2. The following comments on ambiguity, however, rely on knowledge of traditional Hebrew grammar.

Multiple part-of-speech homography.　　Some homographs exhibit *multiple part-of-speech* behavior. Consider the four homographs of עַל shown in the table below, each with its gloss, total incidence count, and a representative context.

עַל *Translation*	*Count*	*Context*	*Citation*
'upon'	4,271	וָאֶתֵּן אֶת־הַכּוֹס עַל־כַּף פַּרְעֹה:	Gen 40:11
'though'	9	עַל לֹא־חָמָס עָשָׂה	Isa 53:9
'Highest'	2	וְאֶל־עַל יִקְרָאֻהוּ	Hos 11:7
'he went'	4	וְדָנִיֵּאל עַל	Dan 2:16

This word can be a preposition, a subordinating conjunction, a proper noun, or an Aramaic verb. In theory, it would be possible to try out each of these possibilities in each context. A parser would rule out several possibilities, or all but one possibility, in a given context. But some contexts would be left formally ambiguous. For example, the clause from Daniel conceivably could be a verbless clause asserting that "Daniel [is the] Highest." Here is the crucial point: since we have world knowledge about "[the] Highest," we assert that the proposed parse is foolish.[15] We, the human over-readers, disambiguate the context and select the verbal sense. We have tried to be thorough in finding and resolving items involving multiple parts of speech. For example, our dictionary of lexemes was, at one point, read against the entries in BDB.

Within-part-of-speech homography.　　Other words exhibit *within-part-of-speech homography* and differ only in their glosses and semantics. For example, the noun עִיר occurs hundreds of times with the gloss 'city' (semantics: geographic), but it occurs a few times with the glosses 'agitation' (semantics: mental state), 'watcher' (semantics: human),[16] 'donkey' (semantics: creature), and 'Ir' (semantics: specific human). In our electronic text, we attempt to resolve this sort of single part-of-speech lexical ambiguity. The sense-resolution process is necessarily incomplete. For example, in the case of עִיר 'city', we do not go on to recognize the several more specific senses found in BDB: 'city', 'town', 'dependent town', 'fortress in a city', 'fortified place', 'inhabitants'. We continue to find instances of confusing or hilariously incorrect glosses. When these are encountered, we resolve the underlying lexical ambiguity.

Pausal Ambiguity.　　Pausal ambiguity can occur at "text breaks," places in the text where a reader pauses for longer than in other places—verse end, *athnaḥ*, and, in long verses, at other

---

15. At base, this is an exegetical assertion, not a linguistic one.

16. This word occurs in Dan 4:10, 20. We assign it "human" semantics as we have done with all angelic beings.

disjunctive accents. Pause is purely elocutionary, and its significance for grammar is minimal. The pausals we have flagged amount to only a fraction of words in pausal *positions* (text breaks that invoke pausal lengthening). Not all nouns that have extra stress because they are in pausal positions have a longer vowel than in other positions. In other words, these nouns are homographic for normal versus pause, but they are all labeled normal. *These homographs have not been resolved.* Many words besides nouns occur in pausal positions, and, as with nouns, only some of them show the normal-versus-pause difference by vowel lengthening. The rest are homographic pairs. (Of course, not all of them—perhaps only a few—are attested in both pausal and nonpausal position.)

An imbalance in our lexeme feature vectors—treating nouns one way and verbs another—is an artifact (arbitrary from the theoretical point of view) forced on us by RAM space limitations in the days when our computers had perhaps eight kilobytes of "core." The sixth place in our feature vectors had to cater to the state of nouns and the person of verbs, so we could not encode the state of verbs. Consequently, pausal verbs were not marked as such. Here is another locus of extensive homography that we did not deal with.

Because of these and other complications, our resolution of homographs is incomplete and frequently uncertain when we have ventured to do it.

Appendix 2

Our Approach to Linguistics

A2.1 *Traditional Approaches to the Syntax of Biblical Hebrew*

A2.1.1 Gesenius and His Successors

The foundations laid by Gesenius nearly 200 years ago have pervaded most of the work on Hebrew and other Semitic languages since then. The first edition of Gesenius's grammar appeared in 1813. Subsequent editions by Rödiger (14th–21st editions), Kautzsch (22nd–28th editions), and Bergsträsser (29th edition), and the English translation of the 28th edition by Cowley (GKC) all retained Gesenius's name as the presiding genius over the whole enterprise. Gesenius supplied grammarians, translators, exegetes, and commentators with many of the categories and terms still in use, but most of all with a way of doing Hebrew grammar that is still the only way that most people learn. We, too, stand in this great tradition. It is part of our eclecticism. It is part of our policy to retain as much of this heritage as we can use, so that we may make the most of the resources found in the vast literature of the field and especially in standard works of reference.

We have no quarrel with much that has been in place in Hebrew grammar since the development of Hebrew philology in the nineteenth century. The way it was done from the beginning continued to influence most of what followed. This is seen in the use of essentially the same template in numerous primers and works of reference. The interest was in *words*, how they were formed and how they were used. Grammar was defined as the study of the ways in which a language used its *words*. Beginning with how they were written (orthography), the next step was how they were pronounced (phonology), and then how they were formed (morphology), how they were classified ("parts of speech"), and how they were used (syntax). Even the syntax was typically driven by listing the various functions of the word classes (verb, noun, pronoun, etc.) and the meanings of each distinct form class (such as the Niphal form). Books on "syntax" such as those by Williams have sections on the functional meanings of each preposition.

A radical difference between this usual approach and ours is that we do not use the term *word* at all to refer to any grammatical entity as such. It is only an accidental outcome of the arbitrary Hebrew writing practice that some *orthographic* words turn up as the units in grammatical constructions. The difference can be illustrated from Gen 24:36. Traditional grammar identifies the *word* "Sarah" as the subject of the verb. Phrase Structure Grammar of the sort that we base our work upon recognizes the *construction* "Sarah, my lord's wife," as a clause immediate constituent that, as a single entity, is the subject of the whole clause.

334

A2.1.2   Traditional Views of Syntax: What Parts of Speech Do

In traditional grammars, syntax consisted of the listing of the grammatical functions of the parts of speech. Thus, A. B. Davidson's justly classic *Syntax* (1894; 3rd ed., 1901) has four sections: Syntax of the Pronoun, Syntax of the Noun, Syntax of the Verb, and Syntax of the Sentence. Similarly, Ronald J. Williams's *Hebrew Syntax: An Outline* has four sections: Syntax of the Noun, Syntax of the Verb, Syntax of Particles, and Syntax of Clauses. Waltke and O'Connor, *An Introduction to Biblical Hebrew Syntax*, has no systematic treatment of the syntax of clauses as such.

A2.1.3   Traditional Views of Syntax: Category Importation

Modern grammars of Biblical Hebrew arose when it was supposed that a language was a means of expressing thoughts in words and that good language use should be "logical." In early editions of Gesenius, one often finds expressions such as "the verbal idea." Grammarians began with "concepts" or "notions" and tried to find out how those "ideas" were expressed in Hebrew.

One of the concepts used in this way was that of *case*. The practice continues. For example, Williams has nominative, genitive, and accusative clauses. Ancestral Hebrew inherited from Proto-Semitic a three-case system in the declension of nouns. This system survived in Classical Arabic, but it disappeared completely from Biblical Hebrew. Biblical Hebrew nouns no longer have case endings, apart from a few fossils. Since case is not a formal syntactic category in Biblical Hebrew, we avoid talk of it. (We do sometimes use the term *nota accusativi* for אֶת.)

In traditional Hebrew grammar there was another way in which the categories did not arise from the linguistic data but were imported from outside by "logic." Inventories of clause types vary from one grammarian to another. Terms such as "reason," "cause," "purpose," and "result" occur alongside "affirmative," "negative," and "relative." They are merely miscellaneous lists. There is no development of a theory of the functions of the various clause types in discourse. This narrow perspective on clause syntax is the outcome of restricting syntactic inquiry to what is going on inside a clause, with little or no interest in what the clause as a whole, as an elementary discourse unit, may be doing in its wider text surrounds. Davidson, at least, makes a distinction between simple sentences consisting of just one clause and sentences consisting of two clauses. But this is as far as it goes. Even so, Davidson's *Syntax* points in the direction of rudimentary discourse analysis, and as such, is still worthy of study. Davidson's discussion of "The Conditional Sentence" (p. 175) begins: "The conditional sent. is compound, consisting of two clauses, the former [or, "protasis"] stating the supposition, and the second [or, "apodosis"] the result dependent upon it (the answer to the supposition)." The subsequent analysis concentrates on the kind of verb used in each clause and the conjunctions found in each kind of protasis [or, "conditional clause"]. Davidson provides a list of "conditional particles."

A2.1.4   Comparatives: The Traditional Approach versus Our Approach

Here is an illustration of the difference between the traditional approach and ours.[1] Williams gives the preposition כ nine meanings (functions) including "comparative."[2] Arnold and Choi give three, including "correspondence": "a comparison that establishes an equivalence between the

---

1. *Note well*: this subsection uses phrase marker concepts that are not introduced in the main text until §1.3.
2. R. J. Williams, *Williams' Hebrew Syntax* (3rd ed.; ed. J. C. Beckman; Toronto: University of Toronto Press, 2007) 49–50.

things that are compared."[3] Elsewhere Arnold and Choi introduce "comparative" in discussing the "degrees" of "adjectives," reporting the use of מִן in this connection.[4] This betrays the starting point of the analysis as the expectation that languages will have ways of expressing "degrees" (*good, better, best*), and the question is: how does Hebrew do this? Not by suffixes on adjectives, such as *-er*, and *-est* in English.

Instead of beginning with the prepositions, we begin with clauses in which there is a "comparative" clause immediate constituent (CIC). We ask: what are the formal linguistic marks of this kind of constituent? We do not locate the notion of comparison in the preposition as such but in the whole construction in which something is compared with something else. If we ask at the same time what the preposition כְּ does, we find a many-to-many relation between form and function. There are other ways to make comparisons besides the use of כְּ, and כְּ is used for other purposes than to make comparisons, as is usually the situation with polysemic/polyfunctional segments such as prepositions and conjunctions. Our phrase markers display all the *constructions* in which כְּ occurs, with full analysis of the syntactic function of the whole phrase that is carried by the preposition. Furthermore, our phrase markers make a clear distinction between constructions in which כְּ marks a comparative constituent within a clause and constructions in which it is a modifier in a noun phrase.

We find 2,682 "comparison" CICs in our text,[5] labeled cmpr in our phrase markers. Of these, 2,397 use the preposition כְּ (89%), so that is clearly the prototypical way of making a clause-level comparison. Phrase marker (A2.1) from Prov 3:12 shows an instance of the use of כְּ in a cmpr CIC.

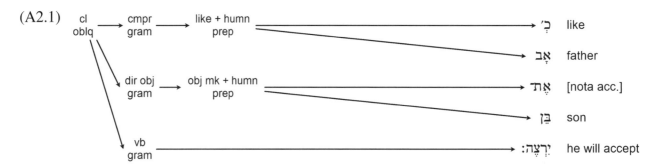

This stirs up interest in two related matters: first, the other ways of marking comparisons; second, the uses of כְּ when it does not mark a comparison.

The other frequent way of showing/marking a CIC as comparative is with מִן—attested 308 times. And, like כְּ, מִן is used also to mark comparison within noun phrases. More than this: comparative מִן is only one (and a very specialized one at that) of the many functions of this preposition. We are in a position to give a full account of all these kinds of constructions. Phrase marker (A2.2) from Judg 5:24 shows the use of מִן in a cmpr CIC.

3. B. T. Arnold and J. H. Choi, *A Guide to Biblical Hebrew Syntax* (Cambridge: Cambridge University Press, 2003) 109.

4. Ibid., 27.

5. Our text is the *Kethiv* text of the Hebrew Bible as attested in the Leningrad Codex, modified as detailed in §A1.2.

(A2.2)

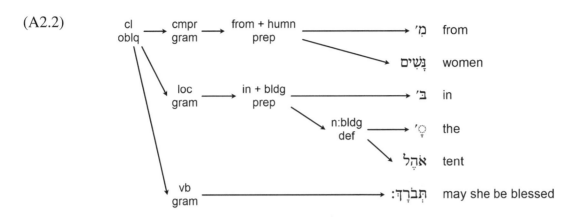

Further investigation consists of two parts. First, how distinctive and categorical is the cmpr CIC? Do the 2,751 instances *include* all the eligible candidates and *exclude* all ineligible candidates? To answer this question, we need to have reliable tests of eligibility. We need to have a clear definition of the "comparison" *function* of a clause constituent in *relation* to the other pole of the comparison—"X is like Y." To say that כ means "like" and makes a comparison is not enough; כ has other meanings, and comparison can be made in other kinds of construction. We may also need to ask if "comparison" is too broad, even too vague, and whether we need to distinguish more than one kind of comparison. Phrase marker (A2.3) from Ruth 1:4 shows the use of כ in a tm int ("time interval") CIC.

(A2.3)

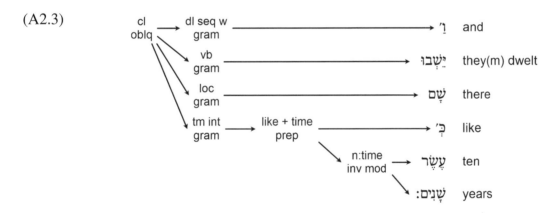

One thing, however, should be clear. These questions cannot be settled a priori, or by importing abstract ideas of "comparison," or by resorting to diagnostics supplied by "deep structure." They must be settled by the data in the texts, augmented as necessary by world knowledge. This is our empirical gospel.

The majority of the comparison CICs have an indubitable *identity*, but their syntactic *function* is often less unequivocal. There is no clean fence between those that "follow the rules" and the exceptions. The former match the definitions—which, since they arise from a disciplined empirical approach, are descriptive not prescriptive. Exceptionality is a matter of degree.

The foregoing highlights a big-picture difference between the tradition and us: for us, the data are the data. The whole text is "Biblical Hebrew." We must have criteria for well-formedness before we can dub something as "less well-formed" or even "malformed." We do not have the easy excuse from further work of setting some corner cases aside as "exceptions," let alone dismissing them as "ungrammatical" or identifying them as a scribal corruption that might be emended according to the rules of some prescriptive grammar.

A2.2 *Phrase-Structure Grammars*

Given that the text of the Hebrew Bible consists of more than 300,000 words, sole reliance on intuition in the working out of syntactic structures would have rapidly led to implementers' catatonia and worse. Consequently, we decided to see how far the phrase-structure grammars commonly used in *computational linguistics* would take us. "Phrase-structure grammars contain rules (PS-rules) which are capable not only of generating strings of linguistic elements, but also of providing a constituent analysis of the strings."[6]

This is not the place to rehearse the details of this work. They are discussed in considerable detail elsewhere.[7] To provide readers a sense of the work, it will suffice to sketch the three major steps that were involved in parsing the text. These were:

1. Design a computational architecture for inferring the syntactic structures of the clauses.
2. Specify the set of rules that describe the possible syntactic structures of Biblical Hebrew.
3. Carry out the parsing and check, correcting errors and completing unfinished work.

A2.2.1 Designing a Sequence of Grammars

Each clause must be supplied to a parsing algorithm (or sequence of parsing algorithms). Rather than trying to produce one all-inclusive grammar, we decided on a divide-and-conquer strategy, using *multiple-pass pipeline parsing*.

Multiple-pass parsing processes each clause through a given grammar multiple times, with each pass building up additional structure. For example, construct chains are dealt with by successively building up their syntactic structures. Given the construct chain "throne of king of Israel," the first pass would form [NP [N *king-of*] [N *Israel*]] while the second pass would build up [NP [N *throne-of*] [NP [N *king-of*] [N *Israel*]]]. *Pipeline parsing* involves a series of grammars, each designed to do one or a few jobs well and further designed to work gracefully as one in a sequence of parsers. In our pipeline parser, we had seven separate grammars. Their competences were as follows:

- Suffixation, hendiadys, adjective phrases, and numbers
- Construct chains and certain apposition constructions
- Preposition and apposition phrases grown backward from clause ends
- Preposition and apposition phrases grown backward from other boundary markers
- Embedded clauses (nominalizations, participles, infinitives construct, etc.)
- Complements identified on the basis of the verb semantics of their main clauses
- Final adjustments (link prepositions with following noun, clean up, etc.)

---

6. D. Crystal, *Dictionary of Linguistics and Phonetics* (5th ed.; Oxford: Blackwell, 2003) 353.

7. F. I. Andersen and A. D. Forbes, "Opportune Parsing: Clause Analysis of Deuteronomy 8," *Bible and Computer: Desk and Discipline* (Paris: Honoré Champion, 1995) 49–75.

A2.2.2   The Specification of Syntactic Rules

Each of the grammars implemented a battery of syntactic rules and built up a structural representation of the clause being parsed. The rules were specified in terms of standard parsing programs. Here is an example of a parsing rule:

$$\text{SnSMD} \rightarrow \text{PtSMD CC PtSMD}$$

which means that when the parser encounters a PtSMD (singular-masculine-definite participle), followed by a CC (coordinating conjunction), followed by a PtSMD (singular-masculine-definite participle), then those three segments should be combined to form a SnSMD (singular-masculine-definite "subjectable" noun). A "subjectable" noun is one that is *available* for later classification as the subject of the clause.

A2.2.3   Computer Parsing

Across the entire Hebrew Bible, the computer did something with 95% of the segments, leaving 5% of the segments stranded. In Deuteronomy 8, the chapter whose parsing we analyzed in detail, about 85% of the structures produced by the computer were correct. As one moves to the left in the resulting phrase markers (toward the root), the error rate climbs, an expected behavior. The computer does a very good job indeed at assembling the simple constituents making up the clauses. It is reliable classification of the clause immediate constituents that proved difficult for our parsers.

A2.3   *The Autonomy of Syntax—Not*

A2.3.1   The Role of Morphology

The term *morpheme* has acquired a central place in modern linguistics. We have not taken this term onboard for use in our descriptions of Hebrew grammatical structures for several reasons. The compact nature of Hebrew morphology imposes limits on the possibilities of formal analysis of "words" down to morphemes as their smallest meaningful components. This is especially so with verbs. A finite Hebrew verb consists of a stem with affixes. The stem consists of a consonantal lattice with stem-forming vowels. The consonantal lattice may be a root or a root augmented by a *binyan*-making morpheme, such as נ for Niphal. So a verb stem may be two or three morphemes—the root, the augmenter, and the vowels. These morphemes are discontinuous and interdigitated.[8] It would be fruitlessly complicated to specify all of these relations, making these morphemes the ultimate constituents of our syntactic constructions. A grammatical feature, such as voice, is distinguished, not so much by the stem vowels as such, but by the systemic *contrasts* between the stem vowels of one verb and another in combination with the consonants of the lattice. So it is better to associate voice with the whole stem as a construction and in contrast to other stems, than to try to isolate a verb's voice as residing in some active or passive morpheme. Voice as a feature of verb morphology is systemic / paradigmatic rather than morphemic.

Likewise with the pronominal affixes. In some verbs, they are suffixes, in others prefixes, and in yet others they are a combination of prefix and suffix. In this last situation, the pronoun is a discontinuous amphifix (or, ambifix, or circumfix). And, even if we isolated these pronominal affixes

---

8. For a full technical discussion of these matters, see George A. Kiraz, *Computational Nonlinear Morphology with Emphasis on Semitic Languages* (Cambridge: Cambridge University Press, 2001).

as entities, they would not be morphemes. Each pronoun has number, gender, and person, but separate morphemes for number, gender, and person cannot be found as segments of these affixes. The prefix ת for instance, with some vowel or other, means either 2nd-person masc. sing. 'thou' or 3rd-person fem. sing. 'she' (it has other combinations, too) but it cannot be analyzed further into three morphemes, one for the value of each feature—one for number, one for gender, one for person. The distinctive meaning of each of these segments as combining the values of three grammatical features is secured by the contrastive patterns among all of them within the pronoun paradigm as a *system*. We leave it as that. Indeed, we leave each finite verb intact as one segment in the vocabulary stock of Hebrew. Each finite verb has nine features: transitivity (valency), voice, tense, aspect, mood, number, gender, person, and semantics. It is not possible to cull out from a finite verb morphemes for each of these features. Instead, we label each verb segment as a whole with a set of features that encodes the specific values for these features in that verb.

A2.3.2 The Role of Semantics

Our inclusion of semantic information in our extended phrase markers originally had nothing to do with the debate about the autonomy of syntax. Our reasons had everything to do with the practical needs of the computer when parsing the texts. Since our focus was on representing the syntactic structures of the clauses making up the text, we happily introduced semantic information when we realized how powerfully it would assist the parsing algorithms. Some details of the presently crude naïve semantics that we used may be found in §3.3.1.

Appendix 3

Alternate Approaches to Positional Syntax

In this appendix, we sketch two approaches to positional syntax considered by us in addition to the fields approach discussed and adapted in §11.3. We also present Connolly's taxonomy of factors that may affect CIC positions.

A3.1 *The Linearization Approach to Positional Syntax*

The concept of linearization is important since it "supports elegant and general linguistic analysis for (relatively) free word order languages, including the possibility of licensing discontinuous constituents."[1] In other words, it is well suited to nonconfigurational languages such as Biblical Hebrew. But, from our perspective, it does have a drawback:

> [M]ost . . . linearization approaches extend the representation of a sign with a so-called *word order domain* in addition to the constituent domain. The theory then includes constraints specifying how word order domains are formed.[2]

We have sought to have our syntactic representation be resolutely *monostratal*, that is, to involve only one level of representation. We have sought to have a What-You-See-Is-What-You-Get representation in the form of our phrase markers. Adding a word order domain alongside the phrase markers would add an unwanted second level to the description of syntax. For this reason, we are disinclined to take the linearization approach to positional syntax.

A3.2 *The Argument Structure Approach to Positional Syntax*

Suppose you were told that a clause, unseen by you, contained a CIC that was a finite verb and were asked what other CICs the clause contained and in what order. Given so little information, you would be unable to answer the questions with any confidence. If, however, you were informed that the finite verb was *intransitive*, then you could state with confidence that the clause would include no direct object. But, if you were instead informed that the finite verb was *transitive*, then you would likely aver that the clause would *probably* include an overt direct object, a non-overt direct object also being possible. Upon being further informed that the finite verb was a member of some *subcategory* of verbs, you would have been supplied information about the makeup of the clause of which the verb was a part. The use of the terminology of subcategorization is illustrated by Manning and Schütze:[3]

---

1. Michael W. Daniels, *Generalized ID/LP Grammar* (Ph.D. diss., Ohio State University, 2005) ii.

2. Frederik Fouvry and Detmar Meurers, "Towards a platform for linearization grammars," in *ESSLLI-2000 Workshop on Linguistic Theory and Grammatical Implementation* (ed. Erhard Hinrichs) 155.

3. Christopher D. Manning and Heinrich Schütze, *Foundations of Statistical Natural Language Processing* (Cambridge, MA: MIT Press, 1999) 104.

We refer to the classification of verbs according to the types of complements they permit as *subcategorization*. We say that the verb *subcategorizes for* a particular complement. For example, *bring* subcategorizes for an object.

When this sort of specifying is refined and generalized, the details of subcategorization emerge. The formalism is central in head-driven phrase structure grammar, in which entries in the lexicon include a list-valued feature called ARG-ST (equals *argument-structure*).[4] Extended selected quotations should make matters clear:[5]

> [T]he ARG-ST list of a verb occurring in a tree contains all of the information about that verb's arguments. . . . It . . . serves to express certain relations at the interface between syntax and semantics. . . . The elements of an ARG-ST list are ordered, and they correspond to phrases in the phrase structure tree. . . . [T]he order of arguments on the ARG-ST list . . . determines their linear order, given the way our grammar works. That is, subjects precede objects and other arguments, direct objects precede other arguments except the subject, and so forth. [The following *sequence*] predicts the linear order that arguments occur in reasonably well: Subject < Direct Object < 2nd Object < Other Complement.

The arguments are "ordered by obliqueness, with the least oblique [argument] being the first element."[6] The sequence above corresponds to "a version of the traditional obliqueness hierarchy."[7] But obliqueness alone does not determine argument order since "the *relative* weight of the [arguments] is important. It is apparent that the spectrum of relative weights interacts with the obliqueness ordering in a gradient fashion."[8] Discourse factors enter the determination of argument ordering.[9] Finally, one should extend the sequence so that adjuncts are included as well as complements, since "adjuncts are more oblique than complements."[10]

The foregoing approach might be developed to suffice for a configurational language such as English, but it needs to be altered if it is to be of use for a nonconfigurational language such as Biblical Hebrew. One proposal is to use "a set rather than a list to represent valence information."[11] That is, the permitted arguments are still listed but no obliqueness order is assigned to them.

A3.3 *Factors That Determine or Affect CIC Position*

A few approaches to positional syntax that rely on summary statements, rules, or sets of constraints purport to determine the ordering of clause immediate constituents. More typically, their developers remark that their formalisms describe usual patterns, typical templates. One reads state-

---

4. Ivan A. Sag, Thomas Wasow, and Emily Bender, *Syntactic Theory: A Formal Introduction* (2nd ed.; Stanford, CA: CSLI, 2003) 205.

5. Ibid., 207, 219.

6. Kordula De Kuthy and W. Ditmar Meurers, "Dealing with Optional Complements in HPSG-Based Grammar Implementations," in *Proceedings of the 10th International Conference on HDPSGC* (ed. S. Müller; Stanford, CA: CSLI, 2003) 91.

7. Carl Pollard and Ivan A. Sag, *Head-Driven Phrase Structure Grammar* (Chicago: University of Chicago Press, 1994) 24.

8. Steven Bird, "Finite-State Phonology in HPSG," *Proceedings of the International COLING* (1992) 79.

9. Carl Pollard and Ivan A. Sag, *Information-Based Syntax and Semantics*, vol. 1: *Fundamentals* (Stanford, CA: CSLI, 1987) 177–79.

10. Ibid., 181.

11. Stefan Müller, "Continuous or Discontinuous Constituents? A Comparison between Syntactic Analyses for Constituent Order and Their Processing Systems," *Research on Language and Computation* 2 (2004) 209–57.

ments such as this: "The order of constituents in free phrase order languages is determined by a set of factors which constitute tendencies rather than clear-cut rules."[12] Just what might these factors be?

John Connolly has produced a taxonomy of factors that can affect constituent ordering.[13] We present it as a tree diagram:

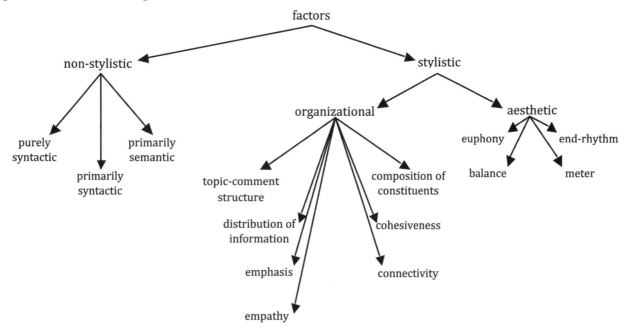

We do not explain the taxonomy but merely provide Connolly's definitions of the nonstylistic factors:

1. *Purely syntactic.*   "[T]he relative position of the two [constituents] is purely a matter of the linear-structural aspect of syntax."
2. *Primarily syntactic.*   "The basic determinant of the choice of position here is the syntactic consideration of whether or not the [constituent] is grammatically dependent on another [constituent], rather than on any directly semantic factor."
3. *Primarily semantic.*   "[T]he cognitive meaning of the sentence depends directly upon the choice of linear syntactic order."

Having examined the definitions and examples for the factors in the taxonomy, we conclude that there are valid reasons to include each. The problem associated with there being so many possibly operative influences is that—as we show for Connolly's rule set (§11.3.1.1)—realistic testing of Connolly's system is out of reach for Biblical Hebrew.

---

12. Ralf Steinberger, "Treating 'Free Word Order' in Machine Translation," *Proceedings of the 15th Conference on Computational Linguistics* (1994) 74.

13. John H. Connolly, *Constituent Order in Functional Grammar: Synchronic and Diachronic Perspectives* (Berlin: Foris, 1991) 9–16.

Appendix 4

Indirect-Object Alternation in the אמר Corpus

We have included this skeletal appendix because it may suggest ways forward for those interested in indirect-object alternations in the אמר corpus.

A4.1 *Indirect Object Alternation as Explained by Jenni and by Malessa*

In §12.4.3.5, we observed that in the אמר corpus, the indirect object occurs with either אֶל (1,276×) or לְ' (645×).[1] Two theories have been advanced to account for the nearly two-to-one ratio of occurrences. Jenni investigated the phenomenon and concluded that the determinative factor in preposition usage was "the relation between the status of the speakers and the status of the listeners."[2] Malessa found problems with Jenni's explanation and proposed his own, based primarily on data from Genesis, 1–2 Samuel, and 1–2 Kings.[3] Malessa's basic thesis is that, in "Earlier Hebrew," when the indirect object does not immediately follow its predicator, then אל is more likely to be used than ל. We reproduce his table 9, translated into our terminology:[4]

Constituent Order	Evidence	PP (אל)		PP (ל)	
Vb-IndObj	128	78	60.9%	50	39.1%
Vb-Sbj-IndObj	300	253	84.3%	47	15.7%

When the subject comes between the predicator and the indirect object, the frequency of use of אֶל is observed to increase by 23 percentage points. In addition to the effect of interpolated constituents, Malessa observed a diminution in the frequency of use of אל in "Later Hebrew" (Esther–2 Chronicles) as compared with "Earlier Hebrew" (Genesis, 1–2 Samuel, 1–2 Kings).[5]

A4.2 *The Jenni and Malessa Explanations: Counterexamples*

Rather than carry out an exhaustive examination of all of the relevant data, we here consider two data subsets that provide counterexamples to the Jenni and Malessa theses.

---

1. It also appears twice with עַל 'upon', in 2 Kgs 22:8 and Jer 23:35.

2. Ernst Jenni, "Einleitung formeller und familiärer Rede im Alten Testament durch *'mr 'l-* und *'mr l-*," in *Vielseitigkeit des Alten Testaments: Festschrift für Georg Sauer zum 70. Geburtstag* (ed. J. A. Loader and H. V. Kieweler; Frankfurt a.M.: Peter Lang, 1999) 25.

3. Michael Malessa, *Untersuchungen zur verbalen Valenz im biblischen Hebräisch* (Assen: Van Gorcum, 2006) 168–91. See also Christo H. J. van der Merwe, "Review of Malessa's *Untersuchungen zur verbalen Valenz im biblischen Hebräisch*," *Review of Biblical Literature* 4 (2007).

4. Ibid., 184.

5. Idid., 188–91.

A4.2.1 Unanchored Predicator . . . Some CIC . . . Indirect Object

Consider the small data set (66 clauses) made up of all clauses in the אמר corpus with the sequence:

unanchored predicator + some CIC (typically the clause's subject, 82%)[6] + *indirect object*

This subcorpus is large enough to allow statistically significant inferences to be based on it. Two observations are germane:

1. *Jenni.* In the 66 indirect-object-shifted אמר clauses, the explicit speaker (sbj) is a deity 47 times, but in all of this superior-to-inferior speaking, the preposition used is אל 26 times and ל 21 times (55% : 45%). In this grammatical context, large social distance does not entail preponderant use of אל.
2. *Malessa.* In the 66 indirect-object-shifted אמר clauses, the indirect object involves אל 34 times and ל 32 times (52% : 48%). Using one or the other of the prepositions is essentially equiprobable. This provides a counterexample to the assertion that dislocating the indirect object away from the predicator leads to a pronounced preference for אל over ל.

A4.2.2 Unanchored Predicator . . . Indirect Object

Next consider the much larger data set (226 clauses) defined by extracting from the אמר corpus all clauses having the sequence:

unanchored predicator followed immediately by *indirect object*

This subcorpus allows statistically significant inference. We find, for instance, that in the 226 indirect-object-adjacent אמר clauses, the indirect object involves אל 118 times and ל 108 times (52.2% : 47.8%). As in the unanchored predicator shifted-indirect-object case, no significant difference in the incidences of the two prepositions is observed in this unanchored predicator adjacent-indirect-object case. We assert that an explanation for a phenomenon should apply not only across all of the pertinent data but also across proper subsets of this data.

---

6. Eight of the 12 interpolated non-subjects are the *manner* SR CIC נָא '[emphatic]' following an imperative.

Appendix 5

Compositional Analysis

A5.1 *Problem*

We have seen multiple instances of CIC-incidence bar charts. It is natural to inquire whether there is a principled way to use the information depicted in a set of bar charts to infer the distances separating the clauses containing the various verbal roots and thereby display the relative affinities, with regard to CIC incidence, of the several verbal roots. (Warning: This appendix is very technical!)

A5.2 *Solution*

In fact, there are ways of computing the distances and using these to devise displays showing the similarities of the involved roots. Carrying out this exercise, however, involves dealing with several subtle intermediate problems. To make matters concrete, we will use incidence data for two sets of clauses, each based on a root/*binyan* combination:[1] the Hiphil actives of שמד 'extermination' (68×) and of רעע 'do evil' (46×). The CIC-incidence bar chart for Hiphil שמד is shown on the top of p. 347.

The Hiphil active of שמד never appears as a noun-verb participle or a purely verbal participle, manifesting only as an anchored verb, an infinitive construct, or an unanchored finite verb. Clauses in which it is the predicator usually contain an explicit direct object (90%) and have an explicit subject one-quarter of the time. They never contain an indirect object, a subject complement, a location, or a movement aim, but a movement origin appears one-third of the time. Rather uncommon are negation (7.4% of the clauses) and comparison (5.9% of the clauses) CICs.

The CIC-incidence bar chart for Hiphil רעע is shown on the bottom of p. 347.

The Hiphil active of רעע never appears as a noun-verb or purely verbal predicator, manifesting as an anchored verb, an infinitive construct, or an unanchored finite verb. Clauses in which it is the predicator contain an indirect object one-quarter of the time. Ditto for negation. Free-standing subjects and direct objects appear about 15% of the time—15.2% and 13.0%, respectively.

A5.2.1 A Proper Sample Space

We ask: in terms of the incidence of their various CICs, how far apart are the sets of clauses having these two roots in their predicators? To highlight a fundamental issue while keeping our example visually accessible, we ask a less wide-ranging question: in terms of the *predicators used,*

---

1. These roots were chosen so that the initial descriptive diagram is in three-dimensional space to allow visualization.

CIC Incidences for שמד Clauses

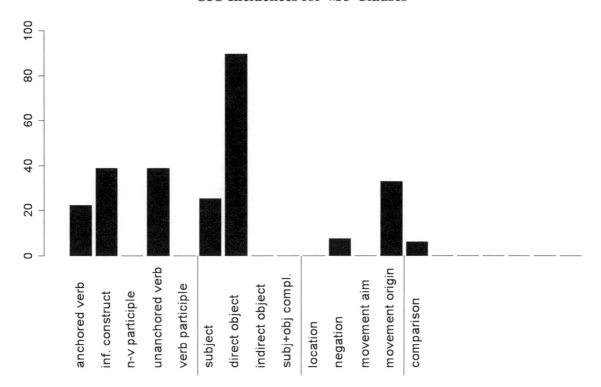

CIC Incidences for רעע Clauses

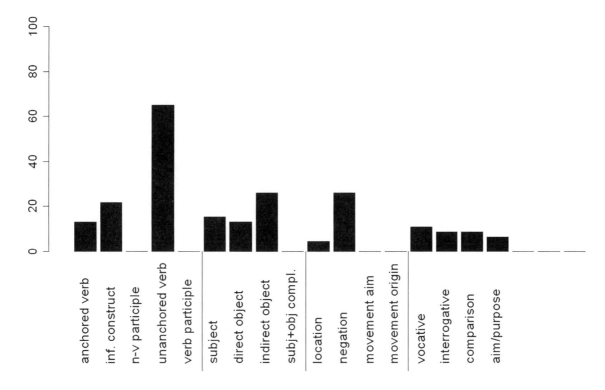

how far apart are these two roots? Only three predicator incidences occur for each root: the anchored verb incidence, the infinitive construct incidence, and the unanchored finite verb incidence.

The usual (naïve) practice would be to normalize the counts to sum to unity and plot a point corresponding to each root in a unit cube.[2] To simplify description, let the unanchored finite verb fraction axis be labeled **U**, the anchored finite verb axis be **A**, and the infinitive construct axis be **I**. The raw and normalized data then are as follows:

Counts		
	שמד	רעע
U	26	30
A	16	6
I	26	10

Decimal Fractions		
	שמד	רעע
U	.3824	.6522
A	.2352	.1304
I	.3824	.2174

When we plot these data in a unit cube sample space, the result looks like this:

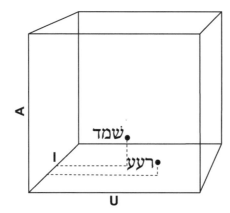

To compute a distance between the points, one typically[3] uses the Pythagorean theorem:

$$d^2 = (\mathbf{U}_{\text{שמד}} - \mathbf{U}_{\text{רעע}})^2 + (\mathbf{A}_{\text{שמד}} - \mathbf{A}_{\text{רעע}})^2 + (\mathbf{I}_{\text{שמד}} - \mathbf{I}_{\text{רעע}})^2$$

Given a large set of roots, one could compute all the inter-root distances and thereby make a distance table of the sort found on most maps. These could then be used to construct an underlying map showing the relative locations of the various roots in "CIC incidence space."

The foregoing yields an estimate of the distance between root/*binyan* incidence proportions, but it fails to take into account a critical constraint met by the data. The predicator incidences are *compositional*. That is, they are constrained to add up to unity:

$$\mathbf{U} + \mathbf{A} + \mathbf{I} = 1$$

The unit-cube sample space does not take this fact into account. Because of this, the distances that result are distorted.

---

2. This unit cube, wherein we plot a data point for each root/*binyan* combination, is our problem's *sample space*.

3. Many other distance metrics are available. For a discussion of the various options, see K. Fukunaga, *Introduction to Statistical Pattern Recognition* (2nd ed.; San Diego: Academic Press, 1990) 441–507.

There are several ways to take the compositionality constraint into account.[4] Each involves transforming the sample space in some way or another. We change our sample space so as to take into account the compositionality of our data as follows. Consider the equilateral triangle diagrammed below. Each of the three variables is associated with one vertex. Data points are constrained to lie within or on the triangle. This ensures that the compositional constraint is not violated. Consider a few possible data point positions:

- Any composition consisting of only one ingredient (a one-component mixture) will have its data point at a vertex. For example, clauses for a root occurring only as an unanchored finite verb will have their data point at the **U** vertex (data point ✻ in the sample space).
- If we are representing a two-component mix, then the data point will lie somewhere along the side opposite the vertex corresponding to the missing component (such as data point ♦ for a **U**-lacking 50%-50% mixture of **A** and **I**).
- An equal-parts three-component mixture will have its data point at the centroid of the triangle, one-third up each angle's bisector line (data point ●).

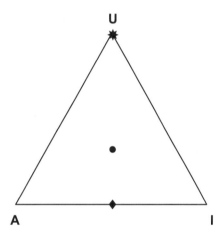

A sample-space triangle such as this is termed a "ternary diagram" or a 3-simplex.[5]

At this point, we encounter a complication not seen until now. For most root/*binyan* combinations, the predicator appears in more than the three forms encountered above. Predicator-incidence data for such root/*binyan* combinations must be plotted in a 4-simplex (also known as a *tetrahedron*), or a 5-simplex, or . . . all the way up to an 8-simplex. The predicators in the standard CIC bar charts provided in chap. 11 (wherein we include only the five most common predicator types overall) require a 5-simplex sample space, which can be embedded in a six-dimensional Euclidean

---

4. For a review of the options, see V. Pawlowsky-Glahn and J. J. Egozcue, "Compositional data and their analysis: An introduction," in *Compositional Data Analysis in the Geosciences: From Theory to Practice* (ed. A. Buccianti et al.; Special Pubs. 264; London: Geological Society, 2006) 1–10. Forbes has used the Bhattacharyya distance in a similar context: A. D. Forbes, "Shards, Strophes, and Stats," in *Fortunate the Eyes That See: Essays in Honor of David Noel Freedman in Celebration of His Seventieth Birthday* (ed. A. B. Beck et al.; Grand Rapids, MI: Eerdmans, 1995) 310–21.

5. A simplex is "a generalized triangle or tetrahedron." Thus, Graham Upton and Ian Cook, *Oxford Dictionary of Statistics* (2nd ed.; Oxford: Oxford University Press, 2006) 393. They go on to provide a mathematically rigorous definition.

space. Fortunately, although we lose the ability to visualize the data when we escalate the dimensionality of the sample-space simplex, the basic mathematics remains the same.

A5.2.2 The Closure Operation

But, wait, there's more! The non-predicator CICs are not compositional, but they are all constrained to lie between zero and one. In our standard bar charts, we display five compositional predicator incidences plus eight always-displayed non-predicator, non-compositional CIC incidences. There is a simple way to convert these mixed data into compositional data—the closure operation: "A vector **w** with positive coordinates is made compositional by the closure operation, which means dividing each coordinate by their sum: $\mathbf{p} = \text{clo}(\mathbf{w}) = \mathbf{w} / \Sigma\ w_i$."[6] This is a trivial operation to carry out.

A5.2.3 The Aitchison Distance Metric

A simplical space is not a Euclidean space, so a new distance metric is required. Martín-Fernández et al. have examined 11 distance metrics and concluded that only 2 meet the requirements for proper statistical analysis in the simplex: the Aitchison metric and the Mahalanobis metric.[7] For the hierarchical clustering we touch on in A5.2.5, they prefer the Aitchison metric.

If $\mathbf{x}_i = \{x_{i1}, x_{i2}, \ldots, x_{iD}\}$ is the compositional vector associated with root i,[8] then the metric is:

$$d_{ij} = \left[\sum_{k=1}^{D} \left(\log\left(\frac{x_{ik}}{g(\mathbf{x}_i)} \right) - \log\left(\frac{x_{jk}}{g(\mathbf{x}_j)} \right) \right)^2 \right]^{1/2}$$

where i and j range over the candidate root pairs and where the geometric mean is:

$$g(\mathbf{x}_i) = \left(\prod_{k=1}^{D} x_{ik} \right)^{1/D}$$

A5.2.4 Sampling Zeros and Structural Zeros

Examination of the definitions of the Aitchison distance and of the geometric mean immediately discloses a potential problem: if any x_{ik} is zero, then the formula yields an indeterminate result. This is because the indeterminate $\log\left(\frac{0}{0}\right)$ then occurs in the definition of the Aitchison distance. Where statistical sampling is involved, zeros are of two sorts: *sampling* zeros and *structural* zeros (or, *essential* zeros).[9] An observed CIC incidence of zero may be the result of having too few clauses in one's sample (yielding a sampling zero), or it may be because occurrence of the particular CIC is impossible with the root/*binyan* combination under consideration (a structural zero). Given our

---

6. Monique Graf, "Precision of Compositional Data in a Stratified Two-Stage Cluster Sample: Comparison of the Swiss Earnings Structure Survey 2002 and 2004," *ASA Section on Survey Research Methods* (2006) 3066. See also Juan M. Larrosa, "A Compositional Statistical Analysis of Capital Stock," *Proceedings of CODAWORK 2003*, section 3.

7. J. A. Martín-Fernández et al., "Measures of Difference for Compositional Data and Hierarchical Clustering Methods," *Proceedings of the International Association of Mathematical Geosciences* (1998).

8. That is, $x_{i1} + x_{i2} + \ldots + x_{iD} = 1$.

9. Alan Agresti, *Categorical Data Analysis* (2nd ed.; Hoboken, NJ: Wiley-Interscience, 2002) 392.

present knowledge of CIC incidence and given the fact that our text is relatively small, we hesitate to declare any observed zero to be structural.[10] This is just as well, since the handling of structural zeros is an active topic of research in the compositional analysis community.[11]

We do encounter sampling zeros. Suppose that we were to search Genesis–Numbers for instances of a subject complement appearing with the verb נתן 'to give'. We would find none and thus would correctly enter zero as the incidence of subject complements in a bar chart for נתן based on the incidences found in the first four books. Sampling the whole of Biblical Hebrew, however, would reveal eight instances of this CIC, yielding an overall incidence of 0.398%. Now, "0.00000" is close to "0.00398." Were it not for the singular behavior produced by the presence of the zero incidence, we could retain it. But the singular behavior is computationally catastrophic, so we must adjust sampling zeros when they are encountered.

There is a principled way of removing sampling zeros, the so-called *multiplicative replacement*.[12] The original measurements, x_j, are replaced by corrected values, r_j, specified by this formula:

$$ r_j = \begin{cases} \delta_j, & \text{if } x_j = 0 \\ x_j \left(1 - \sum_{k|x_k=0} \delta_k\right), & \text{if } x_j > 0 \end{cases} $$

where δ_j is a small "imputed value," typically 0.001 or 0.0005.

A5.2.5 Clusters and Dendrograms

Given M transformed *vectors* of measurements for the M root/*binyan* combinations that one wants to compare—call them r_m, $m = 1, 2, \ldots, M$—one uses the definition of the Aitchison distance to form an MxM array of distances. Once these have been estimated, one may form similarity groups by following, for example:

- a projective geometric path, or
- an agglomerative hierarchical clustering path.

We have discussed these options at length elsewhere.[13] Suffice it for present purposes to observe that the geometrical approach uses the distance matrix to infer a map showing the relative positions of the root/*binyan* combinations. The hierarchical approach uses the distance matrix to infer a tree ("dendrogram") having the root/*binyan* combinations as leaves, with the most similar items closest to each other on this tree. For this book, we rely exclusively on hierarchical clustering. Several classification trees are provided in chap. 17, along with explanations of their significance.

---

10. An example may be helpful. It seems natural to assert that the verb of motion יצא 'to go out' never takes a marked direct object so that the bar chart for יצא would have a structural zero in the direct object position. However, we find five marked direct objects: Gen 44:4; Exod 9:29, 33; Num 35:26; Qoh 7:18.

11. See, for example, J. Aitchison and J. W. Kay, "Possible Solutions to Some Essential Zero Problems in Compositional Data Analysis," CODAWORK 2003.

12. J. A. Martín-Fernández et al., "Zero Replacement in Compositional Data Sets," in *Studies in Classification, Data Analysis and Knowledge Organisation* (ed. H. Kries et al.; Berlin: Springer, 2000) 155–60.

13. See chap. 8 ("Choice of Statistical Methods") of D. N. Freedman, A. D. Forbes, and F. I. Andersen, *Studies in Hebrew and Aramaic Orthography* (Biblical and Judaic Studies from UCSD 3; Winona Lake, IN: Eisenbrauns, 1992) 93–110.

A5.3 *Practicalities*

We make use of two free resources for doing hierarchical clustering with compositional data:

1. SIMCluster (http://xerad.systemsbiology.net/simcluster)[14]

   - *Stand alone.* Supposedly, one may download the package and install it under Linux. We were able to compile but unable to load the software under Fedora FC7.
   - *Web interface.* One may upload data matrices and have dendrograms produced for downloading and printing. This was easy to figure out and use, but it produced idiosyncratic PostScript® diagrams requiring a bit of cleaning up.

2. Compositions (http://www.stat.boogaart.de/compositions)

   - One uses this library of procedures with the public domain R statistics package.
   - One must first download and install the R statistics package from the Comprehensive R Archive Network (http://www.r-project.org). Packages are available for Linux, MacOS, and Windows. Many good books explaining it are available.
   - Then one goes to the Boogaart site, the URL of which is given above. Installation and use is straightforward, although the documentation has some unfortunate errors.

---

14. This suite of procedures is designed for use in the analysis of gene expression data.

Appendix 6

Two-CIC VLCs as Novel Sentences

Traditional definitions restrict the tripartite verbless clauses to a being a VLC with two nominals and one pronoun. Joüon / Muraoka give this more-inclusive specification:

> The nominal clause of the standard type . . . is a clause with two members: subject and predicate. In Hebrew, as in other Semitic languages, it may become a three-member clause with the addition of a third constituent which can be I) the pronoun of the third person . . . ; II) the demonstrative pronoun for near deixis . . . ; III) the adverbs of existence יֵשׁ and אַיִן . . . ; IV) the verb הָיָה.[15]

We see these matters somewhat differently. In our taxonomy, יֵשׁ and אַיִן are quasiverbals. Clauses containing them were discussed in their own right in chap. 18. Further, we have treated the verb form הָיָה as the predicator in an atypical kind of verbal clause. See chap. 13.

We have adopted a novel representation for certain three-CIC VLC pairs. The middle constituent is shared between the two clauses. It is the *subject complement* of the first clause and the *subject* of the second clause and is called by us the Janus subject complement-subject. Phrase marker (A6.1) shows 1 Chr 6:2 analyzed along these lines.

(A6.1)

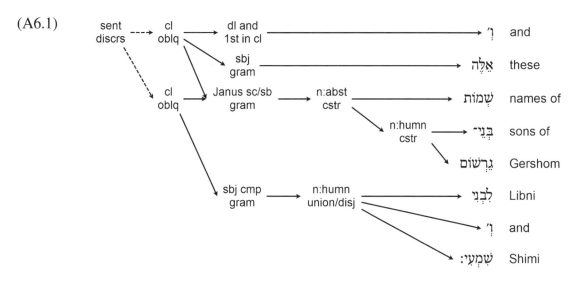

---

15. Joüon, P., / Muraoka, T., *Grammar of Biblical Hebrew,* 538. Williams, *Hebrew Syntax,* 50, takes a similar approach. Van der Merwe et al., *A Reference Grammar,* 252, refer to the use of a 3rd pers. sing. masc. pronoun "between the subject and predicate of a nominal clause with three constituents."

Appendix 7

Enhancements to Our Database

This appendix is a catch-all for three topics that merit brief exposition but do not fit in well elsewhere in the book: our glosses, source ascription, and text-type assignment.

A7.1 *Our Glosses*

Recall that the text segments heading a dictionary entry are termed *types*, while the segments found in texts are "tokens" of these types. As a rule, translators are comfortable if a given text type has multiple translations, each depending on the context in which a token appears. As a rule, lexicographers prefer to recognize as few senses of a given form as possible. Consider the many substantive forms of יָפֶה. The NIV gives nine token glosses for these: 'beautiful', 'handsome', 'lovely', 'fair', 'sleek', 'handsome appearance', 'proper', 'fine', and 'well built'.[1] BDB has four glosses: 'fair', 'beautiful', 'fair one', and 'beauty of'.[2] HALOT has two: 'beautiful' and 'right'.[3] We provide two glosses: 'handsome' and 'handsome of'. Our type glosses are often closer to the Hebrew text than are many translations. For example, in Gen 39:6, for יְפֵה־תֹאַר וִיפֵה מַרְאֶה our glosses read 'handsome of form and handsome of vision' while the NIV reads 'well-built and handsome' and the RSV has 'handsome and good-looking'.

There are places where our glosses are jarring. If we judge the oddity unacceptable, we dissect the involved lexeme and provide better glosses. The parade lexeme for these sorts of situation might be conjunctive כִּי which, until recently, was always glossed by 'because'. This led us to some unsettling and quite misleading gloss texts. For example, in Gen 3:6, וַתֵּרֶא הָאִשָּׁה כִּי טוֹב הָעֵץ לְמַאֲכָל was glossed 'and she saw the woman *because* good the tree to food'. We undertook the resolving of the original lexeme into six distinct lexemes, each assigned its own gloss: 'because', 'but', 'that', 'although', 'when', and 'if'.[4] As a result, we now gloss the clause in Gen 3:6 as 'and she saw the woman *that* good the tree to food'. Readers are alerted, however, that inadequately divided lexemes still exist. The authors will appreciate being alerted to truly unacceptable glosses.

A7.2 *Source Ascription*

A7.2.1 Our Proffered Sources Are the Sources of Eissfeldt

Regarding source ascriptions for the Hebrew Bible, scholars are positioned along a pronounced gradient. At one end are those who have made a bogey out of Wellhausen. Often, they do not real-

---

1. Edward W. Goodrick, John R. Kohlenberger III, and James A. Swanson, *Zondervan NIV Exhaustive Concordance* (Grand Rapids, MI: Zondervan, 1999) 1418, entry 3637.
2. BDB, 421.2.
3. *HALOT*, 423.
4. In the process, we also recognized one new adverbial lexeme and one new modal lexeme (both glossed 'surely').

ize that he stood in a long line of scholars, going back to the earliest stages of the Jewish-Christian debates, through the medieval rabbis, the Renaissance, the Reformation, and the Enlightenment. At the other end of the gradient are those who claim that the matter of source ascription is passé, and serious scholars do not bother discussing it any more. We find ourselves more in the middle. The problems are still with us, pressing as ever, and still resistant to solution.[5]

We take Eissfeldt as our authority for the hextateuchal sources. Why Eissfeldt? Many great scholars have tried their hand at parceling the Torah into sources. Wellhausen's work was the watershed, and modern research seldom goes behind it to the research of his predecessors. Since Wellhausen, many have tried their hand at refining his results, introducing a lot of confusion and disagreement that has given rise to glee among scholars who claim that the failure of critical scholarship proves that Moses wrote the Torah after all!

There have been two broad trends in analysis. One group of analysts used fine details and small differences to identify more and more sources (or redactors), such as the several "Priestly" authors, or the recognition of another source within J, Pfeiffer's Edomite source, or Eissfeldt's Lay source. This kind of splitting reached its extreme in Noth's work. Some small sections were hard to connect with the main "sources" and thus were isolated as "sources behind the sources" that preserved some of their original distinctiveness (the oracles of Balaam and other old poems).

Others looked at the affinities that made it hard to separate even J from E, represented by Rudolph's work on the Joseph story, even to the elimination of E altogether, seeing J and E as derivations from the same *Grundschrift*. The "source" we call "K" embodies Eissfeldt's indecision about whether its genealogies are L, J, or E.

Our claims are modest. People who do not like JEDP or Eissfeldt do not need to use our source data. It is there for people who might wish to continue to investigate the unsolved problems. By choosing Eissfeldt, we struck a good balance. He remains in the mainstream. Combine his L and his J, and we are still close to Wellhausen. And so on.

A7.2.2   The Hexateuchal Sources according to Eissfeldt

The specifications shown in the table at the top of p. 356 have been extracted from Otto Eissfeldt's *Hexateuch-Synopse*.[6] We have isolated some (ancient?) poems. For example, the Song of Moses (Exodus 15) is given to source "L (poetry)," and the Song and Blessing of Moses (Deut 32:1–43) is given to source "E (poetry)." Eissfeldt considers K (Gen 36:2–3, 10–39) to be a mishmash of L, J, and E. While Eissfeldt takes H = the Holiness Code (Leviticus 17–26) to be distinct from the other sources, Richard Friedman calls it P, except for Lev 23:39–43 and 26:39–45, which he assigns to redactors.[7]

To recover the major sources, one may merge the smaller subsources as follows:

---

5. Consider a problem presented in F. I. Andersen and A. D. Forbes, *Spelling in the Hebrew Bible* (Rome: Pontifical Biblical Institute, 1986) 189–91. There, suffixed forms of the object marker (אות/-את-, etc.) in the P source exhibit odd spellings when compared with the other sources (L, J, E+C, D, and H). Moving from least to most *defective*, the sequence of sources is: D, H, E+C, J, P, L. It must be noted that the sample sizes involved are fairly small, so that one should not infer too much from this sequence.

6. Otto Eissfeldt, *Hexateuch-Synopse* (2nd ed.; Darmstadt: Wissenschaftliche Buchgesellschaft, 1962).

7. Richard E. Friedman, *The Bible with Sources Revealed* (San Francisco: HarperSanFrancisco, 2003) 218–38.

Our Code	Our Designation ("Sources")	Locations
Scattered Sources		
L	Lay	passim
J	Jahwist	passim
E	Elohist	passim
P	Priestly	passim
Block Sources		
D	Deuteronomist	Deut 1–30
B	"Begegnung"	Gen 14
C	Covenant Code	Exod 20:22–23:19
H	Holiness Code	Lev 17–26
K	K genealogy	Gen 36:2–3, 10–39
T	Tabernacle Code	Exod 25:1–31:11; 35:4–40:38

L = L (prose) + L (poetry)
J = J (prose) + J (poetry) + K genealogy
E = E (prose) + E (poetry) + Covenant Code
D = Deuteronomist
H = Holiness Code
P = P (prose) + P (poetry) + B (prose) + B (poetry) + Tabernacle Code

Others may prefer different combinations.

A7.3 *Text Types*

A7.3.1 We-a culpa

It must be candidly admitted that this aspect of our work was poorly formulated, only partially implemented, and imperfectly so at that. We debated whether to include it in our public offering. In the event, we decided that it might be useful to some in spite of its severe limitations. Our work on text types was rather makeshift, not based on good definitions of "text types." Be warned!

A7.3.2 Backgrounds of Our Terminology

In hindsight it seems that a number of our interests became muddled together, with at least six connotations or backgrounds for the term *text type*. These are:

1. There is what the Europeans and Robert Longacre call "text types." The Europeans have basically two types: narrative and discourse. For some, "discourse" is reported direct speech (this is Heller's position), but some (Niccacci) include in discourse non-narrative comments in the story line. At latest count, Longacre has about nine types, some with subtypes. His types tend to be literary.
2. We are not aware of any systematic classification of literary types that might include story types: myth, legend, epic, saga, history, biography, parable, or fable. There are very few of these sorts of categories in our markup.

3. Of a more linguistic flavor is the difference between prose and poetry. We have not set things up for separating poetry from prose, except for a few labels on (archaic) poems in the Primary History. A great quantity of prose is found in "narrative," the most populous text type. Most of the poetry, though not labeled as such, can be accessed in the poetry books: Psalms (minus titles, which are labeled), Job (minus the narrative that carries the speeches, which are all poetry), Proverbs, Lamentation, and the Song of Songs.

4. There is a little bit of speech-act theory in some of our text types, such as greeting, request, instruction, and supplication. But we have not singled out *interrogation* as a text type. At least interrogative clauses can be found by the presence of interrogatives in them. We have not worked out the sociolinguistic aspects of speech-act theory by introducing the dimension of *register*. It may be expected that the texts for use in the cult (mainly Psalms) are in the high style, but it has not been shown as far as we know that there is a distinct *Hofstyl* (linguistically speaking) for use with royalty (human or divine). There could be a vernacular register in the dialogue of ordinary people in popular stories. But there could be fancy talk even by peasants as a literary artifice (Ruth). As far as protocol and etiquette are concerned, there may have been conventions to mark social distance (perceived or affected). All verbal interactions might be roughly classified as: (1) superior to inferior; (2) equal to equal; (3) inferior to superior. This would be useful. It would need a new dimension. The only move we have made in this direction is to distinguish the voice of the narrator: divine speakers, human speakers, and preternatural beings (angels, talking animals).

5. The numerous text types we now have in place reflect Andersen's background with regard to *Gattungsforschung*. This enterprise is in disarray, moribund, or even defunct. There never was a canonical list of agreed text types for the Hebrew Bible, with definitions and diagnostics. Even among the text types used by most of the best practitioners, there was much disagreement over the identification of distinct pieces and their classification.

6. Students of Biblical Hebrew may associate "text type" with form criticism (we have a few terms from that enterprise) and complain that our treatment of this system is very amateurish. "Text types" is relatively new. Even so, the term has been around long enough to be used differently by different schools of "text linguistics." It is still sufficiently generic to serve our needs. But there is certainly no canonical meaning for it.

A7.3.3 Final Observations on Text Types

Under the best circumstances, there may be, say, 10% of some text type, such as "blessing," that we have misclassified, whether by mistake or indeterminacy. As a result, the present tally of "blessings" may be 10% short. And the 90% may include some strays. Even so, the 80% of true blessings in the crop should be enough to show up any distinctive / contrastive syntax in "blessings." This may be too sanguine. With "divine oracle" more likely to be a generic default, it may contain half the divine blessings in Biblical Hebrew. Even so, the half that we have correctly identified may be enough for a study.

Finding out how things stand with divine oracles may involve more work than it is worth. There are 12,059 clauses (or, "occurrences"), and it would be a gigantic job to make sure they are all spoken by God, to identify pieces that are clearly text types of a more particular kind (such as "divine accusation"), and to relabel them. No matter. We suspect that, while the criteria for *Gattungen* are primarily social-functional, the differences are more likely to be in vocabulary (content, topics, characteristic of certain text types) than in syntax. If some test studies of the text types we now have located on squishes show that their syntax is not really on a gradient but that they are pretty homogeneous syntactically, this will certainly be an interesting, albeit somewhat negative, result. We can then collapse them, and even collapse them all as "Divine oracle," giving us a block of material more likely to produce robust statistics.

As far as we are aware, nobody else has done anything like this, especially in the dimensions provided by the variables narrative / discourse; divine / human speaker; divine / human addressee; and about 17 text types in the more technical sense (five squishes). The possibilities for combinations and collapsing are all that we could possibly wish to have, especially when we add the choice of "source" (whether Eissfeldt's, text portions, or entire books). They supply a huge number of options. It would be interesting to see if correlation studies of the syntax of Biblical Hebrew, cut in all kinds of ways, come up with affinity trees that make intuitive sense. The heterogeneity of Biblical Hebrew syntax (on a diapason of homogeneous syntax provided by the syntax in which all portions are the same) is not likely to fall neatly on the prose-particle cline.

Glossary

A

accompanier — A participant who shares in the activity of the subject.

active — In active voice, the actor is the subject of the verb, and the undergoer is the object.

adjective — A segment that specifies an attribute of a noun or may function as a noun itself.

adjunct — An optional or peripheral clause immediate constituent; often an adjunct is an adverb or prepositional phrase.

adverb — A segment that functions primarily to modify a verbal construction or secondarily to modify an adjective, etc.

adverbial —A clause constituent that functions like an adverb.

affix — Typically, a prefix or a suffix.

agential — Refers to the doer of an action when the verb is passive.

aim / purpose — A constituent that discloses an intended goal.

all — Refers to the Hebrew segment כֹּל.

also (גם) — When functioning within a clause, this distributionally complex segment expresses inclusion of some number of following constituents.

alternate / surrogate — Refers to a replacement for a person or thing.

†amplifier — An infinitive absolute used to augment a noncognate verb (that usually follows).

apposition — Licenses a construction in which two constituents involve an identical reference. We apply this relation to prepositional phrases as well as nominal phrases. Example: "in Jerusalem, in the city of David" is licensed as an apposition.

Aramaic *binyanim* — The following stem forms are peculiar to Aramaic: Aramaic uses the prefixes א, שׁ, and ת in place of Hebrew ה in *itpeal*, *afal*, *shafal*, and *tafal*.

area — 2 dimensions: "ten cubits by ten cubits"

aspect — The way a verb portrays the temporal structure of an event.

†aspectualizer — An infinitive absolute used to specify the temporal structure of an event.

*attaches higher — A node of out-degree zero, positioned to alert users to the fact that a syntactic edge has been omitted, typically because the dependence is too long-range to represent conveniently.

B

basic phrase — A group of two or more segments joined together at a single node on the basis of a single licensing relation.

beneficiary — Refers to the recipient of a beneficial action.

binyan — A distinct form of a Hebrew verb stem.

Authors' note: In this glossary, an entry marked with an asterisk (*) is interim terminology, representing the current state of the work in progress; it is therefore subject to change. An entry marked with an obelisk (†) defines a concept that has not yet been systematically applied.

bonded correlation — Licenses constructions of the form "not X, but Y."

bound — Refers to pronominal suffixes.

but-rather — A construction in which something is negated and a preference replaces it.

C

cardinal numeral — A segment that expresses the size of a set (*one*, *two*, etc.).

cause — That which brings about an event.

city — Identifies a specific city, town, or village.

clause — Typically, a syntactic unit that includes a predicator and the clause immediate constituents that accompany it. Biblical Hebrew also evidences clauses having no predicator ("verbless" or "nominal" clauses).

clause immediate constituent (CIC) — An immediate constituent of a clause. For example, the grammatical subject of a clause is a CIC. We distinguish 14 sorts of CIC: predicators, aspectualizers, subjects, objects, complements, other participants, movement, space, time, scoping operators, enriching information, phrasal "discourse units", syntactic isolates, and impermanents.

closed interrogative — An interrogative that allows only a yes or no response.

cognitive complement — An indirect report of a thought or speech that (1) completes a verb of cognition / utterance or (2) is part of a question. Examples: (1) "Jeremiah proclaimed that *Israel was doomed*." (2) "Who is David that *we should serve him*?"

cohortative — A first-person expression of a strong intention (*let us, I will*).

"cohortative" sequential — A cohortative verb form with a consecutive ו; the same in function as *wayyiqṭōl*.

collective — The number category that refers to a class or group consisting of individual members (e.g., flock, herd).

common gender — Gender that is either masculine or feminine in an individual occurrence or is indeterminate.

common noun — A noun that is the name common to all members of a group or class of nouns (e.g., a prophet) as opposed to a proper noun that names specific member(s) of this group (Isaiah).

comparison — A clause immediate constituent that indicates that something is like something else.

complement — A constituent that is traditionally viewed as *completing* the action specified by a verb. We also recognize complements of objects / subjects and complements within certain questions.

complement of aspectualizing verb — An infinitival construction that completes an aspectualizing verb. Example: "He added to speak" (= "He spoke again").

complex phrase — A phrase containing two or more nodes, each specifying a licensing relation. Example: "sound of the horn, pipe, zither, lyre, . . . " (Dan 3:7).

†**compound cue phrase** — Two or more immediately adjacent cue phrases that function as a unit. Adjacent cue phrases are not necessarily compound, since they may be operating at differing levels.

concessive — A constituent that concedes something, typically with "although" as a cue phrase.

†**condition** — A discourse unit that is a protasis ("the condition"). Example: "If the Lord be for us. . . ."

conjoined phrases — Created by joining basic phrases and / or segments by juxtaposition, union, or disjunction.

conjunction — A segment that connects segments or constructions.

consecutive ו — A conjunction that combines with an attached finite verb to indicate temporal sequence.

constituent — A linguistic unit in a clause, not itself a clause, that typically combines with other constituents to form a larger construction.

construct — A noun in the construct state governs a following noun, noun phrase, or nominalized constituent. Traditionally said to express a *genitive relation*, as in "house of David" = "David's house."

construction — The grammatical structure of a constituent as represented by a set of elements (nodes, in our case) and the relations among them.

construction / constituent identifier — The first part of a node label identifies the structure immediately dominated by the node. There are two basic kinds of construction / constituent identifiers in our phrase markers. One identifies the major syntactic functions. The other identifies the constituents to the right of the clause immediate constituents.

coordinating conjunction — A conjunction that joins two constituents that are usually of the same grammatical status. The most common coordinating conjunction is וֹ.

cophenetic correlation coefficient (CCC) — A statistical measure showing the degree to which cluster analyses are representative of relations in the data used to produce them.

cost — A constituent that specifies the value of something.

†cue phrase — A conjunctive segment or phrase (such as because, but, although, if, but indeed) that serves to link discourse units. Also called a *discourse marker*.

†cue phrase absent — Indicates a place in a text where a unit is not "introduced" by a cue phrase.

*cue phrase present — Either licenses the creation of a supra-clausal unit or indicates that a unit is preceded by a cue phrase (there being no possibility of confusing the two situations). This is an interim licensing relation.

D

daughter node — If one node immediately dominates another node, then the second is the daughter of the first.

definite — When a noun (or verbal noun) has a definite article prefix, the noun is definite: "the king."

definite article — A segment that acts as a determiner in order to identify or particularize a substantive.

definiteness — Specifies a particular individual by marking a segment with a prefix in Hebrew (the prefixed definite article) and a suffix in Aramaic (the determined suffix).

definite with ה — A segment that is marked as definite with the consonant prefix ה.

definite without ה — A segment that is marked as definite with only a vowel; that is, without the ה of the definite article.

demonstrative — A pronoun that points to an entity. In the clause "this is the word of the Lord," *this* is a demonstrative pronoun. Referred to as a "demonstrative adjective" when used in apposition with a noun.

deprivation — Removal of something, resulting in a loss.

derived adverb — The suffix ם- added to a noun in order to derive an adverb.

determined — In Aramaic, a segment that is marked as definite with a vowel + א suffix; this suffix has not been split off as a separate segment.

discontinuity — Refers to the splitting of a constituent by the intrusion of another constituent. For example: "From the fruit of the tree . . . ," said God, "you will not eat . . ." (Gen 3:3).

†discourse unit (DU) — A unit of text consisting of a clause or sequences of clauses (or other elementary discourse units). Discourse analysis (also known as text linguistics) seeks to discover and understand the grammatical relations that hold among the discourse units making up a text.

distributed apposition — Licenses the assembly of apposition constructions wherein a later constituent is in apposition to two or more earlier constituents considered *together*. The resulting construction exhibits multidominance and discontinuity. Example: " . . . to X and to Y, the sons of Z."

distributive — The number category that ascribes a property or action to the individual members of a group rather than the group as a whole. This is in contrast to collective number.

distributive indirect object — A singular nominal indirect object that refers separately to each and every member of a plural indirect object. Example: "To them . . . *to each one*."

distributive object — A singular nominal object that refers separately to each and every member of a plural object. Example: "Them . . . *each one*."

distributive subject — A singular nominal subject that refers separately to each and every member of a plural subject. Example: "They . . . *each man*."

divine — Identifies a specific deity.

doer — The entity, usually animate, that performs the action specified in a clause. Also called the *agent* in the literature.

dominance — In our representation, when two nodes in a phrase marker are joined by one or a series of edges, then the node to the left is said to dominate the node to its right.

doubled — The D or "doubling" stem, so called because one of the consonants of the root is doubled.

dual — The number category that refers to entities that come in pairs.

E

echo (repeat) — Refers to exact repetition of some constituent.

edge — An arrowed line pointing from one node to another node in a phrase marker.

elementary discourse unit (EDU) — According to Polanyi, discourse units can be: (1) clauses with any preposed cue phrase included as part of the basic unit; (2) clauses with any pre-posed cue phrase external to the basic unit; (3) certain phrases; (4) certain fragments.

ethnic — A segment that refers to nationality; also referred to as a "gentilic" noun. Example: "Moabite."

exclamative — A constituent that expresses a sudden or strong emotion.

exclusivity condition — Requires that, for any two nodes in a tree, either one dominates the other or one precedes the other.

†**exocentric absolute** — A constituent that is isolated in front of its clause. It has none of the usual syntactic relations with other constituents in its clause.

experiencer — The entity, a cognizer or perceiver, affected by the action or state specified by a clause's predicator.

F

feminine — The usual grammatical gender of the marked form of a singular substantive. Feminine segments refer to the female when there is a distinction made between male and female.

finite verb — Consists of a stem with pronominal affixes that distinguish number, gender, and person.

***first in main clause** — Marks a "first-in-clause" coordinating conjunction that actually functions outside the clause in discourse. These conjunctions will eventually be promoted to the discourse level.

first person — Used when the speaker refers to himself or herself ("I") and associates ("we").

free — A free-standing pronoun.

G

gender — Allocates substantives into classes, such as animate versus inanimate, or biological sex (where appropriate).

grammar determined — The identification of most clause immediate constituents is licensed by the nonspecific relation "grammar determined."

grammatical function ("**grammatical relation**") — The syntactic function of a clause immediate constituent in relation to other constituents in its clause. Examples: subject, predicator, direct object.

graph — A network consisting of nodes and their connecting edges.

Grund ('**ground**') — The simplest verb stem form, that is, an unmodified root. Sometimes called the "G" stem. Traditionally called the Qal stem.

H

harmed one — Refers to the recipient of a harmful action.

hendiadys — Two constituents joined by a conjunction stating a single complicated notion.

Hiphil — A stem with a ה typically prefixed to and modifying the root.

Hithpael — A stem with both doubling and prefixed הת.

homographs — Forms having the same spelling but differing meanings.

Hophal — A verb stem characterized by an H binyan (see Hiphil) and a passive voice.

human — Identifies a specific human being.

I

immediate constituent (IC) — The immediate constituents of a construction are the smaller constituents out of which it is *directly* composed.

imperative — The verb form that expresses a command.

*impermanent — A subtype of clause immediate constituents that has not been or cannot be fully analyzed and dealt with.

in-degree — A characteristic of a node: the number of edges that enter a node.

includer (*also* אף) — When functioning within a clause, this segment expresses *inclusion* of a number of following constituents.

indefinite — A segment that is not marked as definite.

indirect object — The secondary undergoer of the action of the predicator, typically a recipient.

infinitival predicator — An infinitive that acts as a predicator and may have its own immediate constituents such as direct objects, locations, and so on. Example: "God set them . . . [[*inf.* to dominate] [*dir. obj.* the day and the night]]" (Gen 1:17).

infinitive absolute — An uninflected verb form that can function as an intensifier of a cognate verb (Gen 2:16–17: "*eat* you will eat and *die* you will die"), an amplifier of a noncognate verb (Gen 41:49: "grain like sand of the sea, *in very large quantities*"), an aspectualizer of another verb (Gen 8:3: "the waters receded *steadily*"), or a predicator (Deut 5:12: "Observe the Sabbath day").

infinitive construct — A verbal noun that expresses action without respect to time or person.

infinitive of utterance — The infinitive construct of the root אמר 'to say'. Its object (the object of address) reports direct speech.

*initial coordinating ו — A coordinating *waw* that is typically the first constituent in a clause but that actually functions at the supra-clausal level. (Many of these have already been made supra-clausal.)

insistent imperative — A morphological variant of masculine singular imperatives.

instrument — A constituent that specifies a tool or device used to perform an action.

†**intensifier** — An infinitive absolute used to intensify a cognate verb (that usually follows it).

interrogative — A segment that asks a question regarding a constituent.

inverted modification — Licenses a construction in which the second constituent is characterized more precisely by the first. The first constituent adds information about the second. Example: "six cows."

involved ones — Coparticipants in an event specified by 'between X and between Y' or the like. Example: "between me and between the earth" (Gen 9:13).

isolate, syntactic — Entities that are not integrated constituents of clauses, though they may be loosely related to clauses. In our analysis, they are vocatives, exclamatives, or labels.

J

†**Janus subject-complement / subject** — A constituent that functions as the subject complement in the initial part (constituents one and two) of a three-part verbless sentence and as the subject in the terminal part (constituents two and three). See appendix 6.

jussive — An indirect command to another (that is, to the second or third person).

juxtaposition (list of fused items) — Licenses constructions in which successive constituents are not bridged by coordinating conjunctions and yet belong together. Example: "A B C."

L

label — The name of a literary unit in a heading, colophon, or elsewhere.

land — Identifies a specific country.

lapsus calami — An uncorrected corruption of the text.

leaf node — Phrase marker nodes that dominate no other nodes. Leaf nodes are the only permanent nodes having an out-degree of zero (the exceptions are attaches higher nodes and remainder of address nodes).

length — One dimension: "ten cubits."

licensing relation — The grounds according to which a syntactic construction is identified. For example, a construct nominal phrase has a syntactic license of "construct," indicating that the phrase is licensed by the presence of the construct state. We divide our relation identifiers into six subsets: supra-clausals; obliqueness structures; clause immediate constituents; conjoined phrases (semantics): conjoined phrases (form); and basic phrases.

location — Zero dimensions: "in Jerusalem."

locative ה — The suffix ה- added to a noun to indicate the direction or goal of movement.

M

manner — A constituent that specifies the way in which some action takes place.

masculine — The usual grammatical gender of the unmarked form of a singular substantive. Masculine segments refer to the male when there is a distinction made between male and female.

†**material** — A constituent that specifies what something is made of or from which it is constructed.

middle — In middle voice, the actor is both the subject and object of the verb.

miscellany — A miscellaneous set of parts of speech: exclamative, definite article, or nominalizer.

mixed-level constituents — Many of these constituents have already been appropriately promoted to discourse level, but some remain in clauses. These constituents represent work in progress.

mixed list — Licenses constructions in which some coordinating conjunctions are absent. Example: "A B and C."

modal — A segment or idiom that expresses the speaker's (un)certainty or desire with regard to a statement.

modification — Licenses a construction in which the first constituent is characterized more precisely by the second. The second constituent adds information. Example: "the water under the earth."

mood ("**modality**") — Mood feature(s) signal(s) the degree of confidence a speaker has in his / her statements.

morphology — The analysis of the structure of words / segments.

mother node — If one node immediately dominates another node, then the first is the mother of the second.

mountain — Identifies a specific mountain or mountainous region.

movement aim (target) — Destination: "to Jerusalem."

movement bearing / direction — Orientation: "toward Jerusalem."

movement interval — Movement path: "from Jerusalem to Beth El."

movement origin — Movement starting point: "from Jerusalem."

multidominance — Refers to situations in which the in-degree of a node is greater than one. The multidominated node has more then one mother. For example, in "And there was evening, and there was morning . . . day one," *day one* is multidominated.

N

nebulous — A constituent the meaning and / or significance of which is unclear. The parade example is סֶלָה, as in Ps 55:20.

negative — A segment that negates a constituent. Included are: 'do not' (אַל), [negation] (בְּלִי), and 'not' (לֹא).

†**nested constituents** — Licenses constructions in which successive constituents are nested but are neither in subset nor superset order. Example: "in the second month, on the first day, in the third year."

Niphal — A stem with a נ typically prefixed to and modifying the root.

node — Any point in a phrase marker from which one or more edges leave and / or one or more edges enter. Each of the nodes in our phrase markers holds a node label.

node label — The labels on nodes, other than the nodes that hold the text segments, are bipartite. Each consists of a construction / constituent identifier and a relation identifier.

node names — Five terms make talking about phrase marker nodes easier: root, leaf, mother, sister, and daughter.

nominalization — Licenses the recategorization of some non-nominal constituent into a nominal constituent.

nominalizer — A segment (usually אֲשֶׁר) that enables the following constituent to function as a noun.

nonadjacent construct — A construct noun that is not followed immediately by the noun that it governs. Also referred to by us as "discontinuous construct." For an example, see Hos 14:3: "all . . . iniquity."

normal — A noun that is not marked as construct, suffixed, or pausal.

noun — A segment with a paradigmatic form that includes a suffix (which may be zero) that specifies number and gender. Traditionally, a noun is a word that is the name of a person, place, thing, or quality. Types of nouns include: (1) common noun: a noun that represents a general category of persons, places, things, or qualities (man, house, throne); (2) proper noun: the name of a specific person(s) (Abraham), or place(s) (Egypt), and so on.

noun-verb / noun participle — A participle with noun functions in respect to both the previous and the following context and also verb functions in respect to the following context.

noun-verb participle — A participle with noun functions in respect to the previous context and with verb functions in respect to the following context.

number — The category that distinguishes references to a single entity from references to multiple entities.

number count — A constituent that answers "how many?"

number of times — A constituent that answers "how many times?"

O

object (general or direct) — That which is affected by the event specified by the predicator of a clause—traditionally, the "undergoer" of the action of the predicator. In Biblical Hebrew, the direct object is often marked by the object marker.

object complement — A nominal that completes the direct object. Example: "They made David *king*."

object marker — The segment אֵת, which typically marks a direct object.

object of address — In our representation, a direct speech that is the object of a verb of utterance.

obliqueness — The licensing relation whereby clauses are built up from clause immediate constituents exploiting the obliqueness principle. All clauses and clause-like structures are licensed by this relation.

obliqueness principle — This abstract principle specifies how clauses and clause-like structures are organized and assembled in a given language.

obliqueness structures — We recognize three kinds of obliqueness structures: (1) the clause and clause-embedded structures with predicators that are (2) infinitives or (3) participles.

open interrogative — Constituents that ask questions the possible answers to which are open—in other words, they allow many possible answers beyond the simple "yes" or "no" answers elicited by closed interrogative questions.

ordinal numeral — A segment that expresses rank order (first, second, etc.).

other geographic — Identifies a specific geographical location that is not a land, mountain, city, or river. Example: Eden.

out-degree — A characteristic of a node: the number of edges that leave a node.

P

†paradoxical discourse relation — Licenses structures in which clausal and supra-clausal units paradoxically function *within* clauses.

participial predicator — A participle that acts as a predicator with its own immediate constituents such as direct objects, locations, and so on. Example: "Joseph, the son of seventeen years, [[part. shepherding] [accmp. with his brothers][location in the flock]]" (Gen 37:2).

participle — A segment that has both nominal and verbal characteristics. It belongs to the same number / gender paradigm as nouns do. It is part of a verb system through a common root and binyan.

particle — One of various classes of uninflected segments that generally do not fall easily under the traditional parts of speech. Pronouns are inappropriately called particles. Prepositions and conjunctions are the familiar particles; in addition, there are many other segments with specific syntactic functions. In general, we avoid this nonspecific term.

part(s) of speech — The grammatical classes or grammatical categories of segments. Defined in five ways: ostensive (by listing); semantic (on the basis of "meaning"); paradigmatic (variations in form); derivational (how affixes convert them from other segments); and distributional (the positions in which they occur). Our definitions are mostly ostensive or paradigmatic.

passive — In passive voice, the undergoer is the subject of the verb and the actor is the agent.

patient — The semantic role specifying the entity undergoing an action.

pausal — A segment that receives additional stress at a text break (a place in the text where a reader pauses for longer than in other places), receiving a longer (pausal) vowel in the stressed syllable.

person — Indicates the role of the participant(s) in a situation.

phrasal "discourse unit" — A phrase *within* a clause that acts as a constituent of a discourse.

phrase —A linguistic unit in a clause that is not itself a clause. Equivalent to a constituent.

phrase marker — A two-dimensional diagram that displays the internal hierarchical structure (dominance) and sequential structure (precedence) of a clause and its constituents. Our phrase markers consist of labeled nodes and their connecting edges.

Piel — The D or doubled stem in active voice.

plural — The number category that refers to more than one entity.

possessor — Refers to a participant as the owner of something.

pre-position — Licenses the assembly of prepositional phrases.

precedence — In our representation, when one node occurs above another in the phrase marker, the first node is said to precede the second node. For example, the segments making up a text occur in precedence order, which matches their physical sequence in the text.

predicate — The non-subject part of a clause.

predicative infinitive absolute — An uninflected verb form that functions as a predicator (Deut 5:12: "Observe the Sabbath day").

predicator — A verbal or quasiverbal constituent that specifies equivalence, activity, state, or process.

prefixed (imperfect) — A verb with a prefixed pronoun subject. Traditionally called an "imperfect" or *yiqtōl*.

prefixed (preterite) — A form of the verb that expresses a simple past tense without aspect.

prefixed sequential — A verb with a prefixed pronoun subject and a consecutive ן. Traditionally called an "imperfect sequential" or *wayyiqtōl*.

preposition — A set of segments that generally precede substantives in order to form constructions. We define prepositions ostensively, that is, by listing them. Our list of prepositions strives to be minimal, containing as few segments as possible.

pronoun — A segment that takes the place of a noun phrase. A pronoun typically refers to a nominal phrase that occurs elsewhere in the text.

proper noun — A noun that names specific individual(s) or entity / entities (Egypt, Amos).

Pual — The D or doubled stem in passive voice.

pure noun participle — A participle with no verbal function.

pure verb participle — A participle with no nominal function.

Q

Qal — The simplest verb stem form, that is, an unmodified root (see Grund).

Qal passive — The verb stem characterized by a Grund binyan and a passive voice.

quantity / quantifier — A constituent that answers "how much?"

quasiverbal — A segment that does not have verb morphology, but functions as a predicator. Included are: 'behold!' (הִנֵּה), 'exists' (יֵשׁ), 'still' (עוֹד), 'not-exists' (אֵין) and, strictly speaking, 'where?' (אַיֵּה).

quoter — A constituent in which a quotation is the object of address of an infinitive of utterance.

R

reason — A constituent that provides the rationale for some event.

reference — A default generic constituent used when no other CIC class seems appropriate.

reflexive — In reflexive voice, the undergoer is the actor, with emphasis on the fact that the actor is acting on itself.

relation identifier — The second part of the node label specifies the grammatical relation that licenses the formation of the structure.

*remainder of address — A node of out-degree zero which signals the fact that the remainder of an address has not been embedded with its initial portion in an object of address or subject of address.

resource — A constituent that specifies a source of supply. Example: "from the sons of Benjamin."

restricter (רַק 'only' and many instances of אַךְ) — When functioning within a clause, these segments express *restriction* of a number of the following constituents.

result — A constituent that discloses an outcome without commenting on its desirability.

resumption — Identifies a feature of a text (or construction) within a clause in which a constituent reactivates the referential content of an earlier suspended constituent. For example, "[susp. in the grave] where Abraham buried Sarah—you will bury me [resum. there]" (see also suspension).

river — Identifies a specific river.

root node — The phrase marker node that dominates all other nodes. The root node is the only node having an in-degree of zero.

ruled-over one — Refers to a participant as subject to some authority (typically, a monarch).

S

scoping operator — A segment that operates upon selected constituents or all of the constituents in a clause. Ambiguity of scoping is not uncommon. Examples: ". . . *all of* [the men and the women]," "do *not* [eat and drink]," "*who* [will come and will sit]?"

second object (of two) — The second of two direct objects. Example: "Moses made-wear Aaron the ephod."

second person — Used when the speaker refers to the person(s) being addressed (you, you all).

segment — A word, part of a word, or sequence of words that is an ultimate constituent in our syntactic analysis. For example, dissecting a prefixed preposition and a pronoun suffix off a word yields three segments (e.g., in + house + his). A proper noun may be "ligatured" to form a multiple-word segment. For example, the two-word sequence 'Beth El' forms a single segment, while the two-word sequence 'from-Beth El' forms two segments: 'from' and 'Beth El'.

semantic role — The semantic relation exhibited by a participant in a clause. For example, in "Gorgou smote the wee gozingpol," "Gorgou" has the semantic role of doer and "the wee gozingpol" has the semantic role of patient.

semantics — The study of the *meanings* of linguistic units. Our representation of clauses freely includes both syntactic and semantic information.

*sentence — Two or more clauses exhibiting as-yet-unspecified coherence.

†separation — A constituent that portrays separation. Example: "Deliver me *from sin*."

*sequential ו — A form of the conjunction *and* prefixed to a verb, which indicates that the verb's clause is in a temporal sequence in discourse. Also, known as "*waw* consecutive" (many of these have already been made supra-clausal).

singular — The number category that refers to a single entity.

sister node — If two nodes have the same mother, they are sisters.

state — A Hebrew noun may have several forms, depending on its function or relation to other constituents. We recognize four different states: construct, suffixed, pausal, and normal.

†strictly subsetting constituents — Licenses constructions in which successive constituents are subsets of their predecessor(s). Example: "in the third year, in the second month, on the first day."

†strictly supersetting constituents — Licenses constructions in which successive constituents are supersets of their predecessor(s). Example: "on the first day, in the second month, in the third year."

subject — Often said to be "what is already known in the clause" (its theme). Traditionally, the "doer" of the action of the predicator in a clause.

subject complement — A nominal that completes the subject. Example: "Moses will be *my prophet*."

subject of address — In our representation, refers to those (few) situations in which a speech is the subject of a passive verb of utterance.

*subordinating conjunction — A supra-clausal conjunction or cue phrase that functions (or will function, when our analysis is complete) at discourse level in our analysis. Included are many instances of 'also' (גַּם) and 'or' (אוֹ) plus most instances of 'if' (אִם) and most uses of כִּי: 'because', 'if', 'but', 'that', 'although', and 'when'.

substantive (or nominal) — The superset of nouns, pronouns, and verbal nouns.

suffixation — When a noun (or verbal noun) has a pronominal suffix, the suffix typically expresses possession: "throne-his."

suffixed — A noun (or verbal noun) that has a pronominal suffix.

suffixed sequential — A verb with a suffixed pronoun subject and a consecutive ו; traditionally called a "perfect" or *wĕqāṭal*.

suffixed verb (perfect) — A verb with a suffixed pronoun subject. Traditionally called a "perfect" or *qāṭal*.

supra-clausal — A discourse structure that exists "above" the clause. Supra-clausals are composed of clauses, often linked by cue phrases. At present, structures at this level of analysis are quite provisional and incomplete.

supra-clausal relations — The relations in this subset are associated with the sentence, the discourse unit, or the compound cue phrase and are noncommittal placeholders that will be replaced by information-bearing relations in the discourse-analyzed extension of our database.

suspension — Identifies a feature of a text (or construction) within a clause in which a constituent is left hanging at the onset of a clause. For example, "[susp in the grave] where Abraham buried Sarah—you will bury me [resum there]" (see also resumption).

syntactic isolate — Entities that are not integrated constituents of clauses, though they may be loosely related to clauses. In our analysis, they are vocatives, exclamatives, or labels.

syntax — The study of how linguistic units (be they segments, words, phrases, clauses, or discourse units) relate to one another in constructions.

T

temporal conjunction — A segment that can function as a conjunction or a temporal adverb.

temporal ה — The suffix ה- added to a noun to indicate a time.

tense — The temporal location of an event.

third person — Used when the speaker refers to person(s) or thing(s) (he, she, they) other than the speaker or the person(s) being addressed.

time aim / goal — Ending time: "until evening."

time interval — Time duration: "from morning and until evening."

time origin — Time starting point: "from morning."

time point — A constituent that specifies a point in time. Most are clausal constituents (as in "on the third day"), but some function at discourse level (as in "When David was king . . . ").

transitive — A verb is transitive if it "takes" a direct object, where the force of "take" ranges from mandatory presence of an explicit direct object to complete optionality, depending on the verb under consideration.

tree — A graph constrained to have only one root, in which each node has only one mother node, and no edge (unavoidably) crosses another ("tangling" not allowed). (The exclusivity condition must also be met.) Almost all of our phrase markers are trees.

U

undesired outcome — A constituent that discloses an unfavorable result or consequence.

union or disjunction — Licenses constructions in which successive constituents are bridged by coordinating conjunctions. Examples: "A and B and C"; "A or B or C."

*unit — Typically, a clause or clauses in a construction that are in relation to other similar units in discourse. When formalized, these temporary "units" will be transmuted into properly labeled discourse units.

V

verb — A segment with a paradigmatic form that includes an affix (which may be zero) that specifies the number, gender, and person of the subject. Traditionally, it is a word that portrays an action, state of being, or process.

verbal — The superset of verbs and verbal nouns.

verbal noun — A verb-derived segment exhibiting noun-like syntactic behavior. Example: infinitive construct.

verb frame — A conceptual structure evoked by a particular verb. It consists of a situation, object, or event plus its associated entities (both participants and props).

verbless clause (VLC) — A clause that lacks a predicator. Its predicate is not necessarily a noun phrase.

verbless sentence — A sentence that lacks any predicator and consists of three CICs, the middle one (Janus subject-complement / subject) doing double duty. See appendix 6.

vocative — A constituent in direct speech intended to attract the attention of the one addressed.

voice — An internal inflection of the verb stem that matches the relationship of the actor and undergoer to the action of the verb.

W

word — An arbitrary *orthographic* unit that is traditionally used by scribes in manuscripts and by printers in editions of the Hebrew Bible. A word is bounded by (white) space, line-end, verse-end marker (*sop pasuq*), or dash (*maqqep*). Words have no grammatical significance per se.

Bibliography

Agresti, Alan. *Categorical Data Analysis*. 2nd ed. Hoboken, NJ: Wiley-Interscience, 2002.

Aitchison, J., and J. W. Kay. "Possible Solutions to Some Essential Zero Problems in Compositional Data Analysis." CODAWORK 2003. http://dugi-doc.udg.edu/handle/10256/652.

Albrecht, C. "Die Wortstellung im hebräischen Nominalsatze." *Zeitschrift für die alttestamentliche Wissenschaft* 7 (1887) 218–24; 8 (1888) 249–63.

Andersen, Francis I. *The Hebrew Verbless Clause in the Pentateuch*. Nashville: Abingdon, 1970.

_____. "Lo and Behold! Taxonomy and Translation of Biblical Hebrew הִנֵּה," Pp. 25–56 in *Hamlet on a Hill: Semitic and Greek Studies Presented to Professor T. Muraoka on the Occasion of his Sixty-Fifth Birthday*. Edited by M. Baasten and W. van Peursen. Leuven: Peeters, 2003.

_____. *The Syntax of Biblical Hebrew*. Ph.D. dissertation, Johns Hopkins University, 1960.

Andersen, Francis I., and A. Dean Forbes. "Attachment Preferences in the Primary History." Pp. 167–86 in *Proceedings of the Sixth International Colloquium: From Alpha to Byte*. Leiden: Brill, 2002.

_____. "On Marking Clause Boundaries." Pp. 181–202 in *Bible et Informatique: Interprétation, Herméneutique, Compétence Informatique*. Paris: Honoré Champion, 1992.

_____. "Opportune Parsing: Clause Analysis of Deuteronomy 8." Pp. 49–75 in *Bible and Computer: Desk and Discipline. Actes du Quatrième Colloque international Bible et informatique*. Paris: Honoré Champion, 1995.

_____. "The Participle in Biblical Hebrew and the Overlap of Grammar and Lexicon." Pp. 185–212 in *Milk and Honey: Essays on Ancient Israel and the Bible*. Edited by Sarah Malena and David Miano. Winona Lake, IN: Eisenbrauns, 2007.

_____. "'Prose Particle' Counts in the Hebrew Bible." Pp. 165–83 in *The Word of the Lord Shall Go Forth: Essays in Honor of David Noel Freedman in Celebration of His Sixtieth Birthday*. Edited by Carol L. Meyers and M. O'Connor. Winona Lake, IN: Eisenbrauns, 1983.

_____. *Spelling in the Hebrew Bible*. Rome: Pontifical Biblical Institute, 1986.

_____. "Syntactic Ambiguity in the Hebrew Bible." Pp. 356–67 in *Proceedings of the Fourth International Colloquium: Bible and the Computer—Desk and Discipline*. Paris: Honoré Champion, 1995.

_____. *The Vocabulary of the Old Testament*. Rome: Pontifical Biblical Institute, 1992.

Andersen, Francis I., and David N. Freedman. *Hosea*. Anchor Bible 24. Garden City: Doubleday, 1980.

Andrews, Avery D. "The Major Functions of the Noun Phrase." Pp. 132–231 in *Language Typology and Syntactic Description*, vol. 1: *Clause Structure*. 2nd ed. Edited by Timothy Shopen. Cambridge: Cambridge University Press, 2007.

Anstey, Matthew P. "The Grammatical-Lexical Cline in Tiberian Hebrew." *Journal of Semitic Studies* 51 (2006) 59–84.

Arnold, Bill T., and John H. Choi. *A Guide to Biblical Hebrew Syntax*. Cambridge: Cambridge University Press, 2003.

Asher, Nicolas, and Alex Lascarides. *Logics of Conversation*. Cambridge: Cambridge University Press, 2003.

Baasten, Martin F. J. *The Non-Verbal Clause in Qumran Hebrew*. Ph.D. dissertation, Leuven University, 2006.

Beaver, David, et al., "Bad Subject: (Non-)canonicality and NP Distribution in Existentials." *Semantics and Linguistic Theory* 15 (2005). http://www.linguistics.ucla.edu/salt/.

Ben Zvi, Nahum, ed., *Jerusalem Crown*. Jerusalem: Yad Ben Zvi, 2000.

Bird, Steven. "Finite-State Phonology in HPSG." *Proceedings of the International Conference on Computational Linguistics* (1992) 74–80. http://www.informatik.uni-trier.de/~ley/db/con/coling/index.html.

Blau, Joshua. *Grammar of Biblical Hebrew.* 2nd ed. Wiesbaden: Harrassowitz, 1993.

_____. *Phonology and Morphology of Biblical Hebrew: An Introduction.* Linguistic Studies in Ancient West Semitic 2. Winona Lake, IN: Eisenbrauns, 2008.

Boling, Robert G., and G. Ernest Wright. Anchor Bible 6. *Joshua.* Garden City, NY: Doubleday, 1995.

Bornkessel, Ina, et al., eds. *Semantic Role Universals and Argument Linking: Theoretical, Typological, and Psycholinguistic Perspectives.* Berlin: De Gruyter, 2006.

Breuer, M. *The Aleppo Codex and the Accepted Text of the Bible.* Jerusalem: Mosad Harav Kook, 1976.

Butt, Miriam, and Tracy King. "Null Elements in Discourse Structure." In *Papers from the NULLS Seminar.* Edited by K. V. Subbarao. Delhi: Moti Lal Banarsi Das, 2000. http://csli-publications.stanford.edu/LF6/12/lfg07.pdf.

Cohen, Maimon. *The Kethib and Qeri System in the Biblical Text.* Jerusalem: Magnes, 2007.

Collins, Michael. "Head-Driven Statistical Models for Natural Language Parsing." *Computational Linguistics* 29 (2003) 589–637.

Connolly, John H. *Constituent Order in Functional Grammar: Synchronic and Diachronic Perspectives.* Berlin: Foris, 1991.

Corston-Oliver, Simon. "Beyond String Matching and Cue Phrases: Improving Efficiency and Coverage in Discourse Analysis." *Microsoft Research Tech Report, November 1988.* http://research.microsoft.com/apps/pubs/default.aspx?id=69677.

Cote, Sharon A. *Grammatical and Discourse Properties of Null-Arguments in English.* Ph.D. dissertation, University of Pennsylvania, 1996.

Croft, William. "Parts of speech as language universals and as language-particular categories." Pp. 65–102 in *Approaches to the Typology of Word Classes.* Edited by P. M. Vogel and B. Comrie. Berlin: De Gruyter, 2000.

Crystal, David. *A Dictionary of Linguistics and Phonetics.* 5th ed. Oxford: Blackwell, 2003.

Daniels, Michael W. *Generalized ID/LP Grammar: A Formalism for Parsing Linearization-Based HPSG Grammars.* Ph.D. dissertation, Ohio State University, 2005.

Dareau, M. G. "Glossary," Pp. 419–42 in *Concise Encyclopedia of Grammatical Categories.* Edited by Keith Brown and Jim Miller. Oxford: Elsevier, 1999.

Davison, Mark L. *Multidimensional Scaling.* New York: Wiley, 1983.

De Kuthy, Kordula, and W. Detmar Meurers. "Dealing with Optional Complements in HPSG-Based Grammar Implementations." Pp. 88–96 in *Proceedings of the 10th International Conference on Head-Driven Phrase Structure Grammar.* Edited by Stefan Müller. Stanford, CA: CSLI, 2003. http://csli-publications.stanford.edu/HPS6/4/dekuthy-meurers-optionality.pdf.

Dotan, Aron, ed. *Biblica Hebraica Leningradensia.* Peabody, MA: Hendrickson, 2001.

Dryer, Matthew S. "Clause Types," Pp. 224–75 in *Language Typology and Syntactic Description*, vol. 1. *Clause Structure.* 2nd ed. Edited by Timothy Shopen. Cambridge: Cambridge University Press, 2007.

Duda, Richard O., et al. *Pattern Classification.* 2nd ed. New York, NY: Wiley-Interscience, 2000.

Eissfeldt, Otto. *Hexateuch-Synopse.* 2nd ed. Darmstadt: Wissenschaftliche Buchgesellschaft, 1962.

Everitt, Brian. *An R and S-Plus® Companion to Multivariate Analysis.* Berlin: Springer, 2005.

Falk, Yehuda N. "The Hebrew Present-Tense Copula as a Mixed Category," Pp. 229–41 in *Proceedings of the LFG04 Conference.* Edited by M. Butt and T. H. King. Stanford, CA: CSLI, 2004.

_____. *Lexical-Functional Grammar: An Introduction to Parallel Constraint-Based Syntax.* Stanford, CA: CSLI, 2001.

Fellbaum, Christiane, ed. *WordNet: An Electronic Lexical Database.* Cambridge, MA: MIT Press, 1998.

Fischer, Kerstin, ed. *Approaches to Discourse Particles.* Bingley, UK: JAI, 2008.

Forbes, A. Dean. "The Challenge of Consistency." Pp. 99–115 in *Computer Assisted Research on the Bible in the 21st Century.* Edited by Luis Vegas, Guadalupe Seijas, and Javier del Barco. Piscataway, NJ: Gorgias, 2010.

_____. "Distributionally Inferred Word and Form Classes in the Hebrew Lexicon: Known by the Company They Keep." Pp. 1–34 in *Syriac Lexicography II*. Edited by Peter Williams. Piscataway, NJ: Gorgias, 2009.

_____. "How Syntactic Formalisms Can Advance the Lexicographer's Art." Pp. 139–58 in *Foundations for Syriac Lexicography III*. Edited by Janet Dyk and Wido van Peursen. Piscataway, NJ: Gorgias, 2009.

_____. "Shards, Strophes, and Stats," Pp. 310–21 in *Fortunate the Eyes that See: Essays in Honor of David Noel Freedman in Celebration of His Seventieth Birthday*. Edited by A. B. Beck et al. Grand Rapids, MI: Eerdmans, 1995.

_____. "Squishes, Clines, and Fuzzy Signs: Mixed and Gradient Categories in the Biblical Hebrew Lexicon" Pp. 105–39 in *Syriac Lexicography I: Foundations for Syriac Lexicography*. Edited by A. D. Forbes and D. G. K. Taylor. Piscataway, NJ: Gorgias, 2006.

Fouvry, Frederik, and Detmar Meurers, "Towards a platform for linearization grammars." *European Summer School in Logic, Language and Information (ESSLLI)-2000 Workshop on Linguistic Theory and Grammatical Implementation*. Edited by Erhard Hinrichs et al. http://linguistlist.org/issues/10/10-830.html.

Francez, Itamar. "Semantic structure and argument realization in (mostly Hebrew) existentials." Available on the web at http://home.uchicago.edu/~ifrancez/IATL07.pdf.

Frank, Anette. "Projecting LFG F-Structure from Chunks—or (Non-)Configurationality from a Different Point of View." *Proceedings of the LFG03 Conference* (2003) 1–20. Available on the web at http://citeseer.ist.psu.edu/viewdoc/summary?doi=10.1.1.67.5254

Freedman, D. N., A. D. Forbes, and F. I. Andersen. Biblical and Judaic Studies from the University of California, San Diego 2. *Studies in Hebrew and Aramaic Orthography*. Winona Lake, IN: Eisenbrauns, 1992.

Freedman, David N., et al., eds. *The Leningrad Codex: Facsimile Edition*. Grand Rapids, MI: Eerdmans, 1998.

Friedman, Richard E. *The Bible with Sources Revealed*. San Francisco: HarperSanFrancisco, 2003.

Fukunaga, K. *Introduction to Statistical Pattern Recognition*. 2nd ed. San Diego: Academic Press, 1990.

Gamut, L. T. F. *Language, Logic, and Meaning*, vol. 2: *Intensional Logic and Logical Grammar*. Chicago: University of Chicago Press, 1991.

Gazdar, Gerald, et al. *Generalized Phrase Structure Grammar*. Oxford: Blackwell, 1985.

Gesenius, Wilhelm, and Emil Friedrich Kautzsch. *Hebräische grammatik*. 27th ed. Leipzig: Vogel, 1902. http://www.archive.org/details/wilhelmgesenius03kautgoog.

Gildea, Daniel, and Daniel Jurafsky. "Automatic Labeling of Semantic Roles." *Computational Linguistics* 28 (2002) 245–88.

Givón, Talmy. *Syntax: An Introduction*. Rev. ed. Amsterdam: Benjamins, 2001.

Golumbia, David. "The interpretation of nonconfigurationality." *Language and Communication* 24 (2004) 1–22.

Goodrick, Edward W., John R. Kohlenberger III, and James A. Swanson. *Zondervan New International Version, Exhaustive Concordance*. Grand Rapids, MI: Zondervan, 1999.

Gordis, Robert. *The Biblical Text in the Making: A Study of the Kethib-Qere*. Jersey City, NJ: Ktav, 1971.

Goshen-Gottstein, Moshe H., ed. *The Aleppo Codex*. Jerusalem: Magnes, 1976.

Graf, Monique. "Precision of Compositional Data in a Stratified Two-Stage Cluster Sample: Comparison of the Swiss Earnings Structure Survey 2002 and 2004." *American Statistical Association Section on Survey Research Methods*. http://www.amstat.org/sections/srms/Proceedings.

Grenager, Trond, and Christopher D. Manning, "Unsupervised Discovery of a Statistical Verb Lexicon." *Proceedings of the 2006 Conference on Empirical Methods in Natural Language Processing*. http://acl.ldc.upenn.edu/W/W06/#W06-1600.

Gross, Walter. *Die Satzteilfolge im Verbalsatz alttestamentlicher Prosa*. Tübingen: Mohr, 1996.

Hale, Kenneth. "Warlpiri and the grammar of non-configurational languages." *Natural Language and Linguistic Theory* 1 (1983) 5–47.

Halliday, M. A. K. *Categories in the Theory of Grammar*. Indianapolis, IN: Bobbs-Merrill, 1961.

Hand, D. J. *Discrimination and Classification*. Chichester: Wiley, 1981.

Hartmann, R. R. K., and Gregory James. *Dictionary of Lexicography*. London: Routledge, 1998.

Hartsfield, Nora, and Gerhard Ringel. *Pearls in Graph Theory: A Comprehensive Introduction*. San Diego: Academic, 1994.

Haspelmath, Martin. "Coordination." Pp. 1–51 in *Language Typology and Syntactic Description*, vol. 2: *Complex Constructions*. 2nd ed. Edited by Timothy Shopen. Cambridge: Cambridge University Press, 2007.

Holmstedt, Robert D. *The Relative Clause in Biblical Hebrew: A Linguistic Analysis*. Ph.D. dissertation, Univ. of Wisconsin, 2002.

Huck, Geoffrey J., and A. E. Ojeda. *Syntax and Semantics: Discontinuous Constituency*. Orlando, FL: Academic, 1987.

Huddleston, R. D. "Sentence Types and Clause Subordination." Pp. 329–43 in *Concise Encyclopedia of Grammatical Categories*. Edited by Keith Brown and Jim Miller. Amsterdam: Elsevier, 1999.

Hudson, Richard. "Con PRO, or the virtues of sharing." *University College London Working Papers in Linguistics* 7 (1995) 277–96. http://www.ucl.ac.uk/psychlangsci/research/linguistics/publications.

Jaworska, E. "Control." Pp. 107–10 in *Concise Encyclopedia of Grammatical Categories*. Edited by Keith Brown and Jim Miller. Amsterdam: Elsevier, 1999.

Jenni, Ernst. "Einleitung formeller und familiärer Rede im Alten Testament durch ʾmr ʾl- und ʾmr l-." Pp. 17–33 in *Vielseitigkeit des Alten Testaments: Festschrift für Georg Sauer zum 70. Geburtstag*. Edited by J. A. Loader and H. V. Kieweler. Frankfurt a.M.: Peter Lang, 1999.

Jongeling, B. "L'expression *my ytn* dans l'Ancien Testament." *Vetus Testamentum* 24 (1974) 32–40.

Jongeling, K. "'And It Came to Pass' Again." Pp. 291–329 in *Babel und Bibel* 2: *Memoriae Igor M. Diakonoff:* . Edited by L. Kogan et al. Winona Lake, IN: Eisenbrauns, 2005.

Joosten, Jan. "In Biblical Hebrew the Present Tense is Properly the Domain of the Predicative Participle." *Zeitschrift für Althebraistik* 2 (1989) 128–59.

Joüon, Paul. *Grammaire de l'hébreu biblique*. Rome: Pontifical Biblical Institute, 1923.

Joüon, Paul, and T. Muraoka. *A Grammar of Biblical Hebrew*. 3rd ed. Subsidia Biblica 27. Rome: Pontifical Biblical Institute, 2006.

Keenan, E. L. "The Definiteness Effect: Semantics or Pragmatics?" *Natural Language Semantics* 11 (2003) 187–216.

Kennicott, Benjamin. *The State of the Printed Hebrew Text of the Old Testament Considered*. Dissertation I, Oxford, 1753; Dissertation II, Oxford, 1759.

Kiraz, George A. *Computational Nonlinear Morphology with Emphasis on Semitic Languages*. Cambridge: Cambridge University Press, 2001.

Korpel, Marjo C. A., and Josef Oesch, eds. *Unit Delimitation in Biblical Hebrew and Northwest Semitic Literature*. Pericope 4. Assen: Van Gorcum, 2003.

Kruijff-Korbayová, Ivana, and Mark Steedman. *Information Structure, Discourse Structure, and Discourse Semantics: Workshop Proceedings*. 13th European Summer School in Logic, Language and Information, 2001. http://www.coli.uni-saarland.de/~korbay/esslli01-wsh-final-papers.html.

Kuramae, E. E., et al. "Cophenetic Correlation Analysis as a Strategy to Select Phylogenetically Informative Proteins: An Example from the Fungal Kingdom." *BioMed Central Evolutionary Biology* 7 (2007) 134–44.

Lambdin, Thomas O. *Introduction to Biblical Hebrew*. New York: Scribner's, 1971.

Larrosa, Juan M. "A Compositional Statistical Analysis of Capital Stock." *Proceedings of CODAWORK 2003*. http://hdl.handle.net/10256/652.

Leech, Geoffrey. "Corpora and Theories of Linguistic Performance." Pp. 105–22 in *Directions in Corpus Linguistics*. Edited by Jan Svartvik. Berlin: de Gruyter, 1992.

_____. "The State of the Art in Corpus Linguistics." Pp. 8–29 in *English Corpus Linguistics: Studies in Honour of Jan Svartvik*. Edited by K. Aijmer and B. Alterberg. London: Longman, 1991.

Levin, Beth. *English Verb Classes and Alternations: A Preliminary Investigation*. Chicago: University of Chicago Press, 1993.

Lode, Lars. "A Discourse Perspective on the Significance of the Masoretic Accents." Pp. 155–72 in *Biblical Hebrew and Discourse Linguistics*. Edited by Robert D. Bergen. Dallas: Summer Institute of Linguistics, 1994.

Loewinger, D. S., ed. *Pentateuch, Prophets and Hagiographa: Codex Leningrad B 19ᴬ*. Jerusalem: Makor, 1971.

Lowery, Kirk E. "Relative Definiteness and the Verbless Clause," Pp. 251–72 in *The Verbless Clause in Biblical Hebrew: Linguistic Approaches*. Edited by Cynthia L. Miller. Linguistic Studies in Ancient West Semitic. Winona Lake, IN: Eisenbrauns, 1999.

_____. *Toward a Discourse Grammar of Biblical Hebrew*. Ph.D. dissertation, UCLA, 1985.

Lyons, John. "A note on possessive, existential, and locative sentences." *Foundations of Language* 3 (1967) 390–96.

Malessa, Michael. *Untersuchungen zur verbalen Valenz im biblischen Hebräisch*. Assen: Van Gorcum, 2006.

Manning, Christopher D., and Heinrich Schütze. *Foundations of Statistical Natural Language Processing*. Cambridge, MA: MIT Press, 1999.

Martin, James R. "Cohesion and Texture." Pp. 35–53 in *The Handbook of Discourse Analysis*. Edited by Deborah Shiffrin et al. Oxford: Blackwell, 2001.

Martín-Fernández, J. A., et al. "Measures of Difference for Compositional Data and Hierarchical Clustering Methods." *Proceedings of the International Association for Mathematical Geosciences*, 1998.

_____. "Zero Replacement in Compositional Data Sets." Pp. 155–60 in *Studies in Classification, Data Analysis and Knowledge Organisation*. Edited by H. Kries et al. Berlin: Springer, 2000.

Matthews, Peter H. *Oxford Concise Dictionary of Linguistics*. Oxford: Oxford University Press, 1997.

McCawley, James D. *The Syntactic Phenomena of English*. 2nd ed. Chicago: University of Chicago Press, 1998.

Merwe, Christo H. J. van der. "The Elusive Biblical Hebrew Term ויהי: A Perspective in Terms of Its Syntax, Semantics, and Pragmatics in 1 Samuel." *Hebrew Studies* 40 (1999) 83–114.

_____. *The Old Hebrew Particle* gam: *A Synoptic Description of* gam *in Gn–2Kg*. St. Ottilien: EOS, 1990.

_____. "Review of Malessa's *Untersuchungen zur verbalen Valenz im biblischen Hebräisch*." *Review of Biblical Literature* 4 (2007). http://www.bookreviews.org/bookdetail.asp?TitleId=5540&CodePage=5540.

Merwe, Christo H. J. van der, Jackie Naudé, and Jan H. Kroeze. *A Biblical Hebrew Reference Grammar*. Biblical Languages: Hebrew 3. Sheffield: Sheffield Academic Press, 1999.

Merwe, Christo H. J. van der, and Eep Talstra, "Biblical Hebrew word order: The interface of information structure and formal features." *Zeitschrift für Althebräistik* 15–16 (2002–3) 68–107.

Miller, Cynthia L. "Ellipsis Involving Negation in Biblical Poetry." Pp. 37–52 in *Seeking Out the Wisdom of the Ancients: Essays Offered to Honor Michael V. Fox on the Occasion of His Sixty-Fifth Birthday*. Edited by R. L. Troxel, K. G. Friebel, and D. R. Magary. Winona Lake, IN: Eisenbrauns, 2005.

_____. "A Linguistic Approach to Ellipsis in Biblical Poetry (Or, What to Do When Exegesis of What Is There Depends on What Isn't)." *Bulletin for Biblical Research* 13 (2003) 251–70.

Mosteller, Frederick, and John W. Tukey. *Data Analysis and Regression*. Reading, MA: Addison-Wesley, 1977.

Müller, Stefan. "Continuous or Discontinuous Constituents? A Comparison between Syntactic Analyses for Constituent Order and Their Processing Systems." *Research on Language and Computation* 2 (2004) 209–57.

Muraoka, Takamitsu. *Emphasis in Biblical Hebrew*. Ph.D. dissertation, Hebrew University Jerusalem, 1969.

_____. *Emphatic Words and Structures in Biblical Hebrew*. Jerusalem: Magnes / Leiden: Brill, 1985.

_____. "Reflexions on an Important Study on the Nominal Clause in Biblical Hebrew." *Bibliotheca Orientalis* 63 (2006) 457–58.

_____. "The Tripartite Nominal Clause Revisited" Pp. 187–213 in *The Verbless Clause in Biblical Hebrew: Linguistic Approaches*. Edited by Cynthia Miller. Linguistic Studies in Ancient West Semitic 1. Winona Lake, IN: Eisenbrauns, 1999.

Niles, Ian, and Adam Pease. "Towards a Standard Upper Ontology." *Proceedings of the 2nd International Conference on Formal Ontology in Information Systems (FOIS-2001)*. http://www.ontologyportal.org/pubs.html.

Oates, Sarah L. "Multiple Discourse Marker Occurrence: Creating Hierarchies for Natural Language Generation." *Proceedings of the ANLP-NAACL 2000*, 41–45. http://acl.ldc.upenn.edu/A/A00/A00-3008.pdf.

O'Connor, M. P. "Discourse Linguistics and the Study of Biblical Hebrew." Pp. 17–42 in *Congress Volume: Basel 2001*. Edited by A. Lemaire. Vetus Testamentum Supplement 92. Leiden: Brill, 2002.

Oliva, Karel. "The Proper Treatment of Word Order in HPSG." *Actes de COLING-92*. http://citeseerx.ist.psu.edu/viewdoc/summary?doi=10.1.31.8332.

Orlinsky, Harry M. "The Masoretic Text: A Critical Evaluation." Pp. i–xlv in *Introduction to the Masso-retico-Critical Edition of the Hebrew Bible*, by C. D. Ginsburg; New York: KTAV, 1966.

Palmer, Martha, Daniel Gildea, and Paul Kingsbury. "The Proposition Bank." *Computational Linguistics* 31 (2005) 71–106.

Pawlowsky-Glahn, V., and J. J. Egozcue. "Compositional data and their analysis: An introduction." Pp. 1–10 in *Compositional Data Analysis in the Geosciences: From Theory to Practice*. Edited by A. Buccianti et al. Special Pubs. 264. London: Geological Society, 2006.

Peursen, Wido T. van. "Three Approaches to the Tripartite Nominal Clause in Syriac." Pp. 157–73 in *Corpus Linguistics and Textual History*. Edited by P. S. F. van Keulen and W. T. van Peursen. Assen: Van Gorcum, 2006.

_____. *Language and Interpretation in the Syriac Text of Ben Sira*. Leiden: Brill, 2007.

Polanyi, Livia. "The Linguistic Structure of Discourse." Pp. 265–81 in *The Handbook of Discourse Analysis*. Edited by Deborah Shiffrin et al. Oxford: Blackwell, 2001.

Polanyi, Livia, et al. "A Rule Based Approach to Discourse Parsing." *Proceedings of the 5th SIGdial Workshop on Discourse and Dialogue*, 2004, 108–17. http://www-sigdial.org/biblio/author/224?sort-type&order=asc.

Pollard, Carl, and Ivan A. Sag. *Head-Driven Phrase Structure Grammar*. Chicago: University of Chicago Press, 1994.

_____. *Information-Based Syntax and Semantics*, vol. 1: *Fundamentals*. Stanford: CSLI, 1987.

Radford, Andrew. *Syntax: A Minimalist Introduction*. Cambridge: Cambridge University Press, 1997.

Richter, Wolfgang. *Grundlagen einer althebräischen Grammatik*, vol. 3: *Der Satz*. St. Ottilien: EOS, 1980.

Romesburg, H. C. *Cluster Analysis for Researchers*. Belmont, CA: Lifetime Learning, 1984.

Ruppenhofer, Josef, et al. *FrameNet II: Extended Theory and Practice*, 25 August 2006. http://framenet.icsi.berkeley.edu.

Sag, Ivan A., Thomas Wasow, and Emily M. Bender. *Syntactic Theory: A Formal Introduction*. 2nd ed. Stanford, CA: CSLI, 2003.

Schiffman, Lawrence F., Emanuel Tov, and James C. VanderKam, eds. *The Dead Sea Scrolls Fifty Years after Their Discovery*. Jerusalem: Israel Exploration Society, 2000.

Seleznev, Michael. "Syntactic Parsing behind the Masoretic Accentuation (I)." *Babel und Bibel* 3 (2006) 353–70.

Shiffrin, Deborah, et al. *The Handbook of Discourse Analysis*. Oxford: Blackwell, 2001.

Sinclair, Cameron. "Are Nominal Clauses a Distinct Clause Type?" Pp. 51–78 in *The Verbless Clause in Biblical Hebrew: Linguistic Approaches*. Edited by Cynthia L. Miller. Linguistic Studies in Ancient West Semitic 1. Winona Lake, IN: Eisenbrauns, 1999.

Sokal, R., and P. Sneath. *Principles of Numerical Taxonomy*. San Francisco: Freeman, 1963.

Steinberger, Ralf. "Treating 'Free Word Order' in Machine Translation." *Proceedings of the 15th Conference on Computational Linguistics*, 1994. http://langtech.jrc.it/Documents/Coling-94_Steinberger.pdf.

Stent, Amanda J., and James F. Allen. *Annotating Argumentation Acts in Spoken Dialog*. Technical Report 740. The University of Rochester, Department of Computer Science, 2000. http://www.cs.rochester.edu/research/cisd/pubs/2000/stent-allen-tr740.pdf.

Stoop-van Paridon, P. W. T. *The Song of Songs: A Philological Analysis of the Hebrew Book*. Ancient Near Eastern Studies 17. Leiden: Peeters, 2006.

Thompson, Cynthia A., Roger Levy, and Christopher D. Manning. "A Generative Model for Semantic Role Labeling." *Proceedings of the European Conference on Machine Learning, 2003*. http://dblp.uni-trier.de/db/conf/ecml2003.html.

Toutanova, Kristina, et al. "Joint Learning Improves Semantic Role Labeling." *Proceedings of the 43rd Meeting of the Association for Computational Linguistics*, 2005. http://www.aclweb.org/anthology/p/P05.

Tov, Emanuel. *Textual Criticism of the Hebrew Bible*. 2nd ed. Minneapolis, MN: Fortress, 2001.

Trask, Robert L. *A Dictionary of Grammatical Terms*. London: Routledge, 1993.

_____. "Parts of Speech." Pp. 278–83 in *Concise Encyclopedia of Grammatical Categories*. Edited by K. Brown and J. Miller. Oxford: Elsevier, 1999.

Traugott, E. C. "Grammaticalization and Lexicalization." Pp. 177–83 in *Concise Encyclopedia of Grammatical Categories*. Edited by K. Brown and J. Miller. Oxford: Elsevier, 1999.

Upton, Graham, and Ian Cook. *Oxford Dictionary of Statistics*. 2nd ed. Oxford: Oxford University Press, 2006.

VanderKam, James, and Peter Flint. *The Meaning of the Dead Sea Scrolls*. San Francisco: Harper, 2002.

Van Valin, R. D. Jr. "Functional Relations." Pp. 150–62 in *Concise Encyclopedia of Grammatical Categories*. Edited by K. Brown and J. Miller. Oxford: Elsevier, 1999.

_____. *Exploring the Syntax-Semantics Interface*. Cambridge: Cambridge University Press, 2005.

Waltke, Bruce K., and M. O'Connor. *An Introduction to Biblical Hebrew Syntax*. Winona Lake, IN: Eisenbrauns, 1990.

Wasow, Thomas. "Generative Grammar," Pp. 295–318 in *The Handbook of Linguistics*. Edited by Mark Aronoff and Janie Rees-Miller. Oxford, Blackwell, 2001.

Webber, Bonnie, et al. "Anaphora and Discourse Structure." *Computational Linguistics* 29 (2003) 545–87.

Whaley, Lindsay J. *Introduction to Typology: The Unity and Diversity of Language*. Thousand Oaks, CA: Sage, 1997.

Williams, Ronald J. *Williams' Hebrew Syntax*. 3rd ed. Edited and expanded by John C. Beckman. Toronto: University of Toronto Press, 2007.

Wolde, Ellen van. "The Verbless Clause and Its Textual Function." Pp. 321–36 in *The Verbless Clause in Biblical Hebrew: Linguistic Approaches*. Edited by Cynthia L. Miller. Linguistic Studies in Ancient West Semitic 1. Winona Lake, IN: Eisenbrauns, 1999.

Zwicky, Arnold M. "Isolated NPs." http://www.stanford.edu/~zwicky/isolated.hnd.pdf.

Index of Authors

Index of Scripture

Page numbers in bold typeface are pages on which the Scripture referenced is represented in a Phrase Marker (PM).

Index of Topics

Many topic index terms are found in the glossary. A frequently-occurring subentry is "verb corpora, in" = "in verb corpora." This refers to chaps. 11–15, in which we study the clause corpora associated with five verb roots: עשׂה, נתן, חפץ, היה, אמר.